Red Brick in the Land of Steady Habits

Red Brick *in the* Land of Steady Habits

CREATING THE
University of Connecticut, 1881–2006

Bruce M. Stave

with

Laura Burmeister, Michael Neagle,

Leslie Horner Papandrea,

and Sondra Astor Stave

University of Connecticut

PUBLISHED BY UNIVERSITY PRESS OF NEW ENGLAND

HANOVER AND LONDON

University of Connecticut
Published by University Press of New England,
One Court Street, Lebanon, NH 03766
www.upne.com
© 2006 by University of Connecticut
Printed in the United States of America
5 4 3 2 1

LIBRARY OF CONGRESS CATALOGING-IN-PUBLICATION DATA
Stave, Bruce M.
Red brick in the land of steady habits : creating the University
of Connecticut, 1881–2006 / Bruce M. Stave, with Laura Burmeister
[et al.].
  p. cm.
Includes bibliographical references and index.
ISBN–13: 978-1-58465-569-5 (cloth : alk. paper)
ISBN–10: 1-58465-569-0 (cloth : alk. paper)
ISBN–13: 978-1-58465-570-1 (pbk. : alk. paper)
ISBN–10: 1-58465-570-4 (pbk. : alk. paper)
1. University of Connecticut—History.   I. Burmeister, Laura.
II. Title.
LD1281.C332S73   2006
378.746′43—dc22   2006002878

For all of the

students, alumni,

faculty, and staff

who have joined

together to create the

University of Connecticut

community

Contents

Acknowledgments

This book began with Richard D. Brown's determination that the University of Connecticut should be the subject of a serious academic history not unlike those enjoyed by many of its peer institutions. He developed and promoted the concept and served as chair of the editorial board that guided the book. For that, for his incisive critiques and helpful suggestions, and for his collegiality and friendship over more than three decades, I am most appreciative.

In addition to Dick Brown, the editorial committee consisted of Ralph Arcari, Phillip Barry, Cornelia (Nina) Hughes Dayton, Judy Kelly, Quentin Kessel, Brenda Murphy, Mark Roy, Ronald Schurin, Ronald Taylor, and Thomas Wilsted. Nina and Brenda joined with Dick to form a "close reading" committee, but many of the members assisted with their comments on specific chapters or the entire manuscript. Quentin Kessel, a second-generation faculty member in Storrs who has lived most of his life in the University of Connecticut community, offered a special perspective on events and personalities. He was equally helpful with the written word, which is not inappropriate for the physicist son of an English professor. The assistance of the committee, particularly those who gave close readings to the manuscript, was invaluable.

At the outset of the project, a university-wide advisory committee met twice to discuss the direction and framework of the book. The committee consisted of the following individuals, whom I thank for their time and advice: Cynthia Adams, Gregory Anderson, Alexinia Baldwin, Daniel Blume, Pamela Bramble, Irene Q. Brown, Nancy Bull, Michael Cutlip, John DeWolf, John Feudo, Peter Halvorson, David Herzberger, Carla Hill, Kathleen Holgerson, Deborah McDonald, Monty Shaw, Suman Singha, Charles Super, Morton Tenzer, Timothy Tolokan, Thomas P. Weinland, and Robert Whitlach. Kent Newmyer, Tom Paterson, Milton Stern, Norman Stevens, and Elliot Wolk answered my questions about specific activities in which they were involved.

Without the resources and staff of Archives and Special Collections at UConn's Thomas J. Dodd Research Center, it would have been impossible to write this book. University Archivist Betsy Pittman and Curator of Multimedia Collections Kristin Eshelman were especially helpful in guiding me through a variety of written and photographic sources, respectively. I thank them for their cooperation and demonstration of the value to a historian of outstanding archivists who know well, and share generously, their collections. Kristin's expertise in digitizing photos facilitated their delivery to the publisher. Others on, or previously on, the Dodd Center staff who were always helpful in the Reading Room are Heidi Abbey, Terri Goldich, Laura Katz Smith, and Rutherford W. "Rudy" Witthus. University Photographer Peter Morenus's fine portfolio of recent photos complements the historic photo collection in the Dodd Center and is accessible on the Web site http://photo.pr.uconn.edu.

The university's Office of Institutional Research, under the direction of Pamela J. Roelfs, generously provided statistical and other information. Staff members Lauren Jorgensen and, particularly, Tara Latawic assisted with data collection; Tara went beyond the call of duty in finding historical references as well. The office's volume "Facts About the University of Connecticut since 1881," second edition, edited by Christine Rocco, is extremely useful for exploring the history of UConn. Dana Wilder and Suman Singha of the Provost's Office helped by responding to specific questions that I posed. Ronald C. Schurin, Executive Assistant to the President, made the files of the Austin administration, not yet conveyed to the Dodd Center archives, accessible to me. Gary Lewicki and Lillian Bosques always helped with business matters when needed. Early research received assistance and encouragement from Mark Jones and Bruce Stark of the Connecticut State Library. I enjoyed and learned from Mark Roy's photo history of the university. In preparation for an unpublished centennial history of the university, Evan Hill, then head of the Journalism Department, collected a vast amount of material on deposit at the Dodd Center that was useful in the writing of this volume. I thank him for his effort.

I very much appreciate the contributions of those I interviewed expressly for this study and for earlier oral histories that proved to be useful for understanding the history of the University of Connecticut. They are listed in the note on sources at the conclusion of this book. Some of the earliest interviews were conducted or supervised by my predecessor as the Director of the Center for Oral History, Morton Tenzer, Class of '53, who also served as an interviewee. His collegiality and support since I arrived at UConn in 1970 is most appreciated. Angela Rola of the Asian American Cultural Center and Roger Buckley of the Asian American Studies Institute facilitated interviews with the Japanese American alumni who returned to campus in October 2003. Linda Shopes, my co–general editor of the Palgrave/Macmillan Studies in Oral History series, encouraged my work on this volume and patiently put up with the delays it caused in our collaborative effort. Martha McCormick, manager of Tapescribe, supervised the transcriptions of oral histories with her usual efficiency and was of great assistance in operating the Center for Oral History. Jesse McCormick bailed me out several times when the computer gremlins became particularly rambunctious.

Support and resources for this project came from several sources, including the UConn chapter of the American Association of University Professors (AAUP), the Alumni Association, the UConn Foundation, the University of Connecticut Professional Employees Association, the Dodd Center, and the Office of the President, and I thank them all for their aid. The AAUP began the process with enthusiasm and encouragement. For that I wish to thank the AAUP Executive Committee and especially AAUP Executive Director Ed Marth, who has done so much good, in so many ways, for the University of Connecticut. Phyllis Deutsch, executive director of the University Press of New England, has shown interest in the development of the manuscript and has smoothed the way for publication.

While it is common in the sciences and social sciences to include multiple authors of a study, historians rarely share authorial credit with assistants. I think that is unfortunate and have tried to recognize on the title page the debt I owe to four individuals who worked directly with me as researchers and aides on this study. Three graduate assistants, Laura "Kat" Burmeister, Michael Neagle, and Leslie Horner Papandrea, helped in a variety of ways. Kat did archival research and did the first readings of newspapers (Bill Berger, an undergraduate, also helped with early newspaper research); Leslie conducted archival research and established the group's system of note-taking, which proved extremely helpful; Mike took over when Leslie received her master's degree—he did archival research, wrote photo captions, and helped in many other ways. My wife, Dr. Sondra Astor Stave, as usual did so much to assist me that I am forever in her debt. She encouraged me to undertake the project when I was reluctant to do so. She did the complete initial reading of the thirteen thousand pages of the Albert Waugh journal, which the former provost wrote on a daily basis from 1941 through 1969 (a treasure trove of a source if ever there was one); she served as my initial editor prior to chapters going to the editorial committee; and she helped with revisions. In addition to that, she has put up with me for nearly a half century. While these four share the title page with me, I am fully responsible for the interpretation, and for any errors that may appear. With respect to interpretation, I appreciate the editorial committee's commitment to avoiding censorship. Though it was written for the University of Connecticut's 125th anniversary, this is not an "official history" in the usual sense of the term. Truth-in-packaging requires notice that while the book's subtitle in honor of that anniversary carries the chronology, 1881–2006, writing ceased in the midsummer of 2005; hence, the events of the 2005–2006 academic year must await another history.

Finally, my toddler grandson with the long name, Stratton Braun Astor Stave, has not helped with the making of this book but has provided a wonderfully pleasant distraction for Grandpa Bear, who very much enjoys seeing him run around on the pedestrian mall in front of the Babbidge Library. His parents, Channing and Sara, are pretty nice as well.

B.M.S.
Coventry, Connecticut

Introduction

Why title a book about the historical development of the University of Connecticut *Red Brick in the Land of Steady Habits?* Connecticut has long been called the "land of steady habits," a nickname resulting from the allegedly strict morals of its inhabitants, who in the colony's earliest days and after were governed by rigid blue laws regulating public morality. In a time when blue laws are no more, the "land of steady habits" is sometimes employed with a grain of cynicism but is still recognized from the town of Greenwich at one end of the state to the town of Union at the other, as well as beyond the state's borders, as describing a moderate, middle-of-the-road Connecticut. "Red brick" is a British term. The "red brick" universities refer to those institutions, six originally, that were built in England's industrial cities during the late nineteenth century and achieved university status before World War II; others were established subsequently. Unlike the elite ancient universities of Oxford and Cambridge, or Harvard and Yale, the "red bricks" admitted students without reference to class or religion and concentrated on practical skills, often emphasizing engineering.[1]

The University of Connecticut had its roots in the Storrs Agricultural School, which was founded in 1881 to teach the very practical, real-world skills of farming, in contrast to the established, elite private institutions in the state, Yale, Wesleyan, and Trinity. While Yale served nominally as Connecticut's land-grant college before the school in Storrs seized that mantle in 1893, a story summarized in chapter 1, the New Haven institution graduated very few students of agriculture and emphasized a broader and more classical liberal arts curriculum, to the chagrin of Connecticut's farmers. As a state-supported school, accessible at comparatively low cost to a wide variety of students, the University of Connecticut developed as a "red brick in the land of steady habits." This volume, written in celebration of UConn's 125th anniversary, explores that history and traces how the university developed from local roots and came to extend beyond its regional identity to become a nationally recognized institution.

The last full history of the University of Connecticut marked the fiftieth anniversary of the Connecticut Agricultural College in 1931 and charted the early decades of the institution, before its designation as a university. While the present volume treats the university's entire 125 years, its primary emphasis concerns the decades after 1931 and the ways in which UConn's development represents the transformation of American public higher education during the twentieth and very early twenty-first centuries. In Connecticut's case, this is the story of educators, legislators, and governors creating a complex research university from the foundation of a tiny agricultural college. This history traces the emergence of the leading New England public university from the long and deep shadows cast by Yale, Harvard, and Brown, the region's great national universities, as well as the outstanding liberal arts colleges also concentrated in the region. The story supplies examples of the ways in which New Englanders addressed the challenges of diversity and co-education, affirmative action and racial tensions, as well as academic freedom issues. By analyzing the impact of student protests in the Great Depression, as well as World War II and its aftermath, the McCarthy red scare, and the rancorous demonstrations of the Viet Nam era, the book reveals the interplay of national and local forces in shaping higher education. Similarly, the unionization of the faculty, debates over undergraduate curriculum, and the creation of major research programs, professional schools, and big-time NCAA athletics disclose the particular ways that institutions adapt to changing aspirations and their social and political environments. Though this history concentrates on the University of Connecticut, a New England public university, the narrative reveals many of the ways that twentieth-century Americans generally remade higher education.[2]

The Connecticut story offers a complement to the histories of other state universities written since the end of World War II while simultaneously creating a narrative that illuminates the special characteristics of UConn's development. In New England, the published history of the University of Rhode Island (URI) provides a narrative of the land-grant idea in that state. While the origins of UConn and URI have much in common, the histories of the institutions and how they present themselves to the world differ markedly. Connecticut developed as the larger institution, with more advanced graduate programs and the ultimate distinction of becoming the region's leading public university. URI's history, written in the mid-1960s, does not consider issues of race, ethnicity, and gender, which have become historically commonplace since, and which receive significant attention in this volume. In contrast, the University of Vermont's story, published in 1991, does explore these topics as it investigates the transformation of that institution over two hundred years. That history is an edited anthology that brings together essays by several authors rather than providing a unified story written by a single author. It traces a quasi-public institution with initially elite, liberal arts college aspirations and a substantial out-of-state student body long before Connecticut would move in that direction. Concentrating more on undergraduate than graduate education and research, UVM historically received a smaller percentage of state budgetary support than the University of Connecticut has.[3]

In the Middle Atlantic States, Maryland and Pittsburgh offer representative institutional histories. Unlike UConn, with its roots in a small agricultural school, Maryland's university began in the early nineteenth century as a professional school, the Medical College of Maryland, and later developed into a complex state university offering undergraduate education tied to the land-grant concept. Pitt, with whom UConn today competes athletically in the Big East, began as a private urban institution in 1787 in a frontier town that would became a gritty city defined by its steel mills, and much later by its successful response to de-industrialization. Throughout Pitt's history, the university struggled with dual desires: to serve its city and region and to emerge as a national and international institution of higher learning. Yet Pitt only became state-related in 1966 and, as a consequence, has had a very different history from Connecticut's.[4]

The south boasts higher-education histories that reflect the special dimension of southern society and the impact of the Civil War, Reconstruction, Jim Crow, and desegregation. In the nineteenth-century midwest and west, which were devoid of such private, elite schools as Yale and Harvard, the state universities emerged as the earliest and ultimately the most powerful educational institutions, those that constitute the Big Ten and continue to dominate the Pacific coast. The University of Wisconsin's history, published for its 125th anniversary in 1975, is an edited anthology that does not emphasize social history but offers a portrait of an accomplished research institution long before Connecticut achieved that status. Similarly, the single-authored centennial volume on the University of California tells a story worthy of emulation. Its author begins, "The University of California has enjoyed international eminence for nearly three-quarters of its life, and, by 1964, Californians were no longer the least bit self-conscious when they called it 'great.'" The residents of Connecticut have not yet reached that stage, but the development of their state university offers a distinct sense of pride. This volume attempts to explain the path UConn followed and the terrain it traversed to bring it to its position of regional and national distinction in its 125th year.[5]

The book's organization follows the chronology of the administrations of the University of Connecticut's thirteen presidents. This framework provides for the coherent discussion of a wide variety of subjects embedded in the university's history. Recurring themes as varied as the creation of a major research library, the founding of professional schools, student life, athletics, and national research funding are treated within the context of particular presidential eras. The book traces the impact of the Great Depression, the effects of World War II and the postwar G.I. Bill, the Cold War era, and the economic boom of the 1990s. Throughout, the national and international context shaped events as Connecticut leaders transformed a serene, rural campus, a provincial "safety school," into a competitive and cosmopolitan national research university.

In chapter 1 I explore the beginnings of agricultural education in Connecticut and the influence of the ubiquitous Theodore Sedgwick Gold, as well as the impact of the 1862 Morrill Act, which endowed the nation's land-grant agricultural and technical colleges. I also investigate the origins of the school in the contribution of land, buildings, books, and money by two prosperous brothers, Augustus and Charles Storrs. The state's ascending educational expectations are evident in the successive renamings of the school: the Storrs Agricultural *College* in 1893, the *Connecticut* Agricultural College in 1899, and the Connecticut *State* College in 1933. In this chapter I examine the ideas and politics that led to these formal changes but focus especially on the prominent agricultural interests and their impact on the curriculum; the effects of World War I; and student life. A founding principal, six presidents, and two acting presidents served during this period. Two of the presidents, Benjamin Franklin Koons (1883–98) and Charles Lewis Beach (1908–28), exercised a major influence in shaping the future direction of their modest institution.

In the second chapter, covering the years 1935–45, I begin with student antimilitarism protests in the 1930s, the departure of Charles C. McCracken as president, and the arrival of the young, dynamic Midwesterner Albert Nels Jorgensen. This builder and reformer would lead the institution for twenty-seven years, propelling its transformation from a provincial college to a research and teaching institution that aspired to meet national standards of professionalism. In this chapter I treat World War II and its impact and pay particular attention to women students, the arrival of Japanese American students, and the academic freedom conflicts that developed when a faculty member of German origin was alleged to be a Nazi sympathizer. During this period, the legislature pointed to its own new ambitions by again renaming the college, this time as the University of Connecticut, in 1939.

Chapter 3 covers events during the second phase of Jorgensen's tenure, which extended through 1962. During these years, like many American institutions of higher education, UConn began to reshape itself into a complex university in the transformed educational environment of the postwar years. Throughout the United States citizens supported a vast expansion of public universities, and the University of Connecticut welcomed veterans at a special campus separate from the main campus while simultaneously reshaping the main campus at Storrs. During this period, local manifestations of such national issues as anti-Semitism, racism, and communism challenged administrators, faculty, students, and politicians. The president, the board of trustees, and the faculty responded to an aroused public, as did Governor John Davis Lodge, who sought to root out communism during the McCarthy era. As a consequence of charges of "red" connections, university authorities forced four professors to depart. A few years later, though student and public interest in intercollegiate sports were mounting, the board of trustees and the administration pledged to oppose "big-time" athletics. Instead, they devoted their efforts to the creation of a medical and dental school and acquired an existing law school, which they redeveloped into a full-fledged center of legal studies. Although President Jorgensen enjoyed wide support for his expansive initiatives in the late 1940s, the conflicts of the 1950s led some within the board of trustees, as well as many students and faculty members, to lose confidence in him, and an uncooperative governor made Jorgensen the target of criticism, which led to his ultimate departure.

The fourth chapter is devoted to the presidency of Homer Daniels Babbidge between 1962 and 1972. Like Jorgensen, Babbidge made an indelible mark on the university during his decade of leadership. Shaped by his education at Yale and his service in the national government, Babbidge promoted the state university in the liberal arts, humanistic tradition. His ambition won many supporters, though he also aroused the opposition of some faculty, alumni, and legislators who still envisioned the institution's future as chiefly agricultural and technical. The Babbidge decade is divided into two five-year segments: the first portrays a honeymoon period—stressing library growth, bringing America's leading novelists to Storrs, establishing an art museum, and shaping a new, cosmopolitan image for the university. The second period found UConn caught up in the turbulent political and social currents of the 1960s. Antiwar protests, especially those targeting on-campus recruiting, divided students and faculty and led Babbidge to bring the state police to Storrs. Consequently, though he maintained an unusual degree of popularity compared with many university presidents, Babbidge became the target of an angry minority. Moreover, the disciplining of four activist faculty members and the dismissal of three of them awakened academic freedom issues and left a bitter legacy. Race-based demonstrations heated the atmosphere as black power moved from slogan to action at Storrs and elsewhere across the nation. The movement for women's liberation further revealed ongoing discrimination in hiring, promotion, and salaries. Worn down by the tide of criticism and conflict, Homer Babbidge resigned on October 1, 1971, the ninth anniversary of his becoming president, and after ten years' service he left in 1972.

While Jorgensen and Babbidge shaped the creation of a modern University of Connecticut over the course of thirty-seven years, their next three successors, treated in chapter 5—Glenn W. Ferguson, John A. DiBiaggio, and John T. Casteen III—consolidated the institution's strengths over a seventeen-year period while struggling to maintain earlier advances in the face of declining state budgets. One success was the university's acceptance of collective bargaining in 1976, after a heated campaign between two faculty groups. The legacy of the administration's flexibility has been a productive relationship among the faculty union, the AAUP, and the administration. The faculty union remains a critical balancing force among administration, the faculty, the legislature, and the governor. Twice the union's willingness to forego contracted pay increases has been instrumental in breaking political logjams and preserving university programs.

But in 1978 the new library's faulty construction was an emblematic management failure. A project supervised by the state department of public works, the plastic-wrapped library facade quickly became symbolic of a decaying campus infrastructure. As on campuses across the nation, the challenges of affirmative action, gender equity, racism, and homophobia buffeted the institution. Attention to student life, drinking, and drugs competed with the development of research programs in the natural sciences, engineering, the humanities, and the social sciences.

One dramatic success was the university's response to the Civil Rights Act's Title IX, which opened new vistas for women's athletics. Decisions by DiBiaggio and Casteen laid the foundation for an era of unprecedented success in women's athletics and in men's soccer and basketball. In 1979 the university became a founding member of the Big East conference. It hired two basketball coaches in 1985 and 1986 who would later join the leading ranks of their profession as a result of their achievements at Connecticut. At the end of the 1980s the university embraced big-time athletics as part of its plan to achieve national prominence, constructing a domed basketball arena, the Gampel Pavilion, that opened in 1990 and preparing to enter into new television contracts that, in addition to revenue, promised increased visibility within Connecticut and across the nation.

The final chapter, which covers the administrations of Harry J. Hartley and Philip E. Austin, extends my analysis of the topics treated in the previous one. I explore the genesis and implementation of two major building programs, "UConn 2000" in 1995 and "21st Century UConn" in 2003, which committed a total of $2.3 billion in state bonding. These initiatives were not merely intended to repair an old infrastructure but to transform the campus, providing space for research programs and making the university more attractive and comfortable for its students. Drawing on an expanding regional and national pool of applicants, the university succeeded in raising its admission standards and enrolling students with substantially higher class ranks and standardized test scores than ever before. Greater ethnic diversity in the student body and rebuilt and rededicated library and student union facilities symbolized the campus's vitality despite diminished operating budgets and the difficulties in managing a complex building program. In addition to its improved facilities, national basketball championships by the women's and men's teams in 1995 and 1999, respectively, and the unprecedented 2004 dual championship have attracted national attention to Connecticut's university, as have the upgrade of football to Division I, the building of a new stadium, and the joining of the Big East on the gridiron.

As the new century began, the faculty adopted curriculum reform and the board of trustees acted to replace faculty who left in response to early retirement incentives, a pattern common to a number of public universities, including the University of California. Research successes—for example, as in the field of reproductive genetics—attracted national and international attention and brought research funding to all-time highs. As the University of Connecticut celebrates its 125th anniversary, a once modest agricultural school and then a regional institution has emerged as a national university.

While one might detect a progressive arc in this analysis of UConn, it is not the author's intent to paint a rose-colored portrait in which to set Connecticut's "red brick" university. The purpose has been to etch a balanced narrative and analytical portrait that reveals the positive but does not hide the negative in the university's history. In a few instances in chapters 5 and 6, I participated in the events described; such participation is identified in the appropriate footnotes. Finally, a word about words. On occasion, terms such as "co-ed" or "Negro" are employed, rather than woman student or African American. When they are so used, it is to reflect the terminology of the time period under consideration. Also, some editorial readers have suggested that UConn is a local term that is not entirely respectful of the seriousness of the institution. I disagree with that assessment. I believe that the university has reached a point in its development where when people say "UConn" they recognize that the university is the subject, not the Yukon of the great snowy north. Therein lies the story I tell in the pages that follow.

Red Brick in the Land of Steady Habits

1

In the Beginning: 1881–1935

*T*WO PRINCIPALS, six presidents, and two acting presidents provided leadership to the community of students, faculty, and staff that gathered in Storrs to learn, teach, and serve during the five and a half decades prior to the arrival of Albert Nels Jorgensen in 1935. The small Storrs Agricultural School, established in 1881, became the Storrs Agricultural College in 1893, then the Connecticut Agricultural College in 1899, and finally the Connecticut State College in 1933. University status came six years later. By that time, the foundations, traditions, customs, and culture of the institution had long been set. At several points, the tension between the perceived needs of an agricultural education and the requirements of classical learning clashed and tore at the fabric of community consensus. Indeed, the college, in all of its youthful vigor, began as an exciting and stimulating place and continued as such despite the charge that "the institution was founded in a rock-bestrewn wilderness, three miles from any railroad, and eight from any town of size."[1]

The Storrs Agricultural School

The need for agricultural training in New England resonated throughout the nineteenth century. In the early 1800s, short-lived agricultural schools arose in Maine, Massachusetts, and Connecticut, the last established by Josiah Holbrook in Derby. The idea of "book farming," or agricultural education, found its strongest advocate in Theodore Sedgwick Gold, who, with his father, Samuel, established the Cream Hill Agricultural School in West Cornwall, Connecticut, which operated from 1845 until Samuel's death in 1869. In the face of increasing industrialization and urbanization, the younger Gold desired to preserve agriculture as a way of life. Agricultural education would teach scientific methods so that Connecticut farmers could become more productive, make a greater profit, and remain on the farm rather than move to the city or seek new land in the west. Gold organized farmers' clubs and associations, and he and his wife were charter members and officers of the Cornwall Grange, which met in their home. At the first meeting in New Haven of Connecticut's State Board of Agriculture in August 1866, those present elected Gold the group's first secretary, its most influential position. Not surprisingly, fourteen years later that board recommended to the state legislature that it accept the gifts of land and money from brothers Charles and Augustus Storrs. The Connecticut General Assembly, on April 21, 1881, thus passed legislation to establish the Storrs Agricultural School (SAS).[2]

The ancestors of the brothers Storrs had arrived in Massachusetts from England in 1663 and moved to Mansfield, Connecticut, thrity-five years later, settling on the rolling land that now is home to the University of Connecticut. The brothers grew up on that land but made their fortunes as businessmen in Brooklyn, New York. By the time Charles died in 1884 and Augustus in 1892, their gifts had spawned the SAS. In 1880, Augustus donated 170 acres of land, the school's first structure, Whitney Hall, and several farm buildings; Charles initially contributed $5,000 and shortly thereafter added another $1,000. He also transferred eight hundred volumes from his private collection to initiate the school's library. The site had previously been used as the Connecticut Soldiers' Orphans' Home, the inspiration of the ubiquitous Theodore Gold, who would become the home's secretary and later an influential trustee of the SAS. Edwin Whitney, who had been encouraged to start a boys' school in Mansfield, rebuilt the school after a fire in 1865. He conveyed it as a loan to the state for the orphanage, which enrolled approximately two hundred children prior to its closing in 1875. This shutdown gave rise to a convoluted process in which the trustees of the home "sold" the property, consisting of Whitney Hall and other buildings on fifty acres, back to Whitney's widow for one dollar; she, in turn, transferred it to Augustus Storrs for $5,000. The transaction ended up in court when the initial sale was challenged as violating the terms of Edwin Whitney's will. As a consequence, when Augustus Storrs made his gift to the state, title was not clear and the future of the school hung in the balance, lending ammunition to those who challenged the location and wished to move it elsewhere.[3]

First, however, the institution had to take root. By the end of September 1881, students began to arrive at the two-year vocational school for boys. It held its formal public opening on October 7, when townspeople, a delegation from the Willimantic Farmers' Club, and citizens from around Connecticut filled the Mansfield church for the ceremonies. Thirteen students attended the first fall term. They were required to be at least fifteen years old and to submit a certificate assuring good moral character from a clergyman or a member of the Board of School Visitors in their town. Their parents had to be citizens of Connecticut. Entrance requirements included an examination in reading, spelling, writing, arithmetic, English, grammar, geography, American history, and practical agriculture. It cost $25 a year to attend, or $10 a term for each of the three twelve-week terms that comprised the school year, which began the last Wednesday in September. In addition, the charge for board, including laundry, fuel, and lights, was about $2.50 per week. A staff of three taught the pioneer student body, which came to a school that regarded itself as "unlike . . . any institution existing in this country."[4]

The school's trustees appointed Solomon Mead of New Haven as first principal and professor of agriculture, Dr. H. P. Armsby as vice-principal and professor of agricultural chemistry, and Benjamin Franklin Koons, who would have the most significant impact in Storrs, as professor of natural history. These three scholars presided over a routine that found students rising at 6:30 A.M., eating breakfast at 7:00 followed immediately by prayers, attending classes from 8:00 until noon, lunching at 12:15 P.M., doing manual labor between 2:00 and 5:00 P.M., having dinner at 6:00 P.M., and studying between 7:00 and 9:00 P.M., at which point the kerosene lights were turned off. While reports found students "engaged with zest in their manual labor duties," over the next two decades athletics would replace such chores, to the great approval of the student body. The young men had felt particularly aggrieved by the task of picking up and moving stones, as expressed in the first verse of a popular song:

> A freshman once did come to Storrs,
>   As green as green could be,
> He went to walk in a nice white shirt
>   To see what he could see,
> But when he saw the rocks that lay
>   Scattered all over, he swore
> As a freshman sometimes will and said,
>   I won't pick rocks any more.

> [Chorus]

> I won't pick rocks any more
>   I have picked for years
>   On my father's farm and
> I won't pick rocks any more.

Such sentiment, however, did not easily convince those who believed that a farmer must perform hard labor and students should be prepared to do so as well. Such "instructive labor" fit with the course in agricultural practice assigned by the first trustees, who also recognized the need to teach agricultural science. A graduate of the SAS would be well prepared for all facets of farming.[5]

"Not . . . an asylum for incapables"

Solomon Mead remained principal for only a brief time and was then replaced by Dr. Armsby as acting principal. In 1882, Armsby went before the Connecticut Board of Agriculture to present "a plain, unvarnished account of what the Storrs Agricultural School has done, is doing, and aims to do." Armsby promised that he would not "give a puff for the School—to exaggerate its merits or hide its demerits." He explained it wasn't "a little college" or a scientific school, nor was it a school for the benefit of those who were not smart enough to go to a college or scientific school. "It is not, and will not be made, an asylum for incapables," Armsby contended as he described SAS's "carefully planned" two-year regimen of study. Courses in chemistry, physics, natural philosophy, biology, geology, and mineralogy shared time with classes in scientific cattle feeding and stock breeding, structural botany, vegetable physiology, and bookkeeping. Armsby assured one questioner that the SAS was not a school for the sons of the wealthy; rather, in a precedent that would stand for the next century and a quarter, it aimed to provide access to those of ordinary means. He hoped, moreover, that its graduates would emerge as leaders in their communities and models for successful farmers.[6]

Armsby had little time to oversee such development. His brief tenure as acting principal concluded by the winter term of 1883, when the trustees appointed Benjamin Franklin Koons as principal. Koons, from Ohio, was a Civil War veteran who had been taken prisoner and incarcerated in one of the worst Confederate camps, an experience of suffering and endurance that shaped his later ability to cope with challenges. He graduated from Oberlin College in 1874 and did advanced work at Yale's Sheffield Scientific School, graduating in 1881. In addition to his administrative work at Storrs, Koons, as professor of natural history, taught geology, zoology, and political economy. Over the two decades until his death in 1903, his leadership and teaching made him a favorite of the school's community and its supporters. He guided the school through difficult times and a period of early growth that included its transition into the Storrs Agricultural College in 1893.[7]

The school, ten years after its establishment, enrolled sixty-three students and graduated thirteen of them in June 1891. Despite some interest in moving the SAS from its initial site because of the clouded nature of the original deed, once the title cleared the school's location remained set. The General Assembly's appropriation of $50,000 in 1889 allowed construction the next year of a frame structure, the Main Building (known as "Old Main" and torn down in 1929) and a thirty-room dormitory, named Gold Hall after Theodore S. Gold, which burned down in 1914. The school at Storrs might have continued to grow in this manner, slowly and steadily, without any pretensions of becoming a college.

However, federal legislation, and dissatisfaction on the part of the state grange with Yale's role as a training ground for farmers, would change all that.[8]

Land Grant: Yale's Loss, Storrs's Gain

President Abraham Lincoln signed the first Morrill Act, the Land Grant Act of 1862, on July 2 of that year. Less than six months later, on the day before Christmas, Connecticut became the third state to accept its provisions, which encouraged the establishment of agricultural and mechanical colleges. In the midwest and other regions this act led to the establishment of several new institutions including those that would become the University of Illinois and Purdue University, and led to the inclusion of existing schools such as Iowa State and Minnesota. In New England, however, where "classical" colleges already existed, Dartmouth, Brown, and Yale took on the mantle of the land-grant institution. Yale, established in 1701, operated as Connecticut's land-grant college through its Sheffield Scientific School despite the fact that it had no farm and its admission standards proved to be an obstacle for many farm boys. The Connecticut State Grange, following the lead of its national association's attack on classical colleges as training grounds for farmers, was quick to make this point. In 1886, moreover, it charged that in the twenty-four years since the passage of the Morrill Act, Yale had graduated only seven agricultural course students, and at the prohibitive cost of $180,000, or $25,700 each. On the other hand, the grange praised the SAS and pledged it both "patronage and protection." It also began a campaign to leverage land-grant funds away from Yale and toward Storrs. When the U.S. Congress recognized the need for research as a basis for developing agriculture and passed the Hatch Act in 1887 to authorize federal funding for an agricultural experiment station in connection with each land-grant institution, the money was split between the existing Connecticut Agricultural Experiment Station in New Haven and the newly created Storrs Agricultural Experiment Station; the latter, under the initial directorship of W. O. Atwater, went on to become nationally and internationally distinguished for its research. Then, when the Second Morrill Act in 1890 provided each state with $15,000 annually plus additional funds, giving Connecticut assured federal financing for agriculture of $25,000, the competition between New Haven and Storrs intensified. In 1892, the National Grange expanded its attack on agricultural colleges attached to classical institutions, claiming success for none and asserting some to be "dismal failures" while the independent agricultural and mechanical colleges were "eminently successful." Such an argument must have been persuasive, because on April 21, 1893, twelve years to the day after the SAS had been established, the General Assembly approved the establishment of the Storrs Agricultural College (SAC), assigning to the new college the funds from both the First and the Second Morrill Acts.[9]

Yale did not take the matter lightly. The venerable institution sued but failed in the courts. As a consequence, it invoked a section of the 1893 Connecticut law setting up the SAC, which also created a commission to consider damages. In a two to one decision, the three-member commission awarded the New Haven college $154,604, and the SAC became the sole beneficiary of the Morrill Acts and the state's uncontested land-grant institution. While the court award ended the legal wrangling, hard feelings did not die quickly. The *New Haven Register* would not let the matter rest. Although the *Willimantic Journal* editorialized in 1886 that "No other school offers so much at such small cost," several years later the *Register* carried a complaint that national funds were wasted in Storrs and should be restored to Yale. The indictment contended: "The 'agricultural college' pure and simple is still an experiment from the educational point of view, and not a very successful one at that. . . . Connecticut has managed to acquire an institution that is at once a farce and a fake . . . the faculty collected by the board has been enough to damn any institution. . . . The scholarship has been of the poorest quality. It is a fact that an alumnus, who is also a member of the board of trustees, is unable to spell correctly. . . . A diploma from Storrs has never stood for serious training and high scholarship." The fallout from the "Yale-Storrs controversy" lingered well into the early twentieth century.[10]

Women Come to the College

When the Storrs Agricultural School became the Storrs Agricultural College, Principal Koons became President Koons. His presidency coincided with the arrival of the first women to study and teach at Storrs. Whether this resulted from coincidence or from the fact that Koons had been educated at Oberlin College, the first co-educational college in the United States, is uncertain. Nevertheless, it has been suggested that his training at the Ohio school made him particularly receptive to enrolling women students. Beginning with the spring 1891 term, Mansfield residents Nellie Wilson and Louise Rosebrooks became the first female commuting students to attend courses; a total of twenty women had gone to classes prior to 1893, when the school transformed into the college. Despite an aborted attempt in the State Senate to exclude them, the law establishing the college did not bar women from attending, which offered an opening for their increased matriculation. Once this occurred, the college hired Margaret Kenwill to oversee female education and serve as instructor in music. By October 1896, the campus newspaper, the *Lookout,* reported that Oak Grove Cottage (later simply called Grove Cottage) had been built for "young ladies" and was "the handsomest building upon the campus." It informed male students that they could come calling between 7:00 and 10:00 P.M. on Friday evenings.

Women, however, pondered other matters besides who would "come calling."

Just what did they acquire from studying in Storrs? By the time Bertha M. Patterson, Class of 1899, asked that question, the Morrill Act of 1890 already had encouraged women's study of "domestic science" or home economics at the land-grant colleges as matters akin to the agricultural and mechanical arts for men. Patterson agreed that the SAC prepared "boys" to be farmers and "girls" to be farmers' wives: "We are taught to be good housekeepers," she proclaimed. There was, however, more. Women learned to be better company to themselves "by becoming better acquainted with books and reading" and, thereby, better company to others. Familiarity with "the great world of men and things" negated the idea that "women, as housekeepers, must be narrow-minded and uninterested in things outside their own little domain of kitchen, sewing room, and nursery." They would be better fitted to face the world when they left Storrs than when they entered. From a twenty-first-century perspective, the results of Koons's encouragement of co-education at the end of the nineteenth may seem quaint, but, for its time, it was very advanced.[11]

Koons, Flint, and the "War of the Rebellion"

During the fifteen years of Koons's leadership, the Storrs campus blossomed. Student enrollment expanded from thirty in 1883 to 132 in 1898. Students founded a variety of organizations including the previously mentioned *Lookout,* which began publishing in 1896; a debate club followed a year later. Athletic teams began to carry the Storrs banner in football and baseball during the early 1890s. (Men's basketball started in 1901 with a 17–12 victory over Willimantic High School, and the women initiated play the next year, beating the same school 15–6.) The SAC became a more complex, but far from overwhelming, institution. Koons, however, who was generally well liked by the college community, ran into increasing difficulty with the board of trustees, which was then led by W. E. Simonds of Canton. In early June 1897, The *Hartford Courant* reported rumors of Koons's dismissal. The trustees allegedly were dissatisfied with his methods and contended "that the college needs a more energetic, up-to-date management." They also appeared to find fault with discipline on campus; the newspaper alluded to the expulsion of several students who broke into the college pantry during the previous year. The rumor mill also suggested that the trustees favored A. B. Peebles, a professor of physics and chemistry and graduate of the Michigan Agricultural College (later Michigan State), who for a while had been a minister in Utah, to replace Koons. The alumni, who had been organized into an association since 1888, favored a new president as well, but not if Peebles were the replacement. Shortly after the newspaper report, the trustees accepted Koons's resignation, to take effect at the close of the 1898 school year; they also gave him a $300 raise, bringing his salary in 1898 to $2,800. The alumni agreed to the trustees' action but requested that Koons be retained as a professor because of their admiration for his work as an instructor. He thus remained on the faculty, teaching and serving as curator of the natural history museum, which he earlier had established. In 1899, Koons was paid $2,000. Then, as today, administrators earned more than regular faculty.[12]

The trustees in 1900 paid new president George W. Flint $2,500; hence Koons's successor made less than his own 1898 presidential salary. Connecticut's farmers would probably have argued that he was worth significantly below that amount. Flint's brief administration, from July 1898 to October 1901, became embroiled in a dispute between supporters of classical education and champions of agricultural studies. It became so intense that some irreverently compared the split to the American Civil War, labeling it the "War of the Rebellion." While the "War" had no battle of Gettysburg, Flint's opponents certainly took no prisoners. Flint, the 1871 salutatorian of Bates College, was born in Yarmouth, Nova Scotia, and spent his early years in Maine. He taught there and in New Hampshire and then became the principal of the Collinsville (Connecticut) High School in 1874, a position that he held until his appointment in Storrs. It did not take long for him to emerge as a leading citizen of Collinsville, an influential member of the Congregational Church and the president of the town's Savings Society. His marriage in 1873 to Elizabeth Monteith of McIndoe's Falls, Vermont, would have indirect, but long-range, implications for the school at Storrs when Flint hired his brother-in-law, Henry R. Monteith, to teach English, history, civics, and algebra to freshmen and sophomores. When Flint arrived there in the fall of 1898, his daughter was almost sixteen and his two sons attended Yale as a senior and a freshman. Newspaper reports stated that he "paid intelligent attention to the interests of Connecticut farmers." More tellingly, however, they also referred to his active membership in the Connecticut Association of Classical High School Teachers and his service on its executive committee. Flint was fond of quoting in Latin, Greek, and Old English. Ultimately, his attention to agriculture bowed to his intense interest in classical education, which alienated the grange and other farm groups. The sores of the controversy over the land-grant funds and the farmers' antagonism toward Yale reopened, with the main tension this time being intra-institutional rather than inter-institutional.[13]

Unrest also resulted from the belief among some in the college community that Flint headed an autocratic administration. Koons had been an easygoing leader and the trustees wanted his successor to take a firmer hand over operations. For instance, critics of Koons's benign neglect contended that under his tenure instructors indiscriminately and wastefully ordered supplies, that they and their wives traveled at the state's expense, and that they used the long-distance telephone (a relatively new device) without restriction, piling up high bills for calls for which there was no accounting. Flint clamped down on such activity and quickly made campus enemies. Still, his supporters pointed out that not only was he an efficient manager, but under his presidency the farm department had been equipped with a complete outfit of farm appliances; the poultry department had been thoroughly equipped; and the dairy department had been established in one of the best dairy plants among the New England state colleges. Through his trademark management, he had also been able to erect a new agricultural hall, doing so without a special state appropriation; it later became a section of the Dairy Building. Despite all of this, though, the hue and cry against Flint mounted to the point that at the end of August 1901 the Connecticut State Grange, representing twelve thousand organized farmers and their families, called for his resignation. Petitions followed and a rash of newspaper accounts argued the issue, pro and con. Flint became so controversial that he had little choice but to step down. While he received a year's severance pay, which became a further subject of contention, the situation had grown so charged that the trustees refused to appoint him to a professorship as they had Koons. Nevertheless, as the history of the college at Storrs developed, it would become clear that while Flint had lost the battle, he had won the war.[14]

It is not without consequence that during his administration, on June 14, 1899, the General Assembly changed the institution's name from the Storrs to the Connecticut Agricultural College (CAC). The change, which retained "Agricultural" in the title, reflected the belief that appropriations and general backing for the school would have greater support if the entire state could identify with it. It also acknowledged the aspirations of the institution, its striving to be a college attractive to all residents of the state. Like it or not, an increasing number of graduates did not become farmers, which is probably what caused some of the grange's dissatisfaction with Flint. Koons had begun the process of broadening the mission of the college prior to Flint's arrival, but Flint's administrative and personal style brought the situation to a head. His successor, Rufus Whitaker Stimson, offered once again a more genial style and made certain not to offend the college's agricultural constituency while advancing its development into more than a farm school.[15]

Stimson Sheds Light

Stimson, who was first appointed acting president on October 5, 1901, did not receive the full title until more than a year later. He came to Storrs at the age of twenty-nine as professor of English language and literature. Born in Palmer, Massachusetts, which was close to the Connecticut state line, Stimson received his bachelor's and master's degrees from Harvard, where he specialized in philosophy; in 1897 he graduated from Yale's Divinity School. His talent for public relations suited the college well after the tumult of the Flint administration. As he began his first year in office, he sent a letter to "graduates and friends" to request their assistance in making the CAC better known to citizens across the state. He assured them that faculty vacancies created during the "War of the Rebellion" had been filled "with a full corps of competent instructors" and "our equipment is far superior to anything previously found here." He extolled "with unstinted enthusiasm and with unbounded belief . . . the sterling educational value of the courses of study." Stimson also invited his readers to see for themselves. With a flare for chamber of commerce promotion, he described Willimantic as the most important railway center in eastern Connecticut, noting that it had frequent trains, excellent livery stables, and fine hotel accommodations, "and behind a good horse on a pleasant day, whether in warm weather or in cold, few trips are more delightful than that in the town of Mansfield between Willimantic and the Connecticut Agricultural College at Storrs." If one could not visit, he offered to send reports, announcements, catalogues, and circulars to anyone who put themselves on the CAC mailing list. He also promoted the college by developing its summer school and in particular making it attractive to schoolteachers throughout the state, who would be lured by the emphasis on "Agriculture and Nature Study." Stimson reasoned that the teachers would spread word of the wonders in Storrs to students, parents, and others.[16]

Stimson's need to publicize the college did not prevent him from attending to his smaller administrative duties as well, which illustrate the tasks in the charge of a president during those early years of the college. In March 1904 he wrote to the father of a senior who had broken the rule forbidding ball-playing within a hundred feet of any college building. The senior and a lower classman had used a dormitory wall as a backstop. Before the rule went into effect, stray balls had continually broken windows and split clapboards. In Stimson's words, "The damage was considerable, the inconvenience caused by it was great and the buildings were constantly being disfigured." He offered the student a choice of two penalties: a five-dollar fine or one week's suspension from all college privileges. Records do not reveal which punishment the student accepted, but the letter to his father demonstrates Stimson's recognition of the need to communicate. He regretted having to write but wanted to make certain that the parent understood why the penalty was necessary. In this disciplinary matter, Stimson, while asserting his authority, did not abandon the sense of public relations that marked his administration.[17]

He effectively won the support of the grange for a much-needed new dormitory on campus. As the campus newspaper, the *Lookout,* wrote, "The work of the College has never stood so well with the farmers of the State as it does today." Lack of living space discouraged students from applying to the college, and Stimson realized what was needed to remedy the situation. At the urging of the grange, the General Assembly appropriated $60,000 for the building of Storrs Hall, the first brick dormitory on campus, which provided thirty-three two-bedroom suites, each with a common study.[18]

Contractors also installed wiring for electric lights, the prospect of which delighted the editors of the *Lookout,* who welcomed those already in place in the chapel, library, and dining hall. They marveled that whereas ten years earlier no one gave a thought to electricity, by 1907 it was coming into general use. The electrification of the campus in Storrs served as a model for farmers. "It seems as if money invested by a farmer in electric lights for his farm buildings would be a paying investment when the safety and efficiency of the electric light is compared with the oil lantern," conjectured the college journalists. By the time Stimson, giving notice to the end of the school year, resigned his position in February 1908 to head the new Smith Agricultural School in Northampton, Massachusetts, the college at Storrs not only had a new dormitory and electricity but the beginnings of a horticulture building and greenhouses as well. The purchase of an additional one hundred acres of Storrs property increased the size of the campus. Enrollment shot up to 125 regular students and twenty-five short-term students; ninety-eight even enrolled in the 1907 summer session. Stinson left with the appreciation of the board of trustees and general agreement in the college community with the *Lookout* editorial that stated, "During his term of service the institution has made commendable progress." His successor inherited an institution in significantly better repair then when Stimson himself had taken the reins.[19]

Beach the Builder

Two years prior to the president's resignation, the *Lookout* announced with great regret the departure from Storrs of Professor Charles Lewis Beach, a popular instructor of dairy husbandry whose research had contributed significantly to the dairy science of that day. The student editors wished him success and happiness in his new position at the University of Vermont and wrote, "However attractive his new field may be, we do not believe that his work in Connecticut was done, or that there was not, in this state and College, room for further development in his chosen pursuit." The trustees apparently agreed and brought Beach back to serve as president after Stimson. The *Lookout* editors rejoiced and predicted a hearty welcome from faculty, students, and alumni for the forty-two-year-old native of Whitewater, Wisconsin, who held B.A. and B.S. degrees from the University of Wisconsin. His ten years of experience in the milling business before initially arriving at the college at Storrs in 1896 added to his credentials, which by the time of his return as president made him well suited for the job.[20]

Beach's two decades of leadership at CAC brought a great deal of physical change that culminated in the construction, beginning in 1927, of a $420,000 brick classroom, laboratory, and administration building that opened in 1929, a year after he left the presidency. Named in his honor, Beach Hall replaced Old

Main, which had been demolished in the wake of the new structure. With that, the original wood-structured campus at Storrs, built after 1881, had disappeared. Fire had also taken its toll. Gold Hall, a dormitory, burned in 1914; the Chemistry Building ignited in 1917; the Dairy Barn and Grove Cottage, the women's dorm, fell to flames within forty-eight hours of each other in July 1919. Only Old Main and the Experiment Station survived the conflagrations, with the former falling to the wrecker's ball as a sign of brick-and-mortar progress. New buildings, such as a much-improved women's dorm (Holcomb Hall, 1921), a dining facility ("The Beanery," 1920, now the site of the Benton Museum of Art), and Hall Dormitory (1927), created a campus landscape made of brick. While his efforts would be dwarfed by what would come later to the campus, Charles Lewis Beach was indeed a builder.[21]

The college changed in other ways too. When Beach started as president, 167 students were enrolled at Storrs and thirty-six faculty, including a dozen members of the Agricultural Experiment Station, worked there. The library numbered ten thousand books and the curriculum offered eighty-eight courses, several of them not academic in nature. Two decades later, when he left office, the student body had tripled to five hundred students, a statutory limit set by the legislature. The faculty had more than doubled and the experiment station staff exceeded fifty at the state and county levels. The number of books in the library had doubled and the curriculum had expanded beyond agriculture to include the humanities and the social sciences as well as the physical and biological sciences. This larger faculty was also better trained and taught 250 courses. Improvement was not really that difficult, given the conditions when Beach began his tenure. Assessing the college during Beach's very earliest years as president, Albert E. Waugh, who had a long Connecticut career ranging from 1924 through 1965 that took him from instructor to provost, commented, "In 1912 it was a college but a college which did not require high school graduation for admission and did not award a degree on graduation." This would be remedied after 1914. Although the institution may have seemed a college in name only, it did have a certain distinction. Albert F. Blakeslee, one of the few faculty members of his time to hold a doctorate, came to CAC in 1907 to teach courses in agriculture. This Harvard-educated botanist, among his other achievements, undertook genetic research on plants and in 1913 began teaching one of the first, if not the very first, organized courses on genetics in an American college or university. By so doing, he put the institution on the path toward significant research undertakings with wide-ranging implications. Blakeslee departed Storrs in 1915, but he used his Harvard network to turn President Beach toward Cambridge to replace him.[22]

Beach searched there for a new head of the Botany Department. He selected twenty-seven-year-old Edmund Sinnott to replace Blakeslee and brought the even younger George Safford Torrey with him. Sinnott earned Waugh's assessment as the best scholar on staff and the college's intellectual leader. He headed the Botany Department for twelve years, until he left CAC in 1928 for Barnard and Columbia. In 1940 he joined Yale, from which he retired as dean of the graduate school in 1956. Torrey became Botany Department head in 1929 and remained in that position until 1953. Years later, in October 1980, the university honored him by dedicating the Life Sciences Building in his name. Beach would have appreciated Torrey's long period of service to the institution. When he started his term as president, Beach recognized the need for stability in faculty and staff. Legend had it that personnel had traditionally kept their shipping crates intact because of the college's reputation for rapid turnover. The president's first advice to faculty was "throw away your packing cases." He successfully advocated for higher faculty salaries and actively showed his concern for their welfare. Shortly after Beach left office, he summarized this relationship, remarking modestly that his main contribution to the growth and development of the college was to show good judgment in selecting new staff members: "It was the faculty that made this institution and I soon found out that if the members of the staff are happy and if they are contented and if they feel reasonably safe and secure in their positions and have an opportunity to develop their departments, they will pull a president up and push him over the top. It's the teamwork and cooperation of the faculty of an institution that make it great," he stated, offering his prescription for administrative success.[23]

CAC Fights the Great War

Beach oversaw the changes that had an impact on campus during World War I. The Great War, the name used before the outbreak of World War II for the conflagration of 1914 that the United States entered in 1917, made its mark on the CAC. By one count, 653 Storrs men served their country during the war; half were students, faculty, and alumni, and half were members of the Student Army Training Corps (SATC). Seven men gave their life. The SATC allowed the federal government entrance into over six hundred colleges and technical schools in order to strengthen the military. Students inducted into the SATC became part of the army and took courses appropriate for warfare. By the summer of 1918, the college had in fact suspended all regular courses. Earlier, when faculty and students trained together, the homogenizing effects of military preparedness surprised students when three faculty members drilled with them. Professors Torrey, H. B. Price, an instructor in economics, and F. W. Duffee, an instructor in farm machinery, took their places in the ranks with the student trainees. They asked to be put into the same squad, but the captain in charge refused because of their differences in height. None of them had ever drilled before, but they chose to do so in the event that they would be called in the draft. Despite their loss of status as faculty, these three privates claimed to enjoy the drill as the campus became an army camp.[24]

The college's campaign to teach the scientific supervision of food production and conservation likely proved to be more significant to the war effort than its contribution to military training. During the summer of 1917, the CAC's canning courses attracted nearly six hundred participants, who subsequently spread across the state to preach and practice food conservation. That same year, students left Storrs to serve as garden supervisors around Connecticut. Administrators adjusted the college's schedule so that those trained in agriculture could begin work with the spring planting and stay on the job until harvest time, which meant closing the school early and opening it late in the fall. No vacations, longer class hours, and regular Saturday-morning classes were all accepted as part of the necessary sacrifice for the war effort in order to compensate for the time lost by closing. The summer of 1918 found many students in the field as supervisors or farm laborers. The college also hosted the Boys' Working Reserve, which brought high school students from all over the state for instruction in agriculture and military training. Faculty members served on Connecticut's Committee of Food Supply and the State Council on Defense. Students began a campaign to send copies of the *Connecticut Campus* newspaper and personal letters to all CAC men in service. Liberty bond drives met with great enthusiasm, and the Storrs community exceeded its goals. The women of Grove Cottage purchased thirty-two square yards of bunting to make a service flag showing a star for every CAC man enlisted. Every female student would sew at least one star on the flag as a wave of support bathed CAC in wartime spirit and patriotism.[25]

Women students did significantly more than act as latter-day Betsy Rosses. During the summer, they engaged in varying aspects of war work, filling men's places in offices and factories. They supervised gardens, worked in canning kitchens or demonstrated canning skills, joined "farmerette" units and participated in the Land Army Unit; they also rescued the apple crop in the fall of 1918. Not unlike what would happen more than two decades later during World War II, with the male students in the service, women took on campus leadership positions. For example, President Beach asked Walter Stemmons, the college editor for institutional publications, to organize a female staff to revive the *Campus* newspaper, which had lost its male editors and reporters to the war effort. All forty women studying home economics in 1918 joined Stemmons's journalism class, and from the end of November to February they successfully produced the paper under the leadership of its first woman editor, Helen Clark, with Gladys Daggert as business manager. When the men returned from the service, Daggert remained in her position, but Clark yielded the editorship. While Clark's situation was more typical of the impermanence of women's advances during the war, the organizational status of campus women changed with the Armistice. At 4:30 P.M. on November 21, 1918, women students met in the living room of Grove Cottage to organize the Women's Student Government Association and selected Daggert as president, Flora M. Miller as vice-president, and Ruth S. Buell as secretary-treasurer. This assertion of self-government did not, however, lift many of the restrictive cultural controls then limiting the female student body.[26]

The Culture of "Normalcy" and the Place of Women

President Beach, his wife, Louise Crombie Beach, and the entire campus community celebrated the Armistice in November 1918 by lighting a bonfire that burned an effigy of the German kaiser. By January 1919, the *Connecticut Campus* carried the headline "College Returns to Normal Basis," with the subheads "Men Are Registering for Regular Courses. Indications Are Many S.A.T.C. Men Will Eventually Enter C.A.C." For male students it meant a "return to normalcy," a phrase coined by President Warren Harding in place of the existing "normality." No matter. The college established a reserve officers training corps (ROTC) unit in February 1919, when Captain Claude E. Cranston arrived on campus, in keeping with the land-grant colleges' long standing commitment to military education. Over the years, the maintenance on campus of ROTC would sometimes prove controversial. The students of the 1920s, however, had other, more recreational interests. In an age of Prohibition, which was instituted nationally in 1920, President Beach in 1925 issued a notice that "The unwritten law of the College is that discipline for intoxication on the part of a student is suspension or expulsion from the Institution." The need for such a rule suggests that the enforcement of Prohibition on campus was no more reliable in Storrs than elsewhere in the country. At the beginning of the 1927–28 academic year, the president notified the student body of the board of trustees's action forbidding them from owning or operating motor cars during the college year. As students celebrated the "normalcy" of the twenties and dealt with the restrictions as best they could, women continued to find their behavior even more controlled than men.[27]

Just before the decade began, in April 1919, administrators recommended that a woman student be suspended for the remainder of the school year because of "unseemly conduct" that included dancing on Sunday at the women's dormitory; going out on Sunday evening and giving the faculty the false impression that she was going to church; objectionable dancing in a hallway at Hawley Armory while she was on probation; disobeying regulations while under probation, which required her to ask permission to attend any social function or to walk with any young man; mocking authority by giving young men copies of the letter setting restrictions on her conduct. Four years later, the chairman of the college's Student Affairs Committee recommended suspension for another female student who violated the rules, made by the dean of home economics, that stated: "(1) No girl shall leave the campus without permission. (2) No girl shall attend any function off of the hill without permission and, if accompanied by a man escort, without a chaperone." In 1926, when a father complained about his daughter's suspension for two weeks for smoking a cigarette while she was traveling between Willimantic and Storrs in the company of other college women, President Beach defended the punishment. He replied that although schools like Bryn Mawr allowed smoking, with certain restrictions, "It is doubtful . . . whether public opinion at the present time would approve of or sustain a state institution that permitted its young women students to smoke, particularly as a majority of them are being trained as teachers and for other positions of public service where they will be expected to set an example and supervise the conduct of young people in their charge." A state college was always especially sensitive to public opinion; CAC, in particular, had to be careful. In 1923, in a well-publicized Chamber of Commerce report that advocated more emphasis on technical and agricultural subjects and less on cultural courses, the chamber recommended that women be barred from CAC. The report seriously questioned whether the presence of women contributed to the promotion of agriculture in Connecticut and suggested that, because the women were predominantly in home economics teacher training, the state should subsidize them at Connecticut College for Women or at the state normal schools. Had that occurred, the issue of women's conduct at CAC would of course have become moot.[28]

But the women at Storrs were well established in the home economics program, and in 1922 the first female members had been named to the college's board of trustees. Republican Governor Everett J. Lake appointed Mrs. O. B. Robinson of Willimantic and Mrs. F. O. Vinton of the Eagleville section of Mansfield to the board, where they served until 1924 and 1932 respectively. A week after the appointment of the two female trustees, President Beach received a letter that in contemporary times would be labeled a plea for affirmative action. M. Estella Sprague, the dean of women (for whom a dormitory would be later named), wrote to the president and pointed out an apparent inequity. Each of the eight departments in agriculture had a full professor heading it, but such was not the case for the three departments in home economics. She asked, "Why should not the same hold true? . . . Everywhere it has been rather difficult to have Home Economics raised to the standing of other departments but rapid progress has been made, I am glad to say. If you do not wish to grant full professorships, why not associate professorships?" Two months later, Beach responded that he had randomly surveyed twenty land-grant colleges and found that of 203 home economics faculty members, eleven held the title of dean or director, twenty-five were full professors, eight were associate professors, forty-two were assistant professors, and 116 were instructors and assistants. Based on that, he believed it appropriate to have a dean in charge of administration and a full professor to coordinate and oversee subject matter in the Departments of Food and Nutrition (Household Science), Clothing and Textiles (Household Arts), and Teacher Training. He agreed to make such a recommendation to the board of trustees but warned that further appointments in home economics should be at the instructor or assistant level. Beach, implying a tougher standard, declared, "As a general policy it will be necessary to replace instructors from time to time rather than advance them to positions of higher rank." Ever the diplomat, to settle the matter the president offered one full professorship to women rather than three and, setting a tone, did not offer much optimism in the matter for the future.[29]

Fraternities and a Level Playing Field

Beach did not have to deal with issues of race, as would many of his post–World War II successors. Alan T. Busby, the first African American student to enroll in CAC, entered in 1914 and graduated in 1918. President Beach helped him find a job on the campus farm, but the minority population in Storrs remained miniscule for many years afterward. Beach did face more prosaic issues, however, such as those raised by fraternities and inter-class hazing during the 1920s. Fraternities had been on campus since 1893, and by 1926 there were seven Greek letter organizations and the Shakespearian Club in existence. In that year, 64 percent of college males joined fraternities. Faculty members feared that fraternities could be divisive and wanted them controlled. Early in the decade, fraternity hazing brought outlandishly garbed pledges dressed in petticoats and bloomers or, in one instance, a barrel alone, onto campus. One freshman carried a glass of milk around with him for twenty-four hours; another wandered the campus with a hen under his arm; still others perched in trees and chirped like birds. When a first-year student suffered a severely bruised spine as a result of a paddling, President Beach called for a ban on all hazing. Students lamented the end of the "pajama parade," during which upperclassmen assembled pajama-clad freshmen before their dormitory and walked them around campus to the tune of the song "How Green We Are" amid the resounding paddles of sophomores. It also meant an end to the "pond party," which placed recalcitrant freshmen on an old-fashioned New England ducking stool and dumped them into the water as the entire student body watched. A permitted tradition of the 1920s, the pig roast, had freshmen roasting in open air a fifty-pound-plus pig over a wood fire for at least an hour while sophomores tried to derail them. The rules governing the event did not prevent a fracas or two from breaking out on occasion, and sometimes the pig was not the only casualty. The board of trustees set regulations to control the fraternities, and so President Beach dealt with the silliness as well as the seriousness of student life.[30]

At the beginning of the decade, the college instituted a new system of conducting athletics. While sports were obviously recreational and during the 1920s became national entertainment as well, authorities at CAC saw them as educational, with their ultimate control resting with the college's president. A joint committee of students, faculty, and alumni drafted rules that limited the number of football games at eight; basketball, eighteen; and baseball, sixteen; track was not to exceed two dual meets in addition to some reasonable participation in other intercollegiate meets as well. The committee established eligibility requirements for intercollegiate athletics; in particular, a student had to be in good scholastic standing. Coaches would be considered instructors in the Department of Physical Education. All candidates for any team had to pass a physical examination. There would be an Athletic Council to which the president appointed four members from the faculty, one of whom had to be the director of physical education; the Alumni Association also selected three members; and finally, three members of the Student Athletic Association, the managers of the football, basketball, and baseball teams would each also serve until their season ended. The council, among its other duties, was charged with formulating budgets, overseeing the funds raised for intercollegiate athletics and the property purchased from such funds, ratifying schedules and managers, and recommending coaches. While this framework organized the college's internal structure of athletics, in 1923 the CAC, along with New Hampshire State College, Massachusetts Agricultural College, Rhode Island State College, and the University of Maine formed the New England Conference on Intercollegiate Athletics. The conference anticipated some of the issues concerning contemporary college sports; it dealt, for example, with the "transfer problem." Any student winning a varsity letter at an institution could not play for another. For transfer students who had not previously won a varsity letter, the rule required one year of residence before eligibility. Only bona fide matriculated students could participate in intercollegiate athletics. Unlike today, freshman could not play on varsity teams. While all conference participants were state colleges, and while they often played against each other, the ostensible purpose of the conference was not competition for championships but the encouragement of "high standards of eligibility and in the administration of intercollegiate athletics." On occasion, the president had to remind those involved in CAC sports about such standards.[31]

In January 1924 Beach wrote to Professor A. W. Manchester, chair of the Athletic Council, to point out that the college was collecting a considerable amount of money for athletics. He continued that in a "general sense all athletics are a part of physical education" and suggested that because the college took responsibility for physical education, expenditures should pass through the business office so the college would have a permanent record. He asked the council to develop a plan to deposit all athletic fees and receipts with the college treasurer, to be segregated as a trust fund so that all expenditures from the fund would be on requisitions signed by the director of physical education. In this manner, Beach tried to establish accountability in athletic funding. He then went on to call attention to certain practices that required members of the freshman class to wait on tables in the dining hall and perform other services for members of athletic teams. If they failed to do so, they risked being thrown into the showers by sophomores, which had the approval of the student council and the student body generally. Significantly, athletes called upon freshmen to work on the sport fields in preparation for events. Beach showed concern and remarked, "I am of the opinion that the athletic association should not require any service of any student without rendering due financial compensation. It is a question in my mind, also, whether the College is not subsidizing athletes in awarding them positions for paid labor and permitting the student council to assign substitutes to do their work without compensation." President Beach wanted a level playing field for all concerned, even if they were lowly freshmen, with no advantage reserved for athletes. He took seriously the standards CAC agreed to when it joined the New England Conference.[32]

The Attack on the College and the Retirement of Beach

In 1922 President Beach filed a report with the U.S. Department of the Interior that offered a comparison of CAC with other state educational institutions across the country. At that time, its enrollment of 318 proved to be the lowest of any state college throughout the nation, except in cases where states maintained more than one college. The total working income of the college was $851,156, which was surpassed by thirty-three out of the ninety-six other state colleges. Connecticut had more money, $2,392,792, invested in the college's infrastructure and equipment than eighty-one other state institutions throughout the country. The value of the CAC library (27,000 bound volumes) and scientific apparatus amounted to $202,248, which was thirty-sixth among the other state institutions. Only Iowa equaled the $3,000 salary maximum for instructors at the college, and no other state institution exceeded that figure (although it should be noted that few CAC instructors received the maximum). Clearly, the college did not fare badly in the national comparison. Beach, however, found himself having to beat off attacks on the college from the State Board of Finance in 1921 and the Chamber of Commerce in 1923 and 1925. They raised issues not unfamiliar to those who remembered the "War of the Rebellion," asserting that not enough agriculture and too much "culture" was being taught at Storrs. The critics claimed that too many students came from big cities, and upon graduation they for the most part did not pursue farming. They feared competition with the state's private colleges, although early in the decade the board of trustees had proclaimed, "The college does not aim to be a university. It does not compete

with Yale, Wesleyan or Trinity." In fact, however, during the Beach years and especially in the second half of his tenure as president, CAC moved increasingly
in the direction that the critics claimed. By the middle of the decade, in a win-
win situation, those fearful of the college's expansion welcomed an increased
legislative limitation of enrollment at Storrs at five hundred students. Promises
of a new men's dormitory and a new classroom building served as the quid pro
quo for the trustees' acceptance of the enrollment cap, which benefited the college, which was having great difficulty finding housing for its students. For the
time being, CAC would remain small but gain new facilities.[33]

Health problems plagued Beach during his final period in office. Heart
trouble and difficulty with an enlarged thyroid gland and strokes took their
toll. When his wife of thirty years died in 1924, he "was never the same again" in
the words of Albert Waugh. Beach's devotion to Louise Crombie Beach shaped
his advice about his successor to Walter C. Wood, an influential member of the
board of trustees. He told Wood, who would repeat it to the board during each
of the next three presidential searches, "When you pick a president, be certain
that you look at his wife. His wife is just as important as he is. Get someone who
will fit into the community." Beach had begun purchasing paintings to please his
wife as she was recovering from an illness, and after her death he intensified his
collecting and commissioned a portrait of her done from photographs. Beach
subsequently established a foundation in her name, which continued accumu-
lating art. The Beach Collection, which is especially strong in the American im-
pressionists, became the property of the college and hung in buildings throughout the campus until it was collected in one place to serve as the basis of the
William Benton Museum of Art, which opened almost forty years after President
Beach's death in 1933. Illness forced him to spend several months in a Hartford
hospital beginning in the spring of 1928, and the trustees accepted his resignation on September 15 of that year, when they appointed him president emeritus.
His tenure in office would prove to be the second longest in Connecticut history, exceeded only by Albert Nels Jorgensen's twenty-seven years between 1935
and 1962, a period which transformed the college into a university. Beach did
much to lay the foundation on which his noteworthy successor would build.[34]

Good Works in Storrs on the Fast Track

The trustees moved quickly and appointed Charles Burt Gentry as acting president while promising to search expeditiously for a permanent replacement for
Beach. Gentry had arrived in Storrs in September 1920 as professor of agricultural education and director of teacher training and would go on to carve out a
long and distinguished career as an administrator, ultimately serving between
1939 and 1950 as dean of the university, the equivalent to a contemporary pro-

vost; the Education School Building was also named in his honor. According to Waugh, who succeeded him as provost in 1950, "He was universally trusted." His acting presidency in 1928–29, however, was that of a caretaker. In the spring of 1929, when the trustees announced the appointment of George Alan Works, the *Bridgeport Herald* summarized Gentry's contribution: "Professor Gentry . . . has maintained conditions in the college in a very satisfactory manner. He has made no attempt to dictate policy but succeeded in establishing good will among students and faculty members and in maintaining the status quo."[35]

Works, in his very brief tenure, proved to be very different. He was a mover and a shaker, a person of very high standards with academic experience at quality institutions. At the time of Homer Babbidge's presidency (1962–72), one informed observer, thinking back over many administrations, believed Works had the best mind of any person who had been leader of the institution. Works came to CAC from the University of Chicago, where he had been dean of the Graduate Library School. Prior to joining Chicago in 1927, he conducted a highly regarded survey of college libraries for the Carnegie Foundation. He was a graduate of the University of Wisconsin in 1904, worked at Cornell and the University of Minnesota, and earned his doctorate from Harvard in 1925. Appointed at CAC in April 1929, he began service in Storrs on July 1 of that year and immediately recognized the need to improve the professional credentials of his faculty. Those under fifty years of age without appropriate degrees were told that if they expected to advance in the institution, they had to improve themselves professionally. He advocated stricter standards for appointment, reappointment, and tenure. In short, Works punctured the traditional culture of Storrs. When, at his first meeting presiding over the faculty, Sherman Hollister, a professor of horticulture, rose, as was customary, to announce that the Republican caucus would be meeting at a certain time and place in the town hall, Works responded, "I'm shocked and amazed to hear a political announcement made in a faculty meeting here. I never want it to happen again. It having been made, I want to say that we will not adjourn this meeting until someone has announced a time for the Democratic caucus." His educational philosophy diverged equally from what had been the CAC norm.[36]

In December 1929 Works addressed the Hartford County Farm Bureau. While discussing the proper balance of technical and liberal courses in the curriculum, he announced that he favored developing the liberal arts departments. A few months later, at the beginning of March 1930 the president applied (ultimately unsuccessfully) for the accreditation of CAC by the Association of American Universities (AAU), which helped set the standards of more than twenty leading colleges and universities, including Yale and Chicago. To achieve this, Works had funds allocated to improve CAC library and laboratory facilities. For example, CAC spent less than $3 per student on library books, while the AAU set a minimum limit of $5 per student. Works therefore acted to meet the standard.

AAU teaching load requirements limited instructors to sixteen hours a week, and anyone of professional rank in the faculty needed at least two years of study at a recognized graduate school in their respective fields of teaching. The president also wanted to unify entities in Storrs by ending the separation between the college, the Agricultural Experiment Station, and the Extension Service. Works was in a rush to change an institution that had been born and bred in Connecticut, the "Land of Steady Habits."[37]

At some point, it must have become clear to him that the type of change he desired, if it came at all, would be too slow. On June 9, 1930, he informed Harry G. Manchester, vice-president of the board of trustees, that he would be returning to the University of Chicago to head the department of higher education in its division of education, and he wished to resign, effective July 1. In a prepared public statement, Works offered his appreciation to the board of trustees but attacked the State Board of Finance and Control for destroying the trustees' autonomy, noting that "the political organization of the state is not such" as to permit, in the immediate future, the increased scope that he favored for the college. He argued that the young men and women of the state most needed a general education that would entail strengthening the college in the humanities and social sciences. While many people throughout Connecticut, notably Clifford E. Hough, general manager of the Connecticut Milk Producers Association, did not believe this to be the function of an agricultural college, several influential faculty members supported the president. At the first faculty meeting after Works's departure, a committee comprised of Professors Waugh, Gentry, Manchester, and Torrey introduced a motion that passed unanimously. In it, they thanked Works for his "determination to fight anything, whether in the internal management or the external relationships of the College, which threatened to subordinate the interests of education to administrative inertia or political expediency." In addition, they offered appreciation for his efforts to remedy deficiencies in the library and for a curriculum that was more flexible and better adjusted to the varying needs of the students. They lamented his loss as a leader but clearly made their point: "These and other changes are examples of what must continue here if the College and those who work in it are to attain their greatest usefulness to the public." Works's successor, however, although he served a longer tenure, fared rather worse in gaining such faculty support.[38]

McCracken Is Appointed

The process of Charles C. McCracken's appointment was unusual even in those days before open searches and the public advertising of positions. The trustees, taken by surprise by Works's resignation and the short notice of his departure, asked him to name a successor. He refused, not wanting to make it seem that a new president was "Works's man." The trustees then asked him for the name of someone trustworthy who could recommend candidates. He informed the board that Dr. Kline of the U.S. Office of Education had just completed a study of land-grant colleges and knew all of the administrative personnel worth knowing. The trustees asked Works, because he knew Kline, to write him and get a list of nominees; Works agreed, with the proviso that the list go directly to the board and not to him. The response, however, in error came back to Works, who was surprised that no list but rather only one name had been provided. Kline stated that Charles C. McCracken of Ohio State University was the only man he would consider, and that if the trustees could get him, they should not hesitate. This shocked Works, because he knew that McCracken had just been demoted from a department headship at Ohio State because he could not handle the department. Rationalizing, however, that he had told the trustees he would not take part in the selection process, Works passed along the letter and departed from Storrs. A few weeks later, he learned that Kline had been appointed the new head of the Education Department at Ohio State and was moving McCracken out because he didn't want him in his department. In the meantime, the trustees interviewed McCracken only, and hired him.[39]

On the surface, McCracken appeared well qualified; he certainly had wide experience in secondary and higher education. After graduating from high school in Ohio in 1899, he served as a superintendent in the state's rural school system. He entered Illinois's Monmouth College in 1904 and graduated with first honors in 1908. While there, he headed the Math Department of Lancaster High School in Ohio. In 1911, he received an A.B. degree from Harvard, where he was a university scholar. Between 1911 and 1914, McCracken served as dean of the Normal College of Ohio Northern University in Ada. He then returned to Harvard as an Austin Fellow and earned his Ph.D. in 1916, soon after taking charge of the Department of Psychology and Education at Western College for Women in Oxford, Ohio. From 1917 until his appointment at CAC McCracken taught as a professor of school administration at Ohio State University. He had a strong sense of religion, and in 1928 began more than a year's leave of absence from OSU to act as a research consultant for the Department of Colleges and Training Schools of the Board of Christian Endeavor of the Presbyterian Church. When he first came to Storrs, McCracken told the annual business meeting of the Storrs Congregational Church that he wanted people to know that he was interested in the church. He added, forever winning the enmity of Albert E. Waugh, a committed Christian who nevertheless believed strongly in the separation of church and state, that other things being equal in rank and salary, he intended to give first preference to people who were good Christians and members of the church. Waugh believed this flagrant mixing of religion and academics to be one of McCracken's many flaws.[40]

The future provost explained, with a great deal of indignation, that McCracken quickly outraged all elements of the CAC community and the Connecticut State Legislature. The General Assembly customarily appropriated funds to the college in four or five major categories, such as personal services, contractual services, and capital equipment. Within those categories the institution could dispose of the funds as it wished. In McCracken's case, the legislature passed a budget of over four hundred separate items! The chair of the House Education Committee told Waugh that they took such action because they didn't trust Mc-Cracken and did not want to give him leeway to manipulate the budget. On campus, a like distrust manifested itself early in the new president's term. In the spring of 1931 George H. Lamson, dean of sciences, rose during a faculty meeting at which McCracken was presiding and said, "Mr. President, they say that those who can, do, and those who can't do, teach. Those who can't teach become professors of education, and I want to add that those who are failures at that become college presidents." One could have heard a pin drop as a dean insulted the president before the faculty. According to Waugh, McCracken took pride in misleading the board of trustees by giving them partial information and not the full facts. He offered as an example an incident in which the president and the Alumni Association differed over an issue. The head of the association sent a letter to McCracken expressing their opposition, but when McCracken made his recommendations to the board of trustees, he neglected to inform them that the alumni had an opposing view. He did so on the basis that the association's president signed the letter without listing his title, and explained, "I just decided it wasn't really from the Alumni Association." As a consequence, to Waugh's dismay, McCracken felt it was not lying to say he had no information from the *association* itself.[41]

Such dissembling ultimately caught up with McCracken. Dr. Walter C. Wood, a retired surgeon and influential farmer who chaired the board of trustees, eventually confided in Waugh that the trustees forced McCracken from office. Before board meetings, the president usually circulated an agenda listing items to be considered. At one of McCracken's last, after calling the meeting to order, Dr. Wood asked the president to present the first item on the agenda. Mc-Cracken did, and he gave his recommendation. A board member said, "I move that the recommendation be denied." The motion passed unanimously without discussion. This happened several more times, and then the group adjourned. That night McCracken phoned Wood and asked to meet the next day at Wood's home in New Canaan. In the morning, McCracken explained that he was upset, and that if the trustees continued he would have to resign. Wood did not attempt to convince him otherwise. A short time later, McCracken informed the board chair that he was taking a job as an educational counselor for the Board of Christian Education of the Presbyterian Church. In his public statement, he announced that he was tendering his resignation to "accept an offer [of] a position which provides a much wider professional opportunity and allows me to be of service to a far larger group of college youth in America than is afforded in my present position." Governor Wilbur L. Cross, president ex officio of the trustees, personally accepted the resignation and issued a public statement full of praise, simultaneously noting that McCracken's new position was "most congenial to his temperament. He will now be able to devote his whole attention to educational problems without the worry of finances or the details in the administration of a college." Wood was less kind and more direct. In private, he said that while McCracken was smart, he just couldn't get along with people, and the church job would be better suited for him because he would not have much direct contact.[42]

Accreditation, the B.A., and the State College in Storrs

Despite his deficiencies, however, McCracken's tenure was not without its accomplishments. By the end of 1930, a few months into McCracken's presidency, the New England Association of Colleges and Secondary Schools (NEACSS) accredited the college. Institutional membership in the NEACSS represented the first of its kind for the CAC. It enabled students to more easily transfer and gain admission into graduate and professional schools of association members and members of the four other regional associations throughout the nation. Other colleges in the NEACSS included Amherst, Brown, Bates, Boston University, Bowdoin, Clark, Colby, Dartmouth, Harvard, MIT, Mount Holyoke, Radcliffe, Simmons, Smith, Trinity, Tufts, Wellesley, Wesleyan, Wheaton, Williams, Yale, and the Universities of Maine, New Hampshire, and Vermont. The American Council on Education placed CAC on its accredited list for 1931. In the same year, however, Harvard Law School refused to accept degree holders from CAC because, as a general rule, it refused candidates for admission from agricultural and teachers' colleges. The secretary of the law school informed McCracken that membership in an accrediting association did not affect acceptance, "since conditions here differ materially from those in the other schools of the University . . . [and] our experience has been that a man who devotes most of his college work to vocational subjects is not likely to be successful here." On the other hand, Harvard Medical School accepted the degree, and the medical schools at Yale, the University of Rochester, and Georgetown University actually admitted CAC students that year. The condescending attitude of the Harvard Law School, however, highlighted a sensitive and lingering issue that had plagued the college for many years and continued to inform the debate about agricultural versus "cultural" education.[43]

Events of 1931 through 1933 reshaped the debate but did not end it. In the fall of 1931 the board of trustees accepted a recommendation by the faculty committee on studies and the president to rename the Division of Science as the

Division of Arts and Science, which would then offer study leading to a bachelor of arts degree as well as the already granted bachelor of science. McCracken assured those concerned that the change represented "a normal growth of the college." The new degree required no new administrative change to put the plan into operation, and the college already offered all of the courses that would be required for the new degree. He added that CAC made the change in response to a "very substantial and justifiable demand." McCracken also suggested that a new Philosophy Department would be added to existing CAC study in English, modern languages, and history, but he did not hold out much hope for a Department of Classical Language, pointing out that even Yale had recently dropped Latin and Greek as requirements for the A.B. degree. He acknowledged that the movement for the liberalization of the curriculum reached back to Dr. Beach's administration and was also strongly advocated by George Alan Works. Finally, he remarked that he saw no relationship between the move toward the new degree and a proposal to be considered by the next General Assembly that eliminated the word "agricultural" from the college's name.[44]

That proposal and the decision to offer the new degree, however, seem inextricably linked in the evolutionary process that moved the school in Storrs from its emphasis on agriculture to its broader course of study. The desire for such a change had a long history, going back at least to the Stimson administration; it took on added energy once the students and alumni promoted the idea during the school's fiftieth anniversary year in 1931. When the trustees met in February of that year at the Heublein Hotel in Hartford, they did not formally discuss the subject of a name change, but informally the topic created quite a buzz, with opinions being divided. McCracken attempted to straddle both camps and issued a statement that contended, "The change of name would mean no less emphasis on agriculture . . . it would merely be a change in name that more nearly described what already exists." He added, however, that "it is true that almost all the Land Grant institutions have adopted some title such as 'State College'" and reminded his audience that "Massachusetts and Oregon will change this year."[45]

By April, the Druids, CAC's senior secret society, prepared a brief setting forth why a change of name would be desirable. They sent it to Governor Wilbur Cross, President McCracken, the trustees, and the newspapers. It offered six reasons:

1. The name proposed was a more accurate designation of the college as it actually was. In support, the Druids pointed out that only 20 percent of the students were enrolled in pure agricultural courses, with the remainder in science (49 percent), home economics (19 percent), and mechanical engineering (12 percent).

2. Building on McCracken's assertion, they argued that the proposed change was in keeping with a nationwide tendency.

3. Graduates of the college would find the proposed name to be a distinct advantage. In making this argument, the brief pointed out that many employers assumed that an agricultural college taught nothing but agriculture. During the yearlong debate over the change, Bert Wright, a recent alumnus, *Connecticut Daily Campus* editor, and former Druid who took up roots in Honolulu, gave support to this argument. He wrote to McCracken that "I am now convinced more than ever that the name Connecticut Aggies is a handicap to the alumni of the institution who are seeking employment." While some of the rural Hawaiian gentry had heard of the work carried out at the Experiment Station in Storrs, they didn't associate it with the CAC. The alumnus lamented, "The only eastern colleges whose names are mentioned with much respect are Yale and Harvard. Of course many of the other institutions are known and regarded highly. . . . Almost nobody has ever heard of Connecticut Aggie in these parts."

4. The proposed change would be particularly advantageous to women students. The Druids reasoned that if men were disadvantaged by a degree from a college with agricultural in its title, women would be even more so. They asked, "Will not a prospective employer who knows nothing about the college naturally ask, 'What sort of education can a woman get at an agricultural college?'" They then and answered their own question by noting, "Without seeking an answer to his question he will probably discriminate against her and choose a graduate of another college who is no better trained."

5. Again drawing on one of McCracken's assertions, the brief stated that the proposed change would entail no necessary shift of the curriculum and no increase in the cost of equipment or operation.

6. And finally, they argued that the name "Connecticut Agricultural College" never caught on with the people of the state, who usually referred to it as Storrs College, Aggie College, or State College. The Druids contended that the new name would, simply as a name, be more useful and convenient. They concluded, "Connecticut has today a state college in the most exact sense of that term; why not call it State College?"[46]

Governor Cross, who was influenced in favor of a name change by H. A. Seckerson of the English department, his former student at Yale, established a Change-of-Name Committee, on which McCracken sat, and served as its secretary. It met six times between November 1931 and January 1933. The committee initially considered thirteen names including Storrs College and Nathan Hale College, but ultimately determined to select from a short list of three: Connecticut Agricultural College, Connecticut State College, and the University of

Connecticut. A survey of students, alumni, and faculty revealed a large majority in favor of the designation "University"; on the other hand, the trustees, who had been reluctant about any change at all, favored "College." The committee believed its half century of history proved the institution's accomplishments as a state college but questioned whether the state was ready to support the development of a university, although many aspired to it. It summed up its support of the new name, "Connecticut State College," by concluding, "The dignity of the state, and the reputation of the college, require that the name indicate the accepted status and not the hopes and ambitions which may most properly find fruition in the future." Senate Bill 136, "An Act Changing the Name of the Connecticut Agricultural College," passed the upper house of the General Assembly on February 22, 1933, and the lower house two days later. It was signed by Governor Cross with a quill pen presented to him by President McCracken on Saturday, February 25. The governor congratulated McCracken on being the first president of Connecticut State College (CSC).[47]

While McCracken was only one player out of many in the effort to change the college's name, the renaming stands as a major accomplishment of his administration. His tenure coincided with the first years of the Great Depression, when a general lack of funds permitted little building on campus. He was not a brick-and-mortar president. Like all state employees, faculty and staff suffered a salary cut in the 1933–34 academic year, but McCracken still wrote in August 1934 that "The Connecticut State College has not been affected seriously by the depression." The college filled several new faculty and staff positions during his tenure, but did so at very low salaries relative to other New England colleges. Talented young faculty, desperate for work, joined the staff. Student enrollments increased, and, because of a larger number of applications, CSC could be more selective; the library continued to add books to its collection, although, it would soon become clear, not enough books to satisfy the accreditation standards of the American Association of Universities. The cost of attending the college dropped between 1930 and 1935 and students benefited from New Deal programs like the Federal Emergency Relief Administration, while they stretched CSC's small loan fund to its limit. College life continued almost as usual despite the severe economic downturn. At the end of November 1934 the *Connecticut Campus* announced that a "14 week old thoroughbred Eskimo dog of high pedigree, whose grandfather accompanied Peary to the Pole, has been chosen as the Connecticut State College mascot by an almost unanimous vote of the student body." The dog, a gift of the alumni, was expected to follow the football team when it traveled and would be brought to basketball games played in Storrs. The newspaper suggested that the dog's name be "Husky," based upon its breed, "and that the Connecticut State football team be known as the 'Connecticut Huskies.'" The alumni, however, held a naming contest that selected "Jonathan" in honor of the state's Revolutionary War–era governor, Jonathan Trumbull. The mascot and the name continue to this day, although many dogs have obviously filled the role. The attention given to the mascot reveals the distractions from the Great Depression available to those who shared in Storrs college life. A final episode in McCracken's presidency would be of a more serious nature, testing the limits of academic freedom and bringing national attention to Connecticut State College. It happened in 1935, the year he departed and Albert Nels Jorgensen arrived in Storrs to begin a twenty-seven-year period of change and growth there.[48]

2

From State College to University: 1935–45

During these ten years the college has become
a university in fact as well as in name.
(*Hartford Courant*, 1945)

*T*HE COLLEGE IN Storrs underwent a great deal of change during the decade between 1935 and 1945. A controversy over military training and academic freedom placed it at the center of national attention in 1935. In that year, Albert Nels Jorgensen succeeded Charles McCracken and began his almost three-decade tenure as president. He immediately asserted his leadership and oversaw the transformation of the college into the University of Connecticut in 1939. The coming of World War II, not unlike its predecessor, the Great War, accelerated change, brought the army to campus, and temporarily affected the role of women students. The University of Connecticut became a sanctuary for young Japanese Americans seeking refuge and an education during a time of deep national suspicion of their loyalty. It also had to contend with charges against a German-born language professor accused of Nazi sympathies. Even before the war ended, President Jorgensen and the university community were already planning for peace and the enormous growth that was to come.[1]

"The Gag Rule" and the Revolt on Campus

McCracken's tenure ended amidst a controversy over academic freedom that brought a firestorm of unwanted national attention to the newly named state college. One of those people who visited Storrs during the turmoil remained unconvinced that substantive transformation had actually accompanied the change of name. James Wechsler, the former editor of the Columbia College student newspaper who would go on to edit the *New York Post* in its liberal era commented that the shift from Connecticut Aggies to Connecticut State College had little effect. If a bit of light had reached almost every other educational institution, he claimed, "Connecticut had been careful to prevent the infiltration of more than a chance beam. Its steadfast devotion to the ideal of simplicity, of seclusion, of divorce from the unpleasant strife of the world beyond the hill was vigorously maintained." However, the agitation of the spring of 1935 quickly ended such serenity.[2]

Students around the nation wrestled with issues arising from war, the Soviet Union, and the Great Depression. The last cast a pall over most scholarly and social activity but did not dampen agitation concerning the other two. In Connecticut early in 1935 the legislature took up a bill to ensure a military presence on campus by placing, among others, the state's adjutant-general on the Connecticut State College Board of Trustees. At Storrs, a newly formed "Social Problems Club" mobilized against the bill and with other organized liberal groups successfully assisted in its defeat. Elizabeth Upham, the club's secretary, wrote to the chairman of the legislature's Education Committee that "the adjutant general has no place on the Board of Trustees of an educational institution. His presence, no doubt, would restrict free speech." A teachers' loyalty oath was similarly torpedoed. Early in the spring, the head of the ROTC on campus had discerned an increasing anti-military atmosphere. He complained about attempts to weaken military training by efforts to exempt certain students, and about the faculty's desire to end the commissioning of officers at graduation. By the time of the nationwide student strike against war in April, the board feared radical activity at CSC as well, although there was no strike despite a Social Problems Club meeting on the topic that drew a large crowd.[3]

All over the country on April 12, 1935, students protested against war, militarism, and fascism. New York police estimated that ten thousand people turned out in Manhattan and the Bronx, with the largest demonstrations taking place at Columbia University and the City College of New York (CCNY). In New England, antiwar activities were reported at Dartmouth, Smith, Mount Holyoke, and the Massachusetts Institute of Technology (MIT). Simmons College and Brown University dismissed classes so that students could attend meetings. At Harvard, student pranksters attempted a burlesque counter-demonstration. At Storrs, although there was comparative serenity, the trustees showed concern about what they believed to be agitation against compulsory military training at the college. At their meeting of April 17, the board passed the following motion: "Military training is declared to be a part of the college instruction. Any public agitation or formal public discussions on the campus promoted by individuals on the college staff or individual students, which reflect upon the college military instruction or training, will subject such individuals to cause for removal."[4]

The motion, quickly dubbed the "gag rule," directed President McCracken to advise the college staff of the action taken by the board. McCracken, clearly uncomfortable with the turn of events, stated that there had been very little agitation at Storrs and that the resolution was "preventative and not remedial." He explained to one concerned critic that the motion didn't prevent free discussion in faculty meetings or an expression of personal views by the faculty except in the way of "formal public agitations or formal public discussions on the campus . . . which reflect upon the college military instruction or training." The president reported that the trustees feared agitation against military training, such as that at CCNY and Ohio State University. A speaker from New York who appeared on campus on the eve of the strike may have encouraged their concern when he argued that war was a result of a set of artificial social attitudes kept alive by agencies such as the ROTC. He denied that the Morrill Act, which established land-grant colleges, required compulsory military training. Such apostasy stood in direct opposition to the board's philosophy. Nevertheless McCracken believed that "if we could all keep cool we can work out a reasonable solution and fair interpretations that will prevent an upheaval that might become disastrous to the college."[5]

Others invited attention to the issue from advisors outside of the college. Walter Landauer, a professor of genetics, was delegated to approach leaders in the fields of teaching and research and inform them of what had occurred. He sent copies of the board's motion to all American winners of the Nobel Prize, informing them that many people on the staff were aroused over the issue. He cautioned that the board of trustees' action not only insulted the staff but would have a detrimental effect on their teaching and influence. Not every response may have been welcomed by Landauer, however. Charles G. Dawes, chairman of the Board of City National Bank and Trust Company of Chicago and a former conservative Republican vice-president of the United States, returned Landauer's letter to President McCracken with a comment dripping with sarcasm: "I infer from it that the Board of Trustees of Connecticut State College are not considering abdication and the selection of the faculty to take their place." The president of MIT agreed in principle that any decision restricting the public discussion of academic policies was unfortunate, but he didn't know whether the conditions existed to justify such action. On the other hand, he did know "something of the disingenuous character of at least some of the agitation against military training." As a consequence, he felt it improper to venture a comment on the matter.[6]

Some, albeit not Nobel Prize winners, appeared less reluctant to remark on the situation in Storrs. Western Union brought a flood of telegrams to the president and the board. The Student League for Industrial Democracy at Massachusetts State College protested against the repression of free speech and academic freedom on the CSC campus. Two Radcliffe College students wired their opposition to military training as a part of instruction and to the suppression of free speech. The Simmons College Peace Society attacked the repressive measures that had been taken and proclaimed, "Your action contradicts every American principle and is directly destructive to liberal education." Smith College's National Student League demanded the removal of the ban on free speech. MIT's chapter of the same organization added that such administrative repression was typical of fascism and utterly opposed to American traditions of liberty. Others throughout New England and the nation joined the battle. Connecticut's Governor Wilbur Cross, who by virtue of his office sat on the college's board of trustees and later stated that the board's action did not meet with his approval, received dozens of letters in opposition to the gag rule. A star-studded committee of the American Civil Liberties Union told the governor that no greater violation of free speech and academic freedom in a state university had ever come to its attention; signers of that protest included Reinhold Niebuhr, Horace M. Kallen, and Sidney Hook. Clearly, the events at CSC preoccupied the minds of many of those in the United States who cared about academic freedom.[7]

The student newspaper, the *Connecticut Campus,* suggested that the trustees may have gone off in the wrong direction, because CSC students took pride in their ROTC unit and showed little interest in the propaganda and meetings of a small part of the student body that entertained so-called "radical tendencies." Without questioning the board's motives, the *Campus* editorialized that it had to oppose the board's action. The editors warned that the precedent set by the gag rule opened the possibility of unacceptable future infringements on academic liberty and the freedom of speech. Nevertheless, taking a moderate path, they advised a policy of watchful waiting to see what the trustees, administration, and faculty would do next. The paper counseled, "Let us have no part in the making of this mountain from a mole hill."[8]

The faculty resolved that the trustees' action appeared to be in direct conflict with certain fundamental principles of higher education because of the implied threat to free intellectual inquiry. They also contended that it violated a college bylaw, article 9, section 5, that gave faculty the responsibility over courses of study, cases of discipline, and other matters that pertained to the internal educational wellbeing of CSC. They added, not insignificantly, that the board's resolution was at variance with the rules of tenure, because it added another special cause for dismissal. Finally, in support of the students, the faculty pointed out that "undergraduate life at Storrs was sane and wholesome" and congratulated the students on the competent way in which they had handled the situation. On the other hand, some alumni once again asked to have the state adjutant-general added to the board of trustees as a check against anti-military agitation.[9]

The brunt of the criticism increasingly seemed aimed at President McCracken rather than the trustees. After Hartford's Trinity College student newspaper, the *Tripod,* ran an editorial attacking McCracken, its editor-in chief apologized, having been informed by the president's "many friends at Trinity" that he wasn't personally responsible. McCracken responded that it should be well known that the motion was passed against his advice. He told the president of the University of Maryland that a member of the board presented the resolutions without his previous knowledge and that they were forced through in spite of explanations and protests showing the danger in such action. His position grew increasingly defensive as the issue took on yet another dimension.[10]

When students from twenty-six colleges announced plans to come to Storrs to protest the gag rule on May 13, President McCracken said he would receive them and they would be permitted to hold their meeting, which would feature speeches by Budd Schulberg, editor of the *Daily Dartmouth,* and Jonathan Bingham, son of Senator Hiram Bingham and editor of the *Yale Daily News.* Some pro-military CSC students, however, threatened to stop the visitors, by force if necessary. They quickly retreated from this position, though, and acquiesced in accepting the guests politely, a stance advocated by the *Connecticut Campus.*[11]

On the day of the visit, about 175 students from thirteen colleges actually participated. They first gathered at the State Capitol, but Governor Cross had an appointment elsewhere. They then drove to Storrs. While banners decorated their cars with slogans such as "Storrs Oppressed, Yale Next" and "This is our problem too," the visitors represented a serious gathering, not the typical football-game crowd. The sixty-member Yale delegation comprised the largest group. Smith College made up most of the female contingent. James Wechsler of Columbia won honors as the orator of the day and was described as having the platform presence of a veteran campaigner. According to observers, the protest was orderly, dignified, and sincere in its concern about the loss of academic freedom. A common theme likened the trustees' action to the repressive measures of Hitler and Mussolini. The group presented petitions carrying nearly three thousand names to President McCracken, who agreed to bring them to the board meeting two days hence. Few CSC students, however, were willing to add their names to the petitions. Jules Pinsky, president of the Social Problems Club, scolded his classmates for their lukewarm attitude and criticized their lack of openmindedness. This reaction was in keeping with his feeling in earlier statements that apathy on the part of CSC students would indicate that the institution failed to meet general college standards.[12]

On the eve of the protest, the Committee on Militarism in Education and the Academic Freedom Committee of the American Civil Liberties Union requested permission to have representatives speak at the next board of trustees meeting, on May 15. President McCracken replied that the board members determined who appeared before them to present matters for their consideration and noted that the requests would be placed before the board. The Progressive Education Association wrote to Governor Wilbur Cross, asking that he use his personal efforts to have the gag rule repealed. John Dewey sent his own brief telegram protesting "the interference with academic freedom." Mark May, the director of Yale's Institute of Human Relations and a member of the Connecticut State Board of Education, contended that the trustees' action would diminish academic standards at CSC because good teachers and researchers prefer to work in an atmosphere of academic freedom. He added that the college would attract only conformist students as well, because the intellectually gifted certainly would enroll elsewhere. The small state school in Storrs continued to be an object of national concern and scorn.[13]

When the Social Problems Club held another meeting addressed by James Wechsler, the division among students deepened. After Wechsler's speech in the Community House of the Storrs Congregational Church, Maurice Sussman, chairman of the meeting, read a telegram from the ACLU that said it was prepared to defend any student willing to test the trustees' resolution in an open forum. David Pinsky took the opportunity to do so. A group of ROTC supporters silenced him by throwing Pinsky into the nearby lake. Sussman escaped a similar fate only after a Congregational minister, the Reverend J. Garland Waggoner, intervened on his behalf. Wechsler suggested that anti-Semitism encouraged the bellicose turn. Whatever the reason, the trustees would not back away from their resolution in such an atmosphere.[14]

At their meeting on May 15 the trustees refused to rescind the offending motion of April 17. However, they inserted into the minutes an interpretation of their intent. The board explained that they had full confidence in the loyalty and patriotism of the faculty and students. Their action aimed to prevent public agitation on campus by a small minority that intended to hamper the work of the military or create disloyalty to the nation. The board recognized the individual's right to freedom of speech and emphasized that it had no desire to curb such freedom. Nevertheless, the new interpretation did not mollify the critics of the gag rule. Moreover, it did not prevent the resignation of President McCracken, who publicly and privately claimed that his leaving the college had nothing to do with the board's earlier action. He maintained that he had made his decision before the trustees raised their motion and looked forward to becoming an educational counselor with the Presbyterian Board of Christian Education in Philadelphia. When Fletcher D. Parker, secretary of the Hartford Federation of Churches, complained about the weakness of the May 15 reinterpretation and wrote that his group regretted McCracken's departure, "but we certainly cannot blame you for getting out from under a Board of Trustees of this type," the president replied that he would transmit the initial sentiment but omit the latter. He wanted to make no further waves.[15]

The incident did not die until the following fall and the arrival of a new president. In June, the faculty elected a special committee to confer with the trustees about the ruling. It met in executive session with the board on July 31. By early fall, when the faculty asked for a report, the committee would only state that it had "a most cordial and sympathetic reception from the Board and had engaged in an extended and frank discussion." In actuality, the committee had suggested to the board the desirability of rescinding the gag rule and asked the trustees to provide reasons if they chose not to do so. On October 9 P. R. Brammell, committee secretary, urged Acting President Charles Burt Gentry to explain to the board the need to report to the faculty. Shortly thereafter, Albert N. Jorgensen began his twenty-seven-year term as president. Some suggested the young Midwesterner made rescission of the resolution a condition for accepting the position. It is clear that in an early meeting with the board, Jorgensen emphasized that he stood strongly for freedom of speech. In order for him to earn the faculty's trust, he had to demonstrate that the board had confidence in him to deal with sensitive issues; a gag rule simply wasn't necessary if a capable administrator could handle the situation. One of the trustees, Joseph W. Alsop, confided that after meeting with the faculty committee in July, the board decided to defer action until it hired a new president. With the right person in place, a decision to rescind could comfortably be made.[16]

Jorgensen Arrives, a University Emerges

It appeared that the right person was indeed in place. At its meeting of October 25, the board of trustees rescinded the motion that had created so much turmoil. They noted that the conditions surrounding their initial action had changed, and they had "full confidence in the ability of the administration of the college to deal with such matters in the traditional way." Roger N. Baldwin, the director of the American Civil Liberties Union, congratulated Jorgensen and the board for solving the issue in accordance with the tradition of free speech. He particularly appreciated the role of the neophyte president, telling him, "For your part in bringing about this result, we all express our heartfelt recognition." For students, faculty, and many residents of the state, the new administration thus began on a high note.[17]

That the CSC board selected the thirty-six-year-old as president certainly made sense to a Buffalo newspaper, which pointed out that the advantages of choosing a young man to be president were many: he does not have to unlearn things; he is not afraid to break with tradition when tradition should be broken; he knows better than an old man what makes students tick; and he can initiate and carry to fruition in his own lifetime long-range plans and policies. Albert N. Jorgensen promised to bring change to Storrs. The son of Danish immigrants, he was a smalltown boy from the Midwest, born in Lanark, Illinois, on March 20, 1899, and brought up in Sabula, Iowa, whose population counted less than a thousand people. Both he and his wife, Harriet, received their public school education in the Sabula schools, to which Jorgensen returned as a high school principal. This was after his graduation in 1921 from Coe College in Iowa, where he majored in English, minored in history, and won nine varsity letters in football, basketball, track, and baseball. He later went on to become the superintendent of schools in Arlington, Iowa, a town about the same size as Sabula. He earned an M.A. in psychology from the University of Iowa in 1925 and a Ph.D. in educational administration from Iowa State four years later. Before coming to Storrs, he worked at the university level at Iowa State, Michigan State, and the University of Buffalo, where he began service as professor of educational administration in 1931.[18]

Four years later, on September 12, 1935, the Connecticut State College Board of Trustees formally had Jorgensen's credentials presented to them and agreed to invite him to a meeting at the Hartford Club on September 18. On that day, they voted to appoint him president at an annual salary of $10,200. In addition to the rescinding of the gag rule, Jorgensen set a number of other conditions for his acceptance of the position. He requested support for a reasonable but necessary development and expansion of the college as the state's land-grant institution. He wanted the board to define its role as legislative and his role as that of chief executive and administrative officer, and to agree that the president would represent them before the General Assembly and the departments of state government. Jorgensen also asked that in trustees' meetings he would be able to represent the faculty and students, and that representatives of these two groups could appear only upon request. The new president had a sense of what it would take to move the institution forward, which he quickly attempted to do.[19]

He took to heart the advice of a Stamford attorney who wrote to him that the college was not well known even in its own state and suggested that during the coming year Jorgensen should travel in Connecticut as much as possible and address various groups, including religious, civic, and alumni organizations. In his first years as president, Jorgensen gave hundreds of talks, sometimes two or three a day, advocating for the institution in Storrs. In light of the changes occurring at CSC, he was careful to cultivate the school's agricultural constituency, which feared a shift from the institution's original focus. The newsletter that introduced him to the faculty after his appointment by the board carefully stressed his farm background. It reported that Jorgensen worked his way through school doing farm work, that he currently owned a farm in Iowa, and that he had qualified as a teacher of vocational agriculture in Iowa and taught the subject at the beginning of his career. In an appearance on radio station WTIC shortly after his arrival in Storrs, Jorgensen stated that no expansion at CSC would take place "at the expense of agriculture." He recognized that many federal grants came to agricultural education and that the institution had its beginnings as an agricultural school. Appearing before the Middlesex County Farm Bureau in late November 1935, the president announced that the united support of every farmer in the state was needed for the college to do effective work. Jorgensen reassured the members that "as long as I am president of your state college, agriculture and agricultural education shall not be neglected, it will not be minimized and no other expansion of the college will be made at the expense of agriculture." Their most important crops, he assured them, were their sons and daughters. "Farm boys and girls have been the backbone of our nation. The farms need education, but education needs the farms," he concluded. However, events, and likely intent, would move CSC in other directions.[20]

Jorgensen's welcome to the campus literally seemed to be a baptism by fire. Flames ripped through the Alpha Phi fraternity house at 3:30 A.M. on Sunday, October 13, 1935, and a siren atop Beach Hall woke the entire college community. Furniture and clothing, as well as students, flew through its windows; smoke overcame two of the fraternity dwellers. The incident made the very new president aware of the living conditions on campus and the need for new facilities. In his WTIC radio talk, he said the housing situation was definitely inadequate but would be only a temporary embarrassment. He described to the farm bureau the overcrowded conditions, the women's dorm built to accommodate eighty-four and housing 148, and other students sleeping in basements, attics, and even abandoned chicken houses. Something had to be done about the physical situation at the state college. The trustees painted a grim portrait in 1936 of the minimum outlay needed by CSC for its physical plant alone. The state hadn't made any capital investment in Storrs for a dozen years to relieve the strain on student housing, and no capital allocation had been granted in a decade for classrooms and laboratories. Inadequate engineering facilities threatened that program's very accreditation. Poor library facilities also kept CSC off the Association of American Universities approved list. The college's library collection was barely one quarter of that required to meet instructional demands. The library was too small to house its collection and failed to meet the study-room needs of the student body. The new president faced these major difficulties and more as he began his tenure.[21]

Thus the accomplishments at Storrs, in the few short years before the United States' entrance into World War II, are especially impressive. Entering a legislative arena preoccupied with belt-tightening in January 1937, Dr. Jorgensen introduced plans for a multiple-year building program and won virtual approval for the whole thing. Within three years of that initial legislative session, almost three million dollars worth of buildings and improvements were under way, more than had been spent in the entire period since the school's origins. The Wilbur Cross Library, an engineering building, a home economics building, a girls' dormitory (Edwina Whitney Hall), a boys' dormitory (Wood Hall), and a power plant all took shape. Builders added a new wing to Atwater Laboratory, remodeled several older buildings, constructed athletic fields, and installed new steam lines, sidewalks, and four and a half miles of hard-surfaced roads to replace the dirt roads that had always been mired in mud during March and April.[22]

In making his case for the improved physical plant, Jorgensen confronted an issue that deeply affected higher education in New England. He attacked the entrenched belief that private universities made state institutions superfluous. Drawing on his Midwestern experience, the adopted New Englander argued against the region's traditional preference for the elite privates. Services not found at Yale, Wesleyan, Trinity, and Connecticut College for Women were given at Storrs, he contended, continuing, "If citizens are going to look to private institutions for excellent training and be contented with mediocre training at the State College then I am convinced the reason for continuance of the State College vanishes." He pointed out that certain extension, research, and instructional services could be found only at CSC. He established a University Extension Program based upon his experience at other institutions, which included centers in New Haven and Hartford.[23]

A month before the bombing at Pearl Harbor, when the *Bridgeport Post* asked about Jorgensen's accomplishments, he could point to the rebuilding and expansion of the campus, the extension centers, and other achievements as well. Every division in the school had won full accreditation. At the president's request, the state adopted a policy of erecting dormitories on a financially self-liquidating basis. The General Assembly repealed a statute restricting residence in university dormitories to five hundred students at any one time, a law that had been intended to block expansion. Permission was obtained to create a Self-Supporting Activities Fund, through which the university could generate its own income, which had been previously lost to the state's general fund. A summer school began. The Ratcliffe Hicks School of Agriculture at Storrs, a two-year program, was established largely through private funds. Registration on campus more than doubled to 1,746 students from the 812 present when Jorgensen first arrived. In addition, 150 students were attending the recently acquired College of Pharmacy at New Haven, another 150 in the Freshman-Sophomore Program in Hartford, 205 in advanced and graduate University Extension courses, 284 in the summer session, and 1,292 in non-credit University Extension courses, comprising an overall enrollment of almost 4,000 students. Entrance and scholastic requirements escalated. Most significantly, the legislature had changed the name of the institution from Connecticut State College to the University of Connecticut in 1939.[24]

Two years before the change, Representative Edward D. Seger of Colchester introduced a bill in the General Assembly to establish a university in the State of Connecticut. With an appropriation of five million dollars, it would have established an entirely new institution of land, buildings, and staff. Although initially tabled, the bill was reintroduced in the 1939 session. President Jorgensen suggested that the alumni secretary, George Pinckney, visit Representative Seger and explain to him how CSC had grown and for all practical purposes become a university. Soon convinced, the Colchester legislator offered a bill that called for the change of name from CSC to Connecticut State University and extended the college's property rights to the new university, which would have authority to confer academic and professional degrees. In the committee hearing process, the name Connecticut State University was transformed into the University of Connecticut. Jorgensen argued that the shift to "state college" in 1933 brought no radical or fundamental changes in either policy or procedure, and the move to "university" likewise would not change things much, because "the institution has had for fifteen years a diversified offering greater than that of many small universities."[25]

The momentum for the inevitable change, which grew with each expansion plan announced by Jorgensen since his arrival, passed both houses of the legislature without dissent. Professor Andre Schenker of the Department of History and Government, George Pinckney, the alumni secretary, William F. Crowley, outgoing president of the student senate, Edward V. Finn, the incoming president, and Normand P. DuBeau, editor of the *Connecticut Campus,* enthusiastically joined President Jorgensen in the governor's office for the bill's signing. At 5:19 P.M. on Friday, May 26, 1939, Governor Raymond Baldwin, using a traditional blue and white quill pen and muttering something about a fan dancer while trying to keep the swirling plumes out of the ink, signed the bill. The University of Connecticut would exist as of July 1, 1939, the institution's fifth name since its founding in 1881.[26]

After the celebration, not everyone shared the enthusiasm witnessed at the signing. In the fall, when the university sought bonding for more dormitories, the *New Haven Register* complained that each time the institution at Storrs expanded, it lay the groundwork for yet further expansion, which was costly to the public pocketbook. It concluded by attacking the university's attempt to install an extension program in New Haven and strongly counseled that the expansionists should put on the brakes. Jorgensen privately complained in return that John Day Jackson, publisher of the *Register,* had vigorously opposed the development of the university. He noted that attacks from New Haven were not new and that Jackson had no interest in the welfare of the state and those agencies carrying out its will. Others raised additional concerns. While the president kept trying to cultivate the school's agricultural constituency, a self-described "farm woman," lobbying for a new Agricultural Industries Building, complained that the Agricultural College had been almost entirely forgotten in the recent physical expansion. If she charged neglect, a member of the CAC class of 1918 who headed another institution's Department of Poultry protested the ouster of his counterpart at Storrs. He resented the driving into retirement of those who built the foundation upon which the new university stood, although he recognized the need of the institution in its new form to recruit the most highly qualified faculty. D. H. Horton emphatically stated, "Please accept this as a vigorous protest against the practice which has been in operation since the University ceased to be the Connecticut Agricultural College." In response, Jorgensen invited Horton to visit and see for himself, adding that neither the administration nor the board of trustees had contemplated eliminating older members of the faculty. Clearly, however, all did not welcome the transformation from college to university.[27]

Welcome or not, the university required a more complex organization than that needed by the smaller college in order to achieve the goal of "centraliz[ing] authority for policy making and decentraliz[ing] the administration of details." The reorganization replaced the old college divisions with seven schools and colleges headed by deans: the College of Arts and Sciences, which was divided into seventeen departments; the College of Agriculture, with fifteen departments; the Graduate School; the School of Business; the School of Education; the School of Engineering; and the School of Home Economics. Directors headed the seven divisions that did the other work of the institution: the Library; the ROTC; Publications; the Health Service; the Summer Session, University Extension and Education by Radio; Physical Education; and Student Personnel. The second-in-command to the president, previously called the dean of the division of resident instruction, became the dean of the university, a position held by Charles Burt Gentry, who was advised by the Dean's Council. Others in the central administration were the director of student personnel, the dean of men, the dean of women, the registrar, and the controller. In an effort at shared governance, the plan established a University Senate consisting of the president, the deans, and not more than thirty-six elected members of the faculty. The main concern of the senate related to the educational program of the institution in matters such as the university calendar, minimum entrance requirements, minimum standards of scholarship, and minimum requirements for degrees. The senate could react to, and suggest, new services, new policies, or changes in existing policies to the president, and through him to the board of trustees. With this structure in place, the University of Connecticut began a decade that would witness dramatic change locally, nationally, and internationally.[28]

Storrs Prepares for War

With the outbreak of war in Europe in September 1939, many people in the United States recognized the need for preparedness. By the end of the year, the president of the newly named university began lobbying for a new armory on campus for military training and a hangar at the Willimantic airport so that student pilot trainees would not have to travel to Hartford's Brainard Field. He explained to General George C. Marshall, chief of staff at the War Department, that the current inadequate facilities would force curtailment of appropriate physical education and preparation for service, and he subtly suggested that the requirement of military training might have to be eliminated. Jorgensen con-cluded, "Because of the general world-wide unrest and the need for a national defense program, it would be most unwise to curtail our military program." What he did not mention was that the state's fiscal problems and the unavail-ability of federal works project funds precluded the building of a planned gym-nasium or field house to be shared by the Departments of Military Science and Physical Education. Clearly, however, he recognized that higher education and defense spending would be linked closely in the years to come.[29]

Welcoming the record number of students enrolled in the class of 1944, the president, early in the fall 1940 semester, noted the critical times and urged stu-dents to not falter, despair, or lose their poise in the face of world turmoil. Before a convocation audience of more than one thousand in Hawley Armory, he drew a distinction between universities in dictatorships and those in democracies. In the former, students lacked freedom of inquiry and might be called upon to re-pudiate truth; in the latter, they searched for truth and developed critical atti-tudes, which in turn stimulated creative thinking.[30]

As the international situation increasingly preoccupied the campus, the Selective Training and Service Act of 1940—the draft—emerged as a major con-cern. The act required that all males between the ages of twenty-one and thirty-five register. By early October, over 250 students were scheduled to register for the draft. Selective service would dramatically reduce the number of male stu-dents enrolled at Storrs, decrease the faculty ranks, and drastically diminish the support staff while giving women students temporary leadership roles and bringing soldiers to study on campus. The Student Personnel Division arranged to enroll a large proportion of the men on campus. It also developed a system of deferment forms, and the administration and the division passed on the va-lidity of claims in conjunction with local draft boards. Status as a student alone did not merit deferment; a registrant had to demonstrate that continuance at the university would improve his quality as a "necessary man," that is, one who couldn't be replaced or whose courses were "necessary to the maintenance of the national health, safety, or interest." The exemption referred to students and teachers in engineering, medicine, chemistry, and similar subjects.[31]

Jorgensen informed General S. H. Wadhams, chair of the state and federal Joint Executive Defense Committee, of the university's defense activities. It offered a basic two-year course in military training to about 250 men. Another sixty-five men, awarded commissions upon successful completion of their pro-gram, enrolled in an advanced two-year course. The university trained a third group in the Civilian Pilot Training Program and, because of the success of that program, had been asked to supervise advanced training there as well. Working under the assumption that an adequate defense involved the preparation of in-dustry, the university enrolled 260 apprentices from Hartford's aviation indus-tries in a junior engineering non-degree program. It established a series of Latin

American seminars to broaden understanding of our hemispheric neighbors. A Committee on Nutrition and Health was appointed to deal with problems in those areas that might grow out of a war emergency; the committee chair advised a national group based in Washington. Jorgensen offered to the defense committee the expertise of the university's extension service if problems with agriculture arose. Finally, he placed the entire research facilities of the university at its disposal. More telling evidence of the institution's involvement came several months later, when, in April 1941, three stars of the Connecticut basketball team, Bob Donnelly, John Yusievicz, and Angie Verinis, passed their tests for acceptance into the air corps and were slated to go to Alabama for training following graduation. The *Connecticut Campus* pointed out that the three high-scoring stars formed a team even in enlistment. It continued, "Hereafter their shots will be directed downward from dive bombers instead of zooming up from the middle of a basketball floor."[32]

Following the Japanese attack on Pearl Harbor on December 7, 1941, and the full entrance of the United States into the world war, the ability of many students to concentrate on their studies diminished. Some, like the basketball players, desired to join the fight immediately. Many doubted that they would have the opportunity to complete school; others saw no use in doing so. To head off a very abrupt decline in enrollment in the spring semester, the administration arranged two meetings with the student body and one with the faculty. President Jorgensen attempted to lay out national policy with respect to universities in wartime and attempted to answer a key question in the mind of students—"How can I, as an individual, best serve the nation?" For some, he suggested that immediate enlistment and service was indeed the proper answer. However, for the majority, the more difficult, but less dramatic, task would be to continue their education until called to military service—to hone their skills so they could later contribute again to democracy. He also cautioned against wild rumors and exaggeration. He called for normal behavior at an abnormal time and enthusiastically endorsed President Franklin Delano Roosevelt's admonition: "Young people should be advised that it is their patriotic duty to continue the normal course of their education unless and until they are called, so that they will be well prepared for greatest usefulness to their country."[33]

December 7, 1941, of course began as an ordinary day in Storrs. A number of faculty attended a tea at the president's house, where rumors of war with Japan kept filtering from the radio. The regular Sunday mystery drama, *The Shadow*, began as usual: "Who knows what evil lurks in the hearts of men?" Then an announcer interrupted, "We take you now to San Francisco." Tokyo declared that a state of war now existed between the Empire of Japan and the United States. After the radio reported that the Hartford papers were printing special editions, several Storrs residents drove to the capital and purchased a large number of those "extras" to bring back to the community. In Hartford, the group had been prevented by police from entering radio station WTIC because of the outbreak of war. Albert E. Waugh, the economics professor who later would become arts and sciences dean and university provost, conjectured that constraints on life on the home front were just beginning. Within a few days, those, like him, who rose with the university whistle at 7:00 A.M. no longer could depend on that for a wake-up. The authorities had decided to silence the whistle, except during air raids and blackouts. Life changed in many large and small ways.[34]

In a personal letter to his son, then a student at the Choate prepatory school in Wallingford, Connecticut, Jorgensen counseled his message of restraint in times of crisis, expressed the hope that Al Junior and his friends would not go off the deep end as a consequence of the declaration of war. Winning the war, he advised, involved a tremendous concentration of time and effort on many fronts—including factory, farm, school, and university. The last two shared the obligation of training leaders for the nation, leaders who were necessary if America was to triumph and then rebuild after the conflagration. He confided, "Until a student is called to service in some defensive and possibly offensive war activity, he is obligated to continue as a student and to do his best job as a student." For the president—and for the father—this seemed a moral and patriotic duty. He urged his son to stay the course and not permit anxious anticipation to change his normal mode of life.[35]

Fighting World War II in Storrs

Both publicly and privately in the early days of the war Jorgensen hammered home the same message, that normal functions must go on. Yet the week before Christmas 1941, Storrs was still to see its first blackout, which would not come until February. Two days after the holiday, the president informed a trustee that because of labor shortages in farm and factory, the university had been asked to adjust its calendar to free up a work force. The university shifted its second semester schedule to shorten vacation periods and adjust examinations so that commencement would be held on May 17 rather than June 7, 1942. It planned to open classes in the fall one week later than usual as well, in order to increase the summer recess. At a meeting with faculty members in early January 1942, Jorgensen urged them to familiarize themselves with the selective service regulations and rules on deferment so they could advise their students. He encouraged an improvement of the entire advising system at a time when student morale was likely to be low. He suggested that staff members who had commitments for leaves of absence should continue with their plans but be aware that changes might occur. He worried that the recruiting of a superior faculty would be made more difficult as the army called up more and more men, but he argued nevertheless for maintaining high standards in hiring. Finally, he called for an evaluation of the curriculum so that offerings not absolutely necessary at the moment could be weeded out.[36]

The student newspaper editorialized that its readers could best serve the nation by doing their daily tasks "plus ten percent." Preparing for the inevitable, the paper concluded that when the call for wider national service came, "Connecticut students will remember the great traditions of this University and will rally in overwhelming numbers to their country's call." By the end of 1942, the extra ten percent became apparent. A book drive collected almost seven thousand books for the United Service Organizations (USO). The university joined the rest of the nation in a scrap drive, with the triangle at the junction of Whitney Road and Faculty Row designated as the dump for metal collected by students. The *Connecticut Campus* raised funds to send subscriptions of the newspaper to former students in the armed forces. The university's Audio-Visual Center was designated as the official war-information film depository for the state and distributed reels of film widely to defense groups in its capacity as War Film Depository. President Jorgensen established a University War Council and a Student War Council to consider the university's participation in the war effort. To protect those who would enter military service during a semester, the University Senate instituted a grade of "Inc-S" in each course, unless the student received permission from the dean of the university to take an examination covering the entire course. Upon return, the student could earn credit by passing an examination covering the entire course, or he could drop the class without receiving a failing grade.[37]

Jorgensen had another matter on his mind. Perhaps recalling the anti-German hysteria that had swept the nation during World War I, he encouraged students to remember that all native-born citizens, whether of German, Italian, or Japanese ancestry, were still Americans. Those proven unworthy of that heritage would be dealt with promptly and severely. All others should be shown the spirit of true Americanism. He did not, however, say how aliens should be treated, although the university would later have an opportunity to test its tolerance when a small group of Japanese American students from the West Coast arrived on campus.[38]

More immediately, the university witnessed an increasing number of resignations, with men going into service and both men and women being recruited to civilian government agencies. Rumors spread that the main dining hall would have to be closed because of a lack of staff. While the closure did not occur, adjustments were required. No parents or other guests could be accommodated. No catering for special conferences or parties would be permitted. In a telling comment on the gender relations of the day, staff members who lived on campus and who had wives who could prepare meals were barred from the cafeteria. Precautions for air raids went into effect. Professor George E. McReynolds was appointed university air raid warden, and he made arrangements for the receipt

of warnings and the enforcement of blackouts, the first of which occurred on
Tuesday, February 10, 1942. At about 8:30 P.M., the college whistle blew three or
four short blasts. Within three or four minutes all was dark, the blackout lasting for about fifteen minutes and ending with a long blow on the whistle sig-
naling "All's clear." Lights again began to wink all over campus and in the Storrs
community. A few weeks later, Leland Cable, the town policeman, announced
that some fifty men from the campus and surrounding towns had signed up for
air-raid lookout duty. Each would serve a two-hour watch, scanning the skies
for enemy planes. They would record the number of all planes seen or heard,
whether single-, bi-, or multi-motor, each plane's approximate altitude, the
plane's distance and direction from the observation post, and the direction in
which the plane traveled. A small tower was erected by the town of Mansfield on
the roof of Beach Hall for the observers to use on the twenty-four-hour watch,
which would join the 166 other posts in Connecticut and some twenty thousand
along the East Coast. Change indeed had come to the small community.[39]

Even more change was on its way. Toward the end of January 1942, the War
Department wrote to President Jorgensen about the possibility of billeting air
corps personnel on campus. The department had been in contact with the American Council on Education and the U.S. Office of Education and was writing to
individual institutions to ascertain whether they could furnish space for the
housing and training of recruits, space that would be leased by the air corps for
the duration of the war. The immediate need was for quartering a minimum of
five hundred recruits, sufficient space for a drill area, and institutional facilities
to feed the men. There would be no demand upon the teachers, laboratories, or
classrooms of the host institutions. The recruits would be under the command
of air corps officers. While this possibility did not come to fruition, by December 1942 the university was about to sign a contract with the navy for the training of six hundred naval reserves in a preflight physical fitness program. The
army, however, intervened by determining that all institutions already having
an ROTC unit should become home to the Army Specialized Training Program
(ASTP). Concern then developed that the current students, and particularly the
women, who weren't likely to be soldiers, would be forced off campus to make
room for the ASTP recruits. Jorgensen assured the university community that
room would be made for the army only after the institution accommodated its
regular students.[40]

The ASTP developed when, early in the war, it became evident that the draft
and enlistments had decimated the college ranks and reduced the number of
trained individuals, particularly in fields such as engineering, medicine, chemistry, and bacteriology. The military needed these skills immediately, as would
the nation as a whole in the postwar period. As a consequence, the U.S. administration in Washington D.C., after much consultation with military and
educational agencies, decided on a program of in-service training. Eighteen- to

twenty-one-year-olds capable of higher education were inducted into the army or navy, placed on active-duty status in uniform, and assigned to one of two hundred colleges or universities for military and physical training as well as academic work. The first ASTP unit members arrived in Storrs in late June 1943 and enrolled primarily in engineering courses. They were assigned to three twelve-week terms in the basic course, and upon successful completion they enrolled in nine months more of advanced courses. Thereupon, they became eligible for Officers Candidate School. They lived in the Koons, Hall, and Storrs dormitories and ate in the campus's main dining room. Though they were ineligible for intercollegiate athletics, they otherwise blended into the campus. There were small tensions, too, as many of them had been college students before the call to arms. When members of the ASTP jeered the Connecticut basketball team during a game against Coast Guard in the winter of 1944, regular students took offense. They could not understand how Connecticut's "own unit" would do such a thing; on the other hand, many of the soldier-students didn't regard themselves as part of the university community. From their perspective, they just happened to be stationed in Storrs.[41]

Upon evaluating the many units, the Curricula and Standards Branch of the ASTP pronounced the University of Connecticut trainees "significantly above corresponding means for all institutions tested." Showing faith in the quality of the program, the University Senate voted to extend full college credit for ASTP courses taken (unless they duplicated courses taken at another institution). Ultimately, more than 850 student-soldiers passed through the program. At the end of March 1944 a large number of them departed for unannounced destinations; in September, the seventh and final term for advanced training ended. The *Connecticut Alumnus* commented that the soldiers' presence on campus would long be remembered. Appreciating their clean-cut demeanor, the periodical suggested it was "just possible that a co-ed here and there shed genuine tears at their departure."[42]

President Jorgensen apparently had another perspective on this, however. When Colonel Passmore, the head of military training on campus, came to Jorgensen in June 1943 to ask for a prophylaxis station for venereal disease, the president told him that that was his problem and warned him that the first time one of Passmore's soldiers molested a co-ed, there would be trouble. He recognized, however, that a problem existed because Storrs was isolated, a "dry" town without even a movie house or some other organized recreation, and it had a much larger percentage of women students than usual. Passmore, on the other hand, thought the soldiers could go to Hartford or Manchester for leisure but worried about sending his men to Willimantic, because he believed it to be a wicked city.[43]

While seeing some advantages to having the military on campus, Jorgensen privately showed concern about university autonomy. At the same time that he discussed the co-eds with Passmore, the president seemed anxious about the army wanting to send as many as 1,600 soldiers for training. He insisted that the university, not the army, run the institution and stated that Connecticut would let the facilities by contract but keep control over education. He would tolerate no army jurisdiction there. Moreover, he complained that the army crowded eight men into each suite in which the university housed four, and noted that 246 soldiers resided in Wood Hall, where 100 male college students normally resided. The military presence on campus increasingly appeared to be a mixed blessing.[44]

The Women's War

For women on campus, wartime presented new opportunity, but in no way did it bring a complete break with the past. On one hand, the culture of gender could not be easily erased; on the other, change was occurring even prior to Pearl Harbor. As winter drew to an end in 1940, the university announced a plan to build two new dormitories to accommodate two hundred additional women by the next school year. During the second week of March, women students hosted the co-ed formal and edited a special all-female-staffed issue of the *Connecticut Campus*. At the formal, following the grand march, Dean of Women Mildred P. French announced that six senior women had been selected for a new honorary society at the university. Chosen on the basis of outstanding scholarship, character, and extracurricular activities, the group consisted of Marion Glater, Mildred Haglund, Ruby Morris, Elizabeth Rourke, Katherine Schueler, and Elizabeth Shepherd. Glater was president of Theta Psi Sorority, a member of the Philosophy Club, and a varsity athlete. Haglund presided over the Women's Student Government Association (WSGA) and served as secretary of the Student Senate, was a member of the Outing Club and the Home Economics Club, and also participated in women's sports. Morris had been feature editor of the *Connecticut Campus* and co-editor of the *Nutmeg* yearbook, and she was social chair of Holcomb Hall and a member of Gamma Chi Epsilon. Rourke was former editor of the *Campus* and the *Nutmeg*, president of Pencraft, a literary society, and a member of Gamma Chi Epsilon. Schueler, a member of the Philosophy Club, served on the executive committee of the WSGA and as senior representative of the Student Senate. Finally, Shephard, active in the Women's Athletic Council and in varsity sports, presided over the Women's Varsity Club and was a member of the Pan-Hellenic Council. Rourke had further distinguished herself by becoming the first woman selected for membership in the Druids, the exclusive honorary secret society. An English major who desired a career in journalism, Rourke reported that a number of publishers told her it was a "man's game." Hence, women at the university had accumulated a number of accomplishments in the year before Pearl Harbor, but many stood in a female sphere that was still divorced from a larger universe.[45]

Harriet Jorgensen, the president's wife, seemed to acknowledge this when she confessed to a reporter that the most likely entry for women into the college life she loved so well was through marriage, although she knew some successful women professors. The women on campus also lent support to the formality of gender difference when they complained in April 1940 that men in sweaters and open shirts did not make a favorable impression in the dining hall. Meals, according to them, demanded a suit coat and tie. This led to one outraged male student's claim that women in skirts and blouses appeared equally casual. He contended that female "Sloppy Joe" sweaters were nowhere near as neat as the male garment and concluded that "Until the co-eds are ready to perfect their own appearances, let's not hear anything more about reforming the already henpecked males of this campus!" Such banter did not prevent the organization of a university dating service, which had as its purpose the getting of dates for fellows who wanted to go out but did not know any girls, and for girls who wanted to be introduced to an escort.[46]

Even while gender differences continued to be emphasized, women at the university sought both dignity and equality. For instance, in the summer of 1940 Dean French wrote to President Jorgensen about what might have seemed to be a very trivial matter, but one that nevertheless irritated some of her staff: the title of "house mother." Some felt too young to be labeled a "mother"; others found the term undignified. A committee recommended "house director," a term that French herself employed, though she agreed with Syracuse and Boston University's use of the title "head resident." Jorgensen accepted the suggestion for a switch to "director," although custom frequently continued the offending usage "house mother" at the university. Women also lobbied for their right to smoke. As a result of action taken by the WSGA the authorities legalized smoking for co-eds in selected areas of the campus, provided each woman furnished her own ashtray and protected furniture and furnishings. Women may have made their strongest statement when Betty Cheney, Janet Speirs, Grace Chapman, and Jean Clarke enrolled with twenty-two men in the second-year Pilot Training course offered by the university in conjunction with the nationwide program sponsored by the Civil Aeronautics Authority. This bucked a trend evident in places like Fullerton, California, where all prospective enrollees in the program had to pledge themselves to seek further flight training with the army or navy air corps, thereby eliminating women from contention.[47]

Although the Connecticut co-eds seemed to fare better than those in the Golden State, their treatment continuously raised concerns for the administration. The president informed William J. Haggerty, the director of student personnel, about complaints regarding the entertaining of females in the upper floors of fraternity houses. Fraternity brothers explained to the "house mothers" that it was preferable to entertain their girlfriends in rooms or attics of frat houses than in the bushes on campus. Jorgensen countered that the administration would not condone the entertaining of co-eds in bushes and certainly would not approve of men entertaining women in their rooms; he then threatened to close the fraternity houses. The issue, however, extended beyond parietal rules. When the university was being considered for inclusion on the American Association of University Women's (AAUW) approved membership list, the organization commented on the small number of women on the Connecticut faculty, which had been noted by a representative who had made a site visit to the campus. Jorgensen immediately responded that several new women faculty had been added since the visit. The organization then voted the University of Connecticut into membership at its May 1941 convention. Almost six months later, a list of women staffers eligible for AAUW membership revealed forty-nine names with positions ranging from dean (Mildred French) to stenographers and typists. Tellingly, even those on the secretarial staff held college degrees, and most of them from superior institutions. The academic discipline with the largest representation was home economics. Women had a special place—segregated into fields like home economics or limited to secretarial work.[48]

Under the headline "Profs Concede Co-Eds Are Necessary Evil," six male instructors offered their responses to a female *Campus* reporter who asked, "Do you approve of co-education?" Professor Winthrop Tilley of the English Department, whose courses attracted many co-eds, responded that "huntresses" would not leave the boys alone so that they could study. This offered no disadvantage to the woman, but it hurt the man. While men's scholarship might thus suffer, however, democracy demanded that women have opportunity, and co-ed colleges fulfilled the demands of democracy. Philosophy professor Robert Baldwin thought co-ed institutions preferable to the monastic life experienced at a college like Wesleyan. For him, the artificial segregation of the sexes encouraged exaggerated and unnatural ideas. The general picture of sexual morality on this campus was good, apart from a few cases of dates gone wrong. But because college life was far enough from real living anyway, it would not help matters to keep males and female separated. Hugh Cannon of the Accounting Department, referred to in the article as a "well-known woman-hater and bachelor-at-large," remarked that it made little difference whether or not there was co-education. He reasoned that boys who wanted to see girls would find them somewhere. He also suggested that for most males, athletics and other recreation could substitute for women. Andre Schenker, a professor of history, regretted that the presence of women made for time wasting and scholastic failures. The social contact between male and female had the advantage, however, of permitting them to get to know each other, so that future disillusionment might be avoided. Economist Paul Nichols found no disadvantages and pointed to several advantages in co-education. He thought it led to better overall development—

physically, mentally, morally, socially, culturally and spiritually. Secondly, co-education kept the boys more sober. Professor William Leonard, also of the Economics Department, believed that women of the time were oppressed economically and socially, and men could afford to be patronizing because they paid the bills. Advanced for his day, Leonard asserted that women would be happier if they were more independent and should be given an equal chance in the professions. He added that the only problem with co-ed colleges was that few of the women majored in economics. Such mixed views of co-education offered the framework for the women's roles at Storrs at the outbreak of World War II.[49]

Despite the new opportunities for women, attitudes about a woman's "place" were slow to change. When a graduate assistant unexpectedly left for the navy, Albert Waugh, then head of the Economics Department, interviewed an honors graduate from Massachusetts State to replace him. She made a good impression, but Waugh wondered "how effective a good-looking girl will be handling discussion sections." He concluded, though, that "beggars can't be choosers." When she didn't accept the position, he hired another woman sight unseen who had done graduate work at the New School of Social Research. Also, Beatrice Fox Auerbach, owner of G. Fox & Company, Hartford's leading department store, made certain that at least one of the Auerbach Foundation Scholarships she donated to the university in March 1942 went to a woman. About the same time, a survey of war industry needs in Connecticut revealed that eighty thousand new employees would be required and further recommended that at least 50 percent of them should be women. Later in the year, Waldemar Hagen, head of student placement and armed service representative for the university, predicted that college women would soon be subjected to a labor draft.[50]

Without such a draft, the Cheney Silk Mills in nearby Manchester, Connecticut, attempted to meet its labor needs by attracting women to work there. When an initial attempt to attract university students failed because of the length of the 3:00 to 11:00 P.M. shift, the mill offered to hire co-eds to work two or more afternoons a week on a 3:00 to 7:00 P.M. split shift. Sewing parachutes by machine, during training, paid forty-five cents an hour; after the instruction period, the young women were paid on a piece basis, averaging up to $1.25 per hour. When the mill announced the plan in December 1942, about sixty women showed interest. However, two months later the factory abandoned the effort. The university's director of placement reasoned that although the trial crew of college workers was a success, the work in the mill was so important for war purposes that the co-eds would have to choose between their scholastic efforts and the parachute sewing. They could not do both without jeopardizing their academic records. The Curtiss Wright Corporation of Passaic, New Jersey, advertised in the *Campus* for women willing to leave Storrs. In large, bold type, it told college women, "This is Your Opportunity to take part in war production." On February 1, 1943, the largest manufacturer of war planes, airplane engines, and propellers in the United States would send eight hundred college women to seven of America's finest engineering colleges for a ten-month custom-built aircraft course. A nominal salary, plus tuition, room, and board, would be paid. Once successfully trained, "Engineering Cadettes" would be placed in the engineering department of Curtiss Wright. Applicants had to be eighteen years old, at least a sophomore, and should have successfully completed college algebra or its equivalent. The advertisement added the caveat that anyone already committed for employment with any company engaged in war work should not apply.[51]

For those women not interested in or suited for factory labor, the university served as a home for the Connecticut Women's Land Army (CWLA) as well, which provided farm training. Storrs became the first site in the nation to develop a continuous yearround program using the expertise of the faculty and the facilities of the Agriculture School. The university joined with the CWLA, the U.S. Employment Service, and the Farm Security Administration in getting as many women trained as possible to take up the slack in agricultural labor. It offered continuously held courses, two weeks in length, that would insure a constant flow of woman power to the farms. Initially, planners conceived that twenty women would complete the course every two weeks; later, ten women left every seven days for farm jobs after specializing in one of the following: dairy farming, poultry farming, fruit and truck farming, and dairy plant operation. The CWLA was modeled on the British Land Army. The farm "soldiers" were distinguished from the rest of the student body by the uniforms they wore and quartered in Old Shakes, which had been renovated and re-equipped. They were under immediate supervision of the state CWLA director, Corinne W. Alsop, the wife of a former university trustee, and W. B. Young, dean of the School of Agriculture and director of all agricultural short courses. Raymond E. Baldwin, the governor of Connecticut, told a radio audience about the need to expand the state's food production to make it as self-sufficient as possible. He added that women enlisting in the CWLA would discover "the most approved war-time method in getting that sun tan," besides helping the war effort.[52]

Interest in the CWLA extended far beyond the opportunity for a sun tan. Eleanor Roosevelt surprised the campus when she arrived to inspect the work done by the trainees. Corinne Alsop, her cousin, played an instrumental role in bringing the first lady to Storrs and served as her host at the Alsop home in Avon, Connecticut. Mrs. Roosevelt, who had addressed an audience at Hartford's Bushnell Auditorium the night before her visit, spoke to a capacity crowd at Hawley Armory on the morning of March 23, 1943. She discussed "the youth of America and their world today," extolling the democracy-preserving activity of young people in the military and in civilian life. She praised England's land army and British women's substantial success in increasing food production. The first lady advised her college audience to learn from the mistakes of the past. President Jorgensen, upon thanking her, asked that she carry the following message back to FDR: "We hope with him for an early termination of the war and he has my promise that the students of this University will help to build the future." Then, escorted by the state police, Mrs. Roosevelt, with an entourage, went on a tour of the dairy barns, the poultry houses, and the CWLA dormitory, where she spoke to women farm soldiers. The most famous woman in America made a lasting impression on the rural campus.[53]

Not long after that, the university announced that for the first time in its history enrollment figures showed more women students registered than men. By the next semester, Henrietta "Happy" Spring was elected the first woman president of the Student Senate in an election that featured only women candidates. In previous years, it had been the custom to elect a senior male as president of the senate, but in 1944 no senior men were even members. Leadership opportunities opened for co-eds, and jobs beckoned non-college women during wartime. However, some females thought they already had made the ultimate sacrifice. When a shortage of materials to make cosmetics developed, one co-ed announced, "If the boys can get along without zoot suits, we can get along without painted snoots. We have already done part of our patriotic duty by wearing skirts half as short, and if we have to we can make our lipstick cover twice as much territory." Another, less-willing woman replied, "They just can't expect the girls to go around as they really look." As the war moved into its final year, women grappled with the non-war issues of smoking and the wearing of slacks on campus. The *Campus* editorialized that there was no reason why women should be discriminated against: "They have every right to do things that men are allowed to do." However, for the time being the newspaper argued that the rules regulating women smoking should stay in place. As for slacks, "They, too, will undoubtedly be worn more generally, but at the present time, there is too much public opinion against." While wearing the pants on campus literally remained primarily a male prerogative, whether frivolous or not, women's sacrifice and service took on a transformed, if transient, wartime role.[54]

Nisei on Campus

The war transformed the campus in another way. It brought to Storrs nineteen mostly second-generation Japanese Americans (*Nisei*), who had been attending college on the west coast when FDR signed Executive Order 9066 on February 19, 1942. That order, for which the government apologized in 1990, had deep consequences for civil liberties in America. Resulting from the fears excited by the bombing of Pearl Harbor, and a long history of anti-Asian sentiment not limited to the Pacific coast, the order interned 120,000 Japanese Americans, two-thirds of whom were citizens, in War Relocation Authority centers in isolated areas of America's interior west that some critics labeled "concentration camps." The internees, who had committed no illegal acts, first were rounded up in assembly centers such as the Santa Anita racetrack, where families, stripped of their possessions, dwelled in the horse stalls under the worst of circumstances. Conditions in the camps offered little improvement, but selected college students whose education had been interrupted found an opportunity to leave. With the blessing of both the army and navy, which approved students and the colleges they would attend, the National Japanese-American Student Relocation Council (NJASRC) placed Nisei undergraduates in eastern colleges and universities.[55]

On April 15, 1943, the army placed the university on the NJASRC list of schools that had expressed an interest in accepting Nisei from the camps and thirteen days later cleared Connecticut to accept students. Two days later, when the head of admissions asked Albert Waugh what he thought of admitting some of the students of Japanese descent who had been ousted from the West Coast, the economics professor urged that it be done. He was told that President Jorgensen had raised some concern on the grounds that they were out-of-state students. Another professor joined Jorgensen and voiced reluctance about admission, adding that he would certainly "watch them more carefully than the other students." Despite such reluctance, Connecticut emerged as a leader among institutions enrolling Nisei. (In a reversal of this relationship, Associate Professor of Sociology James H. Barnett temporarily left the university for a position as a social analyst at the War Relocation Center in Jerome, Arkansas, where he planned to study conflict within the incarcerated Japanese community.)[56]

A confidential Student Relocation Council information memo in late winter 1945 described the university as one of the most popular schools among the Nisei and noted that the school had done a fine job for them. It exulted, "The Nisei there have written us exuberant letters about the warmth, friendliness, and complete acceptance they have experienced." It then lamented that the university was seriously overcrowded and was being forced to turn down applications by long-time residents of the state. As a consequence, it would be very difficult for an out-of-state student to gain admission. By that time, the Nisei had left their mark on the institution, and the university in Storrs played a special role in their lives. Two of the men, Bill Hayakawa and Kay Kiyokawa, played on the varsity baseball and football teams. Kiyokawa had been a pitching sensation as a freshman at Oregon State, where he had a record of seven wins and no losses. Unfortunately for Connecticut, he lost his first start for the Huskies in a 1–0 pitching duel against CCNY. While he was fully accepted in Storrs, in a game against the University of Maine in Orono the fans taunted him. When he got up to bat the first time, the crowd screamed "Tojo," referring to the Japanese military leader. It didn't bother him and he got a base hit. The same thing happened his second time at bat. The third time, instead of screaming "Tojo," the crowd yelled "Slugger!" The diminutive pitcher had made his point. George Fukui arrived in Storrs on a cold, overcast fall day in 1944 and would feel a strong attachment to the University of Connecticut for the remainder of his life. His second weekend on campus, he married Yuri Kenmotsu, whom he had met in an internment camp. He began studying dairy science, in which he had majored at the University of California at Davis but shifted to bacteriology under the mentorship of Professor Walter L. Kulp, who treated him like a son and greatly influenced his later career as a microbiologist. Vinton Esten White, an instructor in charge of the labs, also went out of his way to assist the Japanese American student who had been transplanted from the West to New England.[57]

Other faculty helpful to the Nisei included Paul Pfuetz, a Philosophy Department assistant professor who specialized in religion, Erben Cook Jr., a young mathematician, and Professors Harry Seeley, John Lucke, and E. O. Anderson, as well as college physician Dr. Ralph Gilman. Fukui remembered how on one dark night a driver picked up two hitchhiking Japanese Americans coming back from a movie in Willimantic; President Jorgensen was behind the wheel. However, not all of the Nisei students shared in such good fellowship. Tomoko Ikeda Wheaton recollected how certain professors resented the presence of Japanese Americans and how the students had to persevere in the face of hardship. In general, however, they established a strong sense of camaraderie and banded together to overcome any sense of resentment. Conscientious objectors (COs) added to the mix of soldiers and Nisei on campus. The university offered to accept COs from the Friends Society of Philadelphia, and twenty came to Storrs. They worked in the livestock barns, on the grounds, in the dining halls, and in maintenance. The war thus brought a diversity of individuals to the Storrs campus that was not common prior to the bombing of Pearl Harbor. While few African Americans enrolled at that time, the Nisei befriended two, Bob Hill and Amos Turpin, as people of color joined together.[58]

The Siegel Affair

One German-born faculty member, Theodor Karl Siegel, provided a different and less acceptable kind of diversity to the campus, and he ultimately left the university. His case tested tolerance during World War II. Upon arriving from Germany, Dr. Siegel intended to take a job in a bank, but the Great Depression diminished bank employment even more than it did jobs in institutions of higher education. He joined the university as a language instructor in 1931. Siegel had entered the United States that year at the Vermont border; the following year he filed his declaration of intention for citizenship in the Rockville, Connecticut, Superior Court and his petition for naturalization in 1937 at Hartford. He became a citizen on May 4, 1938. Siegel made a number of trips to Europe after entering the United States and was reported in Czechoslovakia during the crisis in that nation, in Spain during part of the Civil War, and in the Polish Corridor just prior to its invasion by Germany. In 1940, during a roundtable discussion before a capacity audience in Beach Hall, the German professor opened by stating that he was not a Nazi and had never had any desire to be a member of the National Socialist party, but he did point out that both England and France had endeavored to encircle Germany, both economically and diplomatically. He explained Germany's action as self-defense rather than aggression and suggested that no nation would be able to endure the trickery of the Allies. Siegel concluded by asking his audience, "What would you do if you were in Germany's place?"[59]

The roundtable occurred prior to America's entrance into the war. However, almost two and a half years into the conflagration, the *Campus* published a story about a textbook, *In Deutschland,* that was being used in the university's third-year German class and glorified Nazi Germany. While the article did not mention Siegel by name, it implicitly indicted the instructor who had assigned the book as well as the authors of the volume. Albert Waugh, in his journal, confided that the extracts published in the paper, taken out of context, surely proved nothing wrong. He thought the faculty "should go out of its way to protect Siegel or any other member of the staff from unjust attacks which are inevitable accompaniments of war hysteria." Nevertheless, suspicion of the German professor increased. Siegel's reputation was further tarnished by an unusual dispute he engaged in with one of his language department colleagues.[60]

Professor Arsene Croteau, whose headship of the Language Department did not instill confidence in his colleagues, charged Siegel with giving his own daughter, Bettina Siegel, a student at the university, advance information about an important language exam. The dispute heated to the point that Charles B. Gentry, the dean of the university, had to appoint a special committee to investigate the situation and make a determination. He chose Professors Sherman Hollister, Marcel Kessel, G. Safford Torrey, and Waugh, who then selected Professor H. M. Scott as their chair. The committee ultimately found Bettina Siegel blameless and allowed her to continue her French course with an instructor other than Professor Croteau. It found her father guilty at most of indiscretion and pointed out the long-standing animosity between the two language professors, highlighting the tension in that department and the need for improved organization.[61]

For those already suspicious of Siegel, it probably came as no surprise when the Department of Justice charged him on January 26, 1944, with swearing falsely in taking the oath of naturalization, alleging that he intended to retain fidelity to the German Reich and did not intend to make America his permanent home. The news, nevertheless, shocked the campus, and some of the talk was tinged with violence, despite Albert Waugh's call for moderation and an opportunity for Siegal to explain himself. Thomas J. Dodd Jr., the special assistant to the U.S. attorney general who signed the complaint, suggested that the revocation of his citizenship would make the German-born instructor liable for internment. The case took on national prominence when Walter Winchell in the fall of 1945 gave it nightly attention on his popular radio program and even challenged President Jorgensen to a debate about Siegel's citizenship. The President did not rise to the bait but did help to persuade Siegel to accept a leave with pay, during which he would remove himself from the campus. To some critics of the president, this more accurately represented a suspension, after much arm twisting. The American Legion had pressured Jorgensen to take action against Siegel after Jorgensen had asked for their help with the legislature in getting funding for dormitories for returning veterans. One of the legionnaires blatantly suggested a quid pro quo when he remarked, "I suggest that we postpone all action on the question of our support for the University's program until we see what they do in the Siegel case." Jorgensen claimed to have refused to bargain, but the next day the newspapers carried a story about how the legion was insinuating itself into the Siegel matter. Then, a federal district judge found that the German professor had obtained his citizenship fraudulently and illegally because he retained a loyalty to the German Reich. Siegel resigned his position, pending appeal, so as not to be of further embarrassment to the university. The appeal was not heard, nor was Siegel, never proven to be a Nazi, deported. He continued to live in the United States with restricted citizenship rights, but he was never permitted to resume his position at the university. The case stirred strong emotions. Many thought him a traitor; others believed his treatment too harsh. When McCarthyism swept the campus during the next decade, the Siegel case resonated in the minds of those who understood the civil liberties implications for both the left and the right.[62]

Jorgensen Plans for Peacetime

While the Siegel affair captured national attention and stirred the campus, normal activity, and particularly athletic events, captured campus interest. Football and soccer were temporarily suspended in September 1943, when it became apparent that the entire football backfield was serving in a detachment of Marines training at Yale. A modified season was permitted the next year, with a team that included men classified 4-F (physically unfit) by their draft boards, and seventeen-year-olds. Basketball continued to draw excited attention. For the first time, the Connecticut basketball team played at Madison Square Garden, before eighteen thousand spectators on January 8, 1944, against the New York University (NYU) Violets. Even gas rationing and other travel hindrances could not prevent a large turnout of Husky fans at the New York City arena. Eighteen-year-olds made up the foundation of the Connecticut team, with the tallest player being 6′2″; the NYU hoopsters included almost all freshmen, many seventeen years old, with the tallest player at 6′4″. Both teams had lost almost every member of their

1942–43 squads to enlistments, the draft, and reserve call-ups. Hence, the contest at Madison Square Garden pitted green players fresh out of high school, but this did not dim the excitement and the respite it provided from news of the war. The seventeen-point underdog Huskies lost 46–45 in a nailbiter. One sports writer claimed the Huskies made an indelible impression on the crowd, many of whom "probably never knew the University of Connecticut even existed."[63]

Another old, tried and true campus activity flourished during World War II: campus politics took on an added edge as President Jorgensen's tenure moved through its first decade. He was no longer the new boy, and his numerous decisions, while appealing to some, alienated other. These touched on appointments, salaries, admissions, his unwillingness to delegate, his handling of the army on campus, and favored treatment for his children. A strong undercurrent of criticism for Jorgensen, known to the faculty but not necessarily to the public, continued to mount through the war years. By the end of 1943, the local chapter of the AAUP considered establishing a Committee on Faculty Morale but dropped the idea because of the unfavorable publicity that would result if too many staff members supported the firing of the president. When word reached Jorgensen, he talked seriously with his wife about leaving Storrs. The job was exhausting, and he felt betrayed by some of his staff. Albert Waugh confided to him that while he thought it would have been appropriate to get rid of former President McCracken, Jorgensen did not deserve such a fate. He claimed that the majority of the staff supported the president. Difficulty with the governor and two of the alumni members on the board of trustees intensified Jorgensen's problems to the point that he submitted his resignation in January 1944, but it was refused by the full board.[64]

Rumors that Jorgensen would leave the university persisted, and stories disparaging him made the rounds of the faculty. The president's lack of precision in his pronunciation exacerbated matters. One example was his saying "exhilarate" when he meant "accelerate." This habit almost convulsed a meeting of the University Senate, which had to collectively restrain itself when Jorgensen remarked, "We have made a good start now in *exhilarating* the programs of our male students, but you must realize that it is just as important for us to *exhilarate* the co-eds. You haven't been doing enough of that aspect of it. We shall have to give the matter our careful attention, and I am sure that you can find some way to *exhilarate* them, too." More seriously, stories spread that Jorgensen had tampered with his son's grades at the university and his daughter's high-school transcript when she applied to college. In addition, critics claimed that he had given his son a scholarship. When one of the trustees went to the president's house to object and warn that if he didn't reimburse the money, the matter would be taken up with the entire board, Jorgensen returned the scholarship.[65]

Despite the cloud that hung over the president's head as the war came to a close, a number of supporters argued that his administration had been quite successful. While Jorgensen did not inspire his colleagues philosophically or academically, he offered a vision for the university's physical growth. He already had achieved much in that respect during the first five years of his administration—the Wilbur Cross Library, the Home Economics Building, and several new dormitories, among other edifices.

Additionally, several programs and schools were added under his leadership. In 1940 he appointed Nathan L. Whetten as dean of the new Graduate School, which had high ambitions for itself despite a modest budget of $600 for a half-time secretary, $100 for supplies and materials, and $50 for "travel, telephone, etc." The Connecticut Legislature, through the Ratcliffe Hicks School of Agriculture, restored the very practical two-year program in agriculture that had been dropped earlier—to the chagrin of the state's farmers. In 1941 the General Assembly authorized the university to take over the New Haven College of Pharmacy, which would become the University of Connecticut School of Pharmacy. The School of Nursing admitted its first class in September 1942. In the same year, the Hartford Colleges of Law and Insurance at 39 Woodland Street in Hartford joined the university, marking the beginnings of the University Law School. Regional campuses, known then as branches, began in New Haven and Hartford in 1939 and in Waterbury in 1942. The board of trustees in 1940 authorized a two-year graduate program to be given at a School of Social Work to be established in Hartford. It began operation immediately after the war. Hence, the president could certainly point to much organizational growth.[66]

He also knew how to work with the legislature. A woman who attended one of his speeches remarked that she had to smile at the way he took advantage of every opportunity to get funds for the university. She—and others—admired him for that. During the war, under his leadership, Connecticut remained the only land-grant college in the area that had anything like a full enrollment. The university's approximate sixteen hundred regular full-time students, the large majority of them women, exceeded the approximately five hundred at Rhode Island State, the seven hundred fifty at Massachusetts State, and the thousand each at Maine and New Hampshire. Authorities expected the Nutmeg State's numbers to escalate at the war's conclusion, with an anticipated twenty thousand veterans and war workers returning to higher education in the state. Future expansion seemed assured, and the university had to build for this future. Otherwise, the president feared that those returning would enroll at the state teachers' colleges in New Haven, New Britain, or Danbury, which were all in more convenient population centers than Storrs. The very practical Jorgensen cast aside the opinion of faculty, who contended that there was nothing to worry about because those schools could not offer an education equivalent to that of the university in Storrs. Unless the university had adequate facilities, he presciently believed students would go to the institution nearest home, and a number of full-blown state colleges would then emerge.[67]

Never one to shy away from promoting his institution and its advancement, at 10:00 A.M. on Friday, September 22, 1944, in Hawley Armory, the president spoke to the first convocation of the year and laid out his plans for the postwar period. He first suggested that demand for future admission would be at a premium and that standards could be raised. Students would be advised to work as hard as possible to keep their place at the school. He then discussed the physical changes that he anticipated—and that actually came to fruition. He told of plans for new faculty and staff housing, new dormitories, a student union building, an auditorium, a field house, two new classroom and laboratory buildings, a new infirmary and health services building, a new stadium, and tennis courts. He also predicted the planning of a community civic center, which would include a restaurant and soda bar, a general store, a barber shop, a beauty parlor, a men's and women's furnishings store, a movie theater, a bowling alley, a local post office, and a college bookstore. A few months later he suggested the future establishment of a medical school, and earlier he had spoken of the need to consider offering doctoral degrees in some fields. He clearly envisioned the UConn that would take form after the war and had done much to shape it already in the decade since his arrival. As the *Hartford Courant* said in 1945 while assessing the progress made under his administration, "During these ten years the college has become a university in fact as well as in name." Emerging from depression and war, new challenges lay ahead for the university that had borne that title for only a half-dozen years.[68]

3

The Jorgensen Transformation:
1946–62

*T*HE YEARS IMMEDIATELY FOLLOWING World War II brought growth and expansion to the University of Connecticut, as they did to colleges and universities throughout the nation; higher education democratized and became widely accessible to America's, and Connecticut's, youth. Graduate and professional schooling proliferated. Returning veterans brought a more mature student into the university mix. Serious national issues such as anti-Semitism, racial discrimination, and America's Cold War contest with communism intruded on UConn and other campuses, although students still had enthusiasm for routine hijinks and varsity sports. Albert Nels Jorgensen rode the winds of change to build a modern campus, but his magic failed by the beginning of the 1960s. He left office considerably less popular than when he had begun his tenure at Storrs twenty-seven years earlier. His legacy primarily was in bricks and mortar, although his long shadow fell on all aspects of the university community.

A Home for Veterans: The Fort Trumbull Branch

The influx of World War II veterans returning to campuses throughout the nation under the G.I. Bill of Rights reshaped American higher education. Small and less established institutions became larger and more recognized; those already acclaimed for the education they provided emerged grander in scale and with renewed missions. The University of Connecticut was no exception. In July 1946, when Connecticut faced the problem of duplicating an entire freshman-sophomore curriculum at a site removed from Storrs, and doing so on a scale comparable to the size of the entire university prior to the war, the task seemed insurmountable. Events at the new Fort Trumbull campus in New London proved that "the impossible only takes longer." And even that aphorism lost credibility as a result of the speed with which a new campus emerged.[1]

On May 15, 1946, the University of Connecticut Board of Trustees agreed to establish an education program for veterans at Fort Trumbull, if the state desired that it be done. The state, recognizing the need to accommodate returning GIs who had delayed their educations while fighting for their country, gave the go ahead. Politics played a role in the decision, as Governor Raymond E. Baldwin feared Democratic charges that the Republicans were unwilling to assist veterans. As a consequence, the GOP standard bearer expedited the opening of the New London facility. A month after the trustees' motion, President Jorgensen represented Connecticut at a meeting in Washington that was attended by more than twenty representatives of the War Assets Corporation, the U.S. Coast Guard, the U.S. Maritime Service, the navy, the U.S. Office of Education, and the Treasury Department. The group discussed the transfer of the former Maritime Officers Training School at Fort Trumbull to the University of Connecticut. Jorgensen, after rejecting two proposals that would have been costly to the state, proposed that the federal government agencies involved retain their title to the site and issue a "use permit" that would allow use of buildings and equipment on a temporary basis. He explained that the state had made no provision for the purchase of the facility. More significantly, while he recognized the emergency needs raised by the returning veterans, he desired to centralize as much of the university as possible at Storrs. A permanent campus at New London would encourage those there who desired a university branch in that locality. While some of the professional schools should be located in Hartford, he told Governor Baldwin that once the veterans had been cared for, "The University branches at Fort Trumbull, Hartford, and Waterbury should be withdrawn and absorbed in the University at Storrs."[2]

The federal agencies accepted the suggestion and issued the university a five-year use permit for barracks dormitories, an administration building, mess halls, an infirmary, a gymnasium and swimming pool, classroom and laboratory buildings (with certain exceptions), an auditorium, a building known as the "Canteen," the post office building, a fire house, and a maintenance building; all existing equipment was also included. When the 1,190 veterans and 111 non-veterans arrived for "the Fort's" first University of Connecticut semester in September 1946, they found a readymade campus on twenty-three fence-enclosed acres. Morton Tenzer, a UConn graduate who later joined the faculty at Storrs, attended his first undergraduate year in New London. He described Fort Trumbull as "a neat little facility, not a regular campus, but compact." Initially, the fence reminded many of the veterans of military regimentation, but their distaste diminished with the passage of time. By March 1949 the all-male school enrolled more non-veterans than veterans, and green freshmen lived with battle-scarred, amputee, and bemedalled vets. J. Dennis Pollack, who enrolled at the branch in the fall of 1948, described his roommates: "One had jumped into Belgium, won the Belgian Croix de Guerre and still had shrapnel pieces coming out of his back, another roommate was torpedoed, adrift for three days with shark bites on his leg, wow, what an awakening! I had just graduated from high school." Perhaps it was not surprising that the battle-experienced vets razzed the non-veteran undergraduates during their mandatory ROTC marching drills on a field within the campus. In general, however, good fellowship reigned and the campus served its purpose.[3]

That purpose was to provide a basic two-year curriculum for students who would move on to advanced work at Storrs or another institution. About two-thirds of the students did just that, taking programs in arts and sciences, engineering, and business administration. Many former GIs began with a preference for engineering because of their service-based technician ratings, which they thought prepared them for the profession. The college-level mathematical aspects of engineering physics, however, dampened their enthusiasm. Only 190 of 500 students who began the engineering curriculum in 1946 finished with the same major. As they moved into other fields, they had to make the best of the library, which had gotten off to a shaky start. Only seven weeks were available in which to set up a library for the first students. Physically, the space for the library offered an excellent venue, which included a large reading room. That opening September, however, there was little to read. Meager time was available to place book orders, and the demand for books from other institutions around the country that were equally flooded by returning veterans created long delays in delivery. Once received, those books had to be processed before circulating. To further exacerbate matters, most of the thirty periodical and newspaper subscriptions that had been ordered did not arrive until months after the term began. Consequently, only about 350 books were ready for circulation and reference in the fall of 1946. Two years later, ten times that many were available, and the library subscribed to sixty-seven periodicals, enough to support the needs of freshmen and sophomores but not the research interests of the sixty-plus faculty who taught at Fort Trumbull.[4]

Attending college at the Fort inspired a great deal of camaraderie. The men lived in dormitories with the seafaring names of old clipper ships, such as *Lightning, Comet, Rainbow, Tradewind, Red Jacket, Flying Cloud, Dreadnaught,* and *Typhoon.* The last, which housed 120 students, burned down in 1948 during the middle of exams, and *Red Jacket* simultaneously suffered extensive water damage. To solve the emergency housing crisis, 152 qualified students were transferred to Storrs, where they were eligible for residence, on an hour's notice. The Fort's administration, led by Director C. A. Weber, acted quickly to resolve the crisis. The first days at the Fort Trumbull waterside campus were hectic. Some rooms were short of beds; others had beds but no mattresses; some had desks but no chairs. Mattresses and pillows had to be sterilized. The famous World War II graffito "Kilroy Was Here" marked the walls of several dorms. Nevertheless, by February 1947 a visitor described how the men were housed by foursomes in big, well-furnished sleeping and studying rooms that were fifteen feet square. Furnishings may have seemed spartan to civilians, with stacked or broken-down double-decker beds, study tables, and bookshelves for each occupant. However, the veterans for the most part recognized that they occupied what had been officers' quarters. By the time university administrators joined with the governor to celebrate the first anniversary of taking over the Fort from the Maritime Service, they not only enjoyed a good steak dinner and a tour of the facility but they declared the campus to be in very good shape.[5]

Clubs of all types formed on campus. Students organized radio station WRUM in 1947, and two years later nearly one hundred students worked to broadcast four to five hours daily, Monday through Thursday. There was an active Student Council, a weekly newspaper, the *Tide*, a band, and a glee club. Those interested in politics could join the International Relations Club, the World Federalists, or the Young Progressive Citizens of America. If one's interest ranged to sports rather than politics, the splendid gymnasium and swimming pool left by the Maritime Training School offered a variety of opportunities. Intramurals attracted students to basketball, volleyball, softball, tennis, bowling, and sailing in the six whale boats, which were also remnants of the Maritime Service. In organized sports, the Fort Trumbull men produced winning basketball and baseball teams; in the former, during one season, the varsity had a record of 18–4 while the junior varsity was 17–2. Rivalry with the junior varsity teams at Storrs was especially strong. Before the football game with the Storrs junior varsity that was won by the New Londoners 6–0, fans from Fort Trumbull spirited away the Storrs Husky mascot, Jonathan, and brought him to the waterfront campus. Despite threats to clip the dog's fur, the captors returned him well fed and unshorn at game time.[6]

Hence, the men of Fort Trumbull had a full college experience in their New London setting, and many regretted the need to move on to Storrs or another place for their junior and senior years. On January 25, 1950, in keeping with his desire to make certain that the New London campus remained temporary, President Jorgensen formally notified Director Weber that the branch would be turned back to the appropriate federal agencies no later than midnight on June 30, 1950, the conclusion of their use permit. He asked the director to initiate promptly needed steps to make the closing of the branch as simple and orderly as possible. This occurred and, with the exception of a problem that arose over the federal government turning over some equipment to the university, all went as planned. Connecticut successfully met the needs of returning veterans and new high school graduates, although perhaps not to the hyperbolic extent claimed by the public relations director at Fort Trumbull, who extolled the branch as "one of the most interesting and successful experiments ever undertaken in higher education." For the university, though, it was an important experiment in instant education. It developed people's loyalty to the institution, which ultimately transcended the New London site, and gave the first teaching opportunity to a number of faculty who later moved on to Storrs to join others in the intellectual expansion of the University of Connecticut. By May 1954, however, observers sadly reported on the pile of stones and splintered lumber that stood on the site of the Fort's dormitories. The wrecker's ball had done its work, and a headline in the *Connecticut Campus* read, "Fort Trumbull Now Tumbling."[7]

Storrs in the Immediate Aftermath of War

At Storrs, the campus endured the growing pains brought about by the post–World War II rush for higher education. In his 1945 opening address to students, President Jorgensen asked for patience regarding the overcrowding on campus and explained that the university admitted only half of the eligible students who applied and less than a sixth of those who inquired about admission. In 1946, campus enrollment increased by 50 percent to almost 3,300. Men outnumbered women two to one, and many highly qualified women were denied admission in an intentional attempt to continue a ratio that favored males. The traditional president's reception had to be held in three parts so that everyone could attend. Of greater significance to students on a campus that was already proud of its strong basketball tradition, seats to games had to be rationed, allowing only part of the student body who wished to attend a game to do so. The Wilbur Cross Library had a seating capacity, furthermore, for only 315. As a consequence, the authorities considered prohibiting students from using the building for any studying not involving library material. Office space for professors was at a premium, with many reported to be without a desk to call their own. In the permanent dormitories, every single room became a double and every double a triple. Twenty-one temporary men's dormitories, mostly army barracks, were erected. One hundred seventeen married veterans found quarters in a Willimantic housing project, originally built for Pratt & Whitney aircraft workers during World War II. Free university buses running four times daily made round trips between campus and home. Those living on South Campus called it "Siberia" and found it reminiscent of an army camp—mud and dirt roads, little hot water, leaky roofs. Prefabricated buildings sprouted up on a daily basis. While conditions proved difficult, one former G.I. remarked, "I figure it's better being here than not being in college at all."

New faculty lived in temporary housing behind a heating plant on North Eagleville Road. Fuel tanks lined the street, and the area quickly became known as "Oil Can Alley." The four-room apartments had insufficient heat, but the residents by and large found it a "friendly, informal atmosphere" that served as a defining experience for a generation of Storrs faculty. By 1956, little remained of the makeshift area. The sandboxes where faculty children played dangerously near to the North Eagleville Road traffic were empty, and the improvised housing conditions had become a memory, although at least one UConn student recognized the difficulty faced by Oil Can Alley residents: "I used to sit across the way from them and feel sorry about the living conditions. And I lived in North Campus!" Albert E. Waugh, who had become dean of the College of Arts and Sciences, and his wife shared the concern about immediate postwar conditions. They watched men setting up new "temporary houses" with cranes. Trucks transported housing sections from Hartford and the sections were assembled. The Waughs found such housing insubstantial and ugly.[8]

Waugh, however, also had other matters on his mind. He discussed with the president how best to return veterans and government administrators to the professional staff. At what rank and salary should those who left Storrs to serve the nation return? Waugh suggested that if a returnee had been doing work of a lower caliber than he would have done on the university's staff, he should be brought back at the rank and salary he likely would have had if he had stayed in Storrs. As a consequence, according to Waugh, a dedicated economist, the university would be paying more than full value, which would be part of the institution's contribution to the war effort. In such instances, the university should be liberal in granting leaves of absence to assist such staff members in "rehabilitating themselves quickly." If, on the other hand, a returning veteran had been doing work that exceeded that which would have occupied him if he remained home, he should be brought back at actual value. Jorgensen agreed with the suggestion.[9]

Throughout the early postwar years, the president recognized the rapid changes taking place at the University of Connecticut and used them as a vehicle for obtaining more resources. Addressing the entire professional staff on a Monday afternoon in November 1946, Jorgensen pointed out that ten years previously, the university had 837 students, no summer session, and no extension program (its regional campuses). Its entire physical plant was valued at $3 million. Annual expenditures came to $1.2 million, 57.1 percent coming from the state, 23.4 percent from the federal government, and 19.5 percent from within the institution itself. In the fiscal year that ended in June 1947, between eight and nine thousand students attended the university; the physical plant was valued at $13.5 million; and the annual budget amounted to $4.9 million, with 39.8 percent from the state, 9.6 percent from the federal government, and 50.6 percent from within the institution itself. He did not comment on the diminished state and federal support but stressed that percentage-wise the university had done more to take care of returned veterans than any other college in the United States.

He anticipated that the strong demand for admission to the university would continue at least until 1951 and discussed plans to increase enrollments by a thousand students at Storrs beginning in 1948, and to run large summer sessions. He emphasized the need for new dormitories to house the increased student body and revealed plans for self-liquidating bonds to fund new faculty housing. His budget request for the next biennium far exceeded the existing one, with requests of $11.9 million for the first year and $7.8 million for the second.[10]

Jorgensen also announced that a university products store would be established to sell fruit, vegetables, milk, eggs, and other things. Warner Brothers planned to have a theater in operation by the following fall, and the First National Stores, a supermarket, wanted to open a branch near campus. Hence, the president predicted a great deal of change for the community. With the shift in the physical landscape, an important intellectual transformation won support as well. The president urged that research must become more important. Reduced teaching loads and/or committee assignments awaited those faculty who demonstrated an interest in and ability for research. The emerging postwar university promised a new emphasis on scholarship as well as new stores and movie theaters.[11]

The Battle Against Racism and Discrimination

The future would not arrive unblemished, however, and the nation's social and political problems did not bypass the rural campus either. Many observers overlooked the underlying tensions of the day and, like Louis Gerson, a young assistant professor of political science who later in his career would become head of that department, complained of student apathy and indifference to non-academic activities. Such critics labeled college students of the late 1940s and 1950s the "Silent Generation," failing to look closely at events affecting the nation's racial climate and other matters. While there were few minorities on campus during those years, the issue of race—and racial prejudice—percolated, as did the matter of anti-Semitism. The latter helped to topple the Druids, the secret honor society in existence since 1921; the former influenced the future development of fraternities and sororities at the university.[12]

The Druid incident unnerved the administration and made headlines across the state. At 10:00 P.M. on February 6, 1952, shortly before he was to go to bed, Provost Waugh received a phone call from Arwood Northby, the director of student personnel. He had been joined by two advisers of the Student Senate, Sumner Cohen and C. A. Weber, who reported on "startling, unexpected, and serious developments involving the University which were of an urgent nature." Waugh agreed to join them and wouldn't return home until 1:00 A.M. He learned that at that evening's Student Senate meeting three members brought charges of anti-Semitism against the Druids. The three, Ruben Deveau of New London, Robert McLeod of Shelton, and Paul Veillete, laid their evidence, including excerpts from secret minutes of the Druid meetings, before the senate, and later before the entire student body by means of circulars slipped under dormitory room doors. Part of their charge read that "the Druids have time and time again during their existence fostered religious discrimination, attempting to purge organizations of their Jewish membership and to limit the enrollment of Jewish students in the university." The minutes they quoted described the size of the university's Jewish enrollment as "deplorable," because Jews made up about 20 percent of the school's population as compared to 6 percent of the state's. The minutes also included Druid objectives to "Eliminate deadbeats from the band, especially Jewish, and get Christian cheerleaders." What the Student Senate was not told, but Waugh soon learned, was that the three accusers claimed that the minutes, if published, would implicate President Jorgensen as well as two trustees who had been Druids while undergraduates, J. Ray Ryan and Elmer Watson. Several members of the faculty were also associated with the Druids. While Jewish organizations began to honor Jorgensen in the immediate postwar period, his early correspondence as president include some hints of an anti-Semitism that was common to much of America during the prewar 1930s. The situation represented an embarrassment to the university, and the suggestion that the minutes also included anti-Catholic allusions increased the potential for damaging publicity.[13]

When later asked about the charges, Jorgensen responded that the Connecticut trustees, administration, faculty, and students "have, by a series of positive actions, contributed greatly to the elimination of discrimination." He did not elaborate by giving examples. The *Campus* newspaper appeared to be as interested in the charge that the Druids controlled all student activities on campus, including handpicking editors of the paper and the *Nutmeg* yearbook, as it did in the accusation of anti-Semitism. The Student Senate, by a 21–0 vote (with four abstaining), passed a motion requesting the trustees and administration to "cease all recognition of any student organization on campus, the membership and/or functions of which are secret." At a Sunday breakfast meeting on February 10, 1952, the six members of the Druids unanimously decided to make known their identity and in turn petition the university administration and the Associated Student Government for recognition as an open senior men's society. Two of the three who brought the initial charges, Veillette and McLeod, revealed themselves as Druids. Veillette, particularly, argued for openness and asserted that discrimination was no longer acceptable; all six vowed not to embarrass the university. They promised that once the group received recognition as an open society, they would burn their minutes and other files (paradoxically hiding the Druids' activity to history). Jorgensen and Northby encouraged them and promised assistance in their effort to establish an open, honorary society.

At the end of March the president endorsed the Archons, the Druids' replacements, which had the same six students as charter members. A new era was emerging. In postwar Storrs, the desirability of open student government intensified, as did the undesirability of anti-Semitism—at least *overt* anti-semitism.[14]

The fight against Nazi racism during World War II encouraged a change in domestic American attitudes, although it did not erase the stain of racial discrimination altogether. Before the war, in 1937, a survey by a sociology student of co-eds at the university found that they preferred a Caucasian husband with $1,000 over Negroes, Indians, or Japanese with $100,000. However, by 1946 a female student complained to Dean Waugh about a professor who had his class read the Book of Genesis when discussing "the Negro problem." He told the class that when Cain slew Abel, the Lord put his mark on Cain, and the mark was a black skin. According to the student's account, the professor claimed that the Lord had set the Negro aside as an inferior race, and that there was no sense in talking about racial equality. He did admit that the Bible was open to other interpretations, but he stood by this one. The administration, already alerted to that particular instructor's other classroom failings, was in the process of reviewing him.[15]

A year later, the campus chapter of the American Veterans Committee investigated the recurring problem of discrimination against African American students from the university by hotels in Willimantic. After finding that "flagrant violations of the State Civil Rights Statutes, which guarantee full and equal accommodations to all persons regardless of race, creed, or alienage in public places," the committee filed a complaint with the State Inter-Racial Commission, which investigated and verified the charges. The hotels promised to observe the laws in the future. In 1950, however, when an African American student attempted to get a haircut in Willimantic, he was turned away, and the campus chapter of the National Association for the Advancement of Colored People (NAACP) learned that barbershops did not fall within the jurisdiction of the anti-discrimination laws. It pledged to work to change the law and, in support, the *Connecticut Campus* argued that the nation was based upon the premise that all men are created equal, and that did not mean "only white men."[16]

The racial question developed even more fully on campus when fraternity discrimination emerged as a critical issue during the late 1940s and early 1950s. Following a trend at other colleges and universities, students Phil Bryzman and Jim Blawie introduced a resolution on discrimination to the Student Senate in January 1949. It read: "That no organization or group, whether it be political, social, honorary, or fraternal, shall discriminate against or exclude a person because of race, religion, or national origin on that land owned by the people of this state, and known as the University of Connecticut, nor shall such groups have the use of University owned buildings or property." After a heated debate the resolution passed the Student Senate, which agreed to forward it to a referendum. Governor Chester Bowles congratulated the students on the anti-discrimination resolution and told them not to underestimate the effect that their action would have on citizens of the state. He proclaimed, "As the students of a highly respected educational institution, your vote will influence others to think about and act on the problem of discrimination." The referendum overwhelmingly passed, 1267–210. President Jorgensen immediately issued a statement congratulating the students on their vote and pointing out that the resolution applied particularly to fraternities and sororities, which have discriminatory clauses in their constitutions or bylaws, these clauses usually having resulted from action by national organizations. He further noted that the twenty-two Greek organizations on campus supported the referendum results and that they notified their national officers, asking that the matter be taken up at the next National Convention of Fraternities and Sororities in the summer of 1951. Assuming that this would provide enough time to resolve all of the outstanding issues, the Greeks were allowed to operate on the UConn campus under their charters until September 1951. After that time, no fraternity or sorority that discriminated on the basis of race, religion, or national origin would be allowed to occupy university-owned buildings, or buildings on university property.[17]

Even in that atmosphere, it does not seem probable that the pledging of Alfred R. Rogers by Connecticut's Upsilon chapter of Phi Epsilon Pi would make front-page headlines. It was less the local's pledging of the accomplished African American student than the national fraternity's "blackballing" of him, and the Storrs group's ensuing challenge, that made the news. Al Rogers served as president of his freshman class at the university and played varsity football in his sophomore year and after. The Manchester native headed Boys State in 1947 and reached prominence in church affairs and music. He was vice-president of the Tolland County Pilgrim Fellowship (Congregational), sang in his church choir, and in 1947 was the only African American member of the All-State High School Band, in which he played baritone horn. Pledge brothers Dan Blume and Marv Lapuk were "proud" to be in the same pledge class. In short, Rogers appeared to be a prize pledge.[18]

While this seemed obvious to the predominantly Jewish fraternity in Storrs, national officials worried about the effect that enrolling a Negro would have on chapters in the South. The president of the Greek letter society's national Grand Council, Louis Traurig, a resident of Waterbury, Connecticut, asked that Rogers's initiation be postponed from February 1950 to September of that year, when he could discuss the matter at the fraternity's national convention. The local chapter agreed to do so. However, Rogers's challengers issued the "blackball" in June, after college had been recessed. As a consequence, the fait accompli influenced the Grand Council meeting at the national convention, and it then sustained the action. Subsequently, Storrs chapter members announced that they would withdraw from the national organization if they were refused permission to initiate

Rogers. They were suspended. U.S. Senator William Benton congratulated the local group on its stand, telling them, "You and your organization have set an example not only for the state of Connecticut but for the entire nation." He continued by remarking that discrimination was no longer a local, state, or national problem and placed it within the context of the Cold War. "It is precisely this kind of discrimination which the Russians use to exploit against us the people of the world. . . . Unfortunately mistakes of this nature add grist to the propaganda mills of the Kremlin," claimed Benton, who would serve as a university trustee from 1953 to 1973. Within the Cold War context, and in his capacity as governor and president ex officio of the university's board of trustees, Chester Bowles urged the national's executive secretary to revoke the local's suspension. He proclaimed, "We in Connecticut pride ourselves on the progress we have made giving Negroes equal rights and opportunities." He hoped that the national organization would prove itself a true supporter of democracy by rejecting racial discrimination and concluded, "With the eyes of the world upon us, it is important that we practice the democracy we preach."[19]

Support developed in other Phi Epsilon Pi chapters for the Storrs position. Three New York locals, at NYU, CCNY, and Queens College, voted to drop out of the national fraternity if the Connecticut brothers did not receive permission to pledge Al Rogers. Dickinson College gave its strong support. A school like Georgia Tech took longer to get on board, but it did, and pressure overall continued to build on the national. At the end of December 1950, fraternity representative Robert Berdon, who later became a justice of the Connecticut Supreme Court, reported that the organization's Grand Council, at its meeting in Philadelphia, unanimously voted to reinstate the UConn chapter and to reaffirm and rededicate the national to its founding principle of universal brotherhood. In so doing, it recognized that membership in Phi Epsilon Pi "shall not be denied to anyone because of race, color, or religious beliefs." The battle had been won. Irving Chaneles, president of the Upsilon chapter, telegraphed President Jorgensen from Philadelphia: "Alfred Rogers May Be Initiated at Any Time." Victory did not come cheaply, though. Rogers admitted to feeling great pressure in trying to play football, make his way through classes, and deal with the pledging issue. He remarked, "I think there was a quiet contract that I kind of entered into with some of the [fraternity] leadership . . . that if you guys are going out this way for me, I'm going to hang in and go with you. And that was locked in steel." He later attributed his success in commanding one of the army's first integrated units during the Korean conflict, and his later productive career in the private sector, to his experience with Phi Ep and his other activities at Storrs: "The whole UConn experience prepared me for that."[20]

By the fall of 1951, the board of trustees deadline for the elimination of all discriminatory practices by fraternities and sororities, President Jorgensen could report that all ten social sororities on campus had eliminated charter or ritual provisions having to do with discrimination. Of the seventeen social fraternities, twelve had no formal references to discrimination already. One had its national organization agree to end its bias. Alpha Gamma Rho's president informed Jorgensen that at a national convention this offending passage was removed from its constitution too: "No person of Negro, Hebrew, or Oriental descent or blood shall ever be elected or initiated into the Alpha Gamma Rho Fraternity." The organization's grand president did not hide his ambivalence about such action. He did not like being coerced and emphasized the inherent right of a group to organize and set up its own qualifications for membership. However, his fraternity as a whole was committed to the policy that the board of trustees tried to encourage. Four other Connecticut Greek organizations were unable to instigate such action and reluctantly withdrew from national affiliation to operate as independents. Some change had come in the racial climate, and Jorgensen hoped "that those groups affected will regard the matter as a milestone marking progress in solving the national problem of racial and religious discrimination."[21]

As the decade progressed, as with the nation generally, prejudice and discrimination failed to entirely disappear in the university community. At the beginning of the 1952–53 academic year, when a white and an African American woman became roommates by chance, the enraged father of the former vehemently objected and threatened to come to Storrs to take his daughter out of the college unless she was transferred to another room. Six months after the Supreme Court's 1954 landmark decision against segregation in the *Brown v. Board of Education* case, the mother of a freshman daughter wrote to President Jorgensen complaining about a "colored manager" at the Clark House restaurant in Willimantic who was constantly on the "make" with white girls. She hoped "a little something can be done to remove such an unpleasant occurance [*sic*]." A year and a half later, Athletic Director J. O. Christian told the president about the conditions surrounding travel for the "colored boys" on the basketball team, who would play that year in the Orange Bowl Tournament in Miami. Although they could stay together with the rest of the team and be fed and housed on the Miami campus, they "would not have social equality" on commercial transportation. Nor could they go to public restaurants, hotels, rest rooms, or beaches there. While the players accepted the conditions, Jorgensen strongly protested and pointed to Connecticut's policy of non-discrimination. The underdog team went on to beat Miami, Stanford, and Pittsburgh and win the Orange Bowl Tournament. More fans rooted for the Huskies than any other team playing, including host Miami. Apparently the racial issues raised by Jim Crow did not dampen their ardor for Connecticut basketball. When the National Interfraternity Council convened toward the end of 1957 and claimed that choosing one's friends is a social right, not a civil right, and therefore not subject to legislation, it reawakened the discrimination issue at UConn. Student senator Florence Wagman, while recognizing that her motion, co-sponsored by eleven other senators, was not new, nevertheless introduced a recommendation that denounced discrimination clauses in the constitutions of University of Connecticut organizations or those of any other state-supported institutions. Her colleague, Richard Cromie, backed the recommendation and stated that it was good to reaffirm beliefs. He argued that discrimination was one of the greatest crises facing the nation and that students had a duty as Americans to stand up for the Constitution.[22]

The McCarthy Era at UConn

Support for the Constitution was tested in another way during the 1950s. As the Cold War preoccupied the world and the contest between the United States and the USSR heated up, McCarthyism swept the nation's campuses, including the University of Connecticut. The anti-communist issue was not new, having first emerged during the 1930s, but the intensity increased to fever pitch during the 1950s. Earlier, it had pervaded discussion of the anti-militarism campaign during the middle of the Great Depression. Shortly afterward, in 1938, President Jorgensen received a hand-printed letter signed "A-Member-of-the-Faculty." It read, "Why don't you look into the Reds around the college and release a few. . . . They are a decided curse to the college. You will find yourself into [sic] difficulty if you don't." About the same time, a faculty member accused of being a communist told his accuser to prove the accusation or retract it. Hence, the pre–World War II period served as a harbinger of the postwar climate of fear.[23]

By early 1947 the FBI displayed an interest in the development on campus of a chapter of American Youth for Democracy (AYD), which was reputed to be a communist organization. The campus policeman, assisting the FBI, claimed that several students from other schools had been sent to start the local chapter, which was reported to have about thirty members. He also wanted to check on faculty members who were alleged to be assisting the organization. By May the University Senate devoted much of its meeting to a discussion of freedom of speech. The matter arose when administrators prohibited a student group from inviting the African American scholar W. E. B. DuBois to campus. By the time of the president's opening convocation address in September 1947, after the usual statements about enrollments and building prospects much of the speech was then devoted to communism. Albert Waugh suggested that Jorgensen's talk might well have been titled "The Threat of Communism in the World Today." The president told his mostly student audience that "a mighty duel" was in progress between the United States and the Soviet Union. He noted the university's commitment to democracy and the search for truth. As a consequence, the University of Connecticut and universities generally could not be communistic, "because communism will resort to deceit and to sabotage on the intellectual plane to attain its ends." With such a warning, the students then began their academic year.[24]

By early 1949, when Jorgensen received a letter from a legislator inquiring about communist meetings on campus, he responded that the university had no communist organizations. He explained that all student organizations had to be registered at the Office of Student Personnel, and no meetings could be scheduled unless they were sponsored by a registered organization. Jorgensen assured the writer that the information he received regarding communist or communist-leaning speakers was in error. When the International Relations Club, more than a year later, scheduled Owen Lattimore, director of the Walter Hines Page School of International Relations at Johns Hopkins, to speak, an alumnus criticized the invitation. "If he is not Red he is certainly Pink and how the University of Connecticut can even think of letting such a person speak on its campus, I am at a loss to understand," remarked the UConn graduate, who then threatened to cut off his financial contributions to the school. The threat did not prevent Lattimore from giving a lecture entitled "Our Foreign Policy, East and West" and telling his listeners, "In American tradition, all sides of problems should be considered and all views heard." The House Un-American Activities Committee (HUAC), however, did not espouse such tolerance. Well before Lattimore's appearance in Storrs, it asked selected colleges and universities, Connecticut among them, to report the names of all texts and reference books used in courses in history, government, and economics. When the order went out calling for the data, many instructors objected. However, the spiderweb of loyalty, anti-subversion, and anti-communism had been cast over Storrs.[25]

The faculty's objection to HUAC's demand to see book lists came before Joseph McCarthy, the senator from Wisconsin, launched his anti-communist campaign in a speech in Wheeling, West Virginia, in February 1950. McCarthyism made earlier anti-communism pale in comparison. The controversial senator developed a devoted following and outraged dedicated opponents. When the UConn alumni group in Washington, D.C., invited him to be an honored guest and main speaker at its meeting, President Jorgensen encouraged the cancellation of the invitation, because McCarthy and Connecticut Senator William Benton were bitter enemies. Provost Waugh worried that the cancellation could have as great a repercussion as did the original invitation. McCarthy cast a long shadow. By 1953, the *Connecticut Campus* editorialized that the tactics used by congressional investigators turned universities into mere shells of their former (and better) selves. The newspaper suggested that it was rare for a college professor to strike out for academic freedom in the classroom, and that "faculty members are gradually becoming reluctant to even discuss the topic among their friends." While that assessment may have been overly harsh, the atmosphere across the nation diminished diversity of opinion. In response to a Collegiate Press national poll, 85 percent of students replied "no" when they were asked,

"Do you think avowed Communist party members should be allowed on college faculties?" When asked about former communists being allowed to teach, 45 percent responded yes and 39 percent no. When a sociology professor resigned in February 1953 for reasons ostensibly having nothing to do with politics, Albert Waugh, by then provost, breathed a sigh of relief. The administration had received word from the FBI that the faculty member was a communist sympathizer. While Waugh recognized the right of someone to be a communist and had no use for "thought control," he confided to his diary the realization that "tempers are such at the moment that the University would be badly embarrassed if it were to be discovered that there was an active communist on the faculty." When representatives of the AAUP came to discuss with Waugh the possibility that colleges and universities would be investigated by congressional committees, the provost agreed that the investigations would not "be carried out in a spirit which will be conducive to the best of American educational tradition. We do not trust the motives of Senator McCarthy, nor his methods." Events would prove his concern accurate and test the integrity of the institution.[26]

On March 12 of that year Paul R. Zilsel, an assistant professor of physics, called Waugh to say that he had to discuss a matter of great urgency. The next morning, he came to the provost's office, closed the door, and said that he might as well come to the point at once. He had been subpoenaed to appear in Washington the next week at a hearing before the Velde Committee, which was investigating communism in American colleges. The thirty-year-old Austrian-born Zilsel explained that he was not presently a communist but had been for a period of something under two years while in college. He wanted the administration to know in advance before the story broke in the newspapers. He had consulted someone at Yale Law School about approaches to take and was offered four alternatives: he could fully cooperate with the committee and answer all questions completely and accurately; he could refuse to answer questions on the grounds that his answer might incriminate him; he could answer that he is not now a communist but refuse to answer questions as to past membership on the grounds of self-incrimination; or he could answer all questions about his own affairs, both past and present, but refuse to answer any questions that might implicate others.[27]

When Waugh counseled that he follow the first alternative, Zilsel agreed that such a path might be best for him personally, but he said that he had an extremely strong moral revulsion to involving others and he recognized that once he stated he had been a communist, he would be asked to name his associates. He explained that when he was brought up as a small boy in Hitler's Germany, he learned that it was unforgivable to inform on others. He understood that if he took the second or third alternatives, the committee would recognize his rights, but if he followed the fourth he would be cited for and convicted of contempt of Congress. Zilsel inquired what the university's attitude would be in each case.

Waugh replied that he couldn't speak for the board of trustees and would have to confer with President Jorgensen. Both administrators worried that the case would adversely affect the university at a time when important legislation was pending in Hartford. They decided that the president should inform the governor's office and several of the trustees so that they weren't taken by surprise, particularly if they were asked for a statement. Waugh got back to Zilsel and reiterated his encouragement to fully cooperate, adding that President Jorgensen agreed. The provost expressed the hope that if such was the case, the university administration and trustees would protect him in his job. He did not tell Zilsel that, if he were to be held in contempt of Congress, President Jorgensen would recommend dismissal, but he did confide that pleading self-incrimination would lead to strong pressure for his removal.[28]

Saint Patrick's Day 1953 found President Jorgensen called away from routine legislative hearings to a three and a half hour command appearance in the governor's office. Aside from Jorgensen and Governor John Lodge, the meeting included two of the governor's assistants, his legal adviser, the state police commissioner, the individual in charge of the FBI for Connecticut, and a special FBI agent from Washington. The others informed Jorgensen that in addition to Zilsel, three other faculty members, Emanuel Margolis, a government instructor already on a terminal appointment, and two men from the Social Work School, Harold Lewis and Robert Glass, both just recommended for tenure by their dean, were communists. Pacing the floor, his arms swinging, and shouting, the enraged governor called for the immediate dismissal of the accused without a hearing. He expressed frustration that he couldn't fire the professors himself and complained about faculty members who earlier had protested against the imposition of a loyalty oath. Lodge would not distinguish between former communists and active ones but wanted instead to get rid of all "reds." Jorgensen, feeling the pressure, consented to take the matter up with the board of trustees. Lodge demanded an immediate special meeting, but Jorgensen put it off until the next regular meeting on March 23.[29]

Meanwhile, the president and the provost met with Dean Harleigh Trecker, who had recommended tenure for Lewis and Glass. He was flabbergasted about the accusations. The two instructors may have been liberals, but they were not subversives, according to Trecker. The documents provided to the administrators by the FBI through the state police proved to be, according to Waugh, "the worst form of gossip and informer's cheap talk." However, the president claimed that the material presented in the governor's office was specific. As a consequence, Jorgensen and Waugh arranged to meet with Glass and Lewis at the Social Work School. Neither instructor knew the purpose of the meeting and must have been surprised when approached in their offices by the president and the provost. After some preliminary conversation, Jorgensen said to Glass, "I merely want to ask you a question or two. First, are you a communist?" Glass asked why the question was raised. The president replied that he had good reason to ask, but he would not provide the reason, and he then asked another question: "Have you ever been a communist?" Glass reiterated that he wanted to know the purpose of the question and reminded his visitors of the importance of protecting staff members against inquisitorial and star-chamber methods. He added that many university administrators had taken stands on such matters. When Waugh suggested that he could respond "yes," "no," "I prefer not to answer," or "I refuse to answer," Glass stated that he preferred not to answer. The president then noted that he was gathering information for the board of trustees and asked Glass if he refused to answer. Glass said that he did. The two administrators then went to Lewis's office.[30]

There, Lewis replied no to both of the same questions asked of his colleague and requested to know why the president made the inquiry. Jorgensen explained that the issue had been raised in the governor's office and that someone claimed that Lewis and his wife had been active communists before coming to Hartford and continue their activity. The three men discussed the current anticommunist atmosphere and Lewis pointed to the tendency to accuse people of "guilt by association." He told his visitors that he had nothing to hide and would welcome an investigation of his past activity and associates. On the way back to Storrs, Waugh told Jorgensen that Glass's reaction might well be that of an innocent man reacting to what he saw as star-chamber methods. On the other hand, the provost suggested that Lewis's response might have been that of an active communist willing to lie. Both men agreed that they had to report to the trustees exactly what had happened. Waugh later told a committee investigating the situation that he feared that the visit had left the two men in a very troubled state of mind because of its abruptness and their lack of prior knowledge of its purpose or any subsequent explanation.[31]

In the meantime, two days later Zilsel explained to Waugh how he had gone to Washington for the hearing with the Velde Committee, which had then become preoccupied with another witness. The committee never got to his case and so he would have to return in April. It became clear that Zilsel would not completely cooperate with the committee, but he would state that he had been a communist but no longer was, then refusing to testify about other matters. However, long before he would return to Washington, the board of trustees developed its policy on the hiring and retaining of communists: (a) it would not knowingly employ a communist; (b) it would not knowingly retain a communist in its employ; (c) any employee accused of or charged with being a communist would be given the right to be heard in his own defense, and if the board became convinced either on its own investigation or on the basis of findings by any competent agency of the federal or state government that the employee was a communist, he would be dismissed immediately. The board accompanied its policy with a lengthy rationale, typical of the era, which, among other things,

recognized the legal right of a citizen to invoke the Fifth Amendment in refusing to testify but questioned the wisdom in doing so. It contended that academic freedom should not serve as a refuge for conspirators who claim its protection to destroy freedom. When the policy became public, sociology associate
professor Arthur L. Wood, the newly elected vice-president of the local chapter
of the AAUP, pointed out that as far back as 1941 the organization held that faculty should not be dismissed except for reasons pertaining to professional competence or moral turpitude.[32]

The board of trustees decided to follow university regulations regarding the
dismissal of faculty members who had tenure, although only one of the four
accused, Zilsel, fell into that category. Provost Waugh met with a Committee of
Three elected by the senate and informed Professors Charles Sedgewick, James
Barnett, and Phil Taylor that they had to select a Committee of Five to investigate the case. By the end of March, the latter group was constituted, with Professor Marcel Kessel as chair, C. Albert Kind as secretary, and Fred A. Cazel Jr.,
Harold G. Halcrow, and Arthur L. Wood rounding out the committee. Ironically, Harry Marks of the History Department had been approached to serve
but declined to do so because he himself had been a communist. With the administration walking on eggs and feeling strong pressure from the governor,
another former communist on staff would have, in Waugh's words, brought
"President Jorgensen to apoplexy." Marks would end up as a cooperative witness testifying before both the local committee and in Washington.[33]

Pressure from Hartford intensified. On April Fools' Day, Jorgensen received
another summons to the State Capitol to meet the next week with the governor, the state police commissioner, and representatives from the FBI. In no uncertain terms, he was told that if he didn't take action satisfactory to the governor regarding the "communists" on staff, the governor would have legislation
introduced to give him or someone outside the university power over such
cases. Jorgensen greatly resented the interference and feared that the governor
had become so alienated at that point that it would affect support for the university's legislative program. When he met with Lodge on April 9, the governor
insisted that the four accused be fired because they were "communists." The fact
that the FBI made the accusation was sufficient to convince the chief executive,
who evidently cared little for due process. He suggested to Jorgensen that the
university get state police clearance on every new staff member. The president
replied that the day such a regulation became effective would be the day of his
resignation.[34]

The Committee of Five began its deliberations on March 30, 1953, and met
twenty-eight times after that. It interviewed all four of the accused, the heads of
their respective schools or departments, and, where appropriate, their colleagues;
it also received letters. Two committee members, Halcrow and Kind, attended
Zilsel's hearing before the House Un-American Activities Committee (HUAC)

in Washington. Upon their return, they reported that Zilsel's testimony agreed fully with what he had told the investigators in Storrs. While a student at the University of Wisconsin in 1946, he joined the Communist Party and was expelled from it in 1948 for extreme disagreement with party policy. He had not been a member since that year and had no interest in rejoining. However, when asked by the HUAC counsel, Robert L. Kunzig, "Mr. Zilsel, have you at any time been a member of the Communist Party?" the physicist replied, "I am not now a member of the Communist Party. The second part of your question I will have to decline to answer on the grounds of the First and Fifth Amendments, and because to answer it would tend to degrade me. I also would like to have it appear in the record that I am pleading the privilege of the Fifth Amendment because I do not want to be put into a position where I have to inform on people whom I consider to be perfectly innocent." While he directly told the University's Committee of Five about his party membership at Wisconsin, his years of membership were derived by HUAC after questions eliminating other years to which he directly said he was not a member. For the 1946–48 period, Zilsel invoked the Fifth Amendment, as he did when he was asked about specific individuals. Kunzig confronted him with an April 20, 1953, *Hartford Courant* article headed "Teacher Admits Being Former Red," which described Zilsel's visit to Provost Waugh (misspelled as *Wahl* in the hearing record) and his voluntary admission of past communist membership. When asked if he was the individual mentioned in the article, Zilsel again declined to answer. He went on to discuss how his youth in Austria before and after Hitler's takeover of that nation influenced his ideological views.[35]

Professors Halcrow and Kind reported back to their committee and to the president that they believed that Zilsel testified freely and cooperatively on all questions except those that legally might have involved self-incrimination. Moreover, according to the two observers, Zilsel's attitude and behavior had reflected well on the university. This, however, did not prevent the HUAC chair, Harold H. Velde, from suggesting that the physics professor was uncooperative because he would not inform on others, and that he might become more cooperative if the university prevented him from teaching. The governor agreed and threatened to take action if Jorgensen and Waugh did not "have the courage to do so." Lodge and his advisers emphatically counseled immediate suspension. Jorgensen bent to the pressure. Waugh phoned Zilsel to inform him of the suspension and reached him just as Zilsel returned home with his wife and newborn baby daughter.[36]

The provost's head throbbed from the inner turmoil created by the Zilsel case. He felt the governor to be hysterical and unreasonable in his position, and he desired to avoid precipitate and unwise action, but he became convinced that "the suspension was necessary as the lesser of alternative evils." He confessed, "Had I been able to handle the thing without any consideration of outside forces

I would not have taken the step." When Zilsel came to his office the day after the suspension had been announced, Waugh explained the terms of the suspension: he had to stay away from classes; he could use his south campus office but should stay out of contact with students; he could get his mail at the main Physics Department office; he would continue to be paid; he would have full rights of hearing by the Committee of Five. Waugh tried to assure him that the suspension was not a pre-judgment of the case.[37]

The decision of the Committee of Five appeared to support that view and demonstrated the value of peer review, although the final judgment remained with the trustees. The committee concluded that there was no evidence that Zilsel was a Communist Party member at the time or had been since 1948. As a consequence, no reason existed under the board of trustees' policy for him not to be retained on the faculty. No evidence demonstrated that his political beliefs influenced his teaching of physics. His colleagues and students viewed him as an individual of high integrity—and someone who was loyal to his adopted country. He was respected as an "exceptionally effective teacher and as an able and productive scholar." While the five believed that he should have fully answered questions at the HUAC hearing, they recognized that from his point of view "invoking the Fifth Amendment was a moral as well as a legal necessity." It should not be cause for dismissal. (Aware of the highly sensitive nature of invoking the Fifth, the committee appended a special statement on the issue to its report, which, among other things, reflected the then-recent AAUP resolution on the matter.) The committee ultimately recommended the lifting of Zilsel's suspension and his retention as a member of the university's faculty.[38]

Students, in the meantime, rallied to his support by endorsing the AAUP statement concerning academic freedom and Congressional loyalty investigations that had passed at its thirty-ninth annual meeting. Student senator Vincent Coates introduced the motion, which passed unanimously after considerable debate, placing the Associated Student Government behind the statement, which emphasized integrity and professional competence in instruction and research when judging faculty. It went further, too, attacking "the application of political tests, standards of conformity, and inquisitorial procedures" in ways that were "appropriate to an authoritarian society, not to a society based upon confidence in the ability of men to choose the paths of truth, reason, and justice."[39]

As to the three other accused, whose cases were less public than Zilsel's, the Committee of Five also recommended that the two social work professors, Glass and Lewis, be retained. Although Lewis did not fully cooperate with the committee, he did assert that he was not a party member and the five could find nothing to substantiate otherwise. The same held for Glass, whom the committee believed may have been charged because he was a socially minded teacher concerned with the underprivileged. Both social work professors received support from colleagues as well, but the case of Emanuel Margolis, an instructor in government and international relations who was already on terminal appointment, revealed the divisive and corrosive effect on faculties of the loyalty investigations. Colleagues testified against him, beginning with Harry J. Marks of the History Department, who recounted a visit to Margolis's home when leftwing New York politician Clifford McAvoy was also a guest. The history professor objected to his host and McAvoy's discussion of U.S. foreign policy as imperialist and their refusal to recognize aggressive action on the part of the USSR. As a consequence of this testimony, the committee decided to meet with three members of Margolis's department who also specialized in international relations, Norman Kogan, Louis Gerson, and Curt Beck. In varying degrees, each called into question Margolis's ability to teach in an unbiased and objective manner. This made the committee more suspicious of the instructor and his objectivity as an academic. Noting he was on terminal appointment, the committee advised against a further appointment, although if he had tenure, they would have recommended retention, because "suspicions and doubts are insufficient grounds for dismissal of a teacher with tenure." They would advise, however, that he be closely monitored.[40]

In the section in its report on "general conclusions," the five recognized the fragility of the charges made during the McCarthy era. The accusations were anonymous and the teacher had no personal accuser to cross-examine. The committee stressed how it tried to adhere to the traditional principle of American justice: that the accused is innocent until proved guilty. While it did try, Paul Zilsel was not reassured. In late June, he told Waugh and Jorgensen that he had one or two job offers elsewhere. He preferred to stay in Storrs, but if he was to be fired for his alleged communist activity, he would resign. In October, his department head visited Waugh to inform him that Zilsel was considering the advisability of accepting offers of either a temporary job in Belgium or a permanent one in Israel. Zilsel felt that any graduate student he accepted at UConn or anywhere else in the United States would be discriminated against because of association with him. Zilsel added that education in Europe was far superior— that mediocre American colleges and universities ran too many sideshows, such as football. In November, the board of trustees accepted Zilzel's resignation as of March 16, 1954. His replacement in Storrs was hired at almost $1,000 more than his salary when Zilsel moved to Haifa, Israel. When he quickly decided he wanted to return to UConn, he was not offered a second chance, even though the board of trustees originally accepted the Committee of Five's recommendation by a close 6–5 vote and reinstated him. It was one thing to protect tenure during the McCarthy era; it was another to welcome back predictable trouble. The two social work professors received terminal appointments by unanimous vote of the board, not the tenure for which they had been recommended; the trustees rationalized their action not on the communist issue (although the FBI to the very end made accusations that the two were active communists) but on the basis of Glass and Lewis's refusal to answer questions when the they appeared before the board of trustees. Emanuel Margolis already had a terminal appointment. Despite the attempts to protect academic freedom, Connecticut's "communist" four, all victims of McCarthyism, did not remain at the university.[41]

The Yankee Conference, Basketball Madness, and No "Big-Time" Athletics

Before the onset of McCarthyism, in his 1946 beginning-of-the-academic-year address to students and faculty, President Jorgensen encouraged students to do their part in the world and to be leaders. He counseled that they should not sell America short, nor should they "sell the football team short. . . . On the field at Harvard Saturday, win, lose, or draw, [the UConn players] will be the best team." The Huskies lost that game 7–0 and did so again by the same score two years later when playing Harvard's traditional and emerging state rival, Yale, for the first time in 1948. For many students and alumni, playing the prestigious private schools had special significance. It validated one dimension of UConn's coming of age as an emerging university rather than an agricultural college. The Yale game took on such importance that it prompted a "Beat Yale Weekend." Festivities began with a huge snake dance and torchlight procession through the entire Storrs campus. The student rally, which freshmen were required to attend, was followed by a faculty gathering in Hawley Armory with the "Prexy" (President Jorgensen) presiding.[42]

Athletic conferences in immediate postwar America, as today, revealed much about an institution. Connecticut Agricultural College, and later Connecticut State College, played in the New England Conference on Intercollegiate Athletics, which had been organized in the 1920s, as did their successor, the University of Connecticut, until 1946. That league originally included the Universities of Massachusetts, Rhode Island, New Hampshire, and Maine; in 1936, Northeastern also joined. After World War II, the New England Conference of State Universities and Colleges, better known as the Yankee Conference, formed in 1946, with Vermont replacing Northeastern in an all-land-grant league. While it brought traditional rivals together, students initially feared that the Yankee Conference too severely limited competition. Games with universities such as Harvard, Yale, and Brown alleviated that concern, and the conference developed a popular following.[43]

Members of the new conference had to abide by a strict code of regulations on matters such as training tables, scholastic requirements, and transfer students. Albert Waugh, then dean of the College of Arts and Sciences, appreciated the need for such a code and was moreover unimpressed by the contests against the Ivies. He complained to his diary that Connecticut overstressed athletics, that athletes had been admitted irregularly, and that the president had personally readmitted athletes who had not met faculty requirements and had been dismissed for scholastic deficiency. He added that there was also great pressure to permit players who were not degree candidates to represent Connecticut in sports. "The 'athletic crowd' rides high, wide, and handsome on all athletic matters, paying no attention whatever to protests from others, secure in the protection of the President," Waugh continued. He decried a creeping emphasis on sports, such as playing basketball at the famous Madison Square Garden, and, reflecting on UConn's 1946 loss in Cambridge, he asserted, "And they [the 'athletic crowd'] have been acting as they now think that we are entirely in the Harvard class because Harvard has taken us on as an unimportant opening game. They do not realize at all that the outcome of the game is almost a matter of indifference at Harvard, and that they play us as we would play Morse Business College in Hartford."[44]

While these sentiments might have represented the view of some academics, the students and alumni marched to a different drummer. In October 1949 one alumnus wrote to Jorgensen from Sandusky, Ohio, that while he agreed with the goal of high scholastic standards, equally high standards were required in sports. Richard Robertson, Class of '43, argued, "In other words, if we are going to have football let's do a good job of it." He identified the problem as poor coaching and supported the growing student movement to rectify the situation. Jorgensen, in turn, explained the restraints on the development of football at UConn, expressed the hope that the problems would be solved, and told the alumnus in terms that would delight the dubious Waugh, "Big-time football is out of the question."[45]

Under pressure from a variety of groups, the president established a special committee to study and evaluate the athletic situation at the university. A communication from the Druids, then still an elite student secret society, initiated the study. The group pointed to friction between football coach J. O. Christian and his players, as well as tension between the coach and his assistants, but Jorgensen thought it inappropriate to focus solely on the coach. He regretted that the situation had erupted during the football season and, probably as a fig leaf, claimed that he planned to initiate such an evaluation after the season had ended. In any event, he established, with the trustees' support, a committee composed of trustees, faculty, alumni, and students. He charged them with looking into scheduling, facilities, the coaching staff, supplies for the teams, financing, alumni support, and public relations. The trustees bridled under what they thought to be the bad publicity generated by the complaints, but they had ultimate responsibility for all action to be taken.[46]

The committee met six times and devoted approximately forty hours to its task. It conducted interviews at UConn as well as with coaches, officials, and sportswriters throughout the state; examined scholarship data; pored over budget and expenditures; and reviewed a student senate survey of the football team.

After such deliberation, it made a series of recommendations: improved athletic facilities (with the consultation of the athletic staff); a common training table for varsity football and basketball players, with a free evening meal also supplied; a review of the administration of scholarships with a policy established that would make certain that all funds were channeled through a University Scholarship Committee; the scheduling of "natural opponents in the New England area" as a general practice, and the desirability of games with Harvard, Yale, and similar schools; the maintenance of membership in the Yankee Conference, as long as UConn could abide by its rules and regulations; the expansion of the Athletic Advisory Committee to include a senior student representative and one alumnus; and the addition of more assistant coaches, particularly in football.[47]

To the cynical, these recommendations were simply window dressing for the final two points made by the committee. While recognizing that J. O. Christian promoted excellent public relations within and outside of the university and that he was handicapped by a lack of assistant coaches and a training table, the committee realistically pointed out that the study they had just performed by its very nature diminished the coach's effectiveness. Moreover, the group found the coach to have been lax in discipline, to have lost the respect of his players, and to have shown favoritism in his use of players. The committee, with three members dissenting on the basis that reassignment of personnel was a function of the administration and the board of trustees, recommended that a new head football coach be appointed. With the same dissent, it also recommended amid a litany of his deficiencies that a new director of intercollegiate athletics be appointed. The ax had fallen—or so it seemed.[48]

The trustees implemented many of the committee's recommendations. In January 1950 Jorgensen, who privately disagreed with the group's findings on personnel, wanted to protect both George Van Bibber, the director of physical education and intercollegiate athletics, and Christian. He announced that the board of trustees had approved a realignment of the athletic situation at UConn. Under the new plan, Van Bibber became director of the new School of Physical Education, which had been established six months earlier, and J. O. Christian became director of intercollegiate athletics. Old wine filled new bottles. However, the university did hire a new football coach. Arthur Valpey of Harvard accepted the position and stayed for one year. Robert Ingalls, whose team would play in the new 15,000-seat Memorial Stadium, which opened in 1953 with a 26–6 win over St. Lawrence University, replaced him after that and remained as coach until 1963. A huge crowd attended the first game, not simply because it inaugurated the stadium but because numerous free tickets were distributed to make an impression. In basketball, Hugh Greer, a 1926 graduate of Connecticut Agricultural College, served as head coach during the postwar Jorgensen era. Taking over in midseason of 1946–47, he led the team to a 12–0 perfect record and a 16–2 season, the most victories in a single season to that time—and the reason for his immediate popularity. The team continued by winning its first four games the next season, until NYU defeated UConn at Madison Square Garden in December 1947.[49]

Hawley Armory was a far cry from the Garden, but it had been the Huskies' basketball home for thirty-four years until a final win against Wesleyan closed it. The team's new home, the "Cage," resulted from the acquisition of two airplane hangars replete with steel supports and tin sheets. A decidedly basic structure, it had an estimated seating capacity of 3,400, which often was exceeded, to the joy of basketball fans who had been excluded from the smaller armory. The "Cage" clearly appeared to be temporary—and a place that could arouse tempers. An important game there in January 1953, when the Huskies, on an eight-game win streak, went up against powerhouse Holy Cross, almost was cancelled because of a near riot. General admission tickets had been oversold and almost one hundred people broke into the arena, pushing the numbers way over the capacity allowed by the fire marshal. Many angry fans with reserved tickets were kept outside and missed a close and exciting contest that was won by the Crusaders, 71–67. The team played its final game there by beating Columbia in March 1954 during a 23–3 season in which junior center Art Quimby led the nation in rebounding. On December 1, 1954, the Huskies beat archrival Rhode Island, 116–77, in a new arena, the 4,500 seat Field House, which remained home court until the opening of Gampel Pavilion thirty-six years later. During the 1950s, the basketball team from Storrs reigned as Yankee Conference champion and, as early as 1951, earned its first invitation to the NCAA tournament and was classified as a "major college" basketball program. Despite that, when one hundred students signed a petition requesting that examinations be cancelled during the tourney and phone calls inundated the administration asking for the cancellation of classes, Provost Waugh (in the president's absence) denied the requests. Hence, while the athletic-friendly president and the trustees expressed their intention not to embark on a program of "big-time" athletics and the less enthusiastic provost, who nevertheless was an avid basketball fan, did all he could to assert academic primacy, UConn clearly had moved toward the goal of developing "physical education and athletic facilities [and programs] commensurate with the growth and development of the University." The university in Storrs, which in 1952 proudly selected National Flag Blue (cable no. 70077 on the Standard Color Card of America, ninth edition) and white as official school colors, began its half-century march toward national athletic prominence during the final decade of the Jorgensen era.[50]

Finding a Place for Doctors, Dentists, and Lawyers

While athletics preoccupied many people on campus, other issues emerged in the postwar era that were highly significant for the development of the university, not the least of which was the establishment of medical and dental schools. In 1944 Governor Baldwin, speaking to the Connecticut State Medical Society, proposed a state-supported school and then established a commission to study the idea, the first of eight such commissions during the period between 1944 and 1959. At the end of 1945, Baldwin, accompanied by Creighton Barker, an officer of the Medical Society and a university trustee, visited Storrs to discuss the establishment of a medical school there. Jorgensen insisted that it would be preferable for others rather than university administrators to show the need for one, that such a school would have to be first class, and that the university didn't desire one if it interfered with the rest of the institution's program. This approach on the president's part would continue until agreement was reached to establish a medical and dental facility to be operated by UConn. While publicly appearing to be reluctant, Jorgensen vigorously promoted the project behind the scenes.[51]

In 1950, the board of trustees took a go-slow attitude, urging a delay in the building of the medical and dental facility until the university's ongoing physical expansion at Storrs neared its completion and the needs of the existing departments had been adequately met. However, Republican Governor John Lodge made a strong case to the contrary. Employing arguments that would be made throughout the decade, Lodge wrote to James W. Hook, the board's chair, that only approximately seventy-five Connecticut students were trained in medicine each year, although the state acquired about 150 new physicians annually. In other words, Connecticut took two from the national pool of doctors for every one it provided. Since more than half of the medical schools in the United States were state-owned or state-operated and favored their own residents for admission, applicants from the Nutmeg State were at a distinct disadvantage; they had approximately thirty-five schools accessible to them, and competition for admission was cutthroat. Yale, the only medical school in Connecticut, admitted a national class; of the 150 new physicians starting practice each year in the state, Yale supplied an average of twelve. Lodge, who had oversimplified and exaggerated the communist issue, here recognized the complexity of the question regarding the establishment of a medical school and appointed a commission to consider the matter.[52]

The provost, two years later, still worried that the expense of a medical school would be tremendous. Waugh pointed out that the cost per semester for a liberal arts major ran somewhere around $50, while a science major cost approximately $200 because of the need of labs and equipment. He recognized that the cost to educate a medical student would far exceed those figures and, while welcoming the opportunity, feared that it would be achieved at the expense of other academic programs. However, Governor Lodge's commission recommended the establishment of university medical and dental schools. By September, at his opening convocation for the academic year 1952–53, Jorgensen went public. He predicted that the university ultimately would have medical, dental, and veterinary schools but emphasized that success depended upon the governor and the General Assembly. He encouraged students to have their parents contact legislators but cautioned them not to try pressure tactics of their own.[53]

The momentum continued when another commission appointed by Lodge in 1953 rejected a regional New England medical complex and recommended that Connecticut build its own. Two years later, a special session of the General Assembly authorized the board of trustees and the State Board of Education to investigate sites in or near Hartford and to estimate costs. Delicate political maneuvering was involved. One influential state senator threatened that the university would not get medical or dental schools unless it stopped "fighting the Battle of Education" and permitted Connecticut's four teachers' colleges to offer graduate work for training secondary school teachers. E. O. Smith, the representative from Mansfield (Storrs), who sat on the legislature's Education Committee and worked closely with Waugh, told of terrible confusion at the end of the 1955 legislative session that prevented appropriations for the medical and dental school bill that year. Apparently, along with the normal politicking, the chair of the Committee on Finance was intoxicated and couldn't find the bills, which were actually in his pocket. Despite such antics, progress continued. When the provost attended a hearing in March 1957 on Senate Bill 9, to appropriate $500,000 to the university for acquisition of a site and preparation of plans for the school, no one appeared in opposition. The key legislative leaders all spoke in favor of it, as did members of the public. Representatives of labor, the state medical, dental, and veterinary societies, and veterans' organizations, as well as school superintendents and principals, strongly supported the effort. President Jorgensen did not appear, and the bill, according to the strategy of a few years earlier, was not submitted by the trustees of the university. Waugh was amused to hear various politicians taking personal credit for the bill, including one who had told the UConn administrators that the medical and dental school was too expensive and not needed, and that he would work to kill the legislation. The bandwagon had taken off and few politicians wished to be left in the dust.[54]

The provost, who was sometimes privately quite critical of the president, had nothing but praise for Jorgensen in this instance. He attributed the progress to Jorgensen's "long, slow, patient work . . . [to his] furnishing data to successive commissions, working with influential people, and in general getting people to understand what the need is. He is now glad to have others think of it as 'their project,'" but the increasing success reflected the president's "foresight . . . planning . . . ingenuity . . . persistence and energy." Waugh saw Jorgensen working in the same manner on the building of a high school (later named after E. O. Smith) adjacent to the university that would become associated with UConn, although it was not an official university project. Again, Jorgensen worked quietly behind the scenes to get it built. Waugh served as his eyes and ears, reporting back on legislative hearings and corresponding with the legislature on behalf of the university. In 1955 he even drafted a suggested substitute for the bills authorizing bonds for a medical and dental school building. In the meantime, endorsements of a UConn medical and dental school flowed in from the Connecticut State Medical Society, the Disabled American Veterans, the Sons of Italy, and other state organizations.[55]

Through Public Act No. 48, the legislature authorized the state to enter into a regional compact, similar to that of the southern and western states, for the establishment of a New England Board of Higher Education with its aim the furthering higher education in the fields of medicine, dentistry, public health, and so on. A special session of the legislature in June 1955 passed House Joint Resolution No. 9, which empowered the UConn board of trustees and the State Board of Education to investigate what sites in or near Hartford were suitable for a medical and dental college; to secure preliminary estimates for the building of such a college; to appraise the clinical and other facilities that would be available to it; and to take any other preliminary steps deemed advisable toward the later establishment of a medical and dental college in the Hartford area. The resolution also authorized the boards to receive any federal or other grants that might be offered to aid in planning or establishing such a college. The last point was significant, because the federal government was initiating programs to encourage the building of medical schools. The committee representing the two boards consulted a document prepared by the American Medical Association entitled "Essentials of an Acceptable Medical School" and used it as a template for what was needed. Recognizing the board of trustee's desire that a veterinary school, if one were established, be built on the main campus in Storrs, the committee recommended three possible sites for the medical and dental school in the city of Hartford: (1) two parcels of land owned by the city, immediately adjacent to McCook Hospital (the city hospital), bordering Coventry Street and Tower Avenue; (2) a section of Keney Park bordering Holcomb Street, immediately opposite McCook Hospital; and (3) two city blocks near Hartford Hospital. The first two properties would provide the opportunity for medical students to utilize the facilities at McCook, the Jones Home for the Aged, the Hartford Rehabilitation Center, the City Health Department, Blue Hills Hospital, Mount Sinai Hospital, and the Hebrew Home for the Aged. The third option offered the nearby facilities of Hartford Hospital and the Institute of Living. Administrators at all four general hospitals in the area, Hartford, Saint Francis, Mount Sinai, and McCook, showed willingness to cooperate in obtaining a medical and dental school.[56]

The general assembly charged the two boards with reporting back by the 1957 legislative session. Just before Christmas 1956, Jorgensen wrote to a Republican leader who had phoned him about the medical and dental school project prior to the writing of the state's Republican Party platform, which ultimately included a favorable plank. The president implored the Republicans not to turn their backs on the matter. He argued, "There is an opportunity here for the Republican party to take a positive, constructive position in the interest of the people of the state in meeting the needs of the present population but also for a rapidly growing population in our state." Three weeks later, the UConn trustees and the State Board of Education formally reported to the General Assembly and recommended the establishment of the medical and dental school; however, they found that the need for the veterinary facility less urgent. Jorgensen again asked for Republican assistance, pointing out that an appropriation of $500,000 would get things under way by allowing for the hiring of an architect to make the necessary plans and specifications for construction and equipment. Such seed money would put the state in a strong position to request federal funds under pending legislation that might equal half or two-thirds of the total cost but probably not exceed $5,000,000. However, the 1957 session of the General Assembly failed to vote any appropriation, and the board of trustees instructed Jorgensen to secure funds from any and all other sources.[57]

During the next several years, after some hesitancy because of a lack of support from Governor Abraham Ribicoff, President Jorgensen pursued funding from numerous foundations. Also, thinking about the medical and dental school took an innovative, but ultimately aborted, turn. The university proposed a two-year medical program that would integrate liberal arts teaching with medical education. The initiators argued that it would reduce duplication, improve the timing of coursework, and avoid the narrowness of the medical and dental education. Jorgensen argued that it would reduce costs, and, given the urgent need, it would turn out doctors and dentists more quickly. In time, the school could become a four-year institution. The student pool would come from those of "high intellectual power and medically-oriented motivation." The president also suggested a "3–2 pattern" of education, which would involve three years of undergraduate work being followed by a two-year professional training program. He explained that the two- year school would ease the physician shortage economically and expeditiously. The annual attrition rate in existing U.S. medical schools was about 10 percent during the first two years. The vacancies in the last two years of existing medical schools could be filled by transfers from the two-year schools. In 1959 alone, room existed for about eight hundred more medical school junior transfers. Jorgensen stressed that proportionately fewer students from New England study medicine than in other parts of the nation because they are unable to gain entrance into state-supported schools. He predicted that the 1960 doctor-patient ratio of 132 to 100,000 would dip to 123 to 100,000 by 1970 if the number of medical school graduates was not increased. Just to maintain the 1960 physician-population ratio, medical schools by 1975 would have to graduate 11,000 physicians, or 3,600 more than they were presently producing.[58]

The argument resonated with at least one source. The W. K. Kellogg Foundation of Battle Creek, Michigan, awarded the university a three-year grant of

$1,037,500 in the belief that the founding of schools of basic medical sciences was a "practical and economic method" of increasing the number of much-needed physicians. However, by the spring of 1961 Jorgensen reversed his position and informed the newly established bipartisan Citizens Committee for a Connecticut Medical-Dental School that he favored a four-year program. He added that while the Kellogg Foundation particularly desired to promote the basic sciences, the grant was not restricted to a two-year school and could be used for the planning of a four-year program. He explained that while getting a four-year school in operation, the institution might begin with the first year, then the first two, then three and four. However, he saw no reason why it should not start as a four-year school, and all the planning should be based on that assumption.[59]

The change of mind paralleled a change of governor in Connecticut to one who favored the establishment and funding of a medical and dental school in the state. With the presidency of John F. Kennedy, Governor Abraham Ribicoff, whose relationship with Jorgensen was strained, became secretary of health, education, and welfare. His lieutenant governor, John Dempsey, succeeded him on January 24, 1961, and, in his first message to the General Assembly several weeks later, committed himself to strong support for the medical and dental school. By June, the new governor made good on his word and signed legislation, the last bill to be approved on the final night of the session, authorizing $2 million to plan and develop a medical and dental school. Helen Loy, secretary of the citizen's committee, remembered sitting with Dempsey in his office after he signed the bill. He said it was a historic occasion for the State of Connecticut. Then he looked at Loy and the founder and chair of the committee, Carolyn Keller, and said, "Now what the hell do I do?"[60]

President Jorgensen provided a sense of what was necessary. He earlier had testified before the legislature's Education Committee and recommended that the new school be independent from any private participating hospital with regard to its location, financing, and management. Once the appropriation passed, the location of the new institution became paramount, and companion legislation created a Site Selection Committee on which Jorgensen would serve. A tug-of-war developed in Hartford. The Saint Francis and Hartford Hospitals battled; others urged placement in the north end of the city, near McCook Hospital. However, that raised conservationist concerns, because parkland would be taken and Governor Dempsey was unwilling to condemn the wooded area. Storrs received mention but was thought to be too remote. Ultimately, the Site Selection Committee chose approximately one hundred acres of property (with an option on an additional 110 acres) in Farmington owned by prominent Hartford businessman Martin O'Meara. Proponents of that choice argued that the medical and dental school was to serve the entire state, not simply the city of Hartford, and that Farmington offered access to Waterbury and Danbury as well as the capital city. Neighbors of the site feared the impact on their pastoral environment. Rumors arose of a political deal, or that O'Meara would be paid an above-market price, which was not the case. His defenders claimed that he would have made much more by selling to a private developer who wished to build houses. After several meetings, residents of Farmington accepted the arguments in favor of the medical and dental facility being erected in their town. For Jorgensen, who first had worked behind the scenes and then quite publicly, a long-time goal had been achieved. His efforts on this matter during his final year as president, however, did not end with the site selection. A few short months later, he sent a telegram to Connecticut's congressional delegation asking for support to ensure the passage of a bill providing federal funds for the construction of facilities and the support of teaching and research in the fields of medicine and dentistry. He pointed out that such legislation was "peculiarly important to Connecticut in view of the decision by [the] last General Assembly to establish [the] medical-dental school as part of the university." The University of Connecticut Health Center was now underway.[61]

As the only academic health center in the nation where medical and dental schools were founded concurrently, the new institution permitted planners to take advantage of their simultaneous evolution. This encouraged medical and dental students to share essentially a common curriculum in the basic medical sciences during their first two years of study, which provided the dental students with an especially strong foundation there. The close ties between dentistry and medicine reflected the beliefs of the dental school's first dean, Lewis Fox, but the imprint of the Jorgensen administration on this development was evident as well.[62]

While the medical and dental school was becoming a reality, President Jorgensen had the uncomfortable task of reporting to the trustees that the university was experiencing an accreditation problem at the Law School. In 1943, a legislative act provided for the university's operation of the Hartford College of Law and the Hartford College of Insurance for a five-year trial period. Then, during a brief ceremony at the Hartford Club on October 27, 1948, attorney Roger Wolcott Davis, president of the board of trustees of the former Hartford College of Law, declared that the University of Connecticut had been "faithful to its trust" and gave Jorgensen the deed to the school property at 39 Woodland Street. The college had acquired the site from Melancthon W. Jacobus, headmaster of the Kingswood School, for both the law and the insurance schools in 1940. Now it became the property of the university, a property that soon would prove to be an albatross.[63]

Laurence J. Ackerman, the talented dean of the School of Business Administration, served as the acting dean of the Law School between 1943 and 1946, until Bert E. Hopkins, who would hold the position for twenty years, was appointed. The administration eventually thought Hopkins meek, quiet, and passive. By 1954, the board of trustees charged the Law School with the task of converting from a local to a regional school. This was a sensitive issue, as it touched upon increasing enrollments to the Law School, the quality of the students to be admitted, and the balance between day and evening sessions. Moreover, it arose at a time when the weaknesses of the school could no longer be hidden. In April of the following year, the Provost told Hopkins about a conversation relayed to him by a dean who had recently served with a representative of the American Bar Association (ABA). The ABA evaluator noted that the UConn law library had about nineteen thousand volumes, which by the next fall would fall below the minimum needed for accreditation. Teaching loads were too high, and the number of full-time staff, five, fell below the minimum of seven needed for accreditation; only 46 percent of UConn's instruction rested in the hands of full-time faculty, while the ABA recommended that 66 percent should be in full-time. A report issued by the Law School three years later told of extremely high attrition rates. Between 1947 and 1957 the day division had an average entering class of sixty, only thirty to thirty-five of whom graduated. The law library then held 26,000 volumes but was in the fourth quintile of 126 libraries in holdings while in the second quintile with respect to enrolled students. At a time when the UConn Law School's enrollment was 277, the Montana State University law library, with eighty-three students, catalogued 32,791 volumes; the University of Missouri, with 162 students, held 107,621 volumes. Waugh had told Hopkins that he didn't want Hopkins to "lie awake nights over the matter," but he and Jorgensen were "anxious to have a quality program in our Law School (as we think we do have) and if you have any problems which you think might raise question with regard to accreditation we would certainly want you to keep us constantly alert to them."[64]

The problems did not easily fade away. When an ABA accreditation committee visited in the spring of 1957, discussion ensued about dropping the Law School from the association's approved list. Formal word came at the beginning of November and Hopkins immediately protested. He regretted that he "did not allot enough of my time during the inspection to bring [the] brighter side of the picture more fully to your attention." The dean pointed out that while the school may have suffered from a shortage of resources, the graduates of the school were successful. The school took pride in its students' performance in bar examinations; its graduates placed well in the profession; alumni were respected by other practitioners and the judiciary. He explained that since the visit, improvements had been made in a variety of areas. Evaluators had found the physical plant wanting; later they described it as "the worst at any state related school in the country with the exception of two Negro schools in the South." Hopkins noted that the General Assembly had allocated $200,000 for an addition to the Law School, which would serve in the interim until a new building on a new site was erected. The full-time faculty had been enlarged. Salaries had gone up, though not yet enough to attract and retain top-notch faculty. Finally, even "minor vexations" had been eliminated; for instance, each faculty member now had a telephone.[65]

Two weeks after this response, Hopkins met with the president and the provost. The atmosphere was tense. Jorgensen, in a twenty-minute introduction, expressed keen dissatisfaction with the operation of the Law School, and especially how the ABA visit had been handled. Hopkins, who had been judged meek, got up and paced the floor and then treated the president and provost to an impassioned lecture. He shouted about what a good school he had, what a fine faculty existed there, and what an outstanding job they had done. At one point he walked over and shook his finger under the president's nose and shouted at him, which led Jorgensen to threaten to throw him out of the office. Hopkins told them that he could successfully handle the matter of accreditation if they didn't interfere. He said that he repeatedly had warned them about problems but received no response. He extolled his staff, noted that salaries were grossly inadequate, and explained that he was already losing some faculty members. If this wasn't remedied, Hopkins predicted that even more would leave. Jorgensen responded that he recognized the high quality of the faculty, the good job they did of training students, and Hopkins's own attributes, but he complained again that because all of this wasn't made clear to the visiting accrediting committee, the university had been embarrassed.[66]

The issue of Law School accreditation hung like a dark cloud over the university for the next several months, and relations between the administration and Hopkins festered. By the end of January, however, Jorgensen and Waugh agreed to special salary increases at the Law School. The president didn't like the idea of retreating on salaries because of "outside pressure," but Waugh saw little choice and reminded Jorgensen that professional associations such as the ABA existed to improve and promote their professions. As a consequence, it was not surprising that they would push for higher salaries. The board of trustees then informed the ABA's Council Section on Legal Education and Admission to the Bar of its "sincere and earnest intention of securing for our School of Law, not only the minimum acceptable requirements, but those resources which will enable the school to offer a completely acceptable program, and one which will in the long run enrich the Bench and the Bar of our area." After Waugh and Hopkins appeared before the ABA council in February 1958—a hearing during which Jorgensen's absence was taken as a sign of disrespect and he was sarcastically criticized—the council ordered a reinspection of the Law School, stressing that real change would indeed be necessary. The provost and the dean informed Jorgensen that "the Council appears to feel that action to save the Law School must be both quick and drastic."[67]

By July 1959, when Hopkins issued his annual report for the 1958–59 academic year, he noted that after a year of searching for the best available site, one had finally been chosen for the new Law School building. It would be located on university-owned property known as the "Goodwin Estate" at 1280 Asylum Avenue, which already was occupied by the Hartford branch of UConn. He anticipated that the new building would be ready for occupancy for the fall term of 1961. The ABA evaluators, who reinspected the school in April, reported back that the new physical plant was an imminent reality and other improvements in staff and curriculum had progressed. However, a year later Hopkins warned Jorgensen that delays in building because of complications (an organized neighborhood opposition) with the Asylum Street site could jeopardize accreditation, which seemed to have been previously reassured. Another year passed before the board of trustees, rejecting the city's efforts to have the school located in Hartford proper, purchased property from Phoenix Mutual Life Insurance in West Hartford lying between Asylum Avenue and Lawler Road near St. Joseph's College. However, before any final action was taken, the siting of the Law School became entangled with that of the medical and dental school, when planners suggested a single metropolitan campus for the major professional schools of the university. Hopkins, the Law School Alumni Association, and various other supporters successfully urged acceptance of the West Hartford site, which was separate from what would emerge as the University of Connecticut Health Center in Farmington. As the Jorgensen era ended, the disciplines of law and medicine developed independently, separated physically from both each other and the main campus in Storrs. However, they progressed together as one university. In May 1962 the ABA evaluator could write, "The School of Law has made remarkable progress in the past three years." This was welcome news.[68]

The development of the professional schools would ultimately lend distinction to the university. The provost, however, wanted even more. He remarked in 1958 that if UConn was to become a real first-rate university, the development of the Graduate School would be a key factor. He was convinced that during the next ten years that development would be the most important one for the institution. He wished for enough money to bring in a half dozen world-famous staff members—Pulitzer and Nobel Prize winners. While the next decade would bring great change to the university in Storrs, it still would have a long way to go to achieve Waugh's desire. First, however, the leader of the institution for twenty-seven years would come upon hard times.[69]

The Fall of the House of Jorgensen

The high hopes expressed by Waugh were characteristic of the man. Jorgensen appointed him provost in 1950, and from that time on he worked hard to encourage higher standards at the university. Although he never completed his doctoral dissertation, Waugh recognized and encouraged quality in scholarship, appreciated the company of scholars, and carried on many research projects that resulted in publication. When in 1954 a dean passed on faculty concerns about promotion and the fear of an administrative policy of "no publication, no promotion," the provost responded clearly and quickly. He laid out a policy that promised to promote into the higher ranks only those who would be considered for promotion at the best institutions in the country. He recognized that institutions differed in quality and some full professors elsewhere would not even be considered for an instructorship at Storrs. On the other hand, he realized that UConn had not yet attained the reputation and stature of a leading university in the academic world. "Every institution of higher learning has to decide for itself the level at which it wishes to operate. Certainly the level to which we aspire is very different today from what it was 15 or 20 years ago."[70]

However, a few weeks earlier, Charles Waring, the head of the Chemistry Department, had expressed serious concern about the sincerity of the administration's intention to raise the university's prestige in teaching and research. He particularly pointed to UConn's ability to provide graduate assistantships in comparison with other institutions. Ohio State provided one hundred assistantships for 3,500 students, and the University of Illinois 140 for 4,500 students, while UConn had eighteen for 1,800 students. At the two Midwestern schools, the ratio thus stood at 1:35; at Uconn, it was 1:100. With such disparity of resources in mind, Waring argued that while he favored a strict policy on promotion and tenure, he counseled the administration "to view the cold light of reality." The chemist argued that to be fair to the faculty, if standards were set comparable to the likes of Harvard, Chicago, Minnesota, and California, commensurate resources had to be provided and policies that would facilitate excellence established.[71]

The provost countered that a great deal of progress had been made, and he found it difficult to understand how this could be missed. He challenged Waring and suggested that he could not instill enthusiasm in his department if he himself felt little enthusiasm for the institution. The difference in perspective, however, reflected more than an administrator's defense mechanism. The previous summer Waugh reflected on the jump in applications to the university– 3,191, as compared to 2,663 a year earlier. He remarked, "Despite the amazing and almost unbelievable expansion of physical facilities at Storrs, we are actually more crowded for space than we were when I came here 29 years ago to what was then the Connecticut Agricultural College." He had witnessed the entire change that accompanied the Jorgensen era to that point, and for him the evolution from small college to aspiring state university was dramatic. As the Jorgensen era came to a close, the provost told Graduate Dean Nathan Whetten about a lesson he had learned from the president. Jorgensen contended that every department had to take risks and gambles and suggested that if the institution had not, it would still be Connecticut Agricultural College.[72]

To his supporters, then, Jorgensen was the agent of change who transformed the state university in Storrs. They agreed with *New Englander Magazine*'s 1960 assessment of his then twenty-five-year tenure, which acclaimed, "While the University began in 1881 as the Storrs Agricultural School with 12 students housed in a former home for civil war orphans, it started to move in 1935 when a *Midwest cyclone* hit the area in the person of Albert Nels Jorgensen." During his tenure as president, the institution changed from a college to a university and expanded from 750 to 13,000 students. The value of the physical plant rose from $3 million to $70 million. The institution came to comprise sixteen schools and colleges, four two-year branches, and almost a score of academic and service divisions and institutes, and it saw the beginning of a medical and dental school. Progress had been made. However, the final two years of Jorgensen's administration found the "Midwest cyclone" strongly buffeted by the winds of discontent.[73]

Students protested the general loss of rights, the administration's control of fees, and the loss of autonomy over student activities, as well as what they perceived as censorship. Faculty complained about low salaries, which made the institution less competitive in recruiting and retaining good people. A faculty union organized. The state's major newspaper carried a series of articles critical of the university. The initial one appeared on the first page of the *Hartford Courant*, with the banner headline "Multi-Millions Fail to Slow UConn's Skidding Standards." The second had the headline "Crisis at UConn," with the longer subhead "Faculty Voice Muffled as Rift with Administration Widens." Readers learned of a litany of problems—poor faculty pay, heavy workloads, and delayed promotion were causing the departure of a large number of faculty. A report of the AAUP showed that between 1958 and 1961, fifty-three UConn faculty members left for other jobs. UConn stood twenty-eighth out of thirty-six state universities and land-grant colleges in average annual faculty salaries in 1960 at $7,373. Even within Connecticut, UConn had the lowest rating for average faculty compensation per fulltime student—$411, as opposed to $699 at Danbury State and $994 at Willimantic State. Sixty-seven teachers—15 percent of the staff—held the position of assistant instructor, a poorly paid rank not even found in most universities. The newspaper reported that many in higher education declared the school to be second rate and quickly becoming third rate.[74]

Much of the problem, according to the *Courant*, rested with the lack of communication between the faculty and President Jorgensen, as well as the absence of real contact between the faculty and the board of trustees. The newspaper pointed to a rising faculty rebellion that resulted in the organization of a chapter of the American Federation of Teachers (AFT) of the AFL-CIO. On October 20, 1960, a young mathematics professor, Elliot Wolk, wrote to Jorgensen in his capacity as president of the fledgling labor chapter. He informed him of its organization and its aims and purposes. In an attempt to win over the president, he informed Jorgensen that the union supported his continuing endeavor to improve higher education and that this could be done more effectively through an affiliation with organized labor. Wolk promised that the union would proceed in a "dignified, informed, and intelligent manner" and would follow Jorgensen's lead in making the state recognize "that the future of American higher education rests with publicly supported institutions; that the public gets precisely what it pays for; that the key to the quality of our educational future is the quality of the faculty; that by the virtue of the fact that the University and its faculty owe a responsibility to the state, the state owes a responsibility to the University and the faculty." He then went on to ask the president for a meeting and concluded that the AFT's support of Jorgensen's efforts "will strengthen our mutual attempt to provide a continually improving quality of education for the State of Connecticut and its citizens."[75]

The administration, however, did not view the AFT's activities as "dignified, informed, and intelligent." At a University Senate meeting in April 1961, shortly after the *Courant* series had appeared and after another faculty member suggested that the administration had been vindictive in respect to matters of merit raises and statements in the press, Wolk stated that the administration had never responded to the AFT's issue regarding salaries. Despite the fact that the union went on to help win a $900,000 legislative appropriation for salary increases, the group and its leader were not welcome and instead seen as an irritating gadfly by the administration. Provost Waugh had a distinct dislike for industrial unions. As for college faculties, unionization was "undignified and non-professional," an act for which he had "disgust and a loathing and revulsion." In October 1961 Jorgensen, claiming that the troubles on campus did not influence his decision, stated his intent to retire no later than October 1, 1963. Shortly after his announcement, he advised the board of trustees chair, John J. Budds, that he had spent time with "responsible leaders within the faculty" and influenced their actions in the University Senate. A report of the Faculty Standards Committee on salary increases refuted "many of the irresponsible statements made by Wolk in the past" and was favorable to the university's policy on salary increases. He also told the chairman that the senate voted down a resolution presented by Wolk, which had to do with the relation of the board of trustees to the faculty. "Wolk has been widely and deeply discredited by the faculty," the president exclaimed. The deans also showed concern about the activities and influence of the union, discussing the issue at a meeting of the Dean's Council. They determined that vigorous support of the AAUP (rather than the AFT) would be useful, as would an orientation program for new faculty to reinforce such support.[76]

Jorgensen had informed Budds that the friendly senate salary report was prepared by a committee chaired by William Orr and emphasized that he had long been active in the AAUP and was president the previous year. The professors' association had a preferred status with the administration, as opposed to the upstart union. Almost a decade earlier, Provost Waugh had written to an

AAUP officer that while the administration and the faculty had different responsibilities, they were both part of the university family and fundamental partners in ventures of common interest. The common interests emerged at the time of Jorgensen's resignation. The association announced that the efforts of the chapter to improve communication between faculty and administration and board of trustees had been rewarded. Just about the time of the critical *Courant* articles, Jorgensen announced at a senate meeting the transformation of an ad hoc committee into a standing Trustee-Administration-Faculty Committee, and the creation of a standing Faculty Advisory Committee to the president. In consultation with the advisory committee, Jorgensen appointed three new faculty committees that had been recommended by the senate: a Growth and Development Committee; a Faculty Standards Committee, and a Student Welfare Committee. The *AAUP Newsletter* proudly pointed out, and the administration certainly recognized, that the chairman of each senate committee was a member of the AAUP.[77]

Clearly, the bad publicity and agitation helped bring about shared governance at the University of Connecticut. However, this did not mean the approval of direct faculty contact with the legislature, which the AFT pursued despite administrative disapproval. When Dorothy Goodwin, the economist and chair of the AAUP Legislative Liaison Committee who would later become a distinguished legislator representing Mansfield, asked Provost Waugh about such activity, he responded politely but without encouragement. He suggested that it was in bad taste to do this, that it could be bad tactics, and that it might not be permissible under the statutes and regulations of the board of trustees. Waugh pointed out how important it was for the university to speak with a single voice. Only trustee designees could represent the university, but he noted that the president and the board always welcomed suggestions from any source concerning the university's programs and policy, including the AAUP. If the AAUP accepted the limitation, however, the AFT considered it a gag rule and stirred the cauldron at the same time that students also were claiming they were oppressed.[78]

This was the atmosphere in which President Jorgensen announced his resignation in 1961. The board chair accepted it and commented that Connecticut could never repay him for his service to higher education in the state, the region, and the nation. The retiring president wasn't shy about suggesting some characteristics to look for in a successor. He confided to trustee William Benton that his successor "should not be over and preferably on the sunny side of 40." The new president should be a scholar in his own right, having published significantly. If possible, he should have had administrative experience, preferably in a land-grant state university. Moreover, with a vision for the present and future status of the university, he suggested, despite his own background in educational measurement and testing, that his successor should not be in the fields of agriculture or education; someone in the sciences would be both acceptable to those in agriculture and appropriate to work with the developing medical and dental schools. He added, "I firmly believe that there is no one in the University at this time who should receive serious consideration."[79]

As the year ended, Jorgensen recognized the difficulty faced by the institution. He confided to Benton that he had spent several miserable hours following the last trustees meeting. The situation had become untenable and many mistakes that were not the fault of the university had been made. Unless matters improved among the trustees, the state administration, the legislature, the UConn administration, and the faculty, Jorgensen insisted that it would be difficult to find and hold a new president.[80]

However, the trustees did find a new president, and someone who would remain for a decade. Homer Babbidge, upon his selection as the eighth president of the University of Connecticut, wrote to Jorgensen that he and his wife were thrilled to be invited to Storrs as the new first family. He praised both the physical and less tangible aspects of Jorgensen's "magnificent leadership of the University." He was "enormously honored to have been selected to fill [his] shoes" and looked forward to devoting his energy and "whatever talents" he had to living up to the standard Jorgensen established. Jorgensen had replied and assured his successor that he would never second-guess him and would only pass on advice and counsel if asked. He explained that he and his wife expected to be away from the university community for at least a year.[81]

Once Babbidge took office, however, he made a request of his good friend John W. Gardner, president of the Carnegie Foundation, who had spoken at his inauguration. The new president asked for a grant of $26,000 to help with the funding of a long-range planning committee. It was needed, Babbidge wrote, because, "As you can imagine, an institution that has been operated out of one man's hat for 27 years is something of a rat's nest to his successor. . . . I find the University without any clear sense of its future. . . . I have a fair idea where we ought to go and how we ought to get there, but I'd like mightily to have those thoughts emerge from a group effort." He received the grant. The Jorgensen era had come to an end, but his legacy remained in the physically transformed campus that was home to an emerging university.[82]

4

Homer's Odyssey—The Babbidge Years: 1962–72

$\mathcal{D}$URING THE WINTER of 1962, after Albert Nels Jorgensen had announced his resignation but before the selection of his successor, many on the Storrs campus worried that a vacuum would exist until a new president was in place. The dean of the School of Education, F. Robert Paulsen, urged that Jorgensen continue planning and decision making, expressing faith in the outgoing chief executive to carry on. Little, however, would transpire until the arrival of Homer Daniels Babbidge Jr., who was inaugurated on Homecoming Day, October 20, 1962, and who did much to change the tone and raise the spirit on campus. By the end of his first academic year as president, faculty, students, local officials, and community leaders throughout the state praised the newcomer, and John F. Kennedy had invited him to the White House to meet with other educational leaders for a discussion of civil rights. The freshman university president had quickly made his mark. The Babbidge style continued to develop through his decade in office, but Homer's odyssey would not be an easy one. The cultural, political, and generational fault lines that widened throughout the nation during the tumultuous 1960s touched Storrs, emphatically dividing the first half of Babbidge's tenure from the second.[1]

The Transition to the Honeymoon Years

Shortly after Jorgensen announced his retirement, the board of trustees established a Presidential Selection Advisory Committee headed by Graduate Dean Nathan Whetten and composed of six members of the faculty, three administrators, and three members of the board. Anti-Jorgensen feelings on campus had become so intense that several committee members wanted to prevent candidates who visited campus from meeting with the president of twenty-seven years. Whetten persuaded his colleagues of the awkwardness of such a prohibition, but there was an agreement that no candidate should meet with Jorgensen alone. The committee considered almost three hundred candidates and on March 16, 1962, reported to the board its choice of Babbidge, who had been one of the leading prospects from the outset. After receiving the recommendation, the board, including the governor, adjourned for a social hour and dinner at the Hartford Club with the nominee and his wife. Then the board reconvened for an intense question-and-answer session with Babbidge. When he departed, the satisfied trustees unanimously agreed to offer him the presidency, effective October 1, 1962, at the same salary that it had taken Jorgensen twenty-seven years to achieve, $25,000. On March 22, the board chair, John J. Budds, informed Jorgensen, who was vacationing in Barbados, that Babbidge had accepted their offer. Four days later, Budds publicly announced the appointment to the faculty and staff. Jorgensen and Babbidge then had the pro forma polite exchange mentioned at the conclusion of the previous chapter and afterward met several times in Washington, D.C., where, among other matters, they discussed the perquisites available to the new president. These included a fully equipped and maintained residence, two domestic servants, a car for official use, and an entertainment fund for major receptions and teas that in previous years had been held in the Student Union. More interesting, perhaps, were the perquisites that would no longer be allowed, because "everyone agrees that they are a continuous source of possible personal and family embarrassment." No longer would the president accept agricultural commodities from the various departments of the College of Agriculture, except for flowers to be used for official entertaining; in addition, the provision of newspapers at the president's residence at state expense would also be halted. After the criticism of Jorgensen in his final years, the new president hoped to insulate himself from similar attacks. At best, Jorgensen felt ambivalent about the appointment of Babbidge and his own new status as a "lame duck." Babbidge's desire to be involved immediately in hearings on the university's budget must have intensified his predecessor's concern.[2]

In early May, two reporters from the *Daily Campus* newspaper and the university radio station, WHUS, visited Babbidge in Washington at his American Council on Education office, where he served as vice-president. He lauded UConn's potential to be the leading public institution of higher learning in the Northeast and extolled the importance of research. Babbidge explained that the education of undergraduates was enhanced by the presence of graduate students on a campus, and that high-quality faculty were attracted to a research institution. The president-elect discussed student life and responded to a question about UConn being a weekend "suitcase school" by noting the benefit to a university education of staying on campus seven days a week and enjoying a residential experience. When asked about "liberal living conditions," the quick-witted Babbidge said he believed "in co-education but not in cohabitation." As one might anticipate from someone beginning a new leadership position and desiring a smooth transition, he expressed his enthusiasm for coming to Storrs and his great admiration for his predecessor, President Jorgensen. The reporters concluded their account of the meeting with Babbidge by recognizing his great interest in academics, stating, "He will be instrumental in raising UConn's scholastic standing." They conjectured that his American Council on Education experience with federal grants would help secure more federal aid for UConn. Overall, the president-elect appeared to make a good impression on the reporters, although they, perhaps naively, believed that the most significant point of the interview "was the seeming lack of contact made between the University and Dr. Babbidge since his appointment was announced."[3]

In the meantime, Provost Albert E. Waugh began to make plans for Babbidge's inauguration. At the beginning of May he alerted the professional staff to the date and time of the ceremony: on the morning of Saturday, October 20, following the prior evening's presidential reception for the faculty, the 10:30 A.M. inaugural would precede the homecoming afternoon football game against Maine and an evening Boston Pops concert under the direction of Arthur Fiedler. Waugh promised that the occasion would "be an interesting and colorful one and . . . of great importance in the history of the University." He then informed Jorgensen of the event, which would take place in the Albert N. Jorgensen Auditorium, which had opened in 1955. Waugh explained that the event properly centered around Homer Babbidge, but the inaugural committee also wanted to show continuity with the institution's immediate past. They desired to follow the precedent established in 1929, when George Alan Works was inaugurated. At that time Works and President Emeritus Charles Lewis Beach headed the procession. The committee thought it appropriate for Jorgensen to accompany Babbidge and invited him to do so.[4]

Jorgensen, however, was growing increasingly disenchanted with the board of trustees, and it with him. When he resigned, he announced his retirement effective October 1, 1963, and expressed the hope that his successor would be selected to take office no later than October 1, 1962. He planned to leave the university community by that date but expected to be paid his full salary for another year. The board of trustees, despite the strong reluctance of its chair, John J. Budds, and some other members, granted Jorgensen the leave of absence with pay. Provost Waugh looked askance at what he believed was the outgoing president's "truculence and brazen selfishness." He contended that Jorgensen would have been the first to insist on the impropriety of such an arrangement had it been made for someone else, and Waugh predicted that it would draw criticism from many in Hartford and in Storrs. Waugh had to process an employment authorization for Babbidge and feared that he had no actual vacancy if Jorgensen were to be paid for the year when he didn't work. Governor Dempsey, by law ex-officio head of the UConn board, maintained that the payment was morally wrong and added that he had no notice of the salary plan before the action was taken and no opportunity to participate in the vote. "Had I known about it when it was being discussed, I would have fought against the plan," he complained. At the end of May, the expected criticism exploded onto the pages of the *Hartford Times* and the *Hartford Courant* after reaching a boiling point on campus. Facing the inevitable, Jorgensen drafted a statement to be telegrammed to Budds that he would retire as of October 1, 1962, and showed it to Waugh, who rewrote it to make it stronger and completely unqualified. It stated that, in order to stop further embarrassment for himself and the board of trustees, he was retiring as of October 1, 1962, and would cease all connection with the university at that time. Jorgensen made one change in the revision. He substituted "university" for "board of trustees," because he did not want to spare the board, which he thought had lost faith in him, its embarrassment. Nor did he want to let go. He attempted to appoint himself to the advisory committees for the newly forming medical and dental schools but withdrew after the provost pointed out that only *one* president should be a member. Hence, the outgoing president seemed an unlikely candidate to accompany the incoming president at the inaugural.[5]

The provost, as well as the entire university community, eagerly awaited the new leader. On July 5, 1962, Babbidge, on a brief visit to the university, arrived at Waugh's office at 9:00 A.M. They talked for an hour and then went for a walking tour of the campus. They stopped at the library and looked over plans for an addition to that building; then they walked to the top of Cemetery Hill. They returned, visiting dormitories and the field house before stopping for lunch at Waugh's home. The provost seemed impressed with his new boss. He found Babbidge "highly perceptive, with a keen knowledge of the important questions to ask, with a quick and retentive memory, and with an obvious keen intelligent interest in the job which he is soon to assume." By the end of the summer, the Inaugural Committee completed its plans and a new university tradition was born. Waugh suggested that a university mace be produced for the procession. Several people showed enthusiasm for the idea, particularly two members of the Inaugural Committee, Edward V. Gant and Clark Bailey. Waugh asked Professor Knobler of the Art Department to design it, and Dettenborn Company in Hartford produced it, at a cost of $1,078, replete with shaped oak encrusted with gold leaf, the university seal, laurel leaves, and nutmegs.[6]

Making His Mark

As the time approached for his formal assumption of duties, Babbidge declared that he intended to bring about at least some token changes in the university's capital budget requests, in order to make clear to both the legislature and the faculty that his ideas were not identical with Jorgensen's. The faculty welcomed the distinction between the new and old presidents. On his first day at work, Monday, October 1, 1962, when Babbidge lunched at the Faculty Club, a small group stopped dining, stood, and applauded as he entered, a sharp contrast to what Jorgensen might have expected at that time. During the nineteen days leading up to the inauguration, the new president began to make his mark. Babbidge wanted to meet the student body as rapidly as possible, and on Thursday, October 4, all late-afternoon classes were cancelled and the Student Union closed so that as many students as possible could attend the convocation, at which he delivered his first speech. Introducing the new president, Provost Waugh could not resist telling a joke. He explained how he was reminded of the story of a woman whose husband had died. Just before visiting hours at the undertaking establishment were to begin, she viewed the body and expressed her dismay that her husband wasn't wearing a blue suit, because he had always favored them. She asked the undertaker if a blue suit could be substituted. This was accomplished. After visiting hours, the woman expressed appreciation and said she hoped it hadn't caused too much inconvenience. "No trouble," said the undertaker. "There was a man in the next room with a blue suit, so we simply changed heads." Waugh continued, "We at the University are now changing heads. May I now present our new president, Dr. Babbidge." Babbidge then assured the undergraduates that he was especially eager to understand their views, that their criticism would be heard and respected, and that he regarded them as full partners in making the university great. The thrity-seven-year-old eighth president of the University of Connecticut explained, "I'm not too far removed from my own undergraduate days that I've lost the message. I wouldn't be in the business I'm in if I didn't like students and want to be around them." He concluded by noting that he desired to usher in "a new era of good feeling," an era in which every member of the university family would join together for mutual benefit. The next evening, he and Mrs. Babbidge met students from 9:00 P.M. to 1:00 A.M. at a reception in Jorgensen Auditorium. According to Waugh, a few days later, at Babbidge's first board of trustees meeting on October 10, he dealt with issues of budget and policy and "did an amazing job for a man who has been here but 10 days, showing a fine basic philosophy of education and an almost unbelievable grasp of the University's problems." The inaugural would top off a successful first twenty days.[7]

Saturday morning, October 20, found approximately seven hundred people, including forty-six college and university presidents, several representatives of learned societies, and some five hundred faculty members, comprising the inaugural procession, which began just after 10:00 A.M. The speakers started promptly, and the ceremony ended two and a half minutes earlier than planned. Babbidge's friend, John W. Gardner of the Carnegie Foundation, gave the opening remarks; the new president's former boss, Logan Wilson, head of the American Council on Education, offered words of welcome; Dean Whetten spoke on behalf of the faculty; Kevin Dunne, president of the Associated Student Government, conveyed the greetings of the student body; and Hugh McCann, Class of '33, greeted Babbidge on behalf of the alumni at the ceremony overseen by board of trustees chair John J. Budds. Babbidge, in turn, accepted the mace as a symbol of office and told his audience, "The task of a public university . . . is to wed the new spirit of democracy to the old value of learning. To blend the boldness of the people with the restraint of the scholar, to satisfy the equally valid demands of quantity and quality, to accommodate both the timely and the timeless. . . . We must all appreciate that our task here is not simply to preserve the known good, but to uncover the good that is yet unknown."[8]

The speaker of these words had come a long way since his birth on May 18, 1925, in West Newton, Massachusetts. The son of a merchant sea captain, Babbidge moved to New Haven in 1929 and obtained his early education at the Nathan Hale School. He lived in the Morris Cove section of the city, at 25 Parker Place. When he was four years old, a ball shattered a window near him, showering him with splinters of glass and destroying the vision in his left eye. The injury kept him out of the armed services and also prevented him from driving, but it did not slow down his academic studies. When he was twelve, his family moved from New Haven to Amherst, New York, near Buffalo, where he attended high school. After graduation, he enrolled as a scholarship student at Yale and was a product of that university's wartime acceleration program, receiving his undergraduate degree in political science in 1945. At Yale, he served as president of the Political Union, chairman of the undergraduate radio station, a member of the undergraduate board of deacons of the Church of Christ, and a cheerleader, while also being involved in a number of clubs and honor societies. To earn his board, he waited on tables. During his senior year, Babbidge worked as a research assistant to historian George Pierson, who was writing a history of Yale University. This experience pointed him toward a career in higher education.[9]

Upon graduation, Babbidge accepted a position in the Student Appointment Bureau at Yale and began his graduate studies there on a part-time basis, earning his MA in 1948 and Ph.D. in 1953. His doctoral dissertation was a history of the founding and early years of Swarthmore College. He subsequently taught for several years in Yale's Department of American Studies. His continuing work with the Student Appointment Bureau led to his designation as director of the university's Division of Financial Aid. During those years, Babbidge also served as head resident counselor of freshmen and executive fellow of Pierson College. In 1948 he was a co-founder of the Yale Program of American Studies for Foreign Students. From 1955 to 1961, he served with the U.S. Department of Health, Education, and Welfare, first as special assistant to the U.S. commissioner of education, in 1955–56, then as assistant to the secretary of the department (1957–58), and finally as asssistant U.S. commissioner of education and director of the Division of Higher Education (1959–61). He received the department's Distinguished Service Medal in 1961. Not long before he was called to UConn, Babbidge became vice-president of the American Council on Education, an association of more than one thousand colleges and universities and 145 national organizations in the field of higher education. He married Marcia Adkisson of Seattle in 1956, and when they came to Storrs they were the parents of two daughters, Amy Allison, age two, and Sandra Allalee, age one. (A son, Alexander Adams, was born during Babbidge's first year as president.) In 1959 the U.S. Junior Chamber of Commerce named Babbidge one of the "ten outstanding young men of the nation" in recognition of his work in administering the National Defense Education Act of 1958. His co-authored book, *The Federal Interest in Higher Education,* was well received when it was published in 1962. The man who spoke to his inaugural audience on October 20 therefore came to Storrs with strong credentials. However, he had never before been a college president, and he told this story: "When I took the job I had no idea of what a college president did, and the night before the first day, I asked my wife, 'What do you suppose a college president does?' I came in at 8:30 in the morning and the phone rang. Then I knew."[10]

Whether that tale is apocryphal matters not, because it certainly reflects the situation in which the new president found himself. Issues large and small had to be attended to rapidly. Only ten weeks after he became president, Babbidge testified before a state budget hearing in Hartford. He rolled out a theme that would become his mantra during the first years of his presidency. He told those present very directly that the resources made available to the university during the past decade did not accrue at a rate sufficient to insure sound qualitative work. Enrollment had increased 60 percent, but the instructional staff, which was financed by state general funds, had increased only 36 percent. Later, in his first annual report, Babbidge contended that there was hardly a problem confronting the university that was not traceable back to the size of the faculty. Student motivation and morale suffered because the overburdened faculty members seemed remote, and many classes were too large. The heavy demand of teaching impeded faculty research and public service. Faculty morale also suffered.[11]

Inadequate salaries exacerbated this situation. On the AAUP rankings, full professors at UConn fell into the "C" category, while those at Yale rated "A" and at Wesleyan, Trinity, and Connecticut College rated "B." More significantly, out of ten Connecticut colleges and universities in 1961–62, UConn faculty had the eighth lowest salary per full-time-equivalent students, lower than all of the state colleges and higher only than the University of Bridgeport and New Haven College. The UConn figures also reflected heavy teaching loads. Provost Waugh counseled Babbidge that UConn and Yale were the only two institutions in the state that offered doctoral work, and that if UConn wished to develop a strong graduate program it had to compete for faculty with major private universities and state schools such as Minnesota, Ohio, California, Illinois, Iowa, and Michigan, every one of which outranked UConn in the senior faculty category. He went on to explain how the psychology department tried to recruit a clinical specialist from Ohio State, but his current salary was already $430 above the maximum for full professors at UConn and $1,850 above the highest salary actually paid to any full professor at Storrs. The provost pointed out that while UConn's maximum authorized salary for professor was $17,540, the average actually paid registered at $12,889. Babbidge, who on his fifth day as president had asked the provost about increasing salaries, heard the call and made salaries a key component of his program; by 1966 they had risen to the AAUP "B" level.[12]

Building a Research Library

The library provided as dramatic an example of the deficiency in resources as the number of faculty and their salaries did; it also demonstrated the difference between Babbidge and Jorgensen. From the outset, the new president emphasized the need for a stronger collection of books, not merely the need for a building or building extension to house books and periodicals. He encouraged the shift in UConn's character from a primarily undergraduate institution to a leader in graduate training and research and a center of public service. In early December 1962 Babbidge informed legislators that the library held 400,000 volumes, which, according to the Commission on Library Resources, was substandard compared to similar universities. Between 1952 and 1963 general fund appropriations for the library had increased from $68,500 to $100,000, the latter still a paltry sum in relation to what was spent by UConn's peers. He contended that without a strong library, the university could not attract the faculty essential to a leading institution of higher education. "Major attention must be given to support of the University library. The development of the University as a center of graduate study, research, and effective service to the state cannot precede the availability of a minimal library," he concluded.[13]

Statistics prepared by the U.S. Department of Health, Education, and Welfare, with which Babbidge had worked, spoke to the university's deficiency. The number of library volumes in 1960–61 for a half dozen representative state institutions—Southern Illinois, Kentucky, Florida, Kansas, Rutgers, and Louisiana State—averaged 869,139, with all but Southern Illinois holding more than 900,000 volumes; UConn's library contained 423,214. The six schools added an average of almost 60,000 volumes per year; UConn added less than 20,000. The bookbinding and periodical budget average for the six institutions was three times larger than UConn's, as was their average staff size. While UConn spent less than $30 per student on library expenditures, the other six averaged nearly

$70. In all categories of library spending, the University of Connecticut trailed badly. Babbidge identified these deficiencies and then built persuasive arguments around them.[14]

A related event aided his cause. In early fall 1962 the university librarian, James E. Skipper, resigned. The Advisory Committee on Division of the Library, consisting of Professors Fred Cazel, T. K. Lindsay, I. N. Thut, Kenneth G. Wilson, and A. L. Wood, wrote ten days after Babbidge assumed office that they strongly supported his desire to appoint a person possessing the highest possible qualifications. The committee made suggestions regarding how to attract the best possible candidates. By the end of January 1963 it met with the provost and unanimously ranked John McDonald and another candidate far above the others applying. The position of director was later offered to McDonald, who after negotiations with the provost accepted it. By mid-April, McDonald wrote Babbidge from his position as associate director of libraries at Washington University in St. Louis about how Cornell University had acquired a special library collection for a quarter of a million dollars that had been donated by two benefactors. McDonald remarked, "That's the way it's done in the big league, I guess." He looked forward to bringing UConn into that league of libraries. Philosopically, McDonald was in tune with his new president, who had been hard at work finding resources for the library. A week after officially assuming his post, McDonald thanked Babbidge for making the new biennium budget the most significant gain in operating funds that the Library had ever enjoyed. He especially appreciated the threefold increase in the state appropriation for books. By January 1971, a year prior to Babbidge's resignation, John McDonald could announce that the University of Connecticut library holdings had reached the one million volume mark. At a time when there were about 2,200 four-year colleges and universities in the United States, UConn joined fifty-eight other university libraries with a million or more volumes. In New England, only Harvard, Yale, Brown, Dartmouth, and MIT had larger collections than Connecticut. Indeed, the Babbidge years witnessed a transformation in the status of the UConn library. If it was not yet in the truly big leagues, still the faculty and students no longer had to be embarrassed about the institution's library and frustrated by its glaring inadequacies.[15]

Hardly A Wilderness

Aside from the transformation of the library, Babbidge's arrival also marked a new emphasis on the humanities, social sciences, and fine arts that probably resulted from his own interests and reflected his undergraduate education at Yale and his dissertation chronicling Swarthmore College. To some, his orientation seemed appropriate; to others, like Agricultural College Dean Wilfred B. Young, he was leading the former agricultural college astray, away from its mission as a state land-grant university and toward an Ivy League or small-college model. Whatever the reason, the new president welcomed suggestions such as that made by a dynamic young English department faculty member, Milton R. "Mickey" Stern, in early January 1963. Stern explained that he was teaching a graduate course in modern American literature (English 341) and wanted to bring well-known writers to campus. The names he had in mind would not only attract a large audience and deliver an exciting performance "but also will immediately establish for the University a reputation for the kind of program with which the best institutions of higher learning are identified." Babbidge replied that the suggestion had appeal and "made extremely good sense." If Stern's proposal met with the approval of his department head and dean, it should go forward. However, because finding extra resources for all of the university's courses or departments was of course impossible, it had to be demonstrated that English 341 was an area in which the university could get relatively good mileage from the investment.[16]

Apparently, English 341 passed the test. Stern suggested that, for the publicity value, publishers could get the writers, who lived in or near Connecticut, to campus for only $400 each and asked for about $2,000 for the enterprise. Those who came comprised a star-studded array of mid-twentieth-century novelists who continue to remain giants of American literature: Norman Mailer, then author of *The Naked and the Dead, Advertisements for Myself,* and *The Deer Park;* Ralph Ellison, who wrote *The Invisible Man;* Philip Roth, at that time author of *Goodbye Columbus* and *Letting Go;* Bernard Malamud, who wrote *The Natural, The Magic Barrel, The Assistant,* and *A New Life;* and William Styron, author of *Lie Down in Darkness, The Long March,* and *Set This House on Fire.* The seminar series permitted students to actually confront the novelists. For each session, students prepared papers on the works of the visiting lecturer. The papers served as "jumping off" points for general discussion, and the seminars served as the catalysts for establishing a literary salon–like atmosphere that had been previously unknown at the university. Dinners, public lectures, and private faculty parties completed the schedule. The student newspaper reported that President Babbidge was influential in arranging for the university to cover the costs of the lectures.[17]

The following year, Pulitzer Prize– and National Book Award–winning poet Marianne Moore visited campus to deliver the first annual Wallace Stevens Memorial Lecture, named in honor of the late Hartford insurance executive–poet. In addition to speaking, she presented three Wallace Stevens Awards to undergraduates who submitted the best poems in a university-wide competition. During the 1960s the Brien McMahon Lecture Series, begun in 1957 and sponsored by former senator and UConn board of trustees member William Benton in honor of his late Connecticut colleague in the U.S. Senate, brought leading public figures to Storrs. Former Secretary of State Dean Acheson, former President of Venezuela Romulo Betancourt, Senator William Fulbright, Israel's foreign minister, Abba Eban, and the Indian leader and former president of the U.N. General Assembly, Madam Vijayalakshmi Pandit, all came to Storrs to great acclaim. Eban, for instance, spoke on a perennially relevant topic, "Middle East: Past Agony and Future Hope," to an overflow audience of four thousand in Jorgensen Auditorium. He proclaimed a theme that would continue for decades: "The hour is ripe for the great experiment of peace between Israel and her neighbors."[18]

While Babbidge also encouraged others' lecture series and provided resources to assist them, his vision further served as a catalyst for the transformation of "The Beanery" into the Benton Museum of Art. "The Beanery," the nickname given to the red-brick Main Dining Hall for the Connecticut Agricultural College, had been the most-used building on campus in the 1920s and early 1930s. By the time Babbidge arrived, the building, an example of early collegiate Gothic architecture that was built in 1919 and opened in 1920, had turned into a warehouse as the university expanded and the structure was unable to accommodate large numbers of students for dining. Babbidge immediately recognized that given its central campus location across from the new extension of the Wilbur Cross Library, the building demanded to be more than storage space. He recalled, "I walked in and the minute I saw the interior, I visualized it as an art gallery." Architect Alton V. Rheaume of Stamford welcomed the opportunity to convert what was once the large commons room into 3,600 square feet of exhibition space. He particularly thought the thirty-five-foot ceiling and its massive wooden trusses added "grandeur and warmth to the interior." Two new balconies, one on each end of the building, were designed to provide four studios and wall areas for the exhibition of prints. The architect created special lighting that did not lessen the impact of the exposed roof beams. His plans also called for a new layout suited to the traffic patterns of an art gallery. When the museum opened at the end of November 1966, Nathan Knobler, head of the Art Department, thanked Babbidge for the role he had played in the establishment of the museum and added, "Had it not been for your recognition of the need for a major art exhibition facility on campus and your identification of the Beanery as the logical place to install it, the present museum would not exist." Similarly, Frank B. Cookson, dean of the School of Fine Arts, acknowledged Babbidge's "considerable special help" in bringing a leading European musician, Bronislaw Gimpel, to the University String Quartet as first violinist. Homer Babbidge cherished his role as a patron of the arts, and the institution benefited from his enthusiasm. Such contributions as the cutting-edge lecture series, the establishment of an art museum, and top-level concerts helped counter the view of Storrs as a cultural wasteland. A pamphlet prepared during the mid-1960s for new faculty and staff was entitled "Storrs, Connecticut: Hardly A Wilderness" and began, "When you first considered joining the University of Connecticut staff, you probably took a look at a map and asked yourself, 'Where on earth is Storrs?'" Babbidge worked hard to end the need for such a question.[19]

Developing an Educational Philosophy

The president had a definite philosophy of education and administration, and a sense of direction, that he first imparted to a meeting of department heads in May 1963, a meeting so unusual that Provost Waugh appreciatively recalled it as the first time the heads had been brought together in almost a quarter century. Babbidge took the headship role quite seriously and within a year would propose that every department headship be reviewed every five years, a practice that was soon put into place. He spoke to the gathering about the differences and similarities between land-grant institutions and old-line colleges and universities. He thought the similarities more numerous than the differences but went on to discuss the latter at length. Connecticut served a less selective student clientele, but he in turn argued for greater selectivity. He preferred that the weaker students be siphoned off into the state colleges or technical institutes. He was disturbed that a consistent portion of the student body was dropped as a result of scholastic deficiency. Babbidge argued that because the UConn student level began at a lower base than the more selective private schools, the university had a greater opportunity to contribute. "Those who go to Harvard and become Justices of the Supreme Court might well have become Justices without Harvard. Our students in many cases could achieve but little without our help," he stated. As a consequence, the selection of teaching faculty was vitally important. Babbidge told his listeners that he was less interested in the techniques of teaching than in a genuine interest in students.[20]

He explained that the land-grant universities were founded in large part because of a distrust in the older institutions of the fields of science, engineering, and agriculture. Schools like Connecticut brought about—and won—a revolution in higher education: those fields had now become respectable in all institutions. Babbidge suggested that some pretended their institution did not have that past, and joked, "We try to pretend that we are not Irish at all, but first settlers. We ought not forget our ancestry. We should be proud of it." He then turned to the issue of tenure. He commented on its importance, and on the purpose of the probationary period. In granting tenure, the guiding principle should be to reward those who are better than required by the present institution. Not every faculty member should expect to become a full professor, nor was someone a failure who retired as an associate professor. He promised the department heads that the years to come would be exciting ones and particularly pointed to the establishment of the medical and dental schools. He acknowledged that some people feared that they would drain the other schools of the institution of their support. However, Babbidge contended that the same argument had been made when the Agricultural College expanded into the present institution, but such fears did not deter the change. He emphatically declared, "I judge that the medical and dental schools will strengthen the entire institution." Referring to attempts to recognize higher education in the state, the first-year president concluded his remarks by noting that the most important problem faced by UConn involved the institution's autonomy. He thought the university would win the battle, and ultimately he was proven correct, despite several attempts over the next few decades to weaken its autonomy.[21]

In the freewheeling session that followed, the department heads had an opportunity to ask questions of the president, and Babbidge did not hesitate to respond. Alvin Liberman of the Psychology Department, who later would be named to the prestigious National Academy of Science, asked what would be done to get a larger proportion of the best students. Babbidge shot back, "We ought to tell 'em the truth. If we have attractive programs and staff, we should let it be known. We must try to offer education commensurate with the talents of the better students, so that it will be worth their while to come. We should develop honors programs. We must not let these students come only to be bored or forgotten or lost. We must improve the library." He added, however, that he wouldn't try to buy the best and the brightest. He wouldn't give a bright student money to come unless he or she needed the financial support. Nathan Knobler of the Art Department then asked how UConn could get more out-of-state students. Babbidge responded that 13 percent of the student body was already from other states. He voiced concern that the figure had risen to 49 percent at the University of Colorado, which had then led to difficulty with the state legislature. He wouldn't want UConn's share to fall below 10 percent, but he would shudder at the public relations problem if it ran much above 20 to 25 percent. Foreign students, who have to this day never made up a significant part of the undergraduate body at Connecticut, would be the most attractive. At the graduate level, Babbidge asserted, "We should aim to be completely cosmopolitan." He responded to questions about teaching load at Storrs and the branches by saying a twelve-hour load was not unreasonable if one did nothing but teach classes of reasonable size. He favored lighter loads if a professor's time went into scholarly endeavor, "but not to have it go into working in the garden or playing golf." Babbidge recognized that an attempt had to be made to keep more students on campus during the weekends. When the session ended, Provost Waugh heard enthusiastic comments. The department heads came away with the feeling that they had a president with whom they could communicate.[22]

New Institutions and Blue Bikes on Green Hills

Babbidge saw the need to build new institutions that would enhance the university community and led the move for the establishment of the University of Connecticut Foundation and the Faculty Alumni Center. Babbidge instinctively recognized that public universities would always have great difficulty in attracting the kind of resources from the state that were required to achieve true distinction, especially in New England, where private institutions cloaked in their long traditions monopolized the admiration and the support. He also understood that the university's alumni base was small and young, the median age being about thirty-five. As a consequence, he sought other means to supplement resources. In September 1963 Babbidge told the Council of Deans that a University of Connecticut Foundation was being considered by the board of trustees. It would be financed by private funds and its expenditures would not be under state restrictions. He offered the following examples of how such funds could be used: the acquisition of rare books for the library; the support of faculty excellence in teaching and research; or a discretionary fund for the president. He asked the deans to identify projects needing support and to submit their suggestions to him. A year later, the University of Connecticut Foundation was formed by a group of "prominent friends of the institution to finance those special needs of a major public university which the State's taxpayers cannot be expected reasonably to support."[23]

Lester E. Shippee, a former university trustee, served as the foundation's first president and was joined on the board of directors in October 1964 by Laurence J. Ackerman, former Business School dean and at the time of the foundation's establishment president of the Norwich Savings Society; Harry Archambault, an insurance businessman from Chester; Joseph Burns, vice-president of Hartford's Fuller Brush Company; Ellis C. Maxcy, president of the Southern New England Telephone Company; University of Connecticut board of trustees chair John J. Budds; Carl W. Nielsen, University of Connecticut alumni president; and Babbidge himself. They welcomed the $50,000 gift presented by Alfred C. Fuller, chair of the board of Fuller Brush and a university trustee, to inaugurate the foundation's treasury. However, much more would be required. To attend to the needs of the foundation, Babbidge hired a Yale acquaintance, John G. Rohrbach, as assistant to the president. Rohrbach, with his background in business and publishing, served as the foundation's first executive secretary. He immediately traveled to Purdue and Indiana Universities to learn from their long experience with this type of fundraising entity. Rohrbach returned to tell the directors what they probably already knew, or should have known: Connecticut had been a slow starter, not only in comparison with the Midwestern schools, "but even more to our embarrassment, in comparison with our own sister institutions right here in New England."[24]

To play catch up, the foundation began to organize by holding meetings with a faculty committee, developing a policy statement, preparing publicity, and implementing a fundraising campaign. It also agreed to two major projects: a film about the university and the establishment of a Faculty Alumni Center. The twenty-six-minute film, *The Measure of a University*, cost about $30,000 and reflected Babbidge's belief that UConn was one of the state's best-kept secrets.

He narrated the film, which portrayed life at the University of Connecticut and offered a glimpse into the institution's historic past, a view of student life, and a segment on its newly established honors program. Babbidge then turned to graduate study and research and introduced Professor Heinz Herrmann, who elaborated on them. Another facet of the university, its branches, received some coverage, and an emphasis was placed on the university's commitment to Connecticut's citizens. Returning to Storrs, the camera looked in on a board of trustees' meeting as the body discussed future expansion. It concluded with scenes of the 1965 commencement, as Babbidge outlined his views on the appropriate objectives of a state university in contemporary America. Albert Waugh seemed pleased to appear both at the film's beginning and its end and thought it a job well done, but he also commented, "I am never certain just what purpose is served by such pictures nor whether they justify the expense." Others, including the president, seemed more confident that the film would bring the university's message to the people of Connecticut. It was offered to high school students and counselors, alumni, service clubs and civic groups, and the public generally.[25]

The second major project, the Faculty Alumni Center, generated interest and enthusiasm, although Waugh, a teetotaler, thought its only purpose was "to get a place to sell booze on the campus." The fact that Alfred C. Fuller made his gift (worth $62,000 after the execution of stock sales, rather than the announced $50,000) with the suggestion that it be dedicated to such a facility encouraged the building campaign. Rohrbach and some of the foundation directors met with faculty and the Alumni Association to get the project underway. The association pledged $50,000; individual faculty members, not ordinarily thought of as able to play the role of benefactor, pledged almost $100,000, in the belief that the center would facilitate social and intellectual exchange on campus by providing a convenient meeting place in a casual atmosphere. The faculty's enthusiasm impressed an envious president of the University of Rhode Island, Francis H. Horn, whose institution also was trying to establish such a facility. He wrote Babbidge that the pledge reflected a very high degree of faculty morale, a sea change from what it had been under Jorgensen. Horn congratulated his Connecticut counterpart and said, "You should take great satisfaction in what you've accomplished to improve [morale] in a short time." However, the $600,000 budgeted for the building was not easy to come by, and its commitment to the center diluted the foundation's ability to carry out margin-of-excellence programs in its early years. In October 1969 the foundation's secretary, Robert W. Turcotte, scolded the directors when he remarked, "This Board voted the construction of a $600,000 facility but it apparently did not vote its personal commitment to raise the money." He continued that when construction began in the summer of 1967 they had $364,000 in gifts and pledges, and they now had $457,000—up only $93,000 in over two years. He urged commitment in fundraising.[26]

Despite the sluggishness in fundraising, the center did open in 1970 at its Hillside Road site, which was diagonally across from Jorgensen Auditorium. While it may have met expectations in its earliest days, it suffered from exclusivity and changing lifestyles. Its first bylaws limited active membership to *male* members of the university faculty and staff employed in teaching, research, or extension work. It charged annual dues that were unaffordable to many junior faculty members. It could not overcome the habit of many departments to bag lunches on their home territory. It did not attract the large number of alumni that Babbidge and its founders desired. While it made adjustments over the years, it remained, according to John G. Rohrbach, a "place where administrative types would go," to the exclusion of much of the faculty. It closed in 1990 and was later converted into the university's Admissions Building. In short, it was an institution conceived before the tumultuous changes that would transform the university, and American society, during the final quarter of the twentieth century. These changes would have a tremendous impact on the Babbidge presidency, but in the mid-1960s he still remained a breath of fresh air compared to his predecessor. As one alumnus wrote, "The atmosphere at UConn, especially amongst the faculty, has changed greatly—I take great pride in being an alumnus now. Indeed the work you have [done] and are to do can only bring the University to greater stature nationally and internationally."[27]

In keeping with the new atmosphere, on October 15, 1964, the administration moved to new facilities in a renovated Gulley Hall, which stands handsomely between Beach and Manchester Halls and continues to be the offices of the president and the provost. Funds for the original building were appropriated in 1907, the cornerstone was laid on May 28, 1908, and the building was first occupied in 1909. Named after Alfred G. Gulley, who came to Connecticut from the University of Vermont in 1894 as professor of horticulture and stayed until 1917, the building, in recognition of Connecticut's agricultural school origins, has "Horticulture" chiseled above its entrance. Small things as well as big moves helped to establish the Babbidge style, which pervaded Storrs during much of the 1960s. He transferred the annual tea for retired staff members from the Student Union Building, where President Jorgensen had held it, to his own house, thereby giving it a more comfortable setting. He eliminated the receiving line at the president's reception for the faculty, making the occasion less formal. The Babbidges instituted an annual Easter Egg Hunt on their lawn the day before Easter for the children of all university employees. In 1964, for example, almost three hundred youngsters searched for the one thousand eggs that had been hidden, and they also enjoyed the nine-foot papier-mache rabbit along with the carousel and small ferris wheel that were erected. Babbidge welcomed four mallards to Mirror Lake in 1964 as part of a program to restock the lake, which had been "duckless" for years. In 1967, he also brought one hundred "blue bikes" to UConn. The white-seated Columbia bikes arrived to improve transportation on the rolling, 1,800-acre campus. Authorities established ground rules for their use. During the week, they had to be ridden on an assigned course in academic areas; on weekends, they could be taken anywhere on or off campus as long as they were returned by Monday morning. The rules also asked that bikes be parked in racks planted around campus. Any unoccupied bike was fair game for any member of the campus community. President Babbidge inaugurated the program and rode the first bicycle around campus. Students greeted the experiment with enthusiasm, but within twenty-four hours, twenty of the bikes had landed in the maintenance shop; over the next few days, fifty-nine of them had to go to the mechanics for repair. While breakdowns did taper off, the experiment had a relatively short life, despite "blue-bike" Babbidge's desire to make university life livelier, freer, and more enjoyable.[28]

Assessing Babbidge at the end of his second year in Storrs, Albert Waugh found the president a "delightful chap to talk with." He had good common sense and an unusually fine personality. To the great advantage of the university, Babbidge restored personal contact with faculty members. Waugh, however, worried that this affability might create future difficulty for the president, who would be seen as so approachable that he would be inundated by staff seeking solutions to their problems. At a later time, the provost in his daily journal chided Babbidge for being too nice and unwilling to disappoint candidates for promotion. His charm extended to students, who warmed to the former Yale cheerleader. During his second year as president, Babbidge coached a faculty basketball team that beat student leaders 48–40. At intermission, he danced with cheerleaders to a Beatles tune. When water fights broke out in South Campus during a fifteen-hour power failure, the president called in a band and organized a dance. On his fortieth birthday, four students dressed in "roaring twenties" outfits and carrying toy guns "kidnapped" Babbidge from his office and took him to a surprise birthday party. When UConn played UMass in football in 1966, the president and his wife led a student procession from the Amherst train station to the UMass stadium. He was a president for all people, a "Mr. Chips" who just happened to preside over a middle-sized state university.[29]

"A Warm Athletic Supporter"

As far as intercollegiate athletics were concerned, despite what others might have said, and the invidious comparisons to his predecessor, Babbidge contended that he was "a warm athletic supporter," which led students at one birthday celebration to present him with a jockstrap. Those who did not doubt his enthusiasm for athletics sometimes questioned the former Yalie's loyalty to UConn, as this story, apocryphal or not, seems to suggest. In the fall of 1969, when the Huskies took to the gridiron against the Bulldogs at Yale Bowl, Babbidge was detained by commitments elsewhere and did not arrive until a white-and-blue-shirted player received the opening kickoff and ran it back for a touchdown. Babbidge cheered with great delight until his neighbor in the accompanying seat, Governor John Dempsey, with whom he had a cordial relationship that brought much-needed resources to UConn during the 1960s, incredulously asked, "What's wrong with you, Homer? That was a Yale score." Babbidge's defenders quickly pointed out that the uniforms were strikingly similar, and UConn went on to beat Yale 19–15. Thereafter, Babbidge supposedly pledged to support the Huskies in all athletic dogfights, although some claimed to have seen him sitting in the end zone and cheering for whichever team had the ball.[30]

During Babbidge's tenure, UConn fans saw the baseball team under Coach Larry Panciera go to the College World Series in 1965 and 1972, and the basketball team dominate the Yankee Conference and play several times in the post-season NCAA tournament. In football, the Huskies achieved their first-ever win, 13–6, over Yale in 1965, after sixteen losses; it was the first time in eighty-six games that Yale had lost to any team in the state of Connecticut, so dominant had the Ivy League team been. New coaches who would play significant roles in the school's sports history were named. John Toner became football coach in 1966 and remained in that post until 1970, when he was appointed director of athletics; he would oversee the university entrance into the Big East Conference nine years later. In 1969 Joe Morrone took over as head coach of men's soccer, and he would lead the team to a national championship in 1981. Dee Rowe began coaching basketball in 1969 and went on to compile a 120–88 overall record during the next eight years; he would then remain a key figure in the administration and development of Connecticut athletics into the next century. In accord with UConn tradition, basketball also continued to be a big story, even before Rowe's ascendancy.[31]

Babbidge was called out of a long University Senate meeting on Monday, January 14, 1963, to be told that highly successful and much-respected basketball coach Hugh Greer had died very unexpectedly. The president returned to the debate in progress and whispered the news to Provost Waugh and, at an appropriate break in business, announced Greer's death to the entire senate. The shock did not dampen that body's predilection for debate, however, which continued until nearly 6:30 P.M. Waugh reminisced about Greer, a former student whom he thought to be not only an excellent coach but "a gentleman." Waugh continued, "He never stormed at the officials nor at his players, and was always calm and quiet in appearance, well-dressed, handsome, pleasant to meet, and an all-round good influence on the boys." Nevertheless, a week and a half later, when pressure began to build on Babbidge to name the field house after Greer (which was done), Waugh, who so much admired Greer, ruminated that it was a sad commentary on university life that so much interest and concern attended the coach's death, while that of Harold Knauss, the former head of the Physics

Department, which took place at almost the same time, went almost unnoticed. For the provost, who followed Husky basketball closely as a fan, it reflected "the unfortunate over-emphasis on athletics in academic life."[32]

During the rest of the decade, until Dee Rowe began in 1969, Fred Shabel served as basketball coach. He continued Greer's winning ways, compiling a 72–29 four-season record, but in a much more assertive and combative style. "Huskymania" could not be contained when Shabel led his team to the NCAA tournament in 1964. On Monday, March 9, the University Senate adjourned early, ostensibly so that members could study a report brought before them and be ready to intelligently debate the next week; actually, though, many of them wanted to go home to their radios to listen to a "sweet sixteen" game played in Philadelphia, in which the underdog UConn ultimately beat Temple 53–48. Led by star Dom Perno, who later coached the Huskies, UConn also beat Bill Bradley's Princeton Tigers in a nailbiting 52–50 victory but lost to Duke in the regional finals. A year later, when Toby Kimball starred, the legislature adopted a resolution praising the basketball team and its coaches for their outstanding performance during the 1965 season. This salute led Provost Waugh to comment that the "legislature . . . would have been almost completely uninterested in any exposition of the solid intellectual accomplishment for which they have appropriated the funds." In 1966, however, after the University of Rhode Island defeated UConn for the Yankee conference championship and went on to the NCAA tournament, Connecticut had the opportunity to go to the National Invitational Tournament (NIT). Four decades later, Shabel remembered "that after a post game meeting of administrators, trustees and faculty representatives— 'but not the coach'—UConn issued a statement that it would not accept an NIT bid." He further suggested Babbidge's ambivalence toward "big-time" sports: "Times were different then [compared to the 2003–2004 season] and presidents were debating the role of athletics." Fans still delighted in players such as Wes Bialosuknia, who ended his senior season in 1967 as the all-time leading scorer to that date, with fifty points in a single game against the University of Maine.[33]

Babbidge, after condemning abuses in recruiting athletes, expressed concern about an overemphasis on athletics when he told the UConn Club's Tenth Annual Sports Award Dinner, "We need excellence in our athletic programs, and excellence in turn requires integrity." He went on to elaborate on his views regarding sports within the university. The faculty also demonstrated concern. In March 1965 the University Senate's Committee on General Scholastic Requirements, which was led by Kenneth G. Wilson, the head of the English Department who became dean of the College of Liberal Arts and Sciences and then academic vice-president, issued a report on "Intercollegiate Athletics and Academic Standards." At its February meeting, the senate instructed the committee to investigate and report back on whether there had been "any undue influence by the intercollegiate athletic program upon the University's academic standards in such matters as admission policy, excessive interest in athlete's [*sic*] grade, academic counseling, etc." While it found no abuses in admissions, the committee uncovered questionable practices in other areas, particularly in football and basketball, and made a number of recommendations to rectify the situation. Their report met with the approval of the entire senate and won plaudits from the provost, who found it well written and judicious in tone, but he complained that the university had suffered from an overemphasis on athletics since President Jorgensen had arrived in 1935. Waugh contended that the situation had become worse with the appointments of Rick Forzano, who coached football during the 1964–65 season, and Shabel in basketball. He charged, "They are both high-pressure coaches who are already in the process of seducing alumni and the student body (and to a considerable extent some of the trustees) and the Senate's report arises from some fears among faculty members at the prospects."[34]

By the end of Babbidge's tenure, other issues larger than athletics occupied his and the university community's attention, although the matter of the UConn sports mascot, the Husky, would not disappear in the face of a rising counterculture. Concern arose that the Husky, the school's symbol since 1934, would be replaced by the colonial Yankee. Alan J. Barth, a sophomore student senator, recognized several indications pointing to such a change. First, Babbidge had introduced the colonial three-cornered hat at graduation. Although it failed to become a tradition, at the time it seemed a dangerous omen for Husky supporters. Secondly, the marching band received a message about such a change in the spring of 1970. Finally, there appeared to be a shift in the university's official press abbreviation from UConn to "U of C," which to some represented a move away from the Husky and its tie to the Yukon. While the change never occurred, it continued to preoccupy those concerned with athletic symbolism.[35]

Sex, Booze, and Drugs: The Currents of the 1960s

During the 1960s, however, student concerns focused elsewhere, ultimately on issues of major cultural and political import. Summed up in the phrase "sex, drugs, and rock 'n' roll," enormous shifts occurred in the campus cultural landscape. In 1962 Elizabeth T. Noftsker, the assistant dean of students in charge of women's affairs, wrote to the campus police to help enforce rules that obviously were falling by the wayside:

> "NO PUBLIC DISPLAY OF AFFECTION BEYOND WHAT
> IS GENERALLY CONSIDERED IN GOOD TASTE"—
> Handholding—walking with arms around waists OK;
> Fervent and smothering embraces in either sitting or
> lying positions—NO!

"A SITTING, *NOT* A RECLINING POSITION WHEN
RELAXING ON CAMPUS"—this is "unladylike behavior"
in my book under any circumstances and should be allowed only
in the privacy of the sunbathing area behind Merritt.

"APPROPRIATE CAMPUS ATTIRE WITH THE PUBLISHED
DRESS STANDARDS." See enclosed University rules and
Regulations governing conduct of students. Page 5. Shorts, slacks, etc.
are not to be worn on Sundays or on Mansfield Road
during class hours.

Noftsker then posted a notice to all women students telling them that the Security Department had been notified to turn in the names of all rulebreakers because the uncontrolled public display of poor taste by couples on the campus greens, notably around the lakes, had become a matter of increasing concern.[36]

Alcohol and drinking had long been an issue on the supposedly dry Storrs campus, but a tolerable one. However, in the summer of 1964 the father of a student who would begin UConn in the new academic year complained to President Babbidge that when he told people his son would attend the University of Connecticut, they immediately responded with tales of drinking and sex at the Storrs campus. Because, he claimed, working-class families were most likely to send their children to the university, and that group seemed most strongly to hold this point of view, the father advised Babbidge to hold an open house for workers "and show them that not all students live at Dinah's [*sic*] Pool or drink up the hard earned money which it takes to send a son or daughter to college." A year later, the *Connecticut Daily Campus* editorialized against strict enforcement of the liquor regulations, which would in turn force parties off campus and open students to state and local law enforcement. The paper argued that few campuses were as isolated as Storrs and urged a revision of the regulations in recognition of the students' need for amusement.[37]

However, in the 1960s alcohol began to take a backseat to the student use of drugs. In March 1965 Provost Waugh and other administrators met with representatives of the university's security force. State police narcotics experts had informed the UConn police that a group of perhaps thirty students used marijuana and other drugs—and that they were slowly attracting other students as well. Although formally abiding by university housing rules and renting dormitory rooms, most of them actually lived with "non-student beatniks" in rented places bordering the campus. Until sufficient evidence was gathered, the administrators chose to take no action. However, a year later the *Daily Campus* announced, in bold type, "UConn Narcotics Ring Smashed—Six Arrested, Probe Continues." The state police narcotics squad seized a small quantity of marijuana from an off-campus trailer in which one of the accused lived. Not all were active students, but those who were faced immediate dismissal from the university. President Babbidge expressed deep concern but added that he had confidence in what he termed "the basic integrity and good conduct of the overwhelming majority of UConn students." By 1971 the Security Department would estimate that 65 to 70 percent of the undergraduate population experimented with or were steady users of drugs such as marijuana, hashish, LSD, mescaline, and psilocybin. By then, a President's Ad Hoc Committee on Drug Abuse had been established, with music professor Brian Klitz as chairman.[38]

Babbidge was sensitive to the currents of the 1960s, however, and at the end of March 1966 he sent a confidential memo to the board of trustees urging a "major and comprehensive review of the conditions of student life at Storrs." He explained that in many respects, because of its isolated, pastoral atmosphere, which was admittedly one of the institution's greatest charms, the University of Connecticut stood as an anachronism among larger institutions. It was required to create an entirely self-contained community, and although it made a considerable effort to do so through the provision of recreational, social, and cultural facilities and programs, the weekend exodus of students revealed that a complete community still did not exist. The main campus could not be moved, and it was unrealistic to expect a modern urban community to develop in Storrs. Hence, an atmosphere for living and learning had to be created to make the most of its potentialities, within its obvious existing limitations. With that in mind and in light of the changes sweeping American society, he advocated a more permissive attitude toward undergraduate living. This would include: (1) permitting regulated visiting between the sexes in student rooms; (2) easing the prohibition against liquor in the dormitories, and/or (3) making positive provision for adult drinking of beer and wine on the campus; (4) clarifying the role of resident advisors as advisors, not disciplinarians, and seeking to recruit better-qualified persons for such positions; (5) continuing efforts to enhance recreational and social opportunities in Storrs; and (6) exploring reasonable opportunities for some off-campus living. To achieve these goals, he suggested that the board of trustees appoint a blue-ribbon commission of students, faculty, and citizens to advise them. Finally, he assured the board that he did not present the recommendations as a consequence of any intimidation by rebellious or threatening students but in the belief that they would enhance the living experience of a large number of students.[39]

The suggested committee brought back a package of reforms that recommended students over the age of twenty-one be allowed to drink alcoholic beverages on campus and that, as at many other institutions, a beer-serving rathskeller be established. It advised lifting the ban against "co-eds" visiting the dormitory rooms of male students. It also advocated the construction of dormitories with more single rooms, additional housing for married students, greater contact between the administration and students, better academic counseling, and a fair hearing before any dismissal. Overall, the recommendations of the Committee to Study the Conditions of Undergraduate Life on the Storrs Campus of the University of Connecticut led to the loosening of the doctrine of "in loco parentis" while both reflecting changes already underway and paving the path of future student life in Storrs for the remainder of the century. And it had been initiated by Babbidge, who clearly saw the need for social and educational change. In 1969, when the governor signed a bill to expand the Stamford branch into a four-year regional campus, Babbidge argued that the times called for more than a "conventional" college education. If he were to start a new institution, he would initiate an innovative one, without departments and without conventional courses. Constraints prevented this from happening in Stamford, but the president expressed his ideal to the committee overseeing the transition. His sensitivity to educational change and student issues, however, would be otherwise severely tested as the 1960s came to a crashing conclusion.[40]

The Honeymoon Is Over:
Setting the Scene for Anti-War Protests

Turmoil swept the nation's campuses during the 1960s. Writing about Berkeley during that decade, historian W. J. Rorabaugh remarked, "Students revolted against the University of California, blacks demanded their rights, radicals surged into prominence, and a counterculture of major proportions blossomed. White, red, black, and green—these movements coincided, fed into one another, and reacted against each other in myriad and sometimes surprising ways." On the East Coast by the spring of 1968, Columbia University had ignited. At the end of April, a Students for Democratic Society (SDS) protest forced the closing of the New York City school and led to the takeover of several campus buildings; this, in turn, resulted in a violent clash between demonstrators and the police that scarred the university for many years afterward. Worldwide, other campuses erupted; simultaneously at the end of April the Universities of Paris, Prague, and Tokyo participated in anti–Vietnam War protests, and sit-ins, boycotts, or clashes ripped across the Italian Universities of Rome, Bologna, Venice, Turin, and Bari. The *Chronicle of Higher Education* reported on the predictable reaction at the conclusion of November 1968: "State Campuses Stiffen Stands on Militants." A lead article explained that a backlash against disruptive college students was building among the presidents and other top administrators of the nation's state-supported colleges and universities. The "get-tough" attitude permeated the meetings of the National Association of State Universities and Land-Grant Colleges and the American Association of State Colleges and Universities; the two groups represented 338 tax-supported institutions, including UConn, and enrolled more than half of the nation's college students. The University of Connecticut would not be alone in the drama that unfolded between 1967 and 1972, the second half of the Babbidge presidency.[41]

The anti–Vietnam War movement was well underway throughout the nation when a group of eight students opposing the presence of the ROTC on the UConn campus demonstrated in front of the ROTC hangar on September 21, 1967. David Yam, one of the organizers of the protest, asserted that training military officers was incompatible with the ideals for which the university stood. Others thought, like the UConn protesters of the 1930s, that the corps was nonacademic and that military training should not receive college credit. They passed out anti–Vietnam War literature as well, but that did not seem to faze the ROTC hierarchy. One air force officer stated that "no one was too disturbed by the picketing." Cadets had been cautioned to "behave like gentlemen" around the protesters, and the demonstration ended without incident, although Yam did announce that there would be further demonstrations in the future.[42]

Less than two weeks later Barry Goldwater, the conservative Republican senator from Arizona and losing presidential candidate in 1964, spoke to an overflow crowd in Jorgensen Auditorium. He told them that if the United States lost in Vietnam, there would be worldwide attacks on established governments. He added, "When we win, Communists will think twice for a long time to come." Students questioned him about foreign and domestic policy long after his speech concluded, and many admirers sought his autograph. The campus seemed still willing to tolerate differing opinions on the war. By the end of the week that witnessed Goldwater's visit, the UConn chapter of the SDS, announced that it was supporting participation in, and transportation to, a National Mobilization to End the War in Vietnam rally on October 21, to be held near the Pentagon and "to disrupt the Pentagon war machine." Faculty members volunteered to speak about the war at dormitories and to discuss the importance of dissent as expressed by participation in demonstrations. At the same time as the October 6 SDS announcement, the student newspaper advised that President Babbidge would hold office hours from 2:00 to 4:00 P.M. in Room 217 of the Student Union Building. He moved quickly to make himself accessible to students, perhaps in anticipation of events to come. As the national antiwar movement intensified after the Pentagon rally, so did events at UConn.[43]

After a heated debate at an SDS meeting on Monday night, October 30, the group decided to demonstrate against on-campus recruitment interviewing by the Dow Chemical Company, the manufacturers of napalm, which had become a controversial weapon during the Vietnam War. Fred Wallace, a student, told those assembled that he hoped the interviews would be cancelled, and that "Dow is contributing to the war effort. We don't want the university being used as part of the war effort." Some of the SDS members present, such as Steve Ambler, showed concern for free-speech rights and suggested that students be persuaded not to attend the session rather than that Dow be blocked from entering

Koons Hall, the site of the interviewing. Others argued that Dow should be extended an "open forum" to express its views, but that allowing the interview would make the university complicit in the war effort. Richard Savage, who would play a central role in later protests, proclaimed, "We are setting the stage for discussion on the entire issue of University involvement in the War." On Tuesday, October 31, between 150 and 200 demonstrators lined the entire corridor of Koons Hall and blocked the two Dow interviewers from entering the office assigned to them. After twice asking the demonstrators to move, Provost Edward Gant, who had replaced Albert Waugh upon Waugh's retirement in 1965, informed the Dow representatives that the interviews were concluded for the day. Other arrangements would be made. When Gant informed his predecessor of what had happened at Koons Hall, Waugh confided to his journal that he did not approve of napalm, nor did he approve of the demonstrators' "insolent infringement on the rights of other people, and ultimately it may become necessary to arrest them for obstructing the use of public property." Nevertheless, he thought Gant and Babbidge, to that point, anyway, had handled the matter well.[44]

The president called a meeting with SDS leaders shortly after the demonstration and, convinced of the protesters sincerity, decided to open to public discussion the question of university screening of employers who sought to interview on campus. While Babbidge thought that it shouldn't be the university's responsibility to do so, he stated: "I am sufficiently impressed by the earnestness and depth of conviction of the critics of our present policy" to open the question to university-wide debate. He referred the matter to the University Senate and the Student Senate for consideration. The Student Senate moved swiftly on the president's request, and at a regularly scheduled November 1 meeting unanimously adopted, after a long and rancorous discussion that included an attempt to censure the SDS, a resolution submitted by Scott Fraser, its president. The resolution asserted that by preventing the job interviews, SDS denied other students their right of freedom of speech and action; it urged Babbidge to adopt measures that would prevent such abridgement in the future. It then went on to support the Placement Office's policy regarding interviews and opposed the screening of employers. The next day, Babbidge briefly summarized his position on the "sit-ins" at his annual convocation for faculty. He regarded as "ominous any suggestion that the University place restrictions or limitations on the free flow of ideas or people." The *Connecticut Daily Campus* editorialized against the demonstrators, claiming that they denied the university's and students' right to bring company officials to campus. When some of the mail to Gulley Hall and some editorials from newspapers throughout the state misinterpreted the university's position, Babbidge expanded upon his earlier statements and pointed out that he had conferred with Dow officials about postponing interviews the day before they were scheduled and that there had never been any question that they would eventually be held. With the concurrence of the Dow people, the university had decided that the state police would not be called on campus in order to carry forward with the interviews. The president remarked in a comment that later would return to haunt him, "I have every reason to believe that when next the question arises—as it certainly will—we will be able to demonstrate that this is a University whose freedom is guarded not so much by a President who can call police, as by a community dedicated to the free flow of ideas and the free movement of people."[45]

As the controversy entered its second week, the local chapters of the AAUP and the Federation of University Teachers jointly sponsored a forum about interview policy that was open to the entire university community. After hearing a panel discussion considering the pros and cons of the issue, the audience of over two hundred students and faculty engaged in a spirited debate. However, they adopted no resolutions. The national AAUP, on the other hand, condemned student demonstrations to stop campus interviews and to prevent persons invited to campus from speaking. UConn's Graduate Student Council, which had been established a year and a half earlier, adopted a strong resolution on November 6 supporting the policy of inviting bona fide interviewers to Storrs. It regarded the interviewing system "as a definite service to graduating students who otherwise would find job seeking on their own both burdensome and costly." On the same day, the Alumni Council lauded the president, the provost, the student body, the Student Senate, and the "Faculty" [sic] Senate "for the moderate and judicious manner in which the recent demonstration involving the Dow Chemical Company was handled." The next morning a group of students brought to Gulley Hall a petition signed by two thousand students in support of an open door policy for interviewing. This was followed a day later by the University Senate establishment of a "Select Faculty Committee" to consider the university policy on the access of employers to university facilities for the purpose of interviewing and recruiting.[46]

Elliot Wolk, head of the Mathematics Department and a Federation of University Teachers activist, chaired the committee, which was comprised of tenured faculty only. David Ivry, a professor of insurance, served as vice-chairman, and Rufus Blanshard of the English Department was secretary. Other members included Fred Kort (Political Science), Joel Kupperman (Philosophy), Albert Cohen (Sociology), Gustav Mehlquist (Plant Science), R. Kent Newmyer (History), Fred Cazel (History), and James Scully (English). They moved quickly, holding a hearing on November 9 and reporting to the regular senate meeting on November 13. The report recommended the continued use of university facilities for interviewing and recruiting, although it questioned the use of the Student Union for recruiting purposes; it also recognized that the administrative officers of the university had exhibited "a judicious approach to the recent emergency situation." The committee expressed its confidence that due process in cases of protest and dissent would be respected in the future and counseled that its endorsement of the open placement policy should not be construed as an endorsement of any particular employer or the government's war policy. The full senate supported all of the committee's recommendations except for one, which suggested that if a university group so requested, the university would extend an invitation to an employing organization to come to the campus for open discussions in conjunction with interviewing, and provide facilities for such discussions. The interviewing, however, would not be contingent upon the acceptance of such an invitation. Clearly, Babbidge had strong support for his position to permit placement interviews on campus.[47]

On November 8 the Connecticut Resistance Movement staged a sit-in at Koons Hall to demonstrate against recruiting by the Grumman Aircraft Engineering Corporation, but it also announced that it would not prevent anyone from entering offices and informed all concerned to "carry on your intended business." Navy recruiting and interviews for United Aircraft, however, were postponed. Resistance movement chairman Fred Wallace advocated a teach-in as well, "to show the individual student how he is being used as a cog in the wheels of the war machine." Then, two days later, Babbidge sent a memo to the board of trustees in preparation for their November 15 meeting. He asked them to reaffirm the institution's recruiting and interviewing policy and to make clear to all in the UConn community that willful obstruction of any university activity "is subject to the most severe institutional penalties." Although it was not applied during the 1967–68 academic year, the adoption of the recommendation by the board would have major implications for the following year's events, when protest and dissent erupted in a more explosive fashion. One discontented anonymous faculty member reflected on the significance of Babbidge's recommendation and complained, "Your newly stated policy of firing all faculty and staff who attempt to block recruiting is a most novel course for institutions which are of any stature." The writer went on to criticize Babbidge and the trustees for establishing a police-state atmosphere and for denying faculty their rights by suggesting that they could be fired "for standing in a door," despite tenure and the need for due process. These increasingly vitriolic attacks, launched by a relatively small but vocal, alienated, and angry group of activists would continue throughout the remainder of Babbidge's presidency.[48]

Polarization intensified after Selective Service Director Lewis B. Hershey notified draft boards that anyone who protested the war and the draft by disrupting army induction centers or keeping military recruiters from conducting interviews should lose his deferments and be drafted first. While he did not mention students directly, clearly the edict was directed against them, because most demonstrations took place on or near college campuses. This did not prevent UConn students from joining several hundred others from across the state on December 8, 1967, in a march on the Federal Induction Center in New Haven, where they engaged in acts of civil disobedience. Some went limp when arrested, while others consented to be led away by the police, who arrested thirty protesters on charges of disorderly conduct, including fifteen students and faculty from UConn. Fred Wallace suffered a broken nose at the hand of a club-swinging New Haven policeman. He claimed that he was attacked after being told that he would be peaceably arrested. Those arrested were loaded into paddy wagons, held briefly in jail, and then taken to court, where a judge continued twenty-six cases, fined two people who pleaded guilty $25 each, and dismissed two others. UConn assistant professor of sociology, David Colfax, then thirty-one years old, and twenty-four-year-old, David Yam pled guilty. Allan Toubman, who covered the story for the *Connecticut Daily Campus,* had his case dismissed when it became clear that he was present as a reporter. While the demonstration occurred sixty miles from Storrs, it served as a rehearsal for the UConn activists.[49]

On December 14, 1967, Dow Chemical Company returned to campus to conduct interviews with a dozen students in the Business Administration Building rather than in the usual Placement Office. At 8:00 A.M. the interviewers were met by Provost Gant, Dean Hewes, and Placement Director John Powers, as well as about fifty demonstrators who claimed that the university tried to mislead them about the time and place for the interviews. They held signs that read "Dow Doing Its Patriotic Duty," showing a picture of a child burned because of napalm, and "Dow Lights the Way for LBJ [President Lyndon B. Johnson] in Southeast Asia." Morning interviews were held in room 124; about ten demonstrators sat in front of the door while others carried signs, sat in the corridor doing homework, or talked in small groups. Anyone going into the room had to walk between the sitting protestors. After lunch, about twenty demonstrators created an obstacle course for anyone entering the room. At one point, three protestors walked into the room when the door opened. Two were pushed out by the assistant dean of business, but the third sat down at the conference table where the interviewer met with a job applicant. When the interviewer finally left the room, he looked shaken, but the interviews had been conducted, although under difficult circumstances. Job candidates did have the opportunity to pursue their interests. No one called the police to the building.[50]

Meanwhile, in October 1967 and long before his arrest in New Haven, David Colfax, as a protest against the Vietnam War, had surrendered his draft card. At the time, he was married and the father of two young children. Under Selective Service rules, he was classified 3A, a low category for the draft. However, once he turned in his card his status changed to 1A, the most likely to be called to service, and he faced induction on May 6, 1968. On January 15, the University Senate had gone on record in its opposition to using the Selective Service as a punitive instrument. As the May date approached, the senate passed a resolution specifically deploring and condemning the prospective induction of Colfax, and it urged that the orders be rescinded. In so doing, the senate made clear that its position was entirely independent of its members' views on the propriety of

U.S. involvement in Vietnam or the legality of Colfax's method of expressing his opinions. The senators simply opposed the threat to freedom of expression that punitive drafting represented. On May 2 Babbidge sent similar sentiments to Selective Service Director Lewis B. Hershey and urged the director to make certain that no injustice was done. He recalled that a joint statement by Hershey and U.S. Attorney General Ramsey Clark gave the impression that the Selective Service would not be used in a punitive fashion or to preempt the proper authority of the courts. On the other hand, a group of concerned faculty wrote to Colfax, the senate, and the president to complain about the sociology professor's actions. They disagreed with his "general criticism of the American government, its handling of the Vietnam war, his support of picketing and aid to students relative to the draft and condemnation of the Connecticut State Police." For them, his behavior discredited the profession and the university. Colfax further alienated himself when, at the beginning of May, he reported a threatening phone call to the state police. The caller, whom he described as "middle-aged, well spoken," allegedly told him, "Some of us agree that you shouldn't go into the army and we're going to do something about it. Get the kids out of the house because we're coming to get you and burn the house." He brought his wife and two children to a friend and awaited a trooper, whom he claimed arrived "belatedly," was "rude," and then refused to provide protection for his house. As the trooper drove away, Colfax said he picked up a small rock "and very accurately threw it at the rear window." The trooper attempted to arrest him; Colfax fled and called Babbidge and Gant; that night he joined his family at the friend's house. The next morning he was in hiding, according to him not from the police but from the threatening caller. The incident blew over, however, and the senate's and Babbidge's intervention must have achieved their purpose. Colfax remained a UConn faculty member during the tumultuous 1968–69 academic year.[51]

1968–69: Babbidge's Saddest Day(s)

At the beginning of that school year over one hundred people, including twenty-five newly recruited freshmen, gathered for a UConn SDS meeting in the Student Union. The meeting's purpose was to set goals for the coming year, and the group established four committees to do so. The first aimed at restructuring the university by gaining more power for the Student Senate, which already had at least ten SDS members serving in it. The second desired to establish a "free university" that would not charge for classes and would teach courses on non-traditional subjects, such as narcotics—who uses them, what they are like, where they may be obtained. The third worked to advocate no academic credit for ROTC and, if possible, to ban it from campus. The same committee was charged with the teaching of self-defense, particularly against the police. Finally, the fourth committee considered how to protest against the university Security Department's carrying of weapons; it would also investigate whether that department maintained files on SDS or any other radical group, with the aim of learning what was in them.[52]

Two weeks later, Babbidge delivered his "State of the University" address. He argued that general agreement existed about the need for change at the institution, but that there might be a generation gap as to the *rate* of change necessary. He recounted how things had changed since the time a woman student had been dismissed because she was caught smoking (tobacco, not marijuana) at the Eagleville railroad station. He mentioned how the first fraternity on campus was called the Shakespeare House—a little "free university" of its time—because the study of Shakespeare did not have a place in a college of agriculture. The president noted that it was not just that the over-thirty crowd did not understand the young, but that the young did not understand their elders. With regard to such cultural division, he lauded a curriculum innovation, the "semester of the thirties," that would emphasize the experience of the older generation, with its Great Depression, "swing" music, and the coming of a war that people *did* believe in. Such an emphasis would assist students in contemplating why their parents thought the way they did. He concluded by remarking, "Let's make the most of the potential of this exciting institution. I know it's not fun city. . . . But let's work together to make it '*fun farm.*' And let's not let little knots of unhappy people spoil it for the rest of us."[53]

Exactly one month later, the Storrs campus was anything but "fun farm." Demonstrators celebrated the first anniversary of the 1967 Dow protest by engaging in a larger and more significant one when the company's recruiters returned to Storrs a year later to the day. One group threatened to napalm a puppy when the recruiters arrived, but it proved to be a hoax. The state dog wardens and Humane Society officers who had arrived to protect the dog departed quickly, but some students opposed to the demonstrations stayed, increasing the tension. Others supporting the protest commented that the puppy received more sympathy than the humans in Vietnam did. The demonstration started before 8:00 A.M. at Koons Hall, where protestors held signs reading "Dow Shall Not Kill," "Tao, Not Dow," and "No Dow on Campus—No War in Vietnam." It quickly became clear that the recruiters were not present at Koons Hall, so a number of demonstrators went to Gulley Hall to learn their whereabouts. About that time John Manning, the assistant dean of men's affairs, was distributing leaflets stating the official university policy concerning the disruption of placement interviews. The leaflet read, "Those who would jeopardize the free conduct of university affairs jeopardize their own place in the University community." The warning did not stop about 150 protesters from moving to the Engineering Building when they learned that it was the location of the interviews. They crossed the campus in an orderly column, spread out in the mall in front of the building, and lined the stone steps to the main entrance. When they learned that interviews were being conducted in room 111, the protestors crowded inside.[54]

Manning tried to appeal for quiet by announcing that fellow students were taking exams in the area, but sociology professor John Leggett found that to be no excuse for silence. He countered by drawing an analogy to the Germans who stood by when Jews were suffering during the 1930s, remarking, "We must not allow ourselves to follow the same pattern. We must make our stand now. I'm a teacher and I guess that makes me an old timer, because I approve of students taking tests. However, a time like this, I feel that what we have to say here is more important than tests." The crowd grew increasingly boisterous. They sang "We shall overthrow" to the tune of "We Shall Overcome" and substituted "today" for "some day." They chanted a four-letter word, followed by "Dow." They entered the interview room and taunted the Dow recruiter, a slightly built man with glasses. He asked them to leave. One demonstrator rhetorically asked him how he felt about his job and remarked, "I'd rather quit than work for a company that makes napalm." Dean Manning read the policy statement and warned that if the protestors didn't leave, they would be considered to be breaking university rules. Max Putzel, head of the University Committee on Placement, told the demonstrators that he agreed with their views but feared their action would create a backlash "on everything you are trying to do." Manning announced that he would be forced to take the names of the protestors. David Colfax then replied, "How can you tell the keepers from the kept?" Charles Brover of the English Department told the group that though the night before the SDS had determined to keep the demonstrations legal and quiet, Manning's presence had changed that: "I think that the administration's actions have worked to provoke tension." Leggett again compared the situation to Germany in 1938. Colfax claimed that the group acted as a "Committee of Safety" to protect the Dow representatives "against irresponsible acts by uncontrollable elements on the Storrs campus." When another student entered the room for an interview, Provost Gant joined him and declared that the protestors were trespassing on private property. Leggett replied that he wanted real freedom, not just academic freedom. He alluded to factory and shop managers who would not allow the employees to assemble and proclaimed, "We and only we have the right to decide if we should be here."[55]

In a further response to Gant's declaration, David Colfax added that when he left home in the morning, he promised his wife he would not get involved, but the provost's statement, which exposed violators to a severe punishment, would create an unfortunate split between the administration and faculty. Leggett added, "If we don't do something about the dying in Vietnam then we must live with the guilt. If I don't stay here now, I wouldn't be able to face myself in the mirror or face my students in class tomorrow." He and the rest of the crowd stayed until many of them followed the Dow representative to the nearby Commons dining hall. Feeling uncomfortable eating lunch before such an audience, the recruiter left quickly for his car. The demonstrators followed. One carried an effigy of a Vietnamese child that he lit with a match and placed on the pavement near the Dow man's car. As the recruiter drove away, the crowd gave fascist salutes and cried "Seig heil!" Later that day, President Babbidge issued a statement that the group, in the judgment of the provost, had obstructed Dow recruiting despite their familiarity with university policy and the repeated requests to vacate the premises. He regretted the necessity of initiating disciplinary action, which would be done in accordance with established university procedures, "including the assurances of due process as defined by University policies." The dean of students would request the Committee on Student Conduct to review the status of each student involved. Staff members faced the possibility of dismissal under a board of trustees policy established the previous year. He would ask the appropriate committee under university bylaws, the Committee of Five, to determine whether cause for dismissal existed. In the interim, Babbidge directed the provost to meet with those faculty charged with obstruction to determine who should be placed on probation pending the findings of the committee. This action set off a situation in which Babbidge, as both a liberal and a disciplinarian, personified the system under attack by the demonstrators and then became a main target for their discontent.[56]

An SDS member asserted, "Dr. Babbidge has neglected the integrity of the institution and has put Dow Chemical Company above the students." While concern bubbled about the eight students and four faculty members facing discipline, campus anxiety over job recruitment appeared to ease when Babbidge announced that Grumman Aircraft would hold its scheduled interviews off campus. He concluded his announcement by stating, "How rationally others respond to this gesture will determine our prospects for success." One short-lived group, the UConn Students For Reason, disagreed with the movement off campus, believing that it catered to the SDS, a small though vocal minority. Reason and rationality, however, would not be the order of the day. In the early evening of November 11, about seventy demonstrators occupied Gulley Hall in an effort to win amnesty for the Dow dozen. They locked and chained the doors and then barricaded them with a table. As many as two hundred students opposed to the occupation gathered outside the building. They smashed a window, which would be the only real damage done. The occupiers used a mimeograph machine to print periodic bulletins and "liberated" an IBM keypunch machine to print slogans such as "The czar's winter palace has been liberated; what will the czar do now?" and "This computer has been liberated; it demands amnesty for the twelve." Babbidge came to Gulley Hall a little after 9:00 P.M. from an open session at the Student Union, where he had addressed a friendly crowd that cheered his message that "at a time like this reason and rationality cannot be surrendered, especially in a university community, or in our society." With his offices occupied, he set up headquarters in the nearby Home Economics Building and prepared for a "long cold night."[57]

The next morning witnessed the end of the occupation. In a written statement, Provost Gant told the demonstrators that unless they vacated by 9:15 A.M. the Connecticut State Police would arrest everyone inside Gulley Hall. The occupiers didn't move—and the police didn't come. Shortly thereafter, Babbidge pleaded with the demonstrators to leave. They wouldn't listen and wanted a written statement. In writing, then, he informed them that the occupation had left him with little choice but to call the state police. He had taken this action only after discussions throughout the night with "dedicated faculty members." Because every attempt to bring about a reasonable consideration of the issues failed, he had no alternative. The provost also issued a warning of trespass, but the protestors remained adamant. As a consequence, the state police were a last resort. An effort by the Committee of Five to negotiate that morning aborted when its spokesman, David Ivry, was turned away from the front door of Gulley. At 11:15 A.M. State Police Commissioner Leo Mulcahy issued a statement asking those inside "to submit quietly" or be arrested. He explained that he didn't desire to force his way in, but he had enough men and equipment to do so. (While Mulcahy and three UConn security officers wearing riot helmets and carrying billy clubs were visible to the protestors, one hundred state police waited at the Mansfield Training School.) The occupiers finally left at 11:30 A.M. and, joined by about 150 others, crossed Route 195, blocking traffic and chanting "Stop society!" while displaying the two-finger "V" peace symbol on their way to the Campus Restaurant in the commercial bloc across from the university.[58]

The occupation did not achieve the protestors' goal of amnesty for the eight students and four faculty members, the latter identified as Colfax, Leggett, and Jack Roach, all of the Sociology Department, and Charles Brover, SDS faculty advisor and member of the English Department. Richard Savage, one of the SDS student leaders, proclaimed the Gulley Hall sit-in a success, because "We had a large turn out and we are still together," adding that "getting busted" was not a goal. Leggett thought the demonstration a "victory" because it raised important questions and won publicity for the movement. However, one demonstrator did not share the optimism. He complained, "We were led to believe that we would have a confrontation. We lost and Babbidge won because there was panic in the ranks." He would not be disappointed for too much longer.[59]

Amnesty negotiations continued in Gulley Hall over the next several days. When they broke down at about 9 P.M. on November 14, Babbidge met at their request with about 450 students and faculty in Von der Mehden Hall at 11:30 P.M. for three hours. The president was asked why only twelve people had been identified out of the many that had participated in the Dow demonstration. He responded that "all those persons whom they could unequivocally identify under oath were identified." He defended "democratic process" and "academic due process" as well as the fairness of the committees investigating both students and faculty. As a parting statement, he told the seventy or eighty people in the audience who remained until 2:30 A.M., "Some of you are asking me to sell proven processes down the river, and I'm not going to do it." He added, "I don't think you're doing anything wrong in asking for amnesty, but I will be doing wrong in granting amnesty."[60]

Demonstrations continued during the next few days; negotiations between the administration and the protesters sputtered. The potential for violence increased, and it finally came on November 26, when demonstrators attempted to besiege a building where placement interviews for the Olin Mathieson Corporation were taking place. Among the preparations for the impending protests, a mimeographed flyer was circulated that asked, "Will You Allow Your University to Be a Service Station for Munition Makers?" It went on to describe Olin's manufacture of M-14 and M-1 rifles and propellants for the air force's Titan missile and air force and navy planes; it also discussed the company's links to the military-industrial complex. Alluding to Babbidge's own phrase, the flyer concluded, "The *Fun Farm* Players Will Meet the War Profiteers at Koons Hall, Monday, November 25, at 10:00 A.M. If You Liked Dow, You'll Love Olin Mathieson. Keep the Corporations Off Campus!" "Babbidge Escalates!" headed another call to action. The flyer then directed its anger against the president:

It is now clear that Babbidge, the Faculty Senate and the State Legislature want blood. The recruiting issue has hit a nerve—*Money!* They would rather bust heads and arrest students and faculty than jeopardize their precious Placement Service.

If Babbidge wants his University to be a bloody whorehouse for Big Business, then we will make it obvious that a bloody whorehouse is what it is.

We will not allow recruitment on this campus! There is a state agency equipped to handle such interviews in Willimantic (the State Employment Security Division), but then Babbidge and the Faculty Senate would have no excuse to bust heads and arrest "troublemakers."

They have escalated again after SDS asked for De-escalation! We are all into it now!

Blood for Blood!!

Mass Meeting at V.D.M.—Monday—8:00 P.M."[61]

Such heated rhetoric anticipated the violence that would culminate a month's escalation of campus turmoil, including demonstrations, marches, midnight meetings, and a sit-in. The Olin Mathieson visit began on Monday, November 25, at Koons Hall. About 10:00 A.M. demonstrators outside performed a brief guerrilla theater skit, and then several people entered the building in search of the Olin recruiter, who was interviewing a student. Approximately a dozen of them occupied the interview room and, according to Provost Gant, shouted, climbed on the desk, and disrupted the interviewing. At that point, Dean of Students Robert E. Hewes intervened, extricated the recruiter, and guided him safely off campus, which aborted that day's interviewing. In the afternoon, President Babbidge released a statement in which he noted the rescheduling of the interviewing for the next day; precautions would be taken to insure that there would be no disruptions. Following advice from the Committee on Recruitment and Placement, which had been appointed to look into the situation and find ways to ameliorate the tension, the administration scheduled the Tuesday interviews at 7 Gilbert Road, a recently vacated residence not central to the classroom area but close enough to be convenient for interviewees. Babbidge issued a detailed set of regulations in which he recognized the right of peaceful protest but distinguished it from willful obstruction and disruption. Under the regulations, 7 Gilbert Road was open only to persons authorized by the Placement Office. Unauthorized persons could not enter the building and trespassers on its porch or stairs would be subject to penalty, including the possibility of arrest and prosecution. Anyone obstructing entrance to, or exit from, the site would be equally penalized. With these rules in place, everyone awaited the next day.[62]

Interviews began on schedule at 9:00 A.M. with the provost, the dean of students and others from his office, and members of the university's Security Department present to assure a peaceful day. A little more than an hour later, anti-recruiting demonstrators appeared, and a crowd followed. The administration distributed copies of Babbidge's regulations. Six security officers, without helmets or riot sticks, took position at the front steps to assure potential recruits free access to the building. At about 10:20 A.M. several protestors, including Jack Roach, mounted the front steps. Roach asked one of the security officers to arrest him. The officer refused and Roach tried to climb onto the porch over the railing next to the steps. He was stopped and pushed off the porch onto the ground. He climbed back onto the steps, turned to the crowd, and remarked that he hadn't been pushed, that he had slipped. The crowd remained relatively calm, but several individuals began beating on the windows and made loud noises. Just before 11:00 A.M. those demonstrators on the stairs locked arms and prevented a student appearing for his interview from entering. According to the provost, the student attempted to mount the side of the porch but was tackled by protestors. Violence broke out as some people tried to occupy the porch; the crowd heaved bricks and other missiles, wounding a security officer in the head. The officers received orders to protect themselves and were issued riot sticks; they cleared the porch and then went inside, after battering the heads of two students, who, bloodied, were carried away by fellow demonstrators. Bricks and rocks broke more windows and "cherry bombs" followed; at least one exploded inside. Injuries occurred among the crowd outside. A *Hartford Times* reporter on the scene said it was not clear, from a vantage point thirty yards from the porch, whether police clubs or student rocks were used first. In any event, John Ring, the assistant director of university security, read the riot act through a bullhorn from an upstairs window of the house. That act enjoined all persons assembled to depart immediately for their residences or places of business. Anyone remaining was subject to arrest. Minutes later state troopers arrived under the direction of Commissioner Mulcahy. The crowd greeted them with shouts of "Here come the pigs," and the troopers, their badges and name tags removed, moved in two columns through the crowd, making arrests. Other troopers in riot gear formed a line in front of the house, but the violence had ended, and by 2:00 P.M. the area had been cleared. Twelve persons, including Professors Colfax and Roach and SDS leader Richard Savage, were arrested immediately, and nine more arrests followed. (In an ironic twist of UConn history, when the arrests would be contested later in the courts, one of the lawyers defending the demonstrators was Emanuel Margolis, who, as described in the previous chapter, had lost his political science position at the university during the McCarthy era.)[63]

Later that afternoon, Babbidge, referring to the need to summon the state police because "the situation was clearly beyond control," remarked, "*This is the saddest day of my life . . .* to feel that it was necessary to introduce an element of force on the campus of an institution dedicated to reason and rationality." To some on campus, the president had breeched academic propriety by bringing in the police; others thought he did the right and necessary thing to preserve the university's obligation to maintain open access for all; still others, such as Carlton D. Blanchard, a former member of the Governor's Commission on Youth Services, found Babbidge "soft on hippies and Yippies." As was the case with so many university officials in the critical year of 1968, when it seemed that the center would not hold, Babbidge found himself caught in a buzz saw of student unrest and campus turmoil.[64]

The semester ended with additional demonstrations, arrests, and an aborted pre-Christmas student strike that fell victim to "the flu, biting winds, and the yen for holiday vacations." The critical irritant, which remained throughout the academic year and long after, turned on the fates of the four professors who had been arrested during the Dow demonstrations, later at the Olin protests, and in other instances as well. In the aftermath of the state police's Olin arrests, Provost Gant asked Kenneth G. Wilson, dean of the College of Liberal Arts and Sciences, to contact Professors Colfax, Brover, Leggett, and Roach. Brover and Leggett referred all conversation to their attorney and would not meet with the dean. With his department head, Lewis Killian, present, Roach, unknown to his colleagues in the protest, did meet with Wilson. The dean came to Roach's house in an attempt to persuade him to refrain from obstructing university activities in the future. Roach, who suffered battered fingers as a result of a beating by a security officer when he was attempting to remove a student who was being bludgeoned by police officers at the Olin demonstration, flatly refused. According to Wilson, Colfax spoke with him by phone and outlined why he couldn't agree to the dean's request about avoiding future obstruction. First, he believed that the provost and the president had been unfair and were "out to get him." Second, the Committee of Five appointed to investigate the situation, which had been established according to university bylaws, was not creditable because it had no final power and could only make recommendations. Third, he contended that the university deliberately intended to pick off the leaders of the recent demonstrations. Finally, unless the university was prepared to make concessions, further discussion would not be fruitful. These arguments would continue to serve as sources of campus polarization.[65]

As the raw New England winter settled in, the board of trustees took action concerning the four faculty members at its meeting of January 25, 1968. Prior to that meeting, Babbidge telegraphed the AAUP national office and requested that a regional AAUP representative be present; the national agreed to appoint a faculty member from Columbia University. This did not sit well with Leggett and Roach. Leggett, distrustful of liberal institutions in the manner of the New Left, told the *Hartford Times* that the AAUP at all levels had "no guts," and its lack of courage had been evident in his and Roach's cases. He pointed to the UConn local AAUP's assessment that the administration had granted them due process and suggested that AAUP participation at the meeting would be "as a disguised partisan for the administration and not as a neutral observer of events or as a champion of the charged faculty." He asked why he could not choose a group such as the Federation of University Teachers, which had questioned university disciplinary procedure, to represent him. Leggett then launched what was becoming an increasingly common attack on a single target, the president. He charged, "it would appear that President Babbidge is once again up to his old practice of hatcheting people silently while appearing fair publicly." Authority figures did not fare well during this period of late-1960s campus unrest, and Babbidge appeared very much an authority figure to the dissidents at UConn.[66]

The trustees, the holders of final authority at the university, placed the four faculty members on probation. They had to carry out their normal assigned duties and not engage in, contribute to, or incite others to impair or prevent the lawful functioning of the university. They further had to comply with all lawful instructions, regulations, and orders issued with due notice by the president or any other officer of the university. Violation would lead to their prompt dismissal. The board was quick to point out that it could have dismissed all four under its 1967 policy on willful obstruction but had refrained from doing so. However, it did vote that Leggett, whose activity had been found to fall within the definition of willful obstruction, should not be reappointed for the academic year 1969–70. Roach had already received tenure, and Brover's and Colfax's fates would be announced at the regular board meeting in March that considered tenure, promotion, and reappointment on the basis of academic performance and potential. Both, however, received warnings that the board had serious reservations regarding the desirability of their renewal. None of the four accused chose to appear before either the Committee of Five, whose report was central to the trustees' deliberation, or the board itself, but they and others would still be heard loudly with respect to the decisions still to come.[67]

Roach, Brover, and about twenty faculty and students did, however, picket the board meeting at Gulley Hall, even though they did not appear before the trustees. Roach then had an altercation with the WTIC-TV news staffers, who pursued him with questions, to which he responded "No comment" with an obscene gesture to the camera and an obscene word for the microphone. The incident would be considered Roach's fourth disruption of university activities, in what authorities thought was a continuing pattern. Roach also challenged his probation, noting to Babbidge, "That's for criminals, students, or first year faculty. . . . I have tenure and that is that." He considered himself to have the prerogatives of a fully tenured senior faculty member and stated that he planned on continuing to "greet" corporate recruiters such as the one expected from Sikorsky Aircraft in early February. The university responded to Roach by obtaining a temporary injunction that prohibited him from blocking the entrance to a university building, entering a building from which he had been barred, making any unnecessary noise or commotion calculated to disrupt university activities, or engaging in any violence or threats of violence. It also forbade him from making public comments or stating opinions that were "malicious or obscene," and it barred him from carrying signs that bore statements that were untrue, malicious, or calculated to encourage others to participate in unlawful acts. Roach, with the American Civil Liberties Union's assistance, would later challenge the injunction as a prior restraint on free speech. He would, however, limit his actions for several months.[68]

The limitation did not, however, prevent the publication of the obscenely titled newsletter "The Husky Handjob," whose first issue appeared on February 23, 1969, with a cover that read "Today Jack Roach Does Not Have His Civil Liberties. Tomorrow Will You Have Yours?" with a photo repeated a dozen times of Roach with his hands seemingly in prayer. The newsletter aimed to provide a forum for "radical political and social comment, the discussion of strategies for action, and the building of identity within the Movement." Because of the "high potential for political repression," it avoided bylines unless requested. Through heated rhetoric, invective, and barbed humor, it attacked the establishment, especially Homer Babbidge and the board of trustees. The second issue came with a photo of the president's face on the cover, with dotted lines surrounding it and instructions to cut along the lines in order to make a mask. Inside, it included a story that offered "the real reasons why Homer Babbidge wants to recruit on campus." The "real reason" turned out to be Babbidge's membership on the board of directors of the Hartford National Bank, which had substantial stock-holding and director interlocks with the offending corporations. He came in for further criticism when a supporter of Charles Brover remarked how he, Colfax, and Leggett were outstanding teachers, while Babbidge's lectures were "verbal diarrhea." His lecture on education during the 1930s was "dull, drab, and worth-less" and the entire "semester of the thirties" simply tried to detract attention from the 1960s. The writer continued, "Kissing the asses of your corporate friends is your major activity. Your Gestapo police state is shit, and your heavy-handed tactics are apparent to all but your balless [sic] functionaries." Civility had certainly taken a back seat to the zeitgeist of the 1960s and the rhetoric of the extreme New Left.[69]

Organizing in support of causes good and bad flourished, and the four fac-ulty members had their supporters. In early March, a new organization, WIVES (Women Intolerant of Vindictive Educational Suppression), formed. Accord-ing to Barbara Churchill, wife of Thomas Churchill, an English professor, the group emerged when she received heavy support from other area wives for an attempt to raise money for a defense fund to pay the court costs for those ar-rested in the demonstrations. The members of WIVES could "no longer partic-ipate in the conspiracy of silence concerning the current academic purge." They could "no longer sit in our kitchens while our husbands, friends, and children face intolerable and excessive punishments for their dissent." They targeted the administration and the trustees as well as the courts, and pinpointed as egre-gious the probationary status and injunction that had been imposed.[70]

During March, the pot continued to boil. When the board of trustees met to consider tenure, promotion, and reappointment, a crowd of 250 gathered in support of Brover and Colfax. They had been encouraged to attend a "finger-in" to celebrate in parody Jack Roach being "busted for making an obscene ges-ture." An "Ad Hoc Committee for the Spring Finger Mobilization of the Students for Faculty Freedom" asked, "Can this Board withstand the force of hundreds of fingers raised in protest against its existence?" They then proclaimed: "Make an 'obscene gesture' for peace." About fifty of these "committee" members crowded into the trustees' meeting on the second floor of Gulley Hall and surrounded the table at which the board sat. Board members coldly eyed the demonstrators but said nothing until a few began whistling the "Star-Spangled Banner" and "America." Board member Karl Nielson looked up and said to Chairman John Budds, "I'm here to hear a board meeting, not to hear the 'Star- Spangled Ban-ner' whistled. Either it is going to be quiet or the room will be cleared." David Colfax, who had been standing in the doorway, asked everyone to leave because the board was "using the people here as an excuse for intimidation." Colfax, who had been recommended for tenure by the Sociology and Anthropology Department's Promotion and Tenure Committee, explained that the board would not discuss tenure in the presence of demonstrators. After the room cleared, a student representative, Larry Smyle, spoke on his behalf, addressing the group as a "Board of Dictators" and telling them that a teacher should be employed on the basis of his worth and popularity as an educator, not on the basis of his political beliefs. Howard Reed, a history professor, represented a group of "concerned" faculty in the College of Liberal Arts and Sciences who wanted to defer consideration of tenure until a more extensive examination of the issue could be conducted. The board, followed by demonstrators who were locked out, then went into executive session at the Faculty Alumni Center. Following normal procedure, no results of the meeting were released, but that night Colfax said he received a phone call informing him that tenure had been denied. He attributed it to "political pressure in the state." In addition, the trustees did not reappoint Brover.[71]

Yet another a newly formed group, FASTEP (Faculty and Students to End the Purge), collected four hundred student and fifty faculty signatures on a petition that asked for a remedy to what had taken on "the dimensions of a purge." Colfax issued a record of his academic accomplishments to the university community. He told all who would read his message that while he expected to be denied tenure for political reasons, the administration, not satisfied with having him arrested three times "on false charges" and ruining his future at UConn, had begun a "whispering campaign" against him that smeared his scholarship, teaching, and service. He referred to other irritants, including an article about the UConn demonstrations that was critical of the faculty four, written by Journalism Department head Evan Hill and published in the *New York Times Magazine;* also, he complained that the university attorney widely circulated copies of the "unconstitutional" injunction against Jack Roach to colleges and universities throughout the country to be used as a sample weapon against their own protestors. The atmosphere of dissatisfaction by a vocal minority, and the involvement of an awakened majority, continued to the end of the semester.[72]

A Strike Committee on Commencement composed of faculty and students negotiated with the university administration about the form of a demonstration at graduation. They reached agreement that the senior class president, Wally Anderson, and another student, Bill Palmer, would coordinate the presentation of a statement on the strike and the strike demands just before the commencement address. They agreed that the faculty would not lead a walk-out, as originally planned. Students would wear white armbands as a sign of their commitment to end the war, militarism, racial repression, and suppression of dissent. Strike seminars and teach-ins would be held after commencement and after a picnic lunch, at about 1:45 P.M. Certainly the turbulent academic year of 1968–69 marked a critical point in Homer Babbidge's presidency. It tested his leadership,

liberalism—and patience. It brought the "saddest day of his life," when state police had to be called to campus to curb violence. It found that he still retained a
following among students as well, when over fifteen hundred of them, all chanting "Up with Babbidge," marched through campus to protest the demonstrations.
It also revealed a small opposition that held him in ever-increasing contempt.[73]

1969–70: "Love-ins," "Paint-ins," and Keeping the Doors Open

Babbidge, requiring some time off, took a much needed three-month sabbatical beginning in August 1969. Those like him who wished 1969–70 to be calm at
UConn in comparison to the preceding year would be disappointed. On the
antiwar front, October 15, 1969, saw an anti–Vietnam War strike; December 15
found sixteen arrests at a demonstration against recruiting by General Electric;
and, at the end of the school year, the bombing of Cambodia, the killing of students at Kent State University, and the Black Panther trial in New Haven led to
a student strike and the suspension of classes. Protests over racism further added
to the tension.[74]

The October event gathered steam when, in late September, the Student
Senate voted to join the national Vietnam Moratorium Committee and voted
unanimously in favor of a "community strike to protest the war in Vietnam," to
take place on October 15; in doing so, UConn joined about five hundred other
colleges and universities. The Student Senate resolution urged that all classes on
that day be suspended or devoted to the discussion of the Vietnam issue and its
relation to foreign and domestic policies. A few days later, twenty-six faculty
members gathered in the Humanities Building at the call of Milton "Mickey"
Stern of the English Department, Arland Meade of the Agriculture School, psychology professor Alvin Liberman, and zoology professor Norman Davis. They
discussed two types of action in support of the protest: a "community action
program" that would bring UConn students to a city such as Willimantic to
knock on doors and try to talk to residents about Vietnam and related issues and
a teach-in. The latter had almost unanimous support. Stern stressed that those
present represented all aspects of the university's academic community and a
variety of political perspectives. Unity built for the "strike," which Tim Jerman,
president of the Associated Student Government, pointed out was "not a strike
against the University, but a protest against the war in Vietnam." A supportive
Daily Campus editorial agreed. In an unusual move, administrators joined faculty and students and formed the Administrative Staff for Peace. The University
Senate endorsed the strike and the other activities suggested earlier at the meeting of the twenty-six faculty members. Edward Gant, as acting president, issued
a statement to the campus that while the university took no stand on political
issues, he recognized that the need to reflect on, and discuss, the central issue of

the time was perfectly in accord with the objectives of the institution. The day's events that occurred on October 15 brought to Storrs Allard Lowenstein, a New York congressman and the leading progressive of the day, Joseph Duffy, national chair of Americans for Democratic Action, and black comedian and government gadfly Dick Gregory, as well as many other activists. While not a complete love fest, the "strike" reflected more campus unity than other incidents involving anti-war protest. At the end of the month, a real love fest, or "happening," occurred when some four hundred students and faculty gathered at Mirror Lake for a "Dawning of Love and Peace" that included singing, dancing, enjoying nature, and "everybody talking to everybody else." President Babbidge, who had returned from his sabbatical sporting love beads and playing a kazoo, joined the gathering to great applause. He did, however, turn down the opportunity to smoke a marijuana-filled pipe that was being passed around by some of the students. This Age of Aquarius, however, would not bring peaceful times.[75]

The recruitment issue arose again, in somewhat different form, when General Electric attempted to conduct interviews at the skating rink warming hut on December 15. Fifty demonstrators had blocked five students from going to interviews with job recruiters and talked four others out of showing up for interviews. Eleven other students did manage to get their interviews, some after scuffling with picketers outside the building. The issue was less antiwar than labor-related; workers had been on strike at GE for almost two months. At the end of the day, one protest leader said, "We came here to stop the recruitment of scab labor, and we did it." This led the *Hartford Courant* to editorialize that the confrontation had little to do with the war, racial unrest, or campus life. The paper commented, "One can only conclude that the [organizers—the Black Student Union and the SDS] merely wanted to cause trouble and gain attention, thereby sabotaging the orderly process of an academic community." Whatever the motivation, Babbidge quickly stepped in, and with the agreement of GE postponed the interviews until after the Christmas vacation. He announced that the university would ask that warrants be issued for the arrest and prosecution of all persons identified as obstructing placement interviews. UConn security officers and the state police issued sixteen arrest warrants for trespass and breach of the peace, including among them two professors, Charles Brover, the SDS advisor, and anthropologist James C. Faris. The incident continued after the holidays on January 8, 1970, when close to forty-five demonstrators picketed Gulley Hall calling for President Babbidge, who was not in the building, to "Face the masses." While the *Courant* and others approved of Babbidge's quick action in calling for arrests, the president could not escape the seething discontent that motivated some students.[76]

The academic year ended dramatically. On April 30 American troops entered Cambodia, setting off a wave of protests on virtually every major campus in the United States. When national guardsmen killed four students at Kent State

University in Ohio on May 4, an earlier call for a nationwide "student strike" on May 7 took on a new significance. At UConn, in wake of the killings, the Student Senate, the SDS, the Black Student Union, and the United Towers Organization all voted to join the strike and endorsed national demands that advocated the end of the systematic repression of political dissidents such as the Black Panther leader, Bobby Seale; the unilateral and immediate withdrawal from Southeast Asia; and an end to defense research and ROTC at universities. The next day, May 5, other student groups announced their support for the proposed "strike," and the faculty of the College of Liberal Arts and Sciences voted 132 to 99 to suspend classes for the remainder of the semester "so that students and faculty will not be denied the opportunity to respond in a constructive way to this ominous situation." The faculty called for final exams to be given as scheduled but based only on work through May 5. The faculties of several other schools and colleges took positions ranging from general support for the suspension of classes to rejection of any interruption in the academic calendar. In Connecticut, approximately 175 of Wesleyan University's 212 faculty members met with the acting president and voted overwhelmingly to support a student strike of classes; the faculty adopted liberal provisions for grading students for work done until May 4. The faculty senate at the University of Hartford agreed to make classes optional for the remainder of the semester and to base grades on work completed by May 4 for those who chose not to attend. The Trinity College president met with students and stated that the school would remain open despite their strike. Out of state, Princeton University faculty voted to suspend classes for the remainder of the semester and took a stand as a group condemning the war in Southeast Asia. Boston University canceled final examinations and its scheduled May 17 commencement exercises, at which Senator Edward M. Kennedy was to have been the principal speaker.[77]

On Wednesday, May 6, at UConn, a day-long "Metanoia"—a period of active meditation during which classes are cancelled—on racial respect that was planned before the Cambodia episode went on as scheduled. The executive director of the Urban League, Whitney Young, attacked racism and the war in Vietnam but urged students not to close the universities. President Babbidge issued a statement on the proposed strike in which he stated that no classes will be cancelled; because class attendance had long been optional, students would have the right to stay away in protest, but faculty members have an obligation to meet their responsibilities to students who wished to continue their scheduled course work. He expressed the hope that the proposed strike, "as an avowed expression of genuine moral concern, will be non-coercive, and that no one will interfere with the efforts of others to pursue their scheduled programs." When Babbidge that day spoke to a large crowd gathered as part of the Metanoia program on race, he would not discuss the strike, telling the audience, "I am aware that there are some who would exploit this Metanoia for other purposes." Some students responded negatively because the president sidestepped the issues of the strike. Later, about four thousand turned out for a racial respect rally on the Student Union mall.[78]

The next day, Babbidge elaborated on his statement regarding the "strike," recognizing that the "non-coercive strike had won wide support within the community and was being responsibly led." He reasserted that exam schedules would be maintained and recommended to the University Senate, in accordance with the College of Liberal Arts and Sciences suggestion, that it request faculty to cover only materials presented before May 5 in their tests. He called a special senate meeting for the next day and disclosed that he had sent a telegram to President Richard Nixon in which Babbidge reiterated his respect for the strike and his belief that for universities to continue to function responsibly and peacefully, a speedy disengagement from Southeast Asia was required. Picketing began on campus and a cursory survey revealed that many students stayed away from classes in the Humanities and Social Sciences Buildings but attendance was close to normal in the sciences and the professional schools. Many students—one estimate suggested between four and five thousand—gathered at 1:00 P.M. to hear John Froines of the "Chicago Seven" speak at the Student Union mall. He related the situation in 1970 to the period of the American Revolution; referring to the Boston Tea Party, Froines remarked, "Maybe it's time to start throwing things into the water again." That night thousands of students attended a "strike teach-in" at the Field House; smaller teach-ins and workshops met in classrooms, dormitories, the Student Union, and elsewhere. By a close vote, the Student Senate voted to abolish the ROTC.[79]

At a special meeting of the University Senate on Friday, May 8, the body voted to continue classes for all students who wished them and prohibit penalties for students who did not attend, and to limit the content of final exams to coursework presented before May 5. It also provided a mechanism for students not taking the exams to receive an "S" for satisfactory work completed before May 5. Biology professor Jay S. Roth's motion to cancel all classes failed after a great deal of debate; he argued that while continuing classes for those who wished them gave freedom to students, instructors did not have an equal freedom. He continued, "Faculty members also have an obligation to try to right what's wrong in our society. They shouldn't be coerced to attend their classes." The senate received but did not discuss a list of student demands that was supported by an increasing number of organizations that included calls for the end of ROTC and military research at UConn, a free daycare center on campus to be housed in the vacated ROTC building, amnesty for those charged during previous demonstrations, and no further arrests during the current strike. For the more radical students and faculty, the senate still had not done enough. Norris B. Lyle, an assistant professor of history, exclaimed, "Homer Babbidge's illusion of responsiveness to student deaths and American imperialism in Cambodia is to have his 'hack' university bullshit the public." A student, asked what he thought of the University Senate's actions, remarked, "Have you ever seen such a collection of fossils?"[80]

The weekend did not bring rest. On Saturday, May 9, Babbidge brought the Strike Coalition Committee together with representatives of the Connecticut media, elected political leaders, and members of the board of trustees to demonstrate, as the president had suggested in his statement of May 7, that the strike was "not the invention of a small radical minority." The Strike Coalition Committee also presented Babbidge with four additional local demands, which included the establishment of accredited cooperative urban colleges for oppressed people and an increase in minority enrollment, financial aid, and minority campus workers. The following day, Babbidge responded to the strike demands in a lengthy statement. With respect to the war-related demands, he announced that he had directed the university's officer of research development to stop the submission of any new applications for research support from agencies of the Department of Defense immediately, until the formulation of a policy governing them that was generally acceptable to the university community at large. As to the ROTC, he saw that as a complex matter and noted that the University Senate had rejected a motion to abolish them. He did, however, hold out the hope that credit instruction in ROTC-related courses might be brought under the control of civilian faculty, as Curricula and Courses Committee chair John Brand and Liberal Arts and Sciences dean Kenneth G. Wilson, who had conferred with the Defense Department, had confidently suggested. If that didn't happen, the president predicted that ROTC would be discontinued, but he could not take any unilateral action at that moment. He agreed with the need for the daycare center, but not in the ROTC building, and promised to do all that he could to meet it. Regarding amnesty for past unlawful behavior, the president sermonized on accepting the consequences of one's actions. He concluded by stating that while he understood the causes of the strike and was in sympathy on a number of issues, his job was "to keep the doors open." He had to preserve the institution and, as a consequence, could not fully support the strike. Student senators Mark Shapera and Sue Stewart called Babbidge's statement an effort to "skirt the issues." Shapera said the statement was "just a stall technique to wait until things cool down on campus." Stewart added, "He is trying to look like he's supporting the strike, but he's only half-heartedly responding to our demands."[81]

The next week began with a "paint-in" at the ROTC hangar. On Monday, May 11, when at least three thousand students gathered on the Student Union mall to hear four eyewitnesses to the Kent State shootings, a Strike Coalition Committee member read a letter from Babbidge regarding the "paint-in." He noted that some people could understand the peaceful purpose of redecorating the building if you wanted to place a daycare center there, but that the expropriation of public property could not be tolerated. Authorities warned the demonstrators not to enter the building unless they had official business there, but about fifteen hundred people left the mall and went to the ROTC hangar, and about two hundred of them applied paint to the building's interior and exterior in a "daycare" motif. After ninety minutes all but a few left. Those remained until after midnight, when Babbidge was invited to address them. His appearance brought an additional three hundred protestors, who heard the president assure them that no police had been called; he discussed the "strike" issues and warned the occupants that they would be in jeopardy if they did not leave. He left at about 2:00 A.M. with many of those who had been attracted there when they heard he would speak. The remainder filtered out during the early morning hours, so that when the provost and the dean of students arrived at 7:00 A.M. only six remained—and they left upon the arrival of the officials.[82]

The following day, Wednesday, May 13, about forty demonstrators disrupted morning classes at Von der Mehden Recital Hall and at the Social Sciences Building. In the afternoon the dean of students initiated steps to suspend nine students for the disruption. The same afternoon a similar group disrupted an examination in Engineering Building I. The dean of students identified fifteen disrupters but was quick to single out some black students he knew by name. This led to allegations of racism and a march on Gulley Hall. About six hundred protesters converged on the building and about 150 moved inside. Babbidge then discussed the issues outside. One hundred or so demonstrators remained in the building for four hours, and the militants among them damaged telephone lines, window glass, and plastic signs. In the evening, a demonstrator assaulted a cameraman from Channel Three television when he refused to give up some film, injuring him severely enough to require surgery. By 8:30 P.M. the demonstrators departed and other students, including some of the original protestors, returned to clean up the building.

Shortly after midnight, the president met with the University Senate's Executive Committee. According to Mathematics Department head Elliot Wolk, Babbidge, his patience obviously tried, plunked down a bottle of whiskey and asked if the university should be closed. The Executive Committee members said no and issued a statement in which they noted that events had moved from peaceful demonstration to serious disruption and violence. They rejected the alternatives of closing the university or bringing the state police to campus and urged a continuation of scheduled activity. They called upon students and faculty "to preserve your University and to disassociate yourselves from those who would destroy it." Babbidge agreed with the message and broadcast it to the campus in a presidential newsletter beginning "Yesterday was a bad day for the University of Connecticut" and concluding "We can have a freer and better University only if we can demonstrate our ability to weather this storm."[83]

The student senate took a very different approach. On Wednesday evening, it unanimously passed a resolution expressing "no confidence in the will and ability of President Homer D. Babbidge to perform the duties of his position in a manner beneficial to the student community or to the general welfare." Allan Driscoll, acting chair of the Student Senate and sponsor of the resolution, pointed to the deteriorating situation and declared, "The community needs leadership, not hesitation. President Babbidge has failed us too many times." Eileen Pons, another student senator, added, "We realize that he is in a difficult position but his continued failure to act has become intolerable." Classes ended on Friday, May 15. More than three hundred students, clearly less disappointed in Babbidge, signed up to repaint the ROTC hangar in a counterdemonstration. Final exams began the next week, with some students electing to take them in class or at home; others, freed from exams, accepted an "S" grade instead. While the May 1970 strike did not completely close the university, UConn, like so many other institutions across the land, suffered during the trying and disruptive times. It was particularly trying for the university's president, who found himself caught between the proverbial rock and a hard place. His liberal values clashed with the radicalism of the new left. The politics of confrontation created a tension that must have been extremely uncomfortable for Homer D. Babbidge, a decent man who tried hard to preserve the traditions of the University of Connecticut. Tradition, however, was also under siege during the last years of his administration.[84]

Racing Against Race

The impact of the civil rights movement, urban rioting, and the assassinations of Malcolm X in 1965 and Martin Luther King, Jr. in 1968 all brought the issue of race to the fore across the nation. As the May 1970 strike revealed, it had become a major matter along with antiwar sentiment. Earlier in the 1960s race loomed as an increasingly important but less confrontational issue at UConn than it would after a series of incidents that later on involved disruption. With the Black Power movement came new organizations and new ways to demonstrate discontent on the part of the university's African American students. In turn, UConn established a variety of programs in response whose effectiveness depended upon the perspective of the observer. Back in 1963, early in the Babbidge years, John J. Budds, chair of the board of trustees, responded to President John Fitzgerald Kennedy's plea for assistance "in solving the grave civil rights problems faced by this Nation." The board chair told Kennedy, "We have continually concerned ourselves with attempting to provide equal rights and opportunities for all and are proud of the leadership which the University has taken in the field of race relations." He proceeded to delineate a number of ways in which the university had striven to provide equal rights, such as increasing financial aid, improving counseling services, and developing its branches to provide higher education at a lower cost.[85]

In the same year, Babbidge himself called on universities to give "special and favored treatment" to black students. At a meeting of the American Council of Education, he said that institutions of higher learning should "go out of their way to meet Negro students at least three-quarters, and maybe nine-tenths, of the way." Two months later, the Council of Deans discussed the small proportion of African American students and faculty members at UConn and concluded that such students might need special help and guidance and possibly the relaxation of some requirements. A year later, when a Stanford University administrator and personal friend asked Babbidge about what UConn was doing that could be emulated, Babbidge candidly responded, "I regret to say that we are not doing anything here for the higher education of Negroes that I can say is worth emulating." He then elaborated and did remark that the school was looking more carefully at prospective students and paying more attention to them when they came, through counseling and a special attention to reading. He reiterated that UConn was doing nothing dramatic, however, and he doubted dramatic solutions were available: "I'm afraid the only real improvements will come from hard work over time. I think the best first step we can take is to try and make our communities aware of the sad plight of the American teen-age Negro." Then the UConn president offered an analogy that he said could be used to get support for some special effort to improve the racial situation: "We ought to be willing to do as much for a student from an alien subculture as we do for 'foreign' students. In fact, most of the things I can see us doing for Negro students are the things we already do to help the foreign student." This image of the Negro as from an "alien subculture" apparently reflected his private thinking at the time just prior to the urban rioting that would sear America's consciousness, encourage the Black Power movement, and shift the means by which institutions dealt with the issue of race.[86]

Change swept the American landscape—and the campus in Storrs. It arrived first slowly and moderately and then with greater velocity and drama. Black students began to organize. In February 1967 Charles Herbert Smith Jr. told of the establishment of the Organization of Afro-American Students (OAAS), of which he was president. He pointed out that black students comprised less than one percent of the university's student body and that previously they had been scattered throughout campus, with little communication and not much collective identity. The new group included sixty undergraduates and fifteen graduate students and had as a goal to develop "an Afro-American consciousness . . . at the University of Connecticut and improv[e] the cultural and social development of the Afro-American." They initiated activities to tutor underprivileged children, to increase awareness of Negro history, and to recruit minority high school students to the university. They planned community action and employment

programs. Two months later the secretary of the organization, Gwendolyn Sebastian, wrote to Babbidge to thank him for his "generous contribution and
concern for our group," which made possible the first Annual Black Conference.
That meeting dealt with topics such as "Black Civic Leadership," "Greenpower
in Black Hands," "Black Politics," and "Black Students on Connecticut Campuses," and it brought civil rights leader James Farmer to campus as the key-
noter, in addition to a number of state activists. The OAAS explained the conference objectives in terms of the need to build unity for the black community,
which in turn brings new strength to blacks: "We speak of Black Revolution, and
must know where to carry the Revolt. The vanguard of black leadership must
come from youth; accommodationism must Fall before the Fires of militancy."
However, the group pointed out that black students were often co-opted by the
white establishment and became complacent, ignorant, and passive. The conference was a call for action that also desired to provide direction. The statement on objectives concluded with the two simple words: "Black Power."[87]

A year later, OAAS's new president, Ronald Lanier, thanked Babbidge for the
board of trustees grant of $5,000 and the increased financial assistance for in-
coming students. He told how, in cooperation with Director of Admissions John
Vlandis, the OAAS planned to recruit students from the state's high schools. That
occurred shortly after the assassination of Martin Luther King Jr. on April 4,
1968, and the riots that followed. A sense of urgency brought a number of new
initiatives to the university and gave added impetus to existing ones. At its
meeting that month, the board of trustees appointed its first African American
member, William Dehomer Waller, to fill a vacancy created by a resignation.
The appointment responded to pressure from a group called CURE (Connecticut Union for the Revitalization of Education), which called for a board more
representative of Connecticut's heterogeneous population. Babbidge also recommended that the trustees establish a Council on Human Rights and Opportunities; they appropriated $25,000 for it to initiate work. The council would
survey university efforts toward the improvement of human rights and opportunities and evaluate their effectiveness; it would further propose new programs
for the following year, initiate immediate efforts, and offer advice to university
members in order to "heighten the awareness" of the urgency of the racial problem and to formulate a general policy for the university in the area of human
rights and opportunities. The board also authorized initiation of a special leave
of absence program for faculty members, the Community Involvement Program.
It would permit up to twenty-five professors to work in activities designed to
improve community programs and attitudes relating to human rights and opportunities. Babbidge also described existing programs that UConn had in the
area of community involvement. CONNTAC, the Connecticut Talent Assistance
Corporation, operated under a federal grant to scour the state for minority
students with college potential. CONNPEP, the Pre-Collegiate Enrichment Pro-

gram, brought pre-collegiate youths to UConn during the summer for a six- or eight-week intensive program to develop their academic capabilities. The third program, a compensatory program, admitted students who had potential but were deficient in meeting standards. Tutors, such as those provided by the OAAS, worked to help them meet the standards. Babbidge again commented that the number of African American students enrolled at UConn were "disappointingly small."[88]

The initiatives expanded when the university launched the Urban Semester Program in September 1968, which had undergraduate students living in Hartford and receiving credit for their work in a variety of neighborhood agencies. The participants returned to Storrs one day a week to take two regularly scheduled courses. "In some respects their exposure to the urban environment will be more eye-opening to them than the experiences of a group of classmates who have just embarked for a junior year of study in France," proclaimed a press release about the program. Economist Robert Schoeplein, its coordinator, intended that the students would "help build bridges" between residents of the ghetto and their suburban-bred contemporaries. At the end of the 1968–69 academic year, the university announced the appointment of Professor Floyd L. Bass as director of a new Center for Black Studies, which a committee established by Kenneth G. Wilson, dean of the College of Liberal Arts and Sciences, had proposed in March 1969. The Center, because of its interdisciplinary purpose, would be responsible to the provost's office and would be charged, among other tasks, with coordinating new and existing work in black studies, recruiting faculty, and sponsoring special seminars.[89]

Several months prior to the establishment of the center, the OAAS addressed a "Memorandum of Necessary Changes at the University of Connecticut" to Babbidge. Prefacing it with the comment that antiwar disturbances on campus seemed to be obscuring racial issues, the OAAS called for the hiring of black administrators and faculty and listed specific positions to be filled. It asked for the establishment of an Institute of Black Studies, clearly the catalyst for the center, and made several other requests. Babbidge took the requests very seriously. Earlier, when Mike Whalen, news editor for the *Connecticut Daily Campus,* asked him whether he considered the OAAS an authentic voice for black students, Babbidge responded positively, saying that it represented virtually all blacks on campus and spoke for that community. He elaborated, "And I want to say, it's spoken very responsibly and very effectively on behalf of their interest. They have a constructive program—they know what they want, they present their position forcefully and directly. . . . I would urge upon any organization of students that has a constructive program that wants to improve or emulate conditions on this campus, to follow the example set thus far by our OAAS— a very impressive student organization." Not surprisingly the president gave a detailed response to the list of requested changes, including pointing out the appointments of African American administrators such as Frederick Adams as special assistant to the president, Bertram Wilson as administrative assistant to the director of personnel, whose responsibility was the recruitment of black and Puerto Rican classified employees, and James Lyons, director of the new Afro-American Cultural Center for students and black student advisor. Babbidge reaffirmed his belief in the equality of opportunity and remarked that if blacks and whites already had equal opportunity, his favorable response to their requests would be "totally alien to [his] sense of justice." The OAAS replied that they, too, desired equality of opportunity and asked for no change that they thought unfair.[90]

The Council on Human Rights and Opportunities, under the leadership of its chairman, Lawrence L. Parrish, also worked during this period to carry out its charge of ensuring racial social justice. It did so, however, without substantial resources of money and personnel and thus tried to stimulate activity in existing departments rather than serving as an operating agency. It performed as a facilitator and an instrument to raise consciousness about the racial issue. In its first year, which ended in April 1969, the Community Involvement Program, which was open to twenty-five faculty members, attracted only six: Donald Weckstein and Neil O. Littlefield of the Law School, Brian Klitz of the Music Department, Gerald Sazama of Economics, James Scully of English, and Michael Simon of Philosophy. Parrish concluded his first year's report by stating that the sense of urgency that gripped the country in April 1968 "has been much diluted. An important general function which the Council is attempting to perform is to keep the sense of concern, commitment, and urgency alive and strong in this institution." The sense of urgency, however, remained alive and active on the part of blacks, even if the council had to remind some whites about their concern and commitment. During the spring of 1969, students more militant than the OAAS formed the Black Student Union; about thirty "concerned members of the UConn Black community" then occupied the *Connecticut Daily Campus,* preventing its publication on March 21 in an attempt to call attention to what they termed "the unconscious racism and insensitivity of the newspaper toward Black students at the University." About a month later, a confrontation occurred between a group of black students and members of the Lambda Chi Alpha fraternity, which led Babbidge to establish the Committee to Investigate the Possibility of Racial Discrimination at the University of Connecticut. The committee held several hearings and particularly investigated the fraternity and sorority system and general student housing arrangements. It concluded, among several findings, that the Greek network implicitly excluded black students through a carefully designed "preferential selection process." It also found that almost two decades after the Al Rogers incident described here in chapter 3, racial comments and incidents embarrassing to black students still emanated from fraternity and sorority houses. The word "nigger" was used; sorority sisters threw water on black women; a white male appeared nude in the presence of a black couple. Moreover, the "selection process" in student housing throughout the university violated the rights of black and other minority students.[91]

Despite the recommendations made by the committee, the next academic year witnessed two serious racial incidents involving fraternities. The first brought Babbidge back early from his sabbatical. On Thursday, October 9, an estimated fifty to sixty black students damaged lounges and rooms in the Delta Chi fraternity house and Lancaster House. They overturned couches, broke windows, and smashed mirrors. Paint was thrown into some of the rooms at Delta Chi. That incident, which lasted no more than five minutes, stemmed from a confrontation between blacks and whites the previous night. Lew Curtiss, one of the black students, suggested that the disturbance represented an example of "collective defense"—blacks had to be concerned with the protection of black people. The fracas at Lancaster House resulted from insults leveled at a group of black women from the fourth floor. The protesters went directly there, smashing along the way the staircase, doorway, and lounge windows; upstairs windows were also broken, beds knocked down, and a bureau smashed. Three residents received minor cuts on their hands and faces when they met the protestors at the front door. After the incident, however, Lancaster residents issued a statement taking blame for initiating the confrontation and expressing the hope that others would learn from the situation and work to solve the racial problem rationally.[92]

The next morning three hundred white freshmen marched quietly in single file to Gulley Hall to "express . . . deep concern over the failure of the University of Connecticut community to take substantive steps toward ending the racial turmoil and injustice within our community" and the desire that remedies be found. Provost Gant, who had been serving as acting president during Babbidge's sabbatical, called on all to embrace with conviction the spirit of the statement and promised to distribute it throughout campus. Babbidge returned to spend the day of October 10 in conferences with students and faculty to ascertain just what had happened—and to discuss its root cause. He said he could not and would not condone property damage but emphasized, "I must assert that we cannot and will not condone damage to person by racial insult, for whatever reason." The insult was the more truly violent act, the more threatening to public safety, the least comprehensible. The president then announced that he had asked the chairman of the board of trustees to call a special meeting for Sunday, October 12. After meeting in executive session, the board endorsed Babbidge's statement and called on him to give highest priority to remedying the cause of racial tension on campus. It recommended expanded orientation efforts to promote racial understanding; it noted the work of the new Committee for Racial Respect and authorized the designation of an ombudsman to work fulltime with the committee; it supported Babbidge's desire for curriculum changes aimed at enhancing racial respect and understanding "and adequately reflecting the experience and contribution of minorities"; it encouraged reform of housing arrangements; and it authorized administrators to give high priority to human rights and opportunities programs in the next biennial budget. The sense of urgency swelled.[93]

The tension, however, did not abate. In the immediate wake of Babbidge's and the trustees' statements, additional incidents occurred. The Black Student Union warned that black students would "take action into our own hands." Babbidge announced that any student charged with inciting a racial incident would be subject to immediate suspension while they awaited appropriate judicial review. Doug Miranda, a Black Panther leader from New Haven, spoke to an audience of 2,800 people in Jorgensen Auditorium a day after Babbidge's announcement. He explained the slogan "All power to the people!" and asked UConn students to fight white racism. While race seemed to be the paramount issue on campus, Miranda also emphasized the class struggle and called for the destruction of capitalism, the material basis of racism. Whatever the basis, in the fall of 1969 the student newspaper editorialized that racism was so ingrained at the university "that hardly a dent is made by a special freshman orientation program, book lists, Board of Trustees' statements warning that acts of racism would not be tolerated, and visits to white dorms by men of both races . . . who are trying to make white persons aware of the racist nature of their institutions." Toward the end of the academic year, Frederick Adams, who had been appointed university ombudsman, reported on an incident at Sousa House that revealed the explosive and seemingly impenetrable nature of racism at UConn.[94]

On Sunday afternoon, April 19, 1970, two young black women appeared in the lobby of Sousa House, an independent undergraduate dormitory for sixty men, requesting use of the house intercom system to announce a rally in support of the accused Black Panther Bobby Seale. They received permission to do so and departed without incident. That evening, between 8:00 and 9:00 P.M., they returned to repeat the announcement. When they did, a voice on the intercom boomed, "You are sick." The women responded in kind and a stream of obscenities volleyed back and forth. John Kosak, the president of the house, tried to quiet his fellow residents and apologized to the women. He thought all was settled, but about 11:30 P.M. a group of twenty to thirty black students arrived, carrying rocks, pipes, and steel reinforcing rods. The crowd forced Kosak against a wall and inquired who had made the derogatory statements. He claimed not to know the individuals involved, and a brief shoving match ensued, until Kosak went down the stairs while the black students went in the other direction in an attempt to find those responsible. They entered several rooms. At the same time, one of the women students accompanying them started paging, in a very repetitive fashion, the entire house about the Bobby Seale rally. Kosak tried to intervene and placed his hand on hers to get her to stop. With the intercom still on, the woman yelled, "Take your hands off me." This brought the black men from upstairs back down, where they asked, "Did he touch you, sister?" She answered, "Yes." By this time, it was midnight. They asked her to leave the lobby and then a physical confrontation occurred, resulting in Kosak's hospitalization. His attackers first hit him with fists; when he fell on the floor, they stomped on him; then he was strangled and kicked in the face. The incident reflected the heated racial atmosphere and misunderstandings that existed as the year ended and Gulley Hall was occupied once again.[95]

For Babbidge, the situation grew still more complicated because a newly organized independent group, the Committee Against Racism, had charged the university with de facto segregation and complained to Washington that UConn was in violation of the 1964 Civil Rights Act and other statutes. The president, in the institution's defense, told Senator Abraham Ribicoff about all of the programs that had been instituted to provide equality of opportunity, and added, "I would say we are fairly typical of many colleges and universities making a vigorous and sincere, if belated, effort to redress historical inequities." On the other hand, Neil Olcott, the committee's chairman, told the senator, who had been in support of civil rights legislation, "Surely segregation in Connecticut must be fought as strongly as segregation in Mississippi." Babbidge would have agreed with that, but he denied the portrait of a segregated UConn and welcomed any inquiry into the university's efforts toward racial justice. The racial issue was complex and, like the anti–Vietnam War protests, dogged the final years of the Babbidge presidency, making them uncomfortable, disruptive, and sharply contrasting with the earlier honeymoon years.[96]

Liberating Women

In tandem with the antiwar and civil rights movements, the women's liberation movement emerged to bring vast social change to the nation and to the University of Connecticut. Early in his tenure, Babbidge found the proportion of women undergraduates at the university to be capped at 48 percent, a carryover of the traditional belief in male predominance at the state institution, which had seen a substantial dilution during World War II. Sensitive to this inequity, he invited Elizabeth "Betty" Roper, who had headed the state's League of Women Voters, to establish a program of continuing education for women. She recognized Babbidge's intent when she remarked, "If women couldn't come in the front door, he would get them in through the back door." While this might later be looked upon as "tokenism," at the time it represented a sincere attempt to provide greater educational opportunity. As the decade progressed, women students saw the reduction or elimination of parietal rules such as curfews and dress codes. Consciousness-raising groups for both female students and staff members mushroomed. A group of women interested in encouraging feminist ideology and activism on campus promoted the idea of a Women's Center, which was initiated in 1969 and shared cramped space with Betty Roper in the Bishop Center. All of this would be a prelude to a more intense emphasis on gender issues during the final years of the Babbidge era.[97]

In May 1970, based upon information provided to them by an unidentified UConn faculty member, the Women's Equity Action League filed a charge of sex discrimination with Secretary of Labor George P. Shultz against the university. A league spokesman proclaimed, "Women are second class citizens at the University of Connecticut; they are hired in small numbers and are not generally promoted as rapidly as their male counterparts." According to the whistleblower, whose figures may not have been accurate but whose point had impact, the 491 faculty members at the university included only forty-seven women, with a substantial number of these not even on a tenure track: one university professor; two professors; three associate professors; seventeen assistant professors; seventeen instructors; three assistant instructors; seven lecturers; and five one-semester lecturers. The unnamed UConn faculty member went on to say that she or he suspected that salary differentials existed, although no real supporting data was available. Gender issues related to hiring, promotion, and salary would remain prominent for several decades afterward.[98]

At the beginning of the 1970–71 academic year, an audience of over two hundred at a meeting of the UConn Women's Liberation Chapter heard a visitor from Boston's Bread and Roses faction explain the purpose of women's liberation. Liz Benton told her avid listeners, "We believe that women should be autonomous; that we should be judged by our human qualities and not just by our biological reproductive function." She continued with the claim that the national power structure keeps women subservient "because the system is set up not to allow too many women to gain much power. Male chauvinism and the attitude that women are only 'baby-breeders' is important to the support of the capitalistic system of this country." She lauded "women's lib" for encouraging females to have enlightening and loving relationships with other women that break down the traditional separating barriers of age and status. Benton also recommended "that women who know judo and karate teach other women how to defend themselves from attack." Others were less concerned with self-defense than with child care. The creation of a daycare center had been one of the ten local demands during the May 1970 strike. However, two months earlier, a women's group headed by Stephani Schaefer and Wendy Chapple had approached the administration. The two had been working for about seven months on plans to open a children's center to help area wives because "today's 'liberated woman' is perhaps the most isolated woman in history." In their preliminary efforts they found their plans frustrated by the lack of a suitable building; zoning, fire, and health regulations; and economic limitations. Then contacts with UConn officials throughout April and May suggested several ways that the university might be helpful. Babbidge also pointed them toward a building occupied by the department of child development that was going to be vacated, but the possibility quickly fizzled in a tangle of red tape.[99]

Meanwhile, the local Women's Radical Caucus announced plans for a daycare center that would provide its services free to low-income workers. This became one of the ten local demands of the Strike Coalition Committee in May. The demand called for "immediate creation of a free day care center funded by the university for, in the following order of priority, all children of campus wageworkers and then others according to financial need." At that point, Babbidge could not support a center in the ROTC hangar but recognized the need to provide such a service to employees and vowed his assistance. In June, however, he said "no" to opening, for the summer, a state-funded, free daycare center for children of university employees. The decision came on the heels of a report by an ad hoc administrative committee on daycare chaired by Eleanore B. Luckey, head of UConn's Department of Child Development and Family Relations. A survey by the committee found limited interest in the proposed summer program, which persuaded Babbidge to pursue other alternatives. In October, the Department of Community Affairs planned to open a center for low-income families in Mansfield. He also noted the expansion of the Child Development Department's child care program to include openings for about one hundred area children in February. This did not satisfy one faculty member, though, who objected to the expansion because "Mrs. Luckey has frankly said she needs children there for use as guinea pigs in child development research." The issue and the objections lingered as a subcommittee of the University Senate Growth and Development Committee explored the matter in the fall. Its chair, history professor Marvin Cox, said President Babbidge had been friendly to the idea of a daycare center, but he feared the president might have problems about non-university people using it. For Babbidge, there always was the "bent corner." Amidst an enormous array of emotional issues, he could never satisfy everyone.[100]

Claire Berg, an assistant professor of biology who had been hired a few years earlier, sent Babbidge a litany of complaints at the end of March 1972. She began by asserting that his administration had given women's rights a very low priority, which was "especially frustrating in this time of rising expectations." She granted that in the past he had initiated appropriate actions, but they had had relatively little effect, and she offered examples. In December 1970 he had asked deans, directors, and department heads to post permanently in a conspicuous place his memo on "equal treatment for women in personnel practices" and an American Council on Education statement on "discrimination against women in colleges." When Berg complained that the material was not widely posted, the administration did nothing further to publicize the documents. In the spring of 1970, Babbidge had appointed the President's Commission on the Status of

Women but filled its roster with predominantly non-feminists. After some pressure, the president made a few appointments more acceptable to Berg, but then the commission moved slowly because of an inadequate budget and a busy and uncommitted membership. Its existence, however, had a negative impact on the more independent Organization of Faculty and Professional Women (OFPW), which had begun to collect data on discrimination against women at UConn. The OFPW halted its work in deference to the commission and to a University Senate Subcommittee on Faculty and Professional Women, which had official sanction. However, the two accomplished little and the OFPW went on to complete its report anyway. Professor Berg implied that Babbidge had cranked up official machinery to delay real action.[101]

The biologist claimed that the Commission on the Status of Women blocked her suggestion that the charge to the Council of Human Rights and Opportunities be expanded to include women. Babbidge appeared receptive, but would not act until the commission made a recommendation. Berg asked Dorothy Goodwin, a university administrator who sat on the commission, to bring it to the group's attention but later claimed that it was never done. Athletic facilities represented another irritant. An independent university women's group, the Committee of Women's Recreation, asked Babbidge for adequate access to athletic facilities. Again, he lent his weight to the request. Certain accommodations were made and a locker room became available to women. However, the committee believed the Field House facilities to be inadequate, particularly because visiting teams used the women's lockers, and at certain times of year access for women to the Field House was curtailed. They argued that because women students paid university fees as well as men, equal access should be provided. In addition, the women complained about a shortage of lockers and the checking of individual identifications, a practice confined only to women. Despite Babbidge's support, little was achieved, although Lloyd Duff, the director of recreational activities, pointed to a growing interest in athletics on the part of women at the university.[102]

Professor Berg believed that no one in the administration or among the senior faculty could or would look out for the interests of women. The feminist found Dorothy Goodwin "kind, sympathetic and probably effective in correcting isolated inequities" but too concerned with the university's public image to serve as a women's advocate. She suggested that Babbidge publicly affirm his commitment to achieving equitable treatment for women; pledge to make the university's affirmative action plan a public document available to interested individuals; and pledge to appoint a woman who is also a feminist to a visible administrative post, with her primary responsibility being in the area of women's rights. Berg's suggestions took on greater authority when the Department of Health, Education, and Welfare sent a team of inspectors on April 10, 1972, to investigate the existence of possible discrimination against women and minorities at the university. The department required UConn to prepare and file with the government an acceptable affirmative action plan to remedy whatever imbalance and discrimination existed. Then, in early May, Babbidge announced the appointment of Gail Anne Shea as assistant provost of the university, charged with the specific responsibility "to guide the institution in equalizing the status of all women at the University of Connecticut." She would lead UConn to full compliance with all state and federal regulations as they applied to sex discrimination, and she would draft the affirmative action plan called for in those regulations. Moreover, she had the task of "recommending a wide range of plans and strategies to the Provost and the President that will ensure equal rights to women throughout the University, and promote full community awareness and respect for women as students and staff members." The feminists had won their point, or at least it seemed so at the time, and Babbidge escaped the type of confrontations common to the antiwar and racial recognition movements. He would be out of office when two dozen demonstrators occupied Gulley Hall on February 20, 1973, and presented eight women's rights demands to Acting President Edward V. Gant. By then the pressures of the presidency no longer fell on the shoulders of Homer Daniels Babbidge.[103]

On October 1, 1971, the ninth anniversary of his becoming president, Babbidge submitted his resignation, to be effective no later than one year from that date. He told the board of trustees chair, Gordon Tasker, that his years at UConn had been great ones, and it was hard to bring them to a close. But, from the beginning of his tenure, he recognized "the need to view leadership in public affairs as a relay race, in which each man in his turn passes on the baton of leadership." The time had arrived for him to pass the baton. He admitted that much that happened in recent months caused him great concern, "but these developments have argued for staying rather than leaving, fighting rather than switching. I am resigning in spite of, rather than because of, the challenges that face the University today." This may have been the case, but the continuing confrontations related to the Vietnam War and racial issues, and the mounting questions regarding gender equity, must have taken their toll. University presidents became prime targets of discontent during the 1960s. In Babbidge's own words, "it seems that every time an institution befouls itself, the president is dismissed; we might properly be known as the *disposable diapers of American higher education.*"[104]

   Babbidge, however, was not dismissed but rather likely worn out by the incessant hammering of the era's confrontational politics. While he had become the bête noir of campus radicals, he retained his popularity among the large majority of students, over seven thousand of whom signed a petition that stated, "Under your leadership the University of Connecticut is making great progress. Therefore, we deeply regret your decision to resign . . . and we urge you to withdraw your resignation." A special session of the University Senate unanimously asked him to withdraw his resignation. This was high praise in the era of "disposable diaper" university presidents. Babbidge, discussing his future, responded, "I'm not going to move from here to another college presidency, and I have no plans to enter politics." He then tellingly added, "Besides, my brand of politics isn't very popular now." He may have been referring to his liberal differences with the new left, but a turn of events in Connecticut's traditional politics made the comment especially relevant. The state's voters elected Thomas Meskill as governor in 1970; Meskill, a Republican, replaced Democrat John Dempsey, with whom Babbidge had a cordial, and from the point of view of the university, very productive relationship. The change brought a reversal in attitude, one that bordered on antagonism, toward UConn. The new governor proposed that the terms of trustees be shortened (so that he could more quickly take control of the institution), that salaries of faculty members be reduced and their teaching hours increased, and that students be required to pay tuition, something that Babbidge had opposed since assuming office. One close observer suggested that Meskill's ascendancy forced Babbidge to resign.[105]

Certainly the combination of his experience with new left radicals and the newly elected rightwing governor made Babbidge, the liberal man-in-the-middle, happy to announce that his alma mater had appointed him master of Timothy Dwight College and a fellow of the Institution for Social and Policy Studies, effective July 1, 1972. At a dinner in his and his wife's honor, he assured members of the UConn Foundation that Kingman Brewster, Yale's president, agreed that he could root for Connecticut in all Yale-Connecticut athletic contests. Just in case any ambivalence existed on his part, UConn students presented him with a going-away gift sweatshirt that had the University of Connecticut insignia on the front and Yale's on the back. Babbidge stayed in New Haven for about four years, during which he began an ill-fated campaign for the 1974 Democratic gubernatorial nomination that ultimately went to Connecticut's first woman governor, Ella Grasso. In 1976, he became president of the Hartford Graduate Center. Homer Daniels Babbidge Jr. died of cancer at age 58 in March 1984. Shortly after his death, the University of Connecticut Board of Trustees, in a fitting tribute, named the university's new library, which stands central to the campus, in his honor. Homer's odyssey had brought him back to Storrs after an absence of twelve years, where his name, if not always his deeds, is remembered.[106]

5

Holding Its Own—UConn's Years of Consolidation: 1973–90

*T*HE DECADES immediately surrounding UConn's one hundredth anniversary in 1981 found the university consolidating previous gains and struggling to deal with weakened budgets. Three presidents, Glenn W. Ferguson, John A. DiBiaggo, and John T. Casteen III, each serving approximately five years, confronted an array of difficult issues including affirmative action, racial polarization, and collective bargaining. Their era witnessed the beginning of collective bargaining at the university, and the impact of Title IX on women's athletics, changes that would have significant consequences for UConn, as would the building and crumbling of a new library, the erection of a modern sports arena, and the implementation of all-university curriculum reform. The institution would take pride in faculty achievements such as the election of psychologist Alvin Liberman to the National Academy of Sciences in 1976, but it remained an *aspiring* rather than a *great* university during this period. Glenn Ferguson, in a plaint also appropriate for his two successors, remarked, "I have been engaged in putting out fires which were generated by inadequate financial resources and by real expectations which could not be fulfilled. I have been fighting to preserve what we have . . . but the exercise has deteriorated into a holding pattern." By 1990, many more fires had been extinguished, a number of achievements had accrued, and the university had positioned itself for future transformation.[1]

The Ferguson Years

It was not without irony in April 1972 that Homer Babbidge named his entry into the annual Campus Community Carnival turtle race "The Search Committee."

The process to find his successor moved slowly. In May, Gordon W. Tasker, chairman of the University of Connecticut Board of Trustees, announced the appointment of Provost Edward V. Gant as acting president beginning July 1. Tasker said the designation of an acting president should not be taken to imply any problems in identifying Babbidge's successor. "It's just a matter of finding the right man for the position, and having the time to do it," he explained. One university spokesman suggested the possibility that a new president could be appointed by July. His optimism was exaggerated. The trustees did not select a new president until May 1973, and Glenn Ferguson would not actually take office until September 1 of that year.[2]

The search was a troubled one. The Presidential Search Advisory Committee chaired by College of Liberal Arts and Sciences Dean Robert W. Lougee received more than three hundred nominations, including notables such as U.S. Senator Eugene McCarthy, consumer advocate and Connecticut native Ralph Nader, and former U.S. Attorney General Ramsey Clark. When the committee narrowed the list to forty-two, area newspapers printed the names of the candidates, to the dismay of the committee and the trustees. Rumors spread that politics played a greater role than usual in the selection process, and that Republican Governor Thomas Meskill had his own favorite candidate, F. Don James, president of Central Connecticut State University. After the unwanted publicity, the committee, by the early fall of 1972, reduced the number to a short list of six. Deliberations moved slowly, and not until May, when the economy-minded governor cast the decisive vote, did the trustees select the new president, by a slim 6–5 majority. Asked about his role in the selection process, the governor said he made some suggestions about how candidates should be approached and asked only that he be allowed to meet the top candidates. He was introduced to three. Ferguson, a registered Democrat, asserted, "At no point was I asked my political proclivities or registration." If there was no partisan litmus test, another matter appeared more significant. Trustees chair Gordon Tasker remarked that there was a mandate from the public to be "cost conscious," and the new university president would be expected to reduce costs when possible. Ferguson "welcome[d] accountability to citizens on expenditure of tax funds" and advocated "sound management and willingness to approach administration of higher education with management in mind."[3]

His background as an administrator and a manager were attractive to his supporters at UConn. While competing in football, baseball, and track as an undergraduate at Cornell, Ferguson majored in economics. He earned his master's degree in personnel administration there and studied international relations at Georgetown and the Universities of Chicago and Pittsburgh. He received a law degree at Pitt in 1957 and served as administrative assistant to the chancellor and assistant dean in the Graduate School of Public and International Affairs. He then worked as a management consultant for the large consulting firm McKinsey and Company. In 1961, Ferguson became the first Peace Corps director in Thailand. He served as associate Peace Corps director in Washington and special assistant to the Corps director, Sargent Shriver, who would be an important contact for his future advancement. Between 1964 and 1966, he was the first director of Volunteers in Service to America (VISTA). In 1966, President Lyndon B. Johnson appointed Ferguson to be ambassador to Kenya. Three years later, he became chancellor of Long Island University for a brief and stormy tenure, and then he left to accept the presidency of Clark University in Worcester, Massachusetts. Hence, by the time Glenn Ferguson arrived at UConn in 1973, he had held several relatively high-profile positions, each, however, for a very short period of time. Assuming his newest position would not be easy, especially with the support of a bare majority of the trustees. The state's fiscal problems did not disappear when the Democrat and first woman governor Ella Grasso won election and began serving in 1975. Ferguson's poor relationship with Robert Houley, the chair of the General Assembly's Appropriations Committee, would exacerbate UConn's budgetary problems. The faculty found the formal, more private new president less approachable than Homer Babbidge. His first address to them seemed gloomy and lost the confidence of some. One member of his administration committed suicide. His academic vice-president, Kenneth G. Wilson, described Ferguson's plight as analogous to "the wrestler who comes in and gets kicked in the groin the first moment he steps into the ring. From then on, he was bent over, and there just was no way." He indeed faced an uphill battle.[4]

The Coming of Collective Bargaining

The emphasis on "management" and cost cutting during the presidential search reflected the economy of the times, the direction advocated by the governor, and the anticipation of a coming change, unwanted by some in authority at the university, in the relationship between state employees and their employer. While Governor Meskill vetoed a collective bargaining bill passed by the General Assembly in 1972, he established a Commission on Public Employment Relations that was charged with developing a comprehensive system of collective negotiations for state employees. It would take a few years before such a bill became law, but the likelihood of its success seemed good. Pressure for accountability regarding vacation and sick time on the part of UConn's professional staff in the fall of 1972 prompted the newly formed University of Connecticut Professional Employees' Association (UCPEA) to assert, "Collective bargaining appears to be the only alternative to insure an equitable solution." The teaching faculty, on the other hand, was not as easily convinced.[5]

UConn's Federation of University Teachers (FUT), Local 1386 of the American

Federation of Teachers, AFL-CIO, welcomed President Ferguson in its September 1973 newsletter and announced that it would soon have a "get acquainted" meeting with him to explain the history and background, and aims and goals, of the organization. The FUT added that it looked to continue the cordial relations it had had with President Babbidge and Acting President Gant. In the same issue, the FUT also reminded readers about the collective bargaining drive it had begun toward the end of the previous semester. Although no collective bargaining law had yet been passed by the state, the group argued that the courts had repeatedly ruled that state boards and agencies may enter into collective bargaining arrangements with their employees. Rather than wait for passage of a state bargaining law, the FUT distributed cards for their designation as a bargaining agent; if 50 percent of them were signed, the board of trustees would be asked to negotiate with the FUT as the exclusive representative for all faculty; when 30 percent were signed, the union would ask the trustees to hold an election to determine an exclusive representative of the faculty. It reminded everyone that as of March 1973 over two hundred American Federation of Teachers (AFT) College Locals existed. About fifteen of those had negotiated contracts covering roughly 22,000 college teachers. While the National Education Association (NEA) and the American Association of University Professors (AAUP) also served as bargaining agents for a number of universities, the FUT, as part of the AFT, was involved with the two largest, the City University of New York, with 15,000 faculty members, and the University of Hawaii, with 2,600. In union, the FUT contended, there was strength.[6]

Others, however, thought that without a state bargaining law, the union was acting prematurely. Moreover, some faculty strongly believed that collective bargaining was inappropriate and undignified for professionals, especially professors. They argued that a model suited for the factory did not fit the university. The AAUP Executive Committee responded to the FUT's bargaining campaign with alarm. It pointed out first that while the trustees could enter into a collective bargaining agreement absent a state law, they would not *voluntarily* do so. The association believed it better understood the board's attitudes because AAUP observers had attended all board meetings since August 1972, while the FUT did not send representatives. Secondly, even if the trustees entered into an agreement, without a state law it would seem like a negotiation that the state government would not recognize or fund. The AAUP asked, "How is a rump process of collective bargaining with a few thousand employees at Storrs going to change the very firm fiscal policies of Governor Meskill?" Finally, since FUT, the *smallest* faculty organization, undertook its petitioning campaign *alone*—without asking the AAUP or UCPEA to join in the effort—success was unlikely. The association denounced the FUT effort by commenting that it sincerely regretted "that the FUT has chosen to divide and confuse at a time when concerted effort and solidarity are desperately needed."[7]

The AAUP did, however, agree with the FUT on one major point—that the faculty and professional staff wanted a voice in decision making. It proposed that the two groups establish a regular process of consultation with the trustees and the administration by inaugurating a consultative committee and thereby substitute collective *consultation* for collective bargaining. To the FUT, consultation without a contract seemed to be not much of an improvement over what already existed. The AAUP, moreover, saw the suggestion as a stopgap and recognized the inevitability of collective bargaining coming to Connecticut. In November 1974 the organization's president, Anthony T. "Tony" DiBenedetto, told President Ferguson that there was a high probability that the next session of the General Assembly would pass a collective bargaining bill for state employees. He urged that the board of trustees, the administration, and the professional staff organizations work together to shape the bill so that UConn's bargaining unit would negotiate with the trustees. Otherwise, the faculty and professional staff would become "an atypical minority without influence" in a statewide unit. He advocated constructing a bill in that manner to "preserve the professional standards and distinctiveness of the University."[8]

Because all of the New England states except Connecticut had enacted collective bargaining legislation for state employees, and both Connecticut political parties were on record as favoring such action, DiBenedetto's prediction of a bargaining law's passage seemed well grounded. A great deal of support existed for the preservation of university autonomy and the desire for the faculty to bargain with the trustees rather than with a more inclusive educational or governmental unit. The Faculty Standards Committee recommended this alternative to the University Senate in a report that delineated the pros and cons of bargaining for the faculty but didn't reach a conclusion regarding its merits. Among the negative points, which would have to be overcome if UConn adopted bargaining, the committee listed first the destruction of collegiality and the possibility that the significance of the senate and other faculty deliberative bodies would be reduced. Then opponents argued that the process would be run by professional negotiators and union officials, which would have the effect of replacing the existing administration with a two-layered one. The collective nature of bargaining would not be congenial to individualistic and research-oriented faculty and likely would emphasize the interests of teachers more than scholars. It would do little to encourage the principle of a strong merit component in faculty salaries. It would polarize the relationship between faculty and administration rather than encourage an open and consultative one. Unionization would destroy public respect for faculty and support for the university. The effectiveness of unionization hinged in part on outside support from members of other unions. However, the faculty, which was relatively well paid, would receive little support from union blue-collar workers. Finally, the ultimate weapon in collective bargaining, the strike, made little sense for the university. It would hurt the people of the state and destroy the university's mission and public image. These were the arguments that would have to be addressed if UConn were to accept a collective bargaining agent.[9]

As the bill moved to passage, the AAUP lobbied for local self-determination— that is, for the faculty to bargain with the trustees rather than be swallowed up in a broader unit. The final law accepted that principle, and its passage in 1975 set the scene for an intense contest between the AAUP and the FUT to represent the faculty as agent. That contest occurred in an atmosphere in which "no bargaining," which would appear on the ballot as a choice along with the two organizations, seemed a viable option, but certainly an unattractive one to those working hard to organize and become a recognized bargaining agent. A major point of contention derived from the inclusion of librarians in the faculty bargaining unit, a composition common to other institutions with contracts. While both organizations and the librarians themselves supported the idea, the administration vehemently opposed it. If an election were to be held, the matter required resolution. The AAUP, fearful that a delay could extend into the next year and adversely affect the university's budget, offered a compromise to allow an election, with the librarians voting subject to challenge, pending litigation. The FUT immediately attacked the compromise as a "pre-emptive cave-in" to the administration. As the campaign heated up, the dispute led to a series of charges and countercharges that was unusual in academic life at UConn. The AAUP talked about their opponent's "Big Lie" and the "FUT's deliberate and malicious distortion of the truth." The FUT complained about how "the AAUP has unleashed a torrent of exaggerations, distortions, omissions, and untruths concerning negotiations." The contentiousness probably reinforced the belief of some that unionization was inappropriate for the ivory tower campuses of America. On the other hand, it reflected the intensity and importance attached to the issue.[10]

At UConn, the state budgetary situation during the mid-1970s demanded change, and the advocates of collective bargaining thought that it was the right prescription. AAUP representatives appeared before the General Assembly's Joint Appropriations Committee and told the legislators that the university was no longer able to provide adequate services. "Reductions in budgets and costs of inflation mean that cuts are going through the bone and amputations are taking place," they maintained. In constant dollars (based on 1967), the governor's proposed budget for 1975–76 for the university, exclusive of the Health Center, came in at $30.3 million, compared to $34.5 million in 1971–72. Both the AAUP and the FUT saw the economic advantages in unionization. In 1974–75, the AAUP's Annual Report on the Economic Status of the Profession found the University of Connecticut average compensation falling from seventieth in the nation to one hundred ninth. The AAUP promised to restore budgets and to improve salaries and pointed to AAUP first-round negotiated contracts that had resulted in a 12 percent one-year increase at Rutgers, 18 percent over two years at the University of Rhode Island, 21 percent over two years at St. John's University, and 30 percent over eighteen months at Temple University. The association asserted, "A professional staff should be paid professional salaries."[11]

Collective bargaining, however, entailed more than finances. In the scope of negotiations FUT included promotion, tenure and reappointment procedures, academic freedom, and faculty control of academic programs and standards. The AAUP stated that all satisfactory practices and policies such as those included in the university laws and bylaws, flexibility in work assignments, and rules regarding professional consultation should be written into the contract and thus guaranteed. The things that were lacking in the laws and bylaws, such as retrenchment policies, or that needed improvement, such as the grievance procedure, would be bargaining goals. The AAUP stressed the principles of academic freedom and tenure and the primary responsibility of a faculty to determine academic policy. It emphasized its history as an organization that preserved these, stating further, "The record of AFL-CIO Locals [such as the FUT] in supporting tenure in college contracts is dismal, distressing, and downright disastrous." AAUP provided examples such as the contract at Long Island University, which it claimed allowed administrators to terminate tenured faculty by unilaterally declaring financial exigency, and the C. W. Post College contract, which stated, "Tenure quotas may be set by administration; faculty may be put on permanent probationary status." This type of warning resonated with those faculty who thought a labor union inappropriate for college professors; they envisaged the AAUP less as a union than as a professional association with a long tradition of protecting academic freedom and tenure that was beginning to engage in collective bargaining. While the FUT stressed the value of its "clout" in Hartford, obtained through its affiliation with organized labor and its lobbyists at the state capitol, the AAUP demeaned the argument by questioning whether the lobbyists understood the needs of the university, warning, "Their clout can kill us all or turn a University into a glorified High School." Such a threat resonated as well.[12]

The AAUP made its case effectively enough to win the election held at the university between April 6 and April 9, 1976. With the librarians voting separately and ultimately determined not to be part of the unit (so their votes did not count), the AAUP received 549 votes, the FUT 296, and "No Agent" 174. The State Labor Relations Board declared AAUP the collective bargaining agent for the University of Connecticut, and UConn became the second land-grant institution in New England to enter bargaining with its faculty. Whether the AAUP would have achieved its absolute majority without the FUT as opposition is open to question. It is likely that concern about the more militant, labor-oriented AFL-CIO affiliate made the AAUP more acceptable to faculty who otherwise might have voted for "No Agent." While such an interpretation is only conjecture, it was widely held by many active in the election and later union activities.[13]

At the beginning of the fall 1976 semester, the FUT pledged to stand in "constructive opposition" and serve as a very interested observer during the first round of negotiations. It told the faculty, "Since you now must pay part of your salary to the AAUP [under the Agency Shop provision of the state law], the FUT will make certain that you at least get your money's worth." The AAUP had the harder job of negotiating the contract. The board of trustees authorized the administration to negotiate on its behalf, to keep it informed of progress in the matter, "and to reach agreement on a proposed contract that protects the Board's rights and responsibilities under the General Statutes." As was common with collective bargaining, at least as it became practiced at UConn, the negotiations for the first contract languished for quite some time. After months of planning and negotiating, at the end of February 1977 the AAUP reported to faculty that little significant progress had been made at the bargaining table. The stalemate revolved around two sticking points: shared responsibilities and economics.[14]

Since the financial side of such contracts usually did not get resolved until the final hours at the table, the real debate revolved around shared responsibilities. The administration's representatives, Joan Geetter, chair of the team and an assistant vice-president of academic affairs, John McKenna, the university attorney, William Orr, associate provost, and Neil Macy, a management consultant, refused to negotiate personnel policies. They claimed that faculty rights such as due process, peer review, tenure, and promotion should not be subject to joint decision making between the administration and the faculty's representatives. They proposed that personnel policies and procedures be determined by the board of trustees after only "discussion" with the faculty. At the same time, they proposed the following article on past practices: "All prior practices, agreements, and understanding are void and of no force or effect unless they are specifically incorporated herein [in the contract]." This would have invalidated all of the prerogatives the faculty had previously won and, as might be expected, did not sit well with the national association's Collective Bargaining Council (CBC). The AAUP filed a prohibited practice claim charging the administration with failing to negotiate in good faith. The CBC wrote to the administrator most involved in the process, Vice-President for Academic Affairs Kenneth G. Wilson, and complained that his bargaining team, aside from Orr, who had missed several meetings, had little experience with academic procedures, further implying that they did not understand the importance of such procedures to the academy. They urged that Wilson and President Ferguson join the deliberations.[15]

Wilson, although he was a charter member of the FUT in 1960 when it led the battle against President Jorgensen, was unsympathetic to collective bargaining as an administrator. He believed it undermined peer evaluation and perpetuated mediocrity. Because it was adversarial in nature, it encouraged unions to publicly tarnish the university's image. His response to the CBC's request was therefore predictable: neither he nor President Ferguson would "undercut the negotiating teams' efforts by entering private discussion with officers or other members of the AAUP on any matters currently under negotiation. . . . The negotiating team headed by Ms. Geetter [who had earned a doctorate from UConn's English Department] has full authority to bargain with the AAUP team." Geetter, who had little formal training in collective bargaining but learned quickly while understanding that her job made her the "dragon lady" of UConn, then issued a statement to the faculty making the argument for the board of trustees' primacy and their desire to maintain collegiality on campus, which they argued would be destroyed by union control. She also suggested that if the parties did not negotiate a contract before April 1, as requested by the legislature, the opportunity for the General Assembly to review and fund the contract would in all probability be lost until January 1978. By the third week of March 1977, the administration's team began to show a willingness to compromise about shared responsibility, and it then offered a financial package too. The AAUP did not jump at the bait, but the beginning of the end had arrived.[16]

The threat of the April 1 deadline diminished when CBC member Maria Russell, who was well connected to the State Democratic Party, arranged for Tony DiBenedetto to meet with the then-president pro tem of the Connecticut Senate, Joseph Lieberman. Because neither the AAUP nor the board of trustees and administration had experience in collective bargaining, there was legitimate concern about what the legislature would do. The AAUP did not wish to surrender its battle for language regarding shared responsibilities in the contract, but it feared that a financial settlement would be lost if the negotiations took too long. DiBenedetto left the meeting assured that time was not of the essence. Lieberman told him, "If we go out of session and you don't have a contract, we'll have a special session." With that promise, and having some idea of what the other unions across the state were getting in their financial packages, the AAUP could follow its game plan. Although never made public and not in accord with the etiquette of collective bargaining, informal conversations then occurred between the AAUP chief negotiator, Bill Rosen, and Ken Wilson, both members of the university's English Department. The night before the AAUP representatives scheduled one of several mass meetings to discuss the progress of the negotiations with its membership, Rosen met Wilson at a concert. Rosen told the vice-president, "We're at an impasse. We really ought to talk. There's no reason why we can't settle this." They went to Wilson's house after the concert, drank beer, and talked until two in the morning—"and got nowhere, absolutely nowhere." At the last mass meeting before the two sides reached an agreement, Schenker 55, a large lecture hall attached to the Monteith Social Sciences Building, was mobbed with faculty. As Rosen, ever the Shakespearean scholar, borrowed from one of Marc Antony's speeches in *Julius Caesar*, substituting "The contract. The contract" for "The will. The will," an unidentified person put a note on the speaker's table. It read, "When you're finished with your meeting, come over to Gulley Hall." That broke the impasse.[17]

Immediately afterward, DiBenedetto and Rosen walked over to the administration building. Rosen "felt like one of those figures in a Western, the gunslingers going over to Gulley Hall." On their way, a colleague flashed the "V" sign. Things started to come together after that, but then they almost fell apart. After the administration and the AAUP agreed on all of the contract language, the administration team announced the compensation package at a final meeting of the teams late on a Saturday night. As Rosen describes the scene, accounting professor Corrine Norgaard "had a very large calculator and was going bumpety-bumpety-bump and Tony DiBendetto had a medium size calculator going bumpety-bumpety-bump, and Emory Braswell had his smaller size and then suddenly there was an eruption, a scream, a yelling. They were trying to shortchange us." Rosen grew infuriated and called for Wilson's and Ferguson's resignations. He despondently went home, where his wife, Barbara, had waited up. He downed two Scotches and in a slurred voice told her, "Call Ken Wilson." She responded, "Maybe, dear, you ought to call him in the morning. He may not like being called at this hour." Rosen said, "Oh," and went to bed. The next morning, Sunday at 8:00 A.M., President Ferguson phoned DiBenedetto and invited him to breakfast and to reconsider the financial package. Wilson, Geetter, and the university comptroller, Ed Hanna, joined them in recalculating the compensation according to AAUP's expectations. The contending sides reached a full agreement on UConn's first faculty contract, which recognized the rights of the board of trustees and also the necessity of a collegial governance system for faculty in areas of academic concern.[18]

The first round of negotiations and the resulting contract ushered in an era of collective bargaining that encouraged stability for a generation and promoted the wellbeing of the university, despite some predictable ups and downs in union-administration relations. The AAUP, as the faculty union, developed into a critical balancing force among the administration, the faculty, the legislature, and the governor. Twice the union's willingness to forego pay increases, in 1992 and 2003, was instrumental in breaking political logjams and preserving university programs. UConn's twelfth president, Harry J. Hartley, also served as president of the AAUP. UConn's thirteenth president, Philip E. Austin, has remarked, "It's [the relationship between the University and the AAUP] a very good—in my view—mutually satisfactory, mutually advantageous relationship." That a constructive relationship developed between the administration and the union owed much to the AAUP executive director hired in 1986, Edward Marth. Marth, an experienced negotiator who directed the University of Rhode Island's AAUP chapter before coming to UConn, won the confidence of the administration as well as the faculty and served as a bridge between the two. He had an unusual ability to make things work and to solve problems rather than create them. It is unlikely that the players of 1976 and 1977 could have foreseen such a future for the process that many feared and others despised. One thing seems certain. Glenn Ferguson, in his role as university president, wisely left the heavy lifting on this matter to Kenneth G. Wilson, his academic vice-president, and the negotiating team. He was invisible in that process until the final Sunday morning—*except* for the threat of a no-confidence vote wielded by the AAUP during the heat of the battle. Collective bargaining, by helping to increase salaries, played a positive role in the university's later emergence as a national institution. A year before its advent, UConn lagged behind other doctoral granting institutions in faculty compensation at all ranks; by 1985–86, it exceeded salary averages except for the rank of full professor; ten years later, as a result of contract negotiations, it stood above the average at all ranks. As salaries climbed in comparison to other institutions, the university could retain leading faculty and attract a nationally competitive group on which to build its academic reputation.[19]

"The Coalition's" Umbrella

Ferguson's reluctance to play a public role may have reflected wise bargaining strategy, or he may have been gunshy from his three years of prior experience at UConn. He had inherited a number of problems, though some were certainly of his own making. From the time he arrived in September 1973, the new president grappled with a tangled web of issues—discontent with the operation of the university bookstore, a divided Anthropology Department and the specter of racism, a flawed Affirmative Action Plan and the rallying of feminism, and the continued discontent of minority students. In March 1974 a group called "the Coalition" brought these matters together under one umbrella. After a peaceful demonstration at Gulley Hall, it presented Ferguson with a set of demands.

A month later black students occupied the library in the evening; after authorities ejected them, whites, in a show of support, occupied the premises the next night. Ferguson faced many of the same difficulties that confronted Babbidge during his final years as president, but he did so without the reservoir of support his predecessor had enjoyed.[20]

The Birth of the UConn Coop

Bookstore problems predated Ferguson's arrival. In June 1972 the board of trustees, citing the need for more used books and more efficient service, voted to outsource the university-run bookstore to Follett's, a private corporation, which took over that November. State workers lost their jobs in the process. At the end of January 1973 the Bookstore Advisory Committee commented on Follett's under-ordering, the late arrival of books, and books being returned to publishers too soon. The next fall a group dissatisfied with the bookstore established a counter-bookstore/book exchange that proved successful. Protesters picketed Follett's and organized a boycott of non-text items. Almost fifteen hundred students, faculty, and staff signed a petition aimed against Follett's and the contracting out of bookstore services. At the beginning of 1974, a University Senate Committee investigated the situation and found little faculty support for Follett's, as 95 percent of those surveyed sought an alternative. A *Daily Campus* survey also found 98 percent of students in agreement. Then, on the Ides of March, sixty people attended a trustees meeting to demonstrate their stand against the private company and contracting out. The trustees passed a motion recognizing that "the University community deserves, and must have, a book store which provides the best possible service at the lowest possible cost." It directed Ferguson to set up a task force to explore the options, review the purchase agreement with Follett's, and make precise recommendations to insure a high-quality bookstore operation.[21]

Because the trustees wanted the recommendations before the end of the semester, Ferguson immediately asked David Ivry, then councilor to the provost, to organize a task force on the bookstore. Within twenty-four hours, Ivry established a thirteen-member committee comprised of four undergraduates, one graduate student, five faculty members, two administrators, and one classified employee. "The Coalition," which failed in its attempt to give Ivry a list of nominees due to his quick action, then challenged the committee as being unrepresentative and undemocratically selected. As a consequence, three additional "Coalition" nominees joined the group, but they and one of the original thirteen quit a few days later in a disagreement over the emphasis and direction of the deliberations. They felt that a prima facie case had already been made against Follett's and all of the attention should be paid to the alternatives. "The Coalition," which believed "that the allegiance of the University to the interests of big business is in contradiction to its responsibility to the public," called for Ferguson to urge termination of the Follett's contract at the next board of trustees meeting and for the trustees to give the company its ninety-day notice. The president responded by explaining how the task force would proceed by holding public hearings in a timely enough fashion to meet the deadline so that he could make a proposal to the trustees before the end of the semester. At its April 19 meeting, the board gave Follett's one year's terminal notice and authorized a provisional board of seventeen members to arrange for a cooperative bookstore to take over the operations of the university bookstore. Although not fully satisfied, "The Coalition" considered the action a victory. Ferguson had reason to do so as well. In the context of all of the difficulties he faced, at least one problem had a solution. The UConn Coop was born.[22]

Presents of the University of Connecticut

(all photos of the presidents courtesy of University Photo Collection, Dodd Center, UConn Libraries)

Solomon Mead, Principal, Storrs Agricultural School (SAS), 1881–1882

Benjamin Franklin Koons, Principal, SAS; President, Storrs Agricultural College (SAC), 1883–1898

George Washington Flint, President, SAC and Connecticut Agricultural College (CAC), 1898–1901

Rufus Whitaker Stimson, President, CAC, 1901–1908

Charles Lewis Beach, President, CAC,
1908–1928

George Alan Works, President, CAC,
1929–1930

Charles Chester McCracken, President,
CAC and Connecticut State College (CSC),
1930–1935

Albert Nels Jorgensen, President, CSC
and University of Connecticut (UConn),
1935–1962

Homer Daniels Babbidge, Jr., President,
UConn, 1962–1972

Glenn Walker Ferguson, President, UConn,
1973–1978

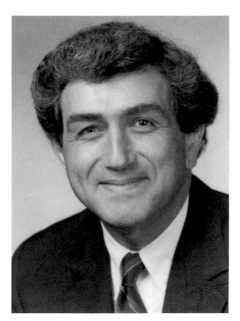

John A. DiBiaggio, President, UConn,
1979–1985

John T. Casteen III, President, UConn,
1985–1990

Harry J. Hartley, President, UConn, 1990–1996

Philip E. Austin, President, UConn, 1996–

FIGURE 1.1 Theodore Sedgwick Gold was an influential advocate and active proponent of a state agricultural school during the mid-nineteenth century. In the face of increasing industrialization and urbanization, Gold wanted to preserve agriculture as a way of life and hoped that agricultural education would help Connecticut farmers become more productive and profitable. He was later an influential trustee when the Storrs Agricultural School opened in 1881. *Photo courtesy of University Photo Collection, Dodd Center, UConn Libraries.*

FIGURES 1.2a, 1.2b Brothers Augustus (photo *a*) and Charles Storrs (photo *b*) were the original benefactors of the Storrs Agricultural School. Both grew up in Mansfield but made their fortunes as businessmen in Brooklyn, New York. Augustus donated 170 acres of land, Whitney Hall, and several farm buildings. Charles contributed $6,000 and eight hundred volumes from his personal library, which were used to start the School's library. *Photos courtesy of University Photo Collection, Dodd Center, UConn Libraries.*

FIGURE 1.3 Whitney Hall, shown in this photo taken during the early 1880s, was the first building of the Storrs Agricultural School when it opened in 1881. Built in the mid-1860s by Edwin Whitney, the building was originally used as the Connecticut Soldiers' Orphans' Home until 1875. The transfer of the building's ownership from Whitney's widow to Augustus Storrs was challenged in court, putting the future of the school at risk almost as soon as it opened. Whitney Hall was razed in 1932. *Photo courtesy of University Photo Collection, Dodd Center, UConn Libraries.*

FIGURE 1.4 Old Main, center, was the signature building on campus soon after its construction in 1890. Here, it is shown flanked by, from left, Grove Cottage, Gold Hall, the Chemistry Laboratory and the Experiment Station Office. Built as part of a $50,000 appropriation by the Connecticut General Assembly, Old Main was eventually torn down in 1929 and replaced by Beach Hall. *Photo courtesy of University Photo Collection, Dodd Center, UConn Libraries.*

FIGURE 1.5 The seeds of the national pastime at the University were planted early in the school's history. The 1890–91 baseball team was one of the few to play with the "SAS" logo across their jerseys. In the program's history, UConn has advanced to the College World Series five times—1957, 1959, 1965, 1972, and 1979. *Photo courtesy of University Photo Collection, Dodd Center, UConn Libraries.*

FIGURE 1.6 The student body of Storrs Agricultural College about 1894, the first year it included female graduates. *Photo courtesy of University Photo Collection, Dodd Center, UConn Libraries.*

FIGURE 1.7 This earliest known commencement photo was taken June 14, 1899, on the college's front lawn. *Photo courtesy of University Photo Collection, Dodd Center, UConn Libraries.*

FIGURE 1.8 CAC President Rufus Stimson holds the reins of Artimon, a three-year-old French coach stallion imported by the Connecticut Agricultural College in 1903. Appointed acting president in October 1901, Stimson received the full title the following year. During his tenure, Stimson devoted much of his administrative attention to the promotion of the fledgling college via correspondence, the development of a summer school, and appeals to schoolteachers throughout the state. *Photo courtesy of University Photo Collection, Dodd Center, UConn Libraries.*

FIGURE 1.9 Nearly a century before it began winning national championships, the women's basketball team first took local bragging rights. The team defeated Willimantic High School, 15–6, in its first game in 1902. This team photo—from 1903 or 1904—includes Coach Steve Crowell, right, chaperone Mrs. Stimson, left, and players Nora Shurtleff, Marjorie Monteith, Lucy Stockwell, Bessie Donovan, Annie Clark, Gertrude Water, and Rose Dimock. *Photo courtesy of University Photo Collection, Dodd Center, UConn Libraries.*

FIGURE 1.10 The *Lookout* editorial staff poses with advisor Henry Monteith, seated at center, in this 1904 photo. The *Lookout* began publishing as a monthly student newspaper in May 1896. *Photo courtesy of University Photo Collection, Dodd Center, UConn Libraries.*

FIGURE 1.11 A blacksmith shop class gathers for a group photo in 1905. *Photo courtesy of University Photo Collection, Dodd Center, UConn Libraries.*

FIGURE 1.12 The Connecticut Agricultural College Cadet Band, which performed at football games and military parades, was organized around 1900. This photo was taken in 1906. *Photo courtesy of University Photo Collection, Dodd Center, UConn Libraries.*

Figure 1.13 A female student's room in Grove Cottage as it appeared about 1906. According to the campus newspaper Grove Cottage had been built for "young ladies" and was "the handsomest building upon the campus." It served as a women's dormitory from 1895 until it was destroyed by fire in 1919. *Photo courtesy of University Photo Collection, Dodd Center, UConn Libraries.*

FIGURE 1.14 The Hawley Armory as it looked about 1912, a time when people were allowed to park their cars right in front of the building. *Photo courtesy of University Photo Collection, Dodd Center, UConn Libraries.*

FIGURE 1.15 The rolling hills of Storrs provided the backdrop for an international egg-laying contest, which was held at the university from 1911 to 1961. *Photo courtesy of University Photo Collection, Dodd Center, UConn Libraries.*

FIGURE 1.16 Daniel E. Noble was instrumental in the development of the first radio station on campus, WABL, whose studio is shown here in this photo taken around the time of its beginning in June 1922. Noble, a graduate and professor at the college, managed the radio station—renamed WCAC in 1925—from 1933–42. *Photo courtesy of University Photo Collection, Dodd Center, UConn Libraries.*

FIGURES 1.17a, 1.17b Killed after being hit by an automobile, Jonathan I was buried on February 8, 1935 (photo *a*), just two months after he was named the school's first mascot. Each of the class presidents served as pallbearers. His successor, Jonathan II (photo *b*) was the first of the school mascots to be an all-white husky. *Photos courtesy of University Photo Collection, Dodd Center, UConn Libraries.*

FIGURE 2.1 For the second time in six years—and the fifth time since its founding in 1881—Connecticut's land-grant college underwent a name change. Connecticut Governor Raymond Baldwin signs a bill changing the name of Connecticut State College to the University of Connecticut effective July 1, 1939. Baldwin used the same quill as did his predecessor, Wilbur Cross, when the school's name was changed from Connecticut Agricultural College on February 25, 1933. Looking on as Baldwin writes are, from left to right William Crowley, Student Senate president; Andre Schenker, professor of history; President Albert N. Jorgensen; George Pinckney, alumni secretary; and Edward Finn, Student Senate president-elect. The new name reflected the expanding variety of educational opportunities available at the school. *Photo courtesy of University Photo Collection, Dodd Center, UConn Libraries.*

FIGURE 2.2 Students congregate in 1935 for a meal at the "Beanery," the dining hall in what is now the Benton Museum of Art. The building had been turned into a warehouse prior to Homer Babbidge converting it to a museum. *Photo courtesy of University Photo Collection, Dodd Center, UConn Libraries.*

FIGURE 2.3 A construction worker puts the finishing touches on chiseling the name of the Wilbur Cross library. The new library was just one example of the improved physical plant on campus during the 1930s at the initiative of President Albert N. Jorgensen, who won approval of a multiyear, multimillion-dollar building program during a time of balanced or shrinking budgets. *Photo courtesy of University Photo Collection, Dodd Center, UConn Libraries.*

FIGURE 2.4 Mildred P. French, center, served as dean of women and dean of the School of Home Economics from 1928 to 1953. She set the tone for female conduct on campus, often strictly enforcing in loco parentis rules. The women flanking her are unidentified. *Photo courtesy of University Photo Collection, Dodd Center, UConn Libraries.*

FIGURE 2.5 Defense and preparation for World War II took place on campus as well. Here, a spotter is on the lookout for planes on an observation perch atop Beach Hall in 1942. Area citizens volunteered for two-hour shifts around the clock to scan the skies over Storrs for enemy planes. *Photo courtesy of University Photo Collection, Dodd Center, UConn Libraries.*

FIGURE 2.6 After a long day on the farm, a Connecticut Women's Land Army (CWLA) trainee shows the calluses on her hands to First Lady Eleanor Roosevelt, who visited the campus in March 1943. The CWLA, modeled after the British Land Army, provided farm training for women during World War II. *Photo courtesy of University Photo Collection, Dodd Center, UConn Libraries.*

FIGURES 2.7a, 2.7b During World War II, nearly 120,000 Japanese Americans were sent to internment camps as a result of anti-Asian sentiment in the wake of the Japanese attack on Pearl Harbor. In photo *a*, William Hayakawa, left, and Kay Kiyokawa, right (shown with baseball coach Dick Wargo), were two of nineteen second-generation Japanese American (Nisei) students who continued their education with the blessing of the American government. In October 2003 Shiro Aisawa, left, and Kiyokawa returned to Storrs for a reunion, as shown in photo *b*.

Photo a courtesy of University Photo Collection, Dodd Center, UConn Libraries. Photo b courtesy of Dollie Harvey/UConn.

FIGURE 2.8 Soldiers march on campus with the flag at half-staff during a memorial service following the death of U.S. President Franklin D. Roosevelt in April 1945.
Photo courtesy of University Photo Collection, Dodd Center, UConn Libraries.

FIGURE 3.1 As this photo indicates, women were a novelty to the students at the Fort Trumbull campus in 1949. The New London facility was created in May 1946 for returning World War II veterans who had delayed their education to fight. Students entered a basic two-year curriculum before moving on to advanced work at Storrs or another institution. The branch, which was designed to be temporary, closed in June 1950. *Photo courtesy of University Photo Collection, Dodd Center, UConn Libraries.*

FIGURE 3.2 In order to accommodate the influx of returning veterans to the student body, many married veterans—such as this couple trying to work their stove—lived in housing off campus in nearby Willimantic. *Photo courtesy of University Photo Collection, Dodd Center, UConn Libraries.*

FIGURE 3.3 Female students exit the Home Economics Building (now Family Studies) in this photo taken during the 1940s. The building and its course of study attracted women students at a time when opportunities for study in other fields were less available to them. *Photo courtesy of University Photo Collection, Dodd Center, UConn Libraries.*

FIGURE 3.4 Before Gampel Pavilion, the Field House was home to the university's men's and women's basketball teams. Both teams played there for thirty-six years beginning in 1954. The Field House is now the site of the Student Recreation Facility. *Photo courtesy of University Photo Collection, Dodd Center, UConn Libraries.*

FIGURE 3.5 The university celebrated its seventy-fifth anniversary with a parade, complete with floats, in October 1956. *Photo courtesy of University Photo Collection, Dodd Center, UConn Libraries.*

FIGURE 3.6 Named for Charles Burt Gentry, former dean of the university and two-time acting president, the Gentry Building was constructed in 1960 and serves as home to the Neag School of Education. It underwent significant renovations as part of Uconn 2000 during the early-twenty-first century. *Photo courtesy of University Photo Collection, Dodd Center, UConn Libraries.*

FIGURE 3.7 The Arjona and Monteith buildings were constructed as mirror images of each other in 1959. Arjona, left, was named for the former head of the Foreign Languages Department, Jaime Homero Arjona, and is also known as the Humanities Building. The Social Sciences Building was named in honor of Henry Monteith, a professor of English and history and advisor to the campus newspaper, the *Lookout*, in the late nineteenth and early twentieth centuries. The buildings are among the most used classroom facilities on campus. *Photo courtesy of University Photo Collection, Dodd Center, UConn Libraries.*

FIGURE 3.8 The reading room at the Wilbur Cross Library is crowded with students in this January 1961 photo. In 1962 the reading rooms were renovated but remained places of study until the library moved from the building in 1978. *Photo courtesy of University Photo Collection, Dodd Center, UConn Libraries.*

FIGURE 3.9 Albert E. Waugh, shown here in this July 20, 1973, photo with his familiar sundial, was an economics professor who served as the dean of arts and sciences as well as provost of the university. He also was active in local and state politics and served as moderator of the Mansfield Town Meeting. His journal, covering the years 1941 to 1969 and housed at UConn's Thomas J. Dodd Research Center, offers a candid look at many campus personalities and issues. *Photo Courtesy of University Photo Collection, Dodd Center, UConn Libraries.*

FIGURES 4.1a, 4.1b University President Homer Babbidge occasionally made appearances at student protest rallies. On one occasion in October 1969 (photo *a*), he played a kazoo—though he declined to smoke a marijuana-filled pipe. In photo *b*, taken in November 1971, Babbidge flashes the Peace sign. *Photo a courtesy of Moe Murray,* Hartford Courant. *Photo b courtesy of University Photo Collection, Dodd Center, UConn Libraries.*

FIGURE 4.2 In 1967, University President Homer Babbidge introduced one hundred "blue bikes" to be used by students for transportation around campus. The ground rules stated that the bikes were only to be used on an assigned course in academic areas during the week, but they could be taken anywhere on or off campus on weekends, provided they were returned to the designated bike racks the following Monday morning. The experiment had its share of snags, however, chief among them maintenance and repairs—within the first twenty-four hours of being introduced, twenty bikes were in the shop; within the next few days, fifty-nine cycles went in for repairs. *Photo courtesy of University Photo Collection, Dodd Center, UConn Libraries.*

FIGURE 4.3 An aerial view of the old South Campus, as it looked before it was razed to make way for the state-of-the-art dormitories that exist today. *Photo courtesy of University Photo Collection, Dodd Center, UConn Libraries.*

FIGURE 4.4 Students repaint the ROTC hanger in June 1970 as a counterdemonstration to a protest staged there the previous month. More than three hundred students volunteered to paint over the protest symbols that had been left on the building's interior and exterior. *Photo courtesy of University Photo Collection, Dodd Center, UConn Libraries.*

FIGURE 4.5 University President Homer Babbidge, left, writer Edwin Teale, center, and Director of University Libraries John McDonald examine the library's one-millionth volume, Teale's *Springtime in Britain*, in January 1971. Out of nearly 2,200 four-year colleges and universities in the country, UConn was one of only fifty-eight with a million or more volumes in its library. In New England, only Harvard, Yale, Brown, Dartmouth, and MIT had larger collections. *Photo courtesy of University Photo Collection, Dodd Center, UConn Libraries.*

FIGURE 4.6 The University of Connecticut Health Center in Farmington began construction in 1966 and graduated its first class in 1972. *Photo courtesy of Peter Morenus/UConn.*

FIGURE 4.7 As student protests increased on campus during the 1960s, so, too, did criticism of University President Homer Babbidge. In this January 15, 1969, protest, two students hold up a banner titled "Why Homer Babbidge Leans To One Side," alleging that Babbidge's association with corporations and other non-university organizations was the reason he allowed them to recruit on campus. *Photo courtesy of University Photo Collection, Dodd Center, UConn Libraries.*

FIGURE 4.8 Students protested against on-campus recruitment by companies whose association with the Vietnam War they opposed. Students rallied against the Grumman Aircraft Engineering Company in November 1967. The Dow Chemical Company and the ROTC were also frequent targets of protest. *Photo courtesy of University Photo Collection, Dodd Center, UConn Libraries.*

FIGURE 4.9 University President Homer Babbidge (seated, fifth from left) addresses the University of Connecticut Board of Trustees during a meeting held March 19, 1969, to consider tenure, promotion, and reappointment. A crowd of approximately fifty protesters gathered in the meeting room in support of Charles Brover and David Colfax, university professors who were charged with obstructing recruiting efforts by Dow Chemical and violating board policy. Despite the recommendation of tenure by the Sociology-Anthropology Department, Colfax was denied tenure by the board. Brover was not reappointed to his position in the English department. *Photo courtesy of University Photo Collection, Dodd Center, UConn Libraries.*

FIGURE 4.10 Amid a large crowd gathered to hear speakers such as Dick Gregory, Allard Lowenstein, and Joseph Duffy, a woman breastfeeds a child, foreground, during an anti-Vietnam War rally held October 15, 1969, on campus. The "community strike" had been unanimously approved by the Student Senate a month earlier in support of the national Vietnam Moratorium Committee. UConn was one of about five hundred other colleges and universities to take part in the protest. *Photo courtesy of University Photo Collection, Dodd Center, UConn Libraries.*

FIGURE 4.11 Sociology professor Jack Roach is led away by police on November 26, 1968, after being arrested for his role in protesting on-campus recruitment by the Olin-Mathieson Corporation. Roach was one of twelve people arrested after protestors engaged in a violent clash with security officers and state police. The need to summon state police to quell the protest caused University President Homer Babbidge to remark that it was "the saddest day of my life." *Photo courtesy of University Photo Collection, Dodd Center, UConn Libraries.*

FIGURE 4.12 The university celebrated "Happy Babbidge Day" on May 18, 1972, to honor President Homer Babbidge's birthday. The celebration underscored the immense popularity Babbidge enjoyed during most of his tenure as university president despite the protests. *Photo courtesy of University Photo Collection, Dodd Center, UConn Libraries.*

FIGURE 5.1 Following a 6–5 vote by the board of trustees, Glenn W. Ferguson became the ninth president of UConn in September 1973. Before coming to UConn, Ferguson, shown here in this December 1977 photo, had held several high-profile jobs, including the first Peace Corps director in Thailand, the first director of Volunteers in Service to America (VISTA), ambassador to Kenya, and president of Clark University. Considered to be more private and formal than his predecessor, Homer Babbidge, Ferguson departed in 1978 to become CEO of Radio Free Europe/Radio Liberty. *Photo Courtesy of University Photo Collection, Dodd Center, UConn Libraries.*

FIGURE 5.2 Upset with the university's administration, more than two hundred black students occupied the Wilbur Cross Library after closing time one night in April 1974. The students were forcibly evicted by state police the next morning. University President Glenn W. Ferguson was roundly blamed for calling in the state police, an action that attracted the attention of the Connecticut Civil Liberties Union and the National Association for the Advancement of Colored People on behalf of the protestors. *Photo courtesy of University Photo Collection, Dodd Center, UConn Libraries.*

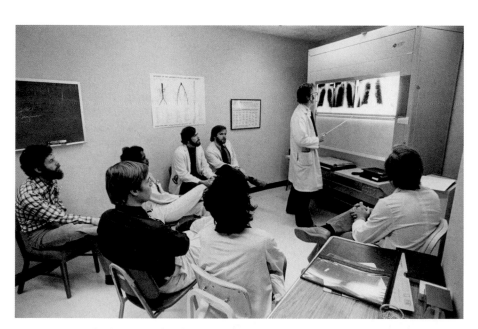

FIGURE 5.3 Medical personnel gather to analyze X-rays in this February 1977 photo taken at the University of Connecticut Health Center. *Photo courtesy of University Photo Collection, Dodd Center, UConn Libraries.*

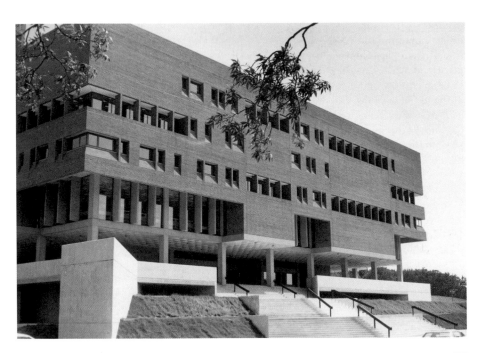

FIGURES 5.4a, 5.4b The Homer Babbidge Library, named for the university's eighth president, shown in photo *a* as it was originally configured. Dedicated in December 1976, the nineteen-million-dollar building replaced the antiquated Wilbur Cross Library. Structural flaws necessitated a host of renovations in ensuing years, as shown in photo *b*. Originally named the University of Connecticut Library, it was renamed in honor of Babbidge after his death in 1984. *Photo a courtesy of University Photo Collection, Dodd Center, UConn Libraries. Photo b courtesy of* Willimantic Chronicle.

FIGURE 5.5 The university moved the Law School from its old quarters in West Hartford to its new campus on the grounds of the former Hartford Seminary in 1984. *Photo Courtesy of Peter Morenus/UConn.*

FIGURES 5.6a, 5.6b The many roles of a university president. In photo *a*, UConn's tenth president, John A. DiBiaggio, celebrates while playing "oozeball"—basically, volleyball in the mud—with students during Spring Weekend of 1985. In photo *b*, DiBiaggio performs a reading with the symphony orchestra during a recital at Jorgensen Auditorium. Before taking over as university president in 1979, the gregarious and outgoing DiBiaggio was a practicing dentist, a university administrator elsewhere, and vice president for health affairs at the University Health Center. *Photos courtesy of University Photo Collection, Dodd Center, UConn Libraries.*

FIGURE 5.7 John T. Casteen shares a moment with his children during his inauguration as UConn's eleventh president in October 1985. Quieter and more reserved than his predecessor, John A. DiBiaggio, Casteen nevertheless shared DiBiaggio's goal of making UConn a top-twenty public research university. By his second year, Casteen, who had three degrees in English from the University of Virginia, began teaching a section of English 109. He left in 1990 to become president of his alma mater. *Photo courtesy of University Photo Collection, Dodd Center, UConn Libraries.*

FIGURE 5.8 A helicopter puts a supporting beam in place on December 1, 1988, as part of the construction of Gampel Pavilion, the long-awaited on-campus arena. Initially approved for funding by the board of trustees in the late 1970s, the facility did not open until January 1990. Despite early estimates of $14 million in 1985, the arena was already projected to cost $21.1 million two years later. In addition to state funds, the project received a $1 million contribution from alumnus Harry A. Gampel, for whom the arena is named. *Photo courtesy of University Photo Collection, Dodd Center, UConn Libraries.*

FIGURE 6.1 Harry J. Hartley, shown here in his familiar UConn jogging outfit with the horse, UC Harry H, was selected as the university's twelfth president in December 1990. During his six-year tenure, Hartley was widely admired by students and the public for his approachability, but some faculty resented what they believed to be his casual style and undue emphasis on sports.

Photo courtesy of Peter Morenus/UConn.

FIGURE 6.2 University President Harry J. Hartley welcomes U.S. President Bill Clinton to the dedication of the Thomas J. Dodd Research Center in October 1995. Clinton was the first sitting U.S. president to visit UConn. The Dodd Center, named for the former U.S. senator from Connecticut, is the archival home for papers, records, and correspondence for a variety of politicians, university faculty members and administrators and businesses. *Photo courtesy of Peter Morenus/UConn.*

FIGURE 6.3 The new law library at the UConn Law School in Hartford, shown in this September 1996 photo, the year it opened and prior to the discovery of problems with its façade. *Photo courtesy of Peter Morenus/UConn.*

FIGURE 6.4 Philip E. Austin—along with former professor of history and mayor of Mansfield Fred Cazel, left, and helpers Amber Travis and Chad Vincinte—takes part in a tree-lighting ceremony behind the Student Union in December 1996, Austin's first winter as the university's thirteenth president. *Photo courtesy of Jonathan Cohen '96/UConn.*

FIGURE 6.5 True to its agricultural roots, one of the university's lead-ing research breakthroughs came in the field of animal science. Led by Professor Xiangzhong "Jerry" Yang, center, a team of animal scientists including, from left, Prof. John W. Riesen, Arnie Nieminen, Yunping Dai and Maneesh Taneja produced Amy, a ninety-four-pound calf who was born on June 10, 1999. She was the first large animal cloned from genetic material extracted from an adult farm animal in the United States. *Photo courtesy of Peter Morenus/UConn.*

FIGURE 6.6 Men's basketball head coach Jim Calhoun holds the 1999 NCAA championship trophy as he and the Huskies celebrated the team's first national title in front of a packed house at Gampel Pavilion. The Huskies went on to win a second NCAA crown in 2004. The following year, Calhoun became the nineteenth coach in NCAA history to win seven hundred games in a career and was inducted into the National Basketball Hall of Fame. *Photo courtesy of Peter Morenus/UConn.*

FIGURE 6.7 Members of the UConn women's basketball team celebrate their 2002 national championship with a parade through downtown Hartford. The success of the men's and women's basketball teams and the positive reaction it inspired led some to believe it was instrumental in spurring the passage of state legislation that allowed for campus improvements, such as UConn 2000. *Photo courtesy of Peter Morenus/UConn.*

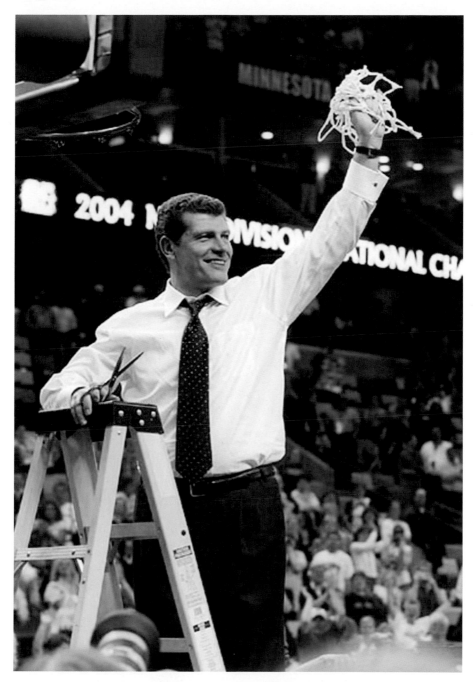

FIGURE 6.8 Women's basketball head coach Geno Auriemma cuts down the net after UConn defeated arch-rival Tennessee in New Orleans for the 2004 NCAA championship. In 1985 Auriemma took over a program that had never enjoyed a winning season before his arrival and built a national powerhouse, winning NCAA championships in 1995, 2000, 2002, 2003, and 2004. *Photo courtesy of Peter Morenus/UConn.*

6.9a

FIGURE 6.9b Memorial Stadium, as shown in photo *a*, was the on-campus home for the UConn football team from 1953 to 2002. In 2003, the Huskies moved from 16,000-seat Memorial Stadium to the 40,000-seat Rentschler Field in East Hartford, shown in photo *b* during their season-opening victory over Indiana. The opening of the new stadium was the culmination of years of debate over the status of the football team, which moved from Division I-AA to I-A in 2000. *Photo a courtesy of University Photo Collection, Dodd Center, UConn Libraries. Photo b courtesy of Peter Morenus/UConn.*

FIGURE 6.10 A memorial vigil was held near the Homer Babbidge Library on the one-year anniversary of the September 11, 2001, terrorist attacks. After the attacks, many Muslim students on campus appealed to University President Philip E. Austin with concerns for their safety and well-being. In response, Austin encouraged a "Metanoia," a time of contemplation and consideration. *Photo courtesy of Peter Morenus/UConn.*

FIGURE 6.11 Students opposed to the U.S. war in Iraq set up "Tent City" on the rolling lawns alongside Route 195 in March 2003 as a form of protest. Approximately 25 anti-war protestors stayed for nearly two months before vandals destroyed it during Spring Weekend. "Tent City" returned in March 2005 to protest the continuing U.S. presence in Iraq. *Photo Courtesy of Peter Morenus/UConn.*

FIGURE 6.12 The UConn Dairy Bar is a popular destination for students and area residents to indulge in fresh ice cream and other summertime treats. *Photo courtesy of Peter Morenus/UConn.*

FIGURE 6.13 Students in this October 2004 photo use state-of-the-art computers at the Information Café at the Homer Babbidge Library. During the early-twenty-first century, the university made a concerted effort to improve information and technology resources to encourage faculty and help attract superior students. *Photo courtesy of Peter Morenus/UConn.*

FIGURE 6.14 A May 2000 view in front of the Homer Babbidge Library shows Fairfield Way, which was converted from a parking area into a pedestrian-only walkway in the center of campus as part of a new master plan. *Photo courtesy of Peter Morenus/UConn.*

FIGURE 6.15 At a cost of more than $12 million, the new residence halls on South Campus were one of the first projects completed as part of UConn 2000. The new dorms opened to students in 1998. *Photo courtesy of Peter Morenus/UConn.*

FIGURES 6.16a-e The UConn 2000 project did not just apply to the campus at Storrs. The university's regional campuses also benefited from major structural improvements, including locations at Avery Point (photo *a*), Hartford (*b*), Stamford (*c*), Torrington (*d*) and Waterbury (*e*).
Photos courtesy of Peter Morenus/UConn.

16b Hartford.

16c Stamford.

16d Torrington.

16e Waterbury.

FIGURE 6.17 The university graduated three more "Huskies" in May 2005. *Photo courtesy of the Willimantic Chronicle.*

Anthropology at War

A more explosive issue igniting pent-up tensions that were linked to Marxism, racism, and academic freedom concerned the university's new Anthropology Department, which was created in 1969 from the combined Department of Sociology and Anthropology. Five faculty members transferred from the earlier department. Norman Chance, the new department head, desired to establish a democratic department that focused on contemporary and third-world issues. With less emphasis on traditional areas such as archaeology and prehistory, linguistics, and physical anthropology, staff recruitment reflected the proposed direction, and five new faculty, several with a strong Marxist orientation, arrived in the specialties of social and cultural anthropology. Two came in archaeology and one, also a Marxist, came in linguistics. Faculty primarily assigned to other departments taught physical archaeology, as did one instructor with a major interest in another area. Several committees, consisting of undergraduate and graduate students and faculty, determined all departmental policy and programs. Students also participated in all department meetings.[23]

Strong personalities among the faculty, advocating divergent and incompatible viewpoints regarding the political and moral obligations of anthropological research and publication, soon divided the department. Outspoken students also added to the tension. Nevertheless, observers found that the department, though "lively, divergent, heterogeneous, and contentious," showed no sign of breakdown in the summer of 1972. At that time, after three years as its head, Norman Chance stepped down and Dennison Nash replaced him, as a "caretaker" for the 1972–73 school year. Nash, one of the faculty who moved from the original Sociology and Anthropology Department, continued Chance's democratic policies, including endorsing all committee decisions. When Jean Aigner, one of the two archaeology appointments, became acting head for the 1973–74 academic year, department members incorrectly assumed that she would also continue in the same fashion.[24]

Aigner had been aligned with William S. Laughlin, who with Benson E. Ginsburg became the object of a vehement anti-racist campaign that divided the Storrs campus and raised important issues of academic freedom. Initiated by a group of students, primarily members of the SDS, which had a large base in the Anthropology Department, and then joined by others, especially the Committee Against Racism, the campaign pilloried the two biobehavioral science professors for their alleged racist writing. Laughlin, who held a joint appointment with Anthropology, resigned from that position. To complicate matters, two anthropologists, Anthony Kroch and James Faris, served as faculty advisers to the SDS. They denied responsibility for, and advance knowledge of, the SDS charges, but later, with students in social and cultural anthropology, they stated their belief that Laughlin's writing was racist. By late fall of 1973, Anthropology Department tensions had heightened as factions hardened and accusations and counteraccusations became more and more public. Aigner added to the tinderbox when she recommended a terminal appointment for Kroch and another instructor. She claimed she based her decision on Kroch's scholarship and teaching, but others considered it political retribution and accused her as well of operating autocratically in other decisions in the previously democratically run department. Laughlin and his defenders believed the charges of racism to be a distortion of his research and an abridgement of his academic freedom. He and Ginsburg complained of harassment to Ferguson, telling the president, "Although the persons on campus involved in these smears constitute a small group, they do have an active mimeograph machine and are achieving national distribution by this means and through some segments of the radical press." Kroch, ultimately supported by the dean and his Advisory Council in winning reappointment, contended that he was a victim of political differences with Aigner. The anthropology crisis took its toll on academic freedom.[25]

In February 1974, ten of fourteen faculty drafted a letter of complaint regarding the acting head. In response, she resigned. The administration refused to accept the resignation but finally began to intervene in search of a resolution to what had become an increasingly embarrassing situation. By the end of the month, a plan calling for separate Anthropology Departments—Social and Biocultural—was proposed that would physically separate personnel and divide resources. The board of trustees adopted the split on a two-year experimental basis at its meeting of March 15, 1974. The bulk of the original department, gathered in the new Social Anthropology offshoot, felt that the decision had been imposed on them, resented the administration's action, and vented against those in the Biocultural Anthropology Department, which Aigner headed and Laughlin joined. The split received wide publicity when Norman Chance and two students sent a letter to the heads of the 116 Anthropology Departments throughout the United States and Canada. It became a cause celebre at the meeting of the North Eastern Anthropological Association at the end of April, when a motion expressing concern about the split passed, although one condemning the UConn administration did not. By then, "the Coalition" had placed repairing the division on its list of demands, along with the acceptance of Aigner's resignation, the reappointment of Tony Kroch, and the call for the restoration of a democratic structure in the Social Anthropology Department, which had been placed in receivership to the Dean's Office because two senior members declined to serve as head.[26]

"The Coalition" maintained that "in establishing a department of biocultural studies, the administration seeks to replace the anti-racist Anthropology Dept. with one that promotes racism." Ferguson patiently denied the accusation and, focusing on the two-year experimental basis, remarked that if the integrity of anthropology as a discipline at the University of Connecticut was to be preserved, "it will have to be restored by anthropologists." A year and a half later, when Julius Elias, dean of the College of Liberal Arts and Sciences, reported to his faculty on the progress made in reuniting the Anthropology Department, he announced that the prognosis was good and most of the preconditions for reunification were in place. Ultimately, unity in structure, if not in esprit, returned; the Marxist faction did not disappear but a quieter atmosphere prevailed. The Anthropology-racism issue in 1973–74, however, proved costly to the university and its president, who became a target for the frustrations of all sides of the question.[27]

Feminists and Ferguson

The complaints regarding women's programs and services at UConn incorporated an equally complex set of issues. The anti-discrimination complaint brought by the national Women's Equity Action League (WEAL) in April 1970, during Babbidge's tenure, charged that women were hired in smaller numbers than men; they were promoted less rapidly than their male counterparts; and the higher that a position was ranked, the lower the proportion of women filling it. WEAL requested that the federal Office of Civil Rights investigate the following in relation to women: admission policies; financial support to women students; placement of graduates; hiring and promotion policies for both staff and faculty; and salary differentials. In November 1972, when Edward Gant served as acting president and well before Glenn Ferguson came to campus, the federal office found that WEAL had probable cause for its allegations. At that time, the university, as a public institution, did not have to have a written Affirmative Action Plan on file. (This would change shortly afterward.) However, the office of Civil Rights required the university to take action to ensure nondiscrimination, to expand employment opportunities for minorities and women, and to comply with all other applicable provisions of Executive Order 11246, which governed what was known as Contract Compliance Review. As a consequence, UConn would have to amass enormous amounts of data and demonstrate that it had corrected all deficiencies. It would have to appoint an Equal Employment Opportunity Officer with specific duties and responsibilities for implementing and monitoring the Affirmative Action Plan. It would have to establish a comprehensive monitoring system to provide for the accurate documentation of all affirmative action efforts. In all, the Office of Civil Rights made nineteen recommendations.[28]

John Bynoe, the federal regional civil rights director, rejected UConn's first attempt at remedying the problem in April 1973 because the university responded in too defensive a manner and did not provide a careful exposition of the policies that would be implemented. The university also omitted or provided inadequate documentation. About the same time, three student organizations filed a complaint with Bynoe's office, charging the university with discrimination in hiring and student enrollment. The Puerto Rican Student Movement, the Organization of Afro-American Students, and Kitty Hawk Unlimited, a student research group that wrote the bulk of the complaint, charged, among other points, that the university failed to inform minority students of the "advantages" of attending its branches rather than Storrs, and had not performed "affirmative minority recruitment" while expanding enrollment. It also complained about the inadequacy of financial aid to minority students, the lack of publicity regarding student labor opportunities for minorities, and discrimination in hiring practices. In sum, although not exactly parallel, it mimicked the WEAL charges regarding women.[29]

Cries of discrimination thus accosted Glenn Ferguson's ears when he arrived in September 1973. To further exacerbate matters, two women's court cases, also not of his making, shadowed his presidency. In March 1972 the university's Organization of Faculty and Professional Women issued a report titled "On the Status of Faculty and Professional Women at the University of Connecticut." Wendy Chapple and Marcia Lieberman co-chaired the group of seven authors, which also included Marianne Barnaby, Claire Berg, Joan Joffe Hall, Gail Shea, and Jacqueline Sachs. It found the university deficient in its employment of women and recommended a number of remedies, the first of which advocated establishment of an autonomous office by a top-level administrator whose mission would be to equalize the status of women at UConn. As a consequence, Homer Babbidge, who was still president at the time, appointed Gail Shea as assistant provost in May 1972. Shea, a doctoral candidate in sociology at Brown University, had come to UConn for a one-year instructor's position after teaching for three years at Georgetown. Marcia Lieberman, a co-author of the report and an assistant professor of English, remarked that "Shea's active feminist work landed this job for her."[30]

Shea promised an investigation of discrimination against women at UConn. She denied reports that she was hired as a "token [women's] libber" because of pressure brought by the Department of Health, Education, and Welfare's Office of Civil Rights. "I think that would be true if I were hired as a presidential assistant," the new assistant provost said, "but the Provost's office is the most powerful department on campus." When a reporter suggested that as part of the provost's office, she had the power to investigate other departments, Shea remarked, "I don't like the word 'investigate' because it means I'm policing the departments," but then she added, "Which, in effect, I am." She recognized "a long, hard battle" before her but believed it would be easier from the provost's office because it offered continuity while the university changed presidents. She observed, "Position and power is what you make it, and I'm going to try very hard to have power."[31]

The continuity and power that Shea expected did not emerge. She contended that she should have been able to improve the status of women by drafting the university's Affirmative Action Plan as it pertained to gender, developing the Women's Center, and forming an Advisory Council. A year after she was hired, Acting President Gant fired her and eliminated the position. She had not been given meaningful input into the Affirmative Action Plan, the Women's Center had been removed from her jurisdiction, and she had to disband her Advisory Council. She contended that she had been promised the position for two years, not one, and Babbidge, in a sworn deposition, did not deny that. Shea then filed a lawsuit in federal court seeking reinstatement, back pay, damages, and legal fees.[32]

The denial of tenure to Marcia Lieberman of the English Department before Shea's dismissal led to another lengthy lawsuit. Formal notice came to Lieberman from the trustees at the end of March 1973. The issue, however, had rankled much earlier as one cause of a dispute between UConn feminists and the school's administrators. "Reinstatement of Marcia Lieberman with promotion and tenure" was the first demand of an ultimatum given to Gant when about fifty demonstrators broke up a meeting in his office on February 19. During an eight-hour occupation of Gulley Hall on February 20 by twenty-one demonstrators, and a demonstration outside the building the next day by more than 120, Lieberman's reinstatement also took precedence. Gail Shea found the denial of tenure "very disturbing." Lieberman's suit brought charges that the English Department used irregular procedures in deciding to deny her tenure because its external evaluators were either out of her field of feminist literature or had a conflict of interest. She sued the university for $100,000 plus attorney's fees for her "mental, emotional and physical stress, embarrassment and humiliation and harm to her professional reputation and economic status." It would not be for quite some time that both lawsuits, eventually lost by the plaintiffs, were ready to go to trial. By then, Ferguson, established in the presidency, had inherited the fury originally aimed at Gant.[33]

Before he officially assumed office in late June 1973, Ferguson wrote to Shea expressing an interest in learning about the situation of women at Storrs. She sent statistical material and replied that she was no longer employed by the university, but she lived in Storrs and invited him to lunch so that they could talk. It was a friendly exchange. Once in office, however, legal propriety necessitated that the new president reject the lunch invitation. Ordinarily, he would have welcomed the opportunity to meet and discuss issues of mutual concern. In light of the lawsuit, however, he wrote, "As a principal officer of the University, it will be necessary for me to assist the University in discharging its role as defendant. Therefore, it will not be possible for you and me to meet independent of the context." That was written in early September. By the end of October 1973, critics upbraided him for indicating, at a meeting of the FUT and AAUP, his opposition to hiring feminists per se. They warned that he needed feminists in policy making and administrative positions "to keep the rest of the administration on its toes. Until Ms. Shea is reinstated, and/or another feminist appointed to a high position, this gap will continue to be omnievident to those who are concerned with equal opportunity." The criticism would build.[34]

By January 1974 the Women's Council, originally Shea's Advisory Council, which had continued operating after her firing, chided Ferguson for saying in a television interview that feminism was not an issue at Storrs. They pointed out that women representing several different UConn groups had sent him a letter in November 1973 requesting that feminists be appointed to administrative positions and also requesting a Women's Studies Program, an equal employment opportunity officer especially for women, and a Women's Center coordinator. They noted that no response had been received, but they set the terms for the continuing struggle. In March 1974 "The Coalition" took up the cry, and by October the council joined as a co-defendant in *Lieberman vs. Ferguson,* Marcia Lieberman's class action suit against the university. The council emphasized that the university's response to the Office of Civil Rights investigations of two years earlier had been unsatisfactory, and none of the Affirmative Action Plans submitted to the Department of Health, Education, and Welfare had been adequate. Despite attempts at reconciliation, Ferguson faced feminist criticism throughout his tenure as president.[35]

Racial Discontent and the Occupation of the Library

The issue of race and racism, as evidenced in the Anthropology Department controversy, preoccupied the president and the campus in other ways as well. In December 1973 Ronald Taylor, an assistant professor of sociology, who a quarter of a century later would serve as UConn's vice-provost for multicultural affairs, discussed the problems of black students in white universities at a colloquium in the International House on campus. He identified five categories of difficulty: identity crises, financial problems, occasional hostile encounters with white students, problems with other personal relations, and a feeling that academic courses were irrelevant to them. He remarked, "Many students find themselves unprepared to cope with dealing with a white majority. Many Black students seem to experience great anxiety about being overwhelmed." Two and a half months later, he participated in a panel discussion by five black faculty members sponsored by the Organization of Afro-American Students. The panelists discussed black solidarity, intellectualism, and the problems of black students when returning to their communities. Taylor argued that black students perceive themselves to be in a "hostile environment," which causes them to "group together for protection."[36]

In April, UConn's black students reacted to the perceived hostility. They wrote to Ferguson, beginning their letter of complaint by stating, "Since this University first initiated an interest in attracting Black Students to this campus, *there appears to be a gross lack of commitment on the part of the University to Blacks.* The Black Community feels that this contradiction is premeditated and continuing in all facets of University Life." The authors appended a list of thirteen demands related to the Anthropology Department controversy, among them the need for a new and more spacious Afro-American Cultural Center, the need for support of black organizations such as the OAAS, Black Voices of Freedom, and Jazz Movers, the need to draw up an acceptable Equal Employment Opportunity Plan for the Office of Civil Rights and the application of an Affirmative Action Plan to the professional schools and to E. O. Smith High School, improved recruiting and financial aid for minority students, and the establishment of a Black and Third World Studies Section in the library. The final demand called for a response within five days.[37]

Ferguson replied point by point on April 16, but he explained that because he had been away and a holiday and weekend had intervened, he had only one working day to respond. He did not intend to procrastinate, however, "but rather to indicate that meaningful programs and responses cannot be devised in a single day." This reply did not satisfy. Several hundred form letters signed by individual students flooded Ferguson's office. They labeled his response "standard administrative procedure for dealing with the concerns and issues that affect us, (vague and ambiguous procrastination)." Regarding the Ginsberg-Laughlin accusations, the students claimed that Ferguson "disregarded the moral responsibility of the University to prohibit teachings that are detrimental to the survival of minority students and the black community at large." The letter writers warned, "Your middle of the road response will serve as impetus to inte[n]sify our protests in the coming days and months." Those protests came quickly.[38]

At midnight on Monday, April 22, just at closing time, more than two hundred black students entered the Wilbur Cross Library and occupied the east side of the building. Ferguson and Gant, along with Vice-Presidents DeHaan and Wilson and Deans of Students Hewes and Manning, assembled to consider the appropriate response. They were later joined by the university's attorney, John Hill, and two African American administrators, Ombudsman Charles Oliver and Equal Employment Opportunity Officer Bertram Wilson. Representatives of UConn's Division of Public Safety and Associate Librarian Norman Stevens remained in the library and shuttled between the students and the administrators. The authorities warned the students that the library was closed and they had to leave. The students refused and explained the purpose of the occupation— not simply to get a definitive response to their demands but to dramatize their need for a Cultural Center "where in we may study together and come together as a group unified in our ethnicity." They would study until 6:00 A.M., when they hoped that Ferguson, Wilson, and Manning would come to the library and address their demands. If the administrators wouldn't come, the students committed themselves to remaining until they did. The administrators offered to meet immediately, but the students insisted on meeting at 6:00 A.M. Then the administrators asked the students to commit to vacating the building once they did speak with the president. At 3:00 A.M. the students received notice to vacate in fifteen minutes; otherwise, they would be in violation of university regulations and state statutes prohibiting interference, disruption, and trespass.[39]

State police arrived about 6:00 A.M., and after attempts to encourage the students' voluntary departure, they forcibly evicted them. Four students reported injuries; one remained in the infirmary for several days. The next night, about seventy white staff and students, part of "The Coalition," showed their sympathy for the evicted blacks by also occupying the library. The administration called the state police to evict them as well. While one professor of animal husbandry wrote that his colleagues and students voiced strong support for Ferguson's action, adding, "If anything, they would not have had the patience nor the magnanimity which you extended to those in direct disobedience," the black reaction was not unexpected. *Contac*, a publication of UConn's Afro-American Cultural Center, published a photograph of a black female protester being dragged down the stairs of the library by state troopers and editorialized, "We deplore the actions taken by President Ferguson in calling state police to evict peaceful demonstrators from the Wilbur Cross Library. . . . the decision to send in State Police to bodily evict the demonstrators and charge them with criminal trespassing and related charges was an act of monumental stupidity and arrogance." The Committee Against Racism began a flyer, "We are disgusted by President Ferguson's police-state response to peaceful protest." The University Council on Human Rights and Opportunities expressed grave concern about the arrests and warned of their effect on the morale of minority faculty. Both the Connecticut Civil Liberties Union (CCLU) and the National Association for the Advancement of Colored People (NAACP) intervened and appealed for leniency on behalf of the demonstrators. A year into his presidency, Glenn Ferguson had become to many, if not to all, the face of a flawed racial policy. Despite university attempts to remedy problems throughout the 1970s and after, it found itself unable to satisfy its critics and catch up with the inequities, seemingly no matter how hard it tried.[40]

Preserving UConn's Autonomy

If Ferguson had to fend off campus protesters, he also had to battle the state legislature's attempt to change the structure of higher education. Governor Ella Grasso appointed a Committee on the Structure of Government, otherwise called the Filer Commission after its chair, John H. Filer, head of the Aetna Life and Casualty insurance company. The plan to restructure state government included the recommendation that UConn and the other institutions of higher education in Connecticut, the state college system, the community colleges, and the technical colleges, be consolidated under a single board of regents rather than operate under their separate boards. In early April 1976 a bill to that effect passed the legislature's Education Committee, where it had been strongly promoted by the committee's chair, Representative Howard Klebanoff. The University of Connecticut Board of Trustees chair, Gordon W. Tasker, and Ferguson immediately spoke out against the bill, and the AAUP Executive Committee at the university also issued an open letter to all Connecticut legislators strongly opposing the bill and asked faculty to mount a telephone campaign to defeat it. Ferguson, fearing that the new structure would impair UConn's independence, scornfully noted that the bill's proponents claimed it would save money but gave no breakdown of how such money would be saved. He attacked it as adding unneeded bureaucracy and additional staff members and concluded that it might violate the state constitution, which specified a state university with a board of trustees to oversee it.[41]

Despite such opposition, the bill passed in the House, with only minor changes, 85–53. Ferguson and the university, through Dorothy Goodwin, the Democratic representative from the Fifty-fourth District, in which UConn was located, called for a further six-month study of higher education before taking action. The area's senator, Audrey Beck, unhappy with the outcome in the House, predicted that the Senate would never support the bill. She proved correct. For the time being, in the spring of 1976, the reorganization, which would be passed a year later in a modified form to establish the state's Board of Higher Education, failed. Ferguson won the immediate battle but was severely criticized for his role by the plan's proponents. The *Norwich Bulletin* editorialized about "Ferguson's Power Play" and charged him with using state funds and publications to lobby against the reorganization. In an attempt at compromise, Ferguson called for the establishment of a coordinating committee that would bring together the boards of UConn and the four state colleges. He recognized that "the time for change had come. It is a coordinating effort, a voluntary effort." When the Coordinating Council met at the president's residence in September 1977, Ferguson's motives seemed clear. He voiced concern about the state colleges embarking on graduate and professional programs already offered at UConn. He wished to avoid duplication and unnecessary expense to the state and obviously strove to protect UConn's turf. In so doing, he served his constituency.[42]

Building a New Library

Ferguson also advocated for a new university library, though plans had been underway since the Babbidge administration. A few months before Ferguson's arrival in Storrs, University Librarian John P. McDonald responded to Acting

President Gant's query regarding whether the design of the facility imposed unusual or avoidable costs upon UConn and the state. McDonald informed him
that Robert S. McMillan Associates "designed a straightforward library building
without the unnecessary ornamentation or monumentality." He explained that
the building was what librarians called a modular design, a system of regularly
spaced columns supporting a number of poured concrete floors. The module
or bay was square, making for economy in construction and flexibility in use.
McDonald pointed out that in planning the building he and McMillan had the
benefit of site visits to several of the best new university libraries in the nation—
the Rockefeller Library at Brown University, the Countway Library of Medicine
at Harvard, the Clark University Library in Worcester, Massachusetts, the University of Minnesota's O. Meredith Wilson Library, the new libraries at North-
western University and the University of Chicago, and the Washington University Library in St. Louis, the last of which McDonald had helped plan in his
previous position.[43]

Shortly into his presidency, Ferguson lobbied strongly for the new library.
Using information and arguments developed by McDonald and Associate Librarian Norman Stevens, he testified before the legislature's Finance Committee that the old Wilbur Cross Library had space for only 753 students, less than
5 percent of the school's enrollment at a time when the American Library Association recommended seating for a minimum of 25 percent of enrollment. Inadequate shelf space for books worsened the situation. Books got scattered or
misplaced because shelves were so tightly packed; twenty-four-hour delays occurred when some books had to be recovered from storage in the Faculty-Alumni
Center basement. Library staff operated in extremely cramped quarters. The
library's collection development officer advised Ferguson that the university
lacked excellent or outstanding research collections, and part of the problem was
the absence of adequate space. The proposed building would contain 385,000
square feet of floor space on seven floors and provide reader seats for 3,000
people and shelf space for 1.6 million volumes, with additional space available
in a sub-basement; it would also include 214 research carrels. Groundbreaking
for the $19 million structure occurred on July 10, 1975. A year and a half later the
governor and other notables participated in a topping-off ceremony, which
consisted of the raising of an evergreen tree at the topmost reaches of the structure and signaled the completion of upward construction. As the opening approached, McDonald faced a major problem—how to move the books from
the Wilbur Cross to the new library. Funds did not seem to be available from the
state. Ferguson wanted to see long lines of students, faculty, and others passing
books like a nineteenth-century bucket brigade, but his suggestion found
little support among library officials. Ultimately, a commercial mover did the
job. More enthusiasm greeted his assistance in undoing the trustees' naming of
the library after Nathan Hale, who had done so in unprecedented fashion with-

out any recommendation from the university's Building Names Committee, which wanted it to be called the University of Connecticut Library. It opened with that name and kept it until the change to the Babbidge Library after Babbidge's death in 1984. By then, Ferguson was no longer at UConn, having left it in 1978 to become CEO of Radio Free Europe/Radio Liberty.[44]

The DiBiaggio Years

Eleven months after Ferguson's departure, UConn chose its tenth president. As the search began, rumors swirled that Homer Babbidge would be brought back. Faculty promoted the idea; William Rosen of the English Department explained that his colleagues suggested "We would like someone like Babbidge," and then "Someone said why not Babbidge himself." Board of trustees chair Gordon Tasker, however, denied that he or any other individuals on the twenty-member committee had had formal contact with the former president. As the search narrowed, Tasker stated that priority consideration would be given to employees of the University of Connecticut. The committee considered insiders such as Acting President Gant, Academic Affairs Vice-President Kenneth G. Wilson, and Harry Hartley, former dean of the School of Education and vice-president of finance and administration. While also considering administrators from American University and the University of Wyoming on their short list, the search committee eventually selected John A. DiBiaggio, who served UConn as vice-president for health affairs at the university's Health Center.[45]

The forty-six-year-old former practicing dentist was born in San Antonio and raised in Detroit. His Italian parents, Ciro and Acidalia DiBiaggio, spoke little English, and the new president would draw upon his immigrant background and success in achieving the American dream to inspire audiences, especially working-class students. He obtained his bachelor's degree from Eastern Michigan University in Ypsilanti and his D.D.S. from the University of Detroit School of Dentistry. DiBiaggio practiced general dentistry from 1958 to 1965 in a Detroit suburb and taught part-time at the University of Detroit Dental School. In 1965, he turned to full-time teaching as an assistant professor while he earned his M.A. in university administration from the University of Michigan. Subsequently, he joined the University of Kentucky as director of continuing education and student affairs; the next year he became assistant dean for student affairs and advanced education and again taught, first as an assistant than as an associate professor. In 1970 he moved to Virginia Commonwealth Dental School as full professor and dean before coming to UConn in 1976, where he was responsible for the institution's medical and dental schools and the John N. Dempsey Hospital in Farmington, as well as associated programs on the Storrs campus and elsewhere.[46]

At the Health Center, DiBiaggio earned respect as an academic leader with an exuberant personality that won him friends at the State Capitol in Hartford. His outgoing demeanor contrasted with Ferguson's reserve, and it was hoped that he would serve UConn better in his relations with the governor and the legislature. Governor Grasso's Italian heritage did not go unnoticed by those who expected it to cement the relationship with DiBiaggio. When the governor and Yale's president, A. Bartlett Giamatti, attended DiBiaggio's 1979 inauguration, Lewis Katz, who spoke for the faculty at the ceremony, pointed out that the audience was in the presence of "a triumvirate unequaled since the days of Ancient Rome."[47]

Battling the Budget and the Library as Casualty

Observers recognized that DiBiaggio had not taken on an easy task by moving from Farmington to Storrs. Tight budgets had plagued the university during Ferguson's tenure as president. The enrollment of students just out of high school had declined. The faculty had become increasingly discouraged by what some believed to be a lack of leadership by the previous administration. DiBiaggio, who took office in June 1979, faced a total budget slightly less than the previous year but was realistic enough not to expect any dramatic increases, although he advocated for more state funding. To compensate, he urged increased corporate and private donations and was eventually successful in leading the Second Century Capital Campaign in which the UConn Foundation, in the institution's first major fundraising effort, collected almost $25 million by the time he left office in 1985. Previously, the school had had almost no endowment. While the $25 million dollars, even when added to what had already been accumulated, was embarrassingly small in comparison with other institutions of higher learning, it served as a beginning for later, more significant campaigns. By establishing a Tuition Fund that permitted the university to maintain control of the tuition it collected, the new president developed another instrument to offset losses in state financing. UConn's financial problems, however, would linger.[48]

In his inaugural address, DiBiaggio expressed concern regarding "the seductive but false hope that all problems can be resolved through the development of more, and more sophisticated technology." He warned that, faced with fiscal constraints, universities and colleges might seek a "quick fix." They might succumb to applied research exclusively and to those programs that solely guarantee students a job after graduation. That approach, he suggested, would produce graduates who would only be able "to cope with the problems of today, while lacking the analytic minds essential to dealing with the problems—not yet imagined—of tomorrow." He wanted more for the institution and stated a theme that would become a mantra for his successors: "As . . . the flagship of the public higher education system, we have a moral and ethical responsibility to serve as a beacon of excellence for all our sister institutions." He did not, however, neglect UConn's service role for the citizens of the state. The speech was crafted to touch all the bases and demonstrated the new president's superior political instincts.[49]

The fiscal realities of the early 1980s muted the effectiveness of those political instincts. A year after the inaugural, Richard Stephenson, a chemical engineering professor, wrote to express confidence in the new president. He said that he learned from his neighbor, Harry Hartley, that DiBiaggio was "a little discouraged about your first year in the presidency." Stephenson added, "We are realistic enough to know that the problems of the university are caused by the financial situation of the state, and not anything you have done or not done." DiBiaggio responded that university presidents sometimes have their "down" days but ended with the upbeat comment that if the university community discusses common goals and shared frustrations "openly and honestly, then we *can* create a better University." By that time, he had spent a year struggling with a reduced budget that had adversely affected the entire institution and the new library in particular.[50]

A *Hartford Courant* headline exclaimed, "UConn Library: Reduced Services in a Fancy New Building," and explained that Governor Grasso, wrestling with a poor economy, had instituted a 2.5 percent budget recision in the fall of 1979. Italian heritage and political contacts could not protect the institution from the damage. Since the state enacted the cut after most of UConn's expected revenues were already committed, the money had to come mainly from equipment and non-contractual labor. The library relied on both (books were categorized as equipment) and as a consequence bore more than its share of the cut. A university-wide freeze on hiring hit it hard, because the library faced an unusually large turnover of staff that fall. As a result, the freeze caught it short-staffed and led to a curtailment of hours open during the spring semester of 1980. A decision to close the building early on Friday and all day on Saturday drew strong criticism. On a Friday night, more than four hundred students staged a sit-in to protest the cutback in hours. Earlier the same day, the Executive Committee of the Graduate School condemned the cuts. Student trustee Steve Donen said the curtailment of hours "could be the most disastrous decision affecting the quality of the university made in the last five years." The chair of the University Senate's Budget Committee laid the responsibility at the door of the governor, but DiBiaggio found it necessary to make a long explanation to State Representative Christopher H. Shays, writing, "I do not believe we have been guilty of poor management." The situation bordered on the desperate.[51]

A combination of budget cuts and inflation during the final years of Ferguson's presidency and the first year of DiBiaggio's seriously depleted the general book fund and hampered the operations of the Special Collections and Serials

Departments. While the library had purchased 25,000 books in 1976, it could afford only 14,000 in 1980. Inflation affected serials (journals and other periodicals essential to a research library) dramatically. The same material that cost $285,750 in 1974–75 cost about $490,000 in 1980. A vast number of periodical subscriptions had to be cancelled. Special collections, which had spent $35,000 in 1974, was allotted only $4,000 for acquisitions in 1980. In 1981, Director John McDonald prepared a report describing the library's declining status compared to that of the other New England state university libraries. Of the five other schools, only the University of Maine received less funding. UMass did best, receiving $1,500,000, almost double UConn's $762,550. On a national basis, of the 101 university libraries belonging to the Association of Research Libraries, UConn dropped from forty-first to sixty-fifth on the list between 1978 and 1981. Ironically, as they slashed hours and book budgets, the authorities, using capital funds, were applying the final cosmetic touches to the building itself. The point was not lost on McDonald, who remarked, "It doesn't make sense for the state to invest eighteen or nineteen million dollars in this building and then withdraw money for operating expenses." The regular opening hours were restored within months, and by 1983 the library had begun a process of rebuilding its collections and, with the acquisitions budget "modestly strengthened," restoring periodicals that had been cut. Nevertheless, the budgetary problems and the library situation did much to explain DiBiaggio's disappointment at the end of his first year in office.[52]

Opportunities for the 80s

Despite this, the DiBiaggio administration's desire for progress remained strong. His vice-president for academic affairs, Anthony DiBenedetto (who had headed the AAUP at the time of the first collective bargaining negotiations and then joined the administration, first as graduate vice-president), developed a planning document, "Opportunities for the 80s." Each unit of the university undertook a self-evaluation and engaged in a planning exercise that charted a course for the institution regardless of the financial resources available to it. Some of the main recommendations included a core curriculum to be required of all students; admission into the professional schools only at the upper division; the designation of twelve academic programs for augmented support based upon their records of excellence and promise of further improvement; the obtaining of additional state and private support for programs, such as engineering, that are of economic importance to the state; the realignment or consolidation of academic programs and the closing of the Torrington regional campus; the maintenance and possible expansion of student enrollment; and faculty and staff development through retraining and early retirement. DiBenedetto made it clear that programs not singled out for support would have to sacrifice for the rest of the university. Later, in 1985, he could report some successes, such as the progress toward a university-wide core-distribution requirement and the fact that the School of Business Administration had become an upper-division school. However, he made no mention of some of the more difficult goals. He reported no program consolidation, and the Torrington campus remained open after a legislative compromise established the Litchfield County Higher Education Center. In higher education, change comes slowly, and at this time in its history the University of Connecticut proved no exception to the rule.[53]

Doctors, Dentists and Lawyers Find their Place

During the 1970s and 1980s change, however, did come for UConn's aspiring doctors, dentists, and attorneys, as those in medicine moved to a newly built campus in Farmington and the law students found a new home on the grounds of what had previously been the Hartford Seminary. The path to the University of Connecticut Health Center (UCHC) was not an easy one. In 1964, after an architectural competition, Vincent G. Kling and Associates of Philadelphia was selected to design the center. Groundbreaking occurred in May 1966, and a year later Lasker Goldman Corporation of New York began construction of the academic wing; two years after that, in 1969, the Kidde-Briscoe Consortium started on the John Dempsey Hospital and its accompanying medical and dental outpatient service units. Construction delays plagued the project, forcing temporary arrangements at the Veteran's Administration Hospital in Newington and at New Britain General Hospital; some dental faculty were also based at Storrs. An eleven-part series in the *Hartford Courant* published at the end of 1970 and the beginning of 1971 alleged theft and underworld activity at the construction site. Cost overruns ballooned. In mid-1965 a UCHC planning team estimated $50 million for construction and equipment. By 1974, when the center had been completed, inflation in construction costs resulted in $67 million for construction alone; equipment, Department of Public Works supervisory charges, site preparation costs, and other expenses brought the total to almost $100 million, of which about a third was paid by the federal government. Lawsuits further took the bloom off the rose. Dr. Morris Cohen, a state representative from Bloomfield and co-sponsor in 1961 of the legislation that created the UCHC, turned against the center. He criticized what he believed to be the wasteful use of space in the impressive building's curved design and what he thought to be an equally wasteful heating system. (It was designed in an elongated "S"-shaped curve and was heated entirely by electricity.) He complained that the center should turn out more students in proportion to the tremendous cost of its physical plant.[54]

Despite such criticism, in its first decade of operation the Health Center made major progress. In the fall of 1966 planners decided to begin teaching classes two years later. The first class entered in 1968 and included thirty-two medical and sixteen dental students. They attended school at McCook Hospital until temporary quarters in prefabricated buildings at the Health Center site became available; four years later, in 1972, permanent quarters at the UCHC complex opened to students. By that time, John Patterson, the second medical school dean (appointed dean in 1965 upon the unexpected death of fifty-one-year-old Dean Lyman Maynard Stowe) was named in 1970 first vice-president for health affairs and executive director of the Health Center. He would influence the development of the UCHC, which held its first commencement in June 1972. John DiBiaggio succeeded Patterson as vice-president for health affairs and executive director in 1975, before DiBiaggio became president of the university. Early that year, the John Dempsey Hospital opened with fifty-five beds. Its ultimate capacity of 232 was a small number for a teaching hospital but was supplemented by the three thousand beds among the eight Hartford-area hospitals in the Capital Area Health Consortium. Ten years after accepting students, the UCHC complex in 1978 served as the base for educational programs for more than one thousand medical and dental students, Ph.D. candidates in medical and dental fields, and medical and dental residents. In addition, twelve hundred practicing dentists and four hundred physicians annually came to the UCHC for continuing education and upgrading of skills. By that time women comprised 25 percent of the medical students and 15 percent of the dental students, as compared to a mere handful in the first class. No minorities appeared in that group, while the class included 6 percent in 1978. Further change would come, but its first decade of teaching medicine and dentistry demonstrated the Health Center's significance in enhancing the reach of the University of Connecticut and contributing to the state's healthcare providers and their patients.[55]

The Law School's move to the Hartford Seminary site involved its own complications but had a most positive resolution. Beginning in 1964, the Law School shared the West Hartford campus with the two-year Hartford Branch (later the Regional Campus) and the School of Social Work. Then the Law School building opened, with 373 students enrolled in forty-six courses taught by fourteen full-time faculty members assisted by sixteen part-time faculty in eight classrooms. By 1980, Phillip I. Blumberg, the school's dean, noted that there were almost twice as many students, more than twice as many teachers, more than twice as many courses, and more than twice as many books, still in the same building but in fewer classrooms by half. There was also a critical shortage of office space for faculty, administration, and student organizations. Part-time faculty had no offices, nor were offices available for distinguished visitors and guest-lecturers. The bookstore, the law review (which did not exist in 1964), and other organizations were all housed inadequately, if at all. The overcrowding in fact jeopardized the school's accreditation; the American Bar Association (ABA) earlier had ordered the

School of Law to show cause why its accreditation should not be revoked. To avoid the sanction, the legislature, in the spring of 1978, authorized the acquisition of the Hartford Seminary Foundation property and its renovation for the use of the UConn School of Law. The ABA then deferred action on revocation of accreditation pending the completion of the construction and renovation program.[56]

Authorities greeted with delight the move in 1984 to the twenty-acre campus, designed by architects Allen and Collens of Boston and built in the mid-1920s in collegiate Gothic style. One administrator suggested that the campus had an "instant Ivy-League" appearance. Dean George Schatzki, Blumberg's successor, remarked that people seemed happier; they "were walking around the campus with smiles on their faces." Associate Dean Peter A. Lane marveled at the renovations, which maintained the impressive building style while creating modern office space inside. When Schatzki invited Governor William A. O'Neill to the dedication ceremonies, he declared, "I look forward to that time when we shall be together and [I] can show off the State's most beautiful campus." The almost $9 million cost for the move seemed worth the funds expended to realize a campus that would be listed on the National Register of Historic Sites. Not only was there a physical improvement, but in the twenty years between locating at 1800 Asylum Avenue, West Hartford, and coming to the Hartford Seminary campus in 1984, academic quality had also improved. Under Howard Sacks's deanship from 1967 to 1972, the school began a clinical legal education program, started its own law review, introduced interdisciplinary courses, and successfully recruited faculty on a national basis; Sacks placed a new emphasis on scholarship while maintaining the school's strong teaching tradition. During Blumberg's tenure as dean, the quality of students rose dramatically and faculty accomplishments continued to honor the institution that Blumberg brought to an impressive new campus, which would serve as the site for continued achievement in legal education over the next two decades.[57]

UCEPI: The Research Park That Wasn't

A program that received a great deal of attention during the DiBiaggio years and later but never came to fruition involved the development of a research park, a hotel conference center, and residential apartments. Arthur Gillis, then vice-president for finance and administration, advanced the idea in 1981. He had just left the University of California, where he had helped attract private industrial research centers that exchanged information and services with the school. DiBiaggio endorsed the concept. Gillis explained the university's purpose as an attempt to find non-state, non-federal, and non-student sources of revenue. DiBiaggio emphasized that the university's principal interest was in basic research, whereas industry was concerned with applied research. He pointed out that technology transfer would be most effective when scientists from both realms worked together in a research park atmosphere.[58]

The idea was not novel. Models of well-established, successful parks could be found in the Stanford Research Park (the first, in 1951), the Princeton-Forrestal Center, the Research Triangle in the Chapel Hill–Durham, North Carolina, area, Yale's New Haven Science Park, and the Huntsville Research Park. Others sprouted during the 1970s and 1980s at Arizona State University, Ohio State, Texas A&M, Washington State, and the Universities of California, Florida, Utah, and Wisconsin. Many others failed or, like UConn's, never got off the ground. In Connecticut's case, the university chose a 390-acre site on the northern edge of campus, bounded by Routes 44A and 195 and Hunting Lodge and North Eagleville Roads. It established a non-stock, nonprofit corporation, the University of Connecticut Educational Properties, Inc. (UCEPI), with directors chosen from the university (and including the president), the greater community, and the state administration. After a nationwide search, the directors selected Sunrise Development Corporation, a subsidiary of Forest City Enterprises of Cleveland, Ohio, as the master developer. Years later, after little progress, the university sued the developer as the project failed. During the DiBiaggio administration, however, the research park, named "Connecticut Technology Park: A University Research Community" (or "ConnTech"), held much promise for enhancing UConn's reputation.[59]

From the outset, the plan encountered difficulty. In February 1983 a plant science professor, A. J. R. Guttay, wrote to his dean reminding him of the state policy to preserve agricultural land. He feared that the research park would be utilizing prime agricultural land. The dean, E. J. Kersting, forwarded the letter to Gillis and mentioned that he and many colleagues in the College of Agricultural and Natural Resources agreed with Guttay's concern about the use of prime agricultural land for the park. While UCEPI reached an agreement with the local agricultural interests respecting the preservation of the farmland, legal issues delayed the transfer of the entire parcel from the university and the state to UCEPI, and therefore hurt the developer's ability to market the project. Later, grassroots groups opposed the development when the proposal was brought to the Mansfield Planning and Zoning Commission. The only part of the plan that was built, the Celeron Apartments, certainly did not justify the vast amount of time and energy spent in trying to bring about ConnTech.[60]

DiBiaggio Departs

Toward the end of his fifth year in office, DiBiaggio prepared a self-evaluation for the benefit of the board of trustees. He recounted some successes—modest, if still insufficient, growth in state funding, the establishment of the Tuition

Fund, the capital campaign, academic planning under "Opportunities for the 80s," an improvement in faculty morale, enhanced student satisfaction, an improved university presence across the state, and his effort to improve UConn's regional campuses. The image of the university throughout the state, however, remained fuzzy. He did not believe that the overall quality of the university had improved significantly during his five-year tenure. Evaluations of the institution revealed that UConn continued to be perceived as average-to-good in most categories. DiBiaggio showed disappointment at a National Research Council evaluation of graduate programs that did not include any of the school's departments in the very top categories, and even more disappointment that none of the UConn departments ranked very high in the improving quality category. Studies such as these gave him pause. In September 1983 his candidacy as one of four finalists for the University of Florida's presidency reached the public, and the board of trustees showed anxious concern. He promised then to continue until the end of the academic year and remained even longer, but in 1985 he did resign to become president of the much larger Michigan State University. Students dedicated the 1985 *Nutmeg* yearbook to the departing president. They praised his efforts to make the university better known: "In between, he came to our dorms for dinner, came to our parties and listened to our complaints about rising tuition and boggling bureaucracy . . . he improved UConn's image . . . and . . . self-image. UConn is more of a community today because of him." The community, nevertheless, had to search again for a new leader.[61]

The Casteen Years

It found one in John T. Casteen III. After a relatively brief search, on June 7, 1985, Dr. Andrew J. Canzonetti, the chair of the board of trustees, wrote to Casteen offering him the position, at a salary of $95,000, plus perks such as the president's residence, which was staffed by a housekeeper, and the promise of a second housekeeper. The successful candidate accepted on July 2 and wrote that he and his family felt "privileged and more than slightly awed to have a part in the University's future." The forty-one-year-old Casteen, a Phi Beta Kappa graduate who held three degrees in English from the University of Virginia, had served as Virginia's secretary of education since 1982 and simultaneously was adjunct professor of English at Virginia Commonwealth University. Prior to that he was the University of Virginia's dean of admissions and taught there and at the University of California at Berkeley and the University of Delaware, as well as Maryland State College. One keen observer noted that Casteen "can read Medieval manuscripts and computer spread sheets with equal understanding (and has) statesmanship which enables him to build bridges between halls of ivy and the halls of Congress."[62]

Casteen praised his predecessor but confessed, "John DiBiaggio and I are very different people." Casteen was quieter and seemed more reserved, perhaps more remote, than the gregarious DiBiaggio, although he was extremely articulate and an excellent extemporaneous public speaker. As Canzonetti remarked of Casteen, "He is not a noisy man." Some on campus would find that appealing; others would come to criticize the style, and the man. By the time he departed for the presidency of his alma mater in 1990, he would have his supporters but also a number of severe critics. Initially, however, Casteen aligned himself behind DiBiaggio's unachieved goal of moving UConn from one of the top sixty public research universities to one of the top twenty. He told the first University Senate meeting he attended in September 1985, "As president, first and foremost I belong to the faculty. It is a fundamental reason I came here." He stressed a core curriculum for undergraduates and the necessity of recruiting more minority students. He recognized that the university must be useful to the state's residents, flexible enough to change with the times, and accountable for the quality of its programs. He quickly made contacts throughout the state and in the business community. On October 12, 1985, Casteen concluded his inaugural address with the challenge, "Let us commit together to assure by our words and our deeds that in this university, whose campus is, as President Jorgensen promised, the entire state of Connecticut, the work of the human mind and hand and the aspirations of the human spirit will flourish together for the common good." In sum, the new president reached out to all of his constuencies.[63]

By his second year in Storrs, Casteen felt comfortable enough to teach a section of English 109, Literature and Composition. Students expressed surprise when they learned the identity of their instructor but also appreciated the unusual presence of a university president in the classroom. One sophomore remarked, "He seems like any other teacher, but knowing that he is the president, I'll work harder." His teaching assistant exclaimed that Casteen's enjoyment of teaching, articulateness, and knowledge impressed students. When he guest-lectured on *Beowulf* to a standing-room-only class of three hundred in Professor Francelia Butler's Children's Literature ("kiddy lit") course, students praised the effort, which included Casteen speaking in Old English and a visit from a costumed Grendel and Grendel's mother, characters from the poem. In 1986 the new president also had success in winning approval from the General Assembly for the university's most favorable budget in years.[64]

Less positive signs that would lead to later restructuring developed as well that year. A report by the New York consulting firm of Peat, Marwick, Mitchell & Company criticized the university's unsophisticated organization, uncertainty about its direction, underdeveloped structure, poor relations with the state, and inadequate fundraising measures. Eva Klein, a manager at the firm, found UConn's external relations to be a major weakness. "This is the only university I've seen in years that does not have a senior management position in external relations." Not surprisingly, and in line with late-twentieth-century trends in higher education, the consultant advised that "The University has to learn to structure itself a little more like a corporation." When Harry Hartley announced in September 1986 that he would step down from his position as vice-president for finance and administration, the *Daily Campus* editorialized that he was the third vice-president to announce his resignation since John Casteen took over more than a year ago, "and that seems a bit strange." A faculty member who sent Casteen lengthy and candid memos of friendly advice told him, "I have heard a few comments about how hard it has gotten to see the President (i.e., you)." At another time, he recounted that a very senior and very well-known history professor asked at the end of October to see the president about an important matter and had one of Casteen's assistants tell him he could have an appointment in mid- or late January. The same writer confided, "I do sense a number of faculty who don't see any vision and/or feel you do not have any strong ideas of your own, whether or not they can be implemented." While griping about administrators had long been a faculty pastime, in this instance a sense of distance set in early.[65]

Carnegie I and Playboy *Number 6*

Events small and large, local and cosmopolitan, would color Casteen's first years at UConn. At the end of September 1985 Hurricane Gloria swept over the campus and caused an unprecedented closing; the space shuttle Challenger exploded at the end of January 1986 and left students, in particular, with a sense of "flash-bulb memory," a term used to describe an event seared into one's mind. UConn's marching band canceled a trip to Europe because of the fear of terrorism associated with Libya's Muammar al-Qadaffy. The board of trustees divested the university's holdings in companies that did business in South Africa after students voted to do so in a referendum and then demonstrated. Feminist and publisher of *Ms.* magazine Gloria Steinem spoke to an overflow audience that had to move from the Student Union Ballroom to the Fieldhouse in order to accommodate all of those interested. Former presidential candidates John Anderson and Jesse Jackson visited campus, and former Yippies Jerry Rubin and Abbie Hoffman squared off in a Yippie-Yuppie debate—Rubin having graduated to Yuppiedom when he became a stockbroker. "Right Stuff" author Tom Wolfe, a founder of new journalism, also visited Storrs as a lecturer. Fast food came to campus when Jonathan's opened in the Student Union in space previously occupied by the Commons Dining Hall. Landscapers transformed the muddy field between the new Coop and the Psychology Building into a Geology Park. Across Route 195, planners proposed a small mall and office complex, Storrs Commons, that would be built on the site of the College Theater south of campus. UConn bustled with life. By the fall of 1987, Casteen would extol the university's rising reputation.[66]

He was thinking of UConn's climb from category two to category one in the Carnegie Corporation's rating of universities. The rating system was the most universal ranking of major research institutions, and Connecticut became the first public institution in New England to receive the category-one ranking. Speaking to about one hundred students in the lounge of Buckley South, Casteen explained that while Yale ranked at the top of category one and UConn stood at the bottom, "It's a good neighborhood to live in." Despite the ranking, however, in 1987 the university slipped nationally from twenty-fourth to twenty-eighth in research spending at public universities. In private funding, on the other hand, it far exceeded the $25 million goal by 1989 set in the Second Century Fund campaign that was started under DiBiaggio; by March 1987 fundraisers had brought in $51.2 million. In a more dubious ranking, *Playboy* magazine also put UConn at number six of the forty top party schools in the United States. Photographer David Chan came to campus searching for models to appear in the magazine's "Back-to-School" issue scheduled for the next fall. As the nation grew more conscious of AIDS, safe sex was promoted at UConn during a week highlighted by "UConndom Day," when free condoms were distributed to students. MTV, the cable video music channel, featured UConn's Spring Weekend on a special program about such events across the country. The reputation of the school in Storrs, for good or for ill, had indeed spread beyond the rolling hills of Connecticut's countryside.[67]

A Nasty Incident and Asian American Awareness

Affirmative action implementation continued with difficulty during the Casteen years. The State's Commission on Human Rights and Opportunities (CHRO) rejected a UConn plan submitted in November 1986. Governor William A. O'Neill noted the rejection of the plan and brought it to the UConn president's attention. He emphasized his belief in the importance of affirmative action and urged Casteen to work closely with the CHRO to bring the hiring plan into compliance. The university's public relations director worried about the impact of the disapproval on the institution's media relations. She warned, "There is no question that almost anything we say may be misinterpreted." Much of the next year was taken up by Casteen and his staffers trying to make things right and bring the plan into compliance with state regulations, which they did. While hiring remained the key issue in question, on another front the admissions director informed the board of trustees in the fall of 1987 of a plan to double the number of minority students on campus by 1990. However, an incident at the end of the year that had long-range implications may have dulled that optimism.[68]

On the evening of December 3, 1987, Marta Ho and seven Asian friends boarded a bus in front of the Belden Hall dormitory to take them to a semiformal dance at the Italian American Club in the neighboring town of Tolland. Ho sat near the back of the crowded vehicle with Lenny Chow and Heidi Hara. Feona Lee and Daniel Shan sat next to them. Ron Cheung, Tina Chan, and Ping Szeto were scattered throughout the bus. Not long after being seated but before the ride began, Lee felt something splash on her face. She thought the roof of the bus leaked but then realized that someone from the back had spat tobacco juice at her. She screamed and demanded to know the identity of her assailants. In response, spit again hit her, this time in the eye. Shan came to her defense, approached two students, football players Sean Doyle and Mark Landolfi, and demanded that they apologize to Lee. They spat at him, called him "Oriental faggot" and "chink," and challenged him to a fight, which did not occur. Most of the students and the bus driver ignored the situation, and a resident assistant advised the Asian students to forget about the matter. When the bus started moving, a wad of spit landed on Ho's hand. Doyle sat down behind her, avoiding her stares each time she turned around. A group of students started singing the Beatles song "We All Live in a Yellow Submarine." Ho, who had emigrated with her working-class parents from Taiwan when she was ten years old, could not avoid interpreting it as a racist taunt, although some of the riders tried to convince her otherwise. At the dance Doyle, apparently drunk, stalked Ho when she began to dance with Szeto and Lee, repeatedly elbowed Szeto in the back, screamed "gook" and "chink," and made monkey-like noises while jumping up and down with his hands flapping. He then dropped his pants, mooned the students, and danced with his penis exposed and directed at Lee. He spat beer into Shan's face. Ho, Hara, and Chan hid in a coat closet for about half an hour. When they finally emerged with the intent to call the police, the midnight bus arrived to take the first batch of students back to Belden Hall. All eight Asian students then boarded, leaving the troublemakers behind.[69]

After the incident, Marta Ho, encouraged by her sister, Maria, a UConn senior and the president of the Asian American Club, sought justice and punishment for the assailants. Initially, the authorities engaged in buck passing. The UConn police saw the incident as out of their jurisdiction because it happened in Tolland, but an officer did make out a "Miscellaneous" report in the event of future problems with Doyle and Landolfi. The resident state trooper in Tolland, once located, advised them to go back to UConn. The Affirmative Action Office claimed no jurisdiction because the matter involved charges of students against students rather than against an institutional official. They then were referred to Dean of Students Frank Ardaiolo. After threatening to go to the press, five of the students were invited to give oral testimony to the dean's assistant, Joanne Quinones, who subsequently asked them to file written statements. The administration's sensitivity to damaging publicity on Asian racial matters had deepened with the increase of Asian American students from 47 in 1976 to 450 in 1988, and with that increase the greater chance for discriminatory encounters. The previous year's need to relocate twenty-nine students from Middlesex Dormitory because of vandalism that included graffiti mentioning a Vietnamese student intensified the concern. The December 3 "semiformal dance incident" would thus have wideranging implications.[70]

Perhaps it was the fear of bad publicity or a belated recognition of the impropriety that finally propelled authorities into action. A week after the incident, the Dean's Office charged Doyle and Landolfi with violating the Student Conduct Code and set a hearing for one week later. The UConn police reconsidered and determined that the case did indeed rest within its jurisdiction. They charged the two football players with disorderly conduct, to which they later pleaded guilty and received a penalty of accelerated rehabilitation. Because of procedural issues and a belief on the part of the victims that was later sustained by a University Senate committee that the Office of the Dean more carefully protected the rights of the accused than of their victims, the internal hearings reverberated much more strongly. The two-day session resulted in Doyle being suspended from school for a year and upon readmission being barred from ever living on campus, while Landolfi was also barred from living on campus and placed on disciplinary probation but allowed to continue on the football team. This led to the charge, unsubstantiated by the senate committee, that Dean Ardaiolo favored athletes and that the Division of Athletics had intervened in the case. The dean claimed he would bar an athlete from a sport only if a violation was related to the sport. The procedural problems at the hearing and the uneven treatment of the accused and the accusers, favoring the former, seemed more egregious; more than a year later Ardaiolo's handling of the matter would come under official investigation.[71]

The Ho sisters, justifiably feeling aggrieved, did not let the matter rest. They began to network with Asian American groups throughout New England and found more support than they ever received at UConn. Back on campus, they organized and presided over an Asian American Student Association. In April about forty Asian American students from UConn and other schools including MIT, Cornell, and Brown gathered in Storrs under the auspices of the East Coast Asian Students' Union. They met with Ardaiolo and demanded an Asian American dean, Asian American studies courses, a racial relations board to handle further problems, an increase in Asian American faculty, and an Asian American cultural center. With respect to the last, students complained that they had nothing comparable to the Afro-American and Puerto Rican Centers. James Lim, a junior economics major, offered their perspective when he remarked, "By not having one, they're not formally recognizing us as a legitimate ethnic group. We don't want to belong in that category of 'other.'" The aftermath of the December 3 incident assured that such would not be the case.[72]

The devotion of the Ho sisters was matched by Paul Bock, an engineering professor of hydrology and water resources, who signed on as faculty adviser to their student group. He also organized an Asian American Faculty Association. Bock pursued the matter with single-minded zeal. Not engaged in campus activism previously, Bock, his consciousness raised, led a crusade to recruit more faculty and students of Asian descent. He also urged the University Senate to investigate the December 3 incident. He led a movement at the May 1988 graduation for the wearing of "Please reduce racism at UConn" buttons, which began with the agreement to do so by President Casteen and the board of trustees. He introduced the Ho sisters to Casteen, and their story encouraged the president to take a more active role in ameliorating the racial tinderbox. Bock inundated Ann Huckenbeck, whom Casteen had appointed to coordinate planning and activities needed to meet the needs of Asian American students, with numerous handwritten memos and requests. He pitched a tent on the Student Union lawn and conducted a hunger strike to call attention to their demands. He obtained seven hundred signatures on a petition to bring about an investigation of the incident. He accused Ardaiolo (who would eventually leave the university for another position) of conducting a "campaign of racism" and pressed for his suspension or dismissal. Some thought Bock had gone too far with his accusations, but he certainly made his point and could not be ignored.[73]

Casteen, initially slow to react to the incident, admitted later that he should have responded more quickly. In May 1988, five and a half months after the ill-fated semiformal, he announced, "I am persuaded that our Asian American students and faculty are correct in their complaints, and I share their sense of outrage and alarm." He said the university abhorred racial abuse and harassment and that it supported the Asian American students and faculty in their efforts to publicize the problem and end it. He eventually announced changes in the Student Honor Code. Suspension or expulsion were instituted as possible penalties for any student accused of discriminatory harassment, and those found guilty, probably as a response to critics of Landolfi's penalty, were barred from playing sports or engaging in other extracurricular activities. Casteen became more "proactive" in attempting to stem racism, visiting dormitories to lecture students after some other, less-publicized incidents. In the wake of the June 1989 Tiananmen incident in Beijing, when the world watched the bloody suppression of student demonstrators, Casteen immediately expressed his support for the campus Chinese community. He explained how the Parents' Fund of the UConn Foundation would provide funds to allow Chinese students and faculty to call family and friends in China. At the end of the month, he informed the UConn community that the campus Chinese Club had established a China Watch Fund and urged others to join him in contributing to it. The fund would be used to support the pro-democracy movement and to document it so that students could preserve the memory and promote understanding of the event.

As a consequence of the attention drawn to Asian American students, UConn later established the Asian American Cultural Center, which emphasized social and cultural programs, and the Institute of Asian American Studies, which encouraged teaching of and scholarship about Asian American themes. Casteen also embraced the need for a comprehensive multicultural training effort. At the same time, however, he recognized that Ardaiolo had done "his best under difficult circumstances" and saw the attacks on him as "bitterly personal and poorly documented." In essence, Casteen attempted to be fair and reasonable in dealing with the explosive issue of race.[74]

Political Incorrectness and Fighting Words

In universities across the nation, the issue of racial bias collided with the right of freedom of speech in what some saw as a growing trend of "political correctness." The matter came home to UConn in 1989 when, somewhat ironically in light of the December 3 incident, an Asian American student, Nina Wu, tacked a handmade poster to her dormitory door that listed the types of people who were "welcome," "tolerated," "unwelcome," and "shot on site." The last category included "bimbos," "preppies," "racists," and "homos." Two women who believed the word "bimbos" was directed at them complained. An official reviewing the complaint brought action because the poster contained the anti-homosexual slur. In April 1989 the university expelled Wu from all residence and dining halls as a result of finding the word "homos" to be a violation of the Student Conduct Code's anti-harassment rule, which prohibited "making slurs or epithets based on race, sex, ethnic origin, religion or sexual orientation." Wu filed a suit in the Federal District Court in Hartford, contending that the school had violated her right to free speech. A settlement reinstated Wu's room and board privileges. It also forced the school to weaken its anti-harassment rule by incorporating language from the Supreme Court's "fighting words" doctrine. The new rule limited offensive speech only if it was made face-to-face and in a way that would likely provoke immediate violence.[75]

Wu's attorney, Karen Lee Torre of New Haven, explained that the rule change represented "a rejection of that school of thought that urges exceptions to the First Amendment as a way to eliminate racism." Susan Bellandese, UConn's interim dean of students, then showed her concern, particularly in light of what had happened on campus. She wondered, "We don't want to restrict free speech, but do we really want a campus where a student can walk up to another student and say to them, 'We don't want niggers at the University of Connecticut'?" Paul Bock exploded in anger at any thought of diluting the condemnation of racism in the name of free speech. The university's lawyer, Assistant Attorney General Paul Shapiro, felt equally strongly that Bock was following the wrong path: "The answer to thoughtless racial (and other) epithets is education—both as an institution, and on an incident by incident basis. Punishing students for speech or communication on the basis of content is unconstitutional and indefensible," he argued. Casteen emphasized parity. He pointed out that "colleges and universities were trying to balance their commitments to First Amendment rights involving free speech and the determination to provide for their students a community free of abuse and harassment." After Wu's settlement, the university had to also drop charges against sixteen students because the incidents did not meet the "face-to-face" standard. Casteen seemed dubious. "We have got to see how it works. I'm not sure that anybody thinks it will work over the long haul," he told a *New York Times* reporter. As with many other university presidents at the end of the twentieth century, Casteen was finding that navigating the rough waters between racial harassment and freedom of speech was proving difficult.[76]

Babbidge Library: Poster Child for Campus Blight

Another difficult situation was presented to Casteen in the crumbling façade of Babbidge Library. Before Christmas of 1988, Casteen wrote to David McQuade, Governor William O'Neill's assistant, to inform him of two structural problems: one at Branford House on the Avery Point Regional Campus, and another, more serious one directly in the center of the Storrs campus. The Babbidge Library was the largest construction project of its time in southern New England under the supervision of the state's Department of Public Works (DPW). It opened in 1978, and problems with its construction became known already in the summer of 1985, although not to their full extent. As a consequence of structural defects in the cantilevered section of the building, the brick veneer that faced the building had begun to pull away from its concrete core. The administration informed the university community that, during a five-month architectural evaluation period, access to the library would be limited to its west side, which faced Hillside Road and a new building that was in the process of construction, Gampel Pavilion. Safety measures included industrial netting to secure the façade over the loading zone on Babbidge Road; a covered pedestrian walkway over the west entrance; and fencing to block the north and south entrances. Sallie Giffen, Casteen's vice-president for administration, apologized to the public for the inconvenience and asked for patience. Patience, indeed, would be needed, as the five-month assessment period ultimately turned into a decade in which the library was a poster child for campus blight. Until its complete renovation and rededication in 1998, the Babbidge Library, wrapped in its plastic tarpaulins, gave the impression of a bombed-out building. The wounded façade, resulting from poor architectural conceptualization and faulty implementation by the DPW, served as an institutional embarrassment. Casteen estimated the repair costs at

$3.5 million, but once UConn decided to completely renovate, the costs mounted to significantly more. Many people agreed, however, that on the second try the architects and builders got it right. This conclusion was long after Casteen had left the university, though, just as the library's troubles had begun long before he arrived.[77]

Saving History: The Thomas J. Dodd Research Center

Another building associated with the library, the Thomas J. Dodd Research Center, opened five years after Casteen's departure. He did, however, play a significant role in its creation. Shortly after the new president's arrival on campus in 1985, John P. McDonald, the director of university libraries, wrote to him about acquiring Senator Christopher Dodd's papers. The idea originated with history professor Thomas G. Paterson, who had met Dodd on Maine's Monhegan Island that summer. Paterson suggested to both Casteen and McDonald that the papers be obtained and a Dodd Center be established. McDonald pointed out that the Connecticut State Library currently held the senator's father's papers and that it was redefining its collection policies, which would permit transferring the late Senator Thomas J. Dodd's materials to UConn. Such acquisitions could spearhead the goal of becoming a major public university by strengthening the library's Historical Manuscripts and Archives Division. The division had been established in 1978 when the move to the Babbidge Library created stack space in the Wilbur Cross building. Its expansion, according to McDonald, who also sought more personnel, would strengthen the library in its ability to support research by faculty and graduate students in the social sciences. At the time, Casteen did not think the Dodd papers made the case for a major change in the library's mission, but he expressed a willingness to reexamine the issue.[78]

Two years later, following a draft prepared by Randall Jimerson, the head of the Historical Manuscripts and Archives Division, Casteen, in a letter to the younger Dodd, reaffirmed UConn's interest in serving as a repository for the papers. The acquisition would not only recognize the Dodds's record of public service but would be "an important step to further our goal of becoming a nationally recognized research center." While the Wilbur Cross Building would have enough space for new acquisitions for a few years, Casteen explained that within a decade the university would need a separate building to house its archival research collections, including the Dodd Papers. He continued that the Dodd materials would form a nucleus around which other political and public affairs papers would be added, and on completion of a proposed Archives Research Center such political collections would take on even greater research value. The archival facility would be centrally located, adjacent to the Babbidge Library, and on the approximate scale of the recently completed United Technologies Engineering Building. After describing what would be in such a building, Casteen suggested that, given certain conditions, it could be named after the elder Dodd. Those conditions related to private fundraising that would supplement funding from the state. He added that there seemed to be substantial interest among potential contributors. Within a short time, the state appropriated $9 million for the building and Dodd's supporters raised another million. The earliest large pledges came from two Holocaust survivors, West Hartford developer Simon Konover and New London automobile dealer Sigmund Strochlitz. While the library and archives staff did much of the heavy lifting in establishing the Dodd Center, Casteen showed vision in his support.[79]

My Old Virginia Home: Casteen Returns to His Alma Mater

Not everyone, however, saw the president in a positive light. By the end of July 1989 the *Hartford Courant*'s perceptive education writer, Robert A. Frahm, published a lengthy article headlined "Casteen's Ability to Succeed Being Questioned." The piece catalogued the president's achievements and noted his considerable intellect and extraordinary grasp of detail, but it also pointed to growing criticism of his "reserved, impersonal demeanor and a demanding, often meddling management style." Associates found him difficult to deal with, an uncompromising boss. Julias Elias, the former dean of liberal arts and sciences who became Casteen's interim vice-president for academic affairs and continually clashed with him before resigning that post, remarked, "He doesn't listen to anybody. He cracks the whip and terrifies people." Elias added that Casteen failed to delegate and drained authority from his administrative associates. Additional irritants included UConn's fall nationally from twenty-fourth to twenty-eighth among public universities in research spending between 1984 and 1987, an inadequate state budget allocation for the university in 1989–90, the deteriorating campus infrastructure, and the state auditor's investigation of improper channeling of research money at the Health Center into the private University of Connecticut Foundation instead of state accounts. Casteen, however, remained optimistic that matters would improve.[80]

At one point, Casteen proclaimed, "I came here believing a substantial number of people in this state want its state university to be a great one in the tradition of Michigan, North Carolina, Wisconsin, Texas. I haven't changed a bit in that belief." He didn't mention Virginia, but it must have been on his mind. According to Julius Elias, Casteen told many people, Elias included, that becoming president of his alma mater was his life's ambition. In early February 1990 Casteen denied rumors that he was a candidate for that institution's presidency. He told the UConn student newspaper that he had no interest in the position and was not talking to the Virginia search committee. "I left there on purpose.

I don't think beyond now," he responded. A month later, he submitted his resignation as of July 31 to Dr. Andrew J. Canzonetti, the chair of the board of
trustees. While the rumors had been rife, the immediacy of his leaving came as
a surprise. The announcement at a hastily called press conference in Virginia took
Connecticut's trustees, administrators, and staff unawares. It irked Governor
William O'Neill, whose spokesman claimed Casteen had given the governor a
promise he would stay for ten years, unlike his two predecessors, who left in half
that time. David McQuade, O'Neill's aide, complained that the governor "didn't
want the presidency of the University of Connecticut viewed as a steppingstone
to any other institution." Campus reaction was mixed, with many feeling abandoned at a time of a severe budget crunch. As Peter Halvorson, a geography
professor and University Senate and AAUP leader, suggested, "When he came,
he and all of us had great expectations that have foundered on a foundering
budget. . . . In his time, he helped us to play a little catchup, but didn't allow us
to move ahead."[81]

Husky Sports: More Than a Holding Operation

Casteen's presidency, however, did coincide with a profound change in UConn
athletics, which witnessed a major transformation during his and his two predecessors' administrations. The impact of Title IX, the joining of the Big East
Conference, the hiring of new women's and men's basketball coaches (in 1985
and 1986, respectively), increased concern about the academic accomplishments
of student athletes, a change in athletic director, and the opening of Gampel
Pavilion marked the Ferguson, DiBiaggio, and Casteen years. At the beginning
of this period, the essential issue in sports was whether UConn would play football in the NCAA's university division as opposed to a college category; the latter would offer fewer scholarships to athletes. The divisions ultimately would
evolve into Divisions I, I-AA, II, and III, but in 1972 had not yet been so refined.
Roger Bradlau, the president of the UConn Club, strongly supported an expanded sports program when he argued, "If the University of Connecticut is
ever to attain the reputation as a *great university,* this can only be accomplished
by taking its proper place in the University division of the NCAA." As the era
ended, UConn moved squarely in that direction. Already by the mid-1980s
Coach Joe Morrone's soccer team had won one national championship and
Coach Diane Wright's women's field hockey team had won two.[82]

Joining the Big East

It was football, however, that was one of the two key sports driving the surge to
Division I during the early 1970s, and there the prospects did not look good. Be-

tween 1965 and 1975, when the Huskies played outside of the Yankee Conference (Maine, New Hampshire, Rhode Island, Massachusetts, and Boston University) against Yale, Holy Cross, Rutgers, and Temple, they had nine wins, nineteen losses, and one tie. The school's overall record counted forty-four wins, forty-six losses, and five ties. According to one observer, the Yankee Conference did not serve UConn well because its games weren't televised, the stadiums had limited seating capacity, and the fan base was small. In basketball, where UConn's record and tradition excelled, the conference affiliation also seemed questionable. At the very beginning of 1975, President Glenn Ferguson told John Toner, the UConn Athletic Director, "I am now convinced that the University of Connecticut should withdraw from the Yankee Conference. . . . With the exception of Massachusetts and Rhode Island, and the possible press coverage in the Boston area when we play Boston University, we do not derive any benefit from our participation in the Yankee Conference." He went on to define "benefit" as the recruitment of students, the development of meaningful contacts, and the nurturing of relationships with comparable institutions. He suggested that playing two basketball games against Rutgers rather than against Maine or New Hampshire would be to UConn's great advantage. By the end of the decade, the opportunity for a new league emerged, although football would not be carried with it and would remain UConn's sole sport within the Yankee Conference.[83]

After four weeks of discussion with groups such as the Athletic Advisory Committee and the Alumni Liaison Committee, on Tuesday, May 29, 1979, John Toner made a commitment to join six other institutions in a new athletic conference, initially dubbed by sportswriters the "Super Conference" before being named the "Big East." He had to respond quickly and remembered, "On the eve of the [Memorial Day] holiday I had it put to me point blank. They wanted a yes or no. I said yes." In addition to UConn, the conference brought together basketball powers Boston College, Georgetown, Providence, Seton Hall, St. John's, and Syracuse, with the expectation that another New England school, such as URI or Holy Cross, and a Philadelphia area institution, such as Temple or Villanova, would join later. It held out great possibility for exciting athletic competition. As a *Connecticut Daily Campus* writer remarked, "It could really be something." And something it became.[84]

Basketball drove the conference, the brainchild of Providence College Athletic Director Dave Gavitt, but NCAA regulations required that six other sports be competed in for championships. While most UConn teams eventually would contest within the Big East, cross country, indoor and outdoor track, tennis, golf, and swimming rounded out the initial competitors. These, however, seemed to be the side show. In the first season of Big East play, Syracuse, St. John's, and Georgetown all registered in the UPI weekly Board of Coaches' Top Twenty basketball ratings. By late February 1980, sixteen of twenty-one conference games had been sellouts. UConn could compete, completing the season with a 20–8 record and getting a bid to the National Invitational Tournament. However, Coach Dom Perno appeared brutally realistic about the new competition when he remarked that fans will have to understand the difference between a loss to St. John's and one to Maine. He elaborated that teams like Syracuse, St. John's, and Providence had been to the Final Four in the NCAAs. Fans "have to be aware of what we're up against. I don't see twenty-five wins again."[85]

By the time Perno became head coach of his alma mater in 1977, taking over from Dee Rowe, the Huskies had already played their first game in the Hartford Civic Center, on January 2, 1976. It was his team and its fans that luckily escaped injury when the snow-burdened roof of the Civic Center collapsed on January 18, 1978, eight hours after a game against UMass. The following November, Perno's Huskies played the first televised game produced by a fledgling sports cable outlet ESPN-TV, when UConn battled Athletes in Action in an exhibition game. In January 1979 the Bristol, Connecticut–based station, which would become a national phenomenon, featured the UConn-Rutgers contest as the first college basketball game aired on national cable television. Perno, with key players Corny Thompson and Mike McKay, would lead the team to three twenty-game-winning seasons in a row between 1979 and 1981, but his coaching tenure encountered difficulty by the mid-1980s. In the spring of 1985, basketball star Earl Kelley was involved in an on-campus incident involving a pistol. On October 1, Kelley pleaded guilty to reduced charges in Rockville Superior Court, but his UConn disciplinary hearing dragged on. Just before Christmas, campus officials found him innocent of the gun charge but guilty of having bullied two students. His punishment moved him off campus but permitted him to remain on the basketball team. When he failed to complete fall semester coursework by the deadline of February 17, he was ruled ineligible for varsity sports. With Kelley gone, the team finished the season with twelve wins and sixteen losses; Perno's nine-year tenure as head coach also ended. After a series of meetings with John Toner in which they "reviewed the entire basketball program," he resigned on April 14, 1986, with a career record of 139–114.[86]

Academics and Athletics

By that time, a special Athletic Task Force had been appointed to review not only the basketball program but the entire athletic operation at UConn. Discontent bubbled up in two directions—athletic competitiveness and the academic achievement of athletes. The Kelley case brought to light that only four basketball players recruited between 1977 and 1986 were graduated, prompting the *New Haven Register* to editorialize, "What has become all too obvious is that UConn isn't meeting its obligation to athletes in revenue producing sports that put extraordinary pressure on those athletes . . . [its] task . . . has become increasingly difficult since UConn started playing a Big East schedule (with frequent TV exposure) that subjects its basketball players to a difficult regimen." The problem of academic standards for athletes was not new to John Casteen. About ten years before he came to Connecticut, the University of Virginia faced a similar problem. Casteen participated in the formation of a committee that unified the campus behind the athletic program and made Virginia a force in the Atlantic Coast Conference (ACC), particularly in basketball and football. Shortly after arriving at UConn, Casteen received a study of graduation rates for student athletes. He asked his vice-president for academic affairs to review the academic provisions and support for athletes. Casteen subsequently established the President's Task Force on Athletics, chaired by a trustee, Dr. Gerard J. Lawrence, a former varsity basketball player at St. John's University.[87]

When the task force held a public hearing in late February 1986 at the campus's Bishop Center, the speakers appeared less concerned with academic standards than with athletic competitiveness. One 1980 graduate tapped his finger at the podium and complained, "I'm sick of mediocrity at this university." Speaker after speaker criticized the school's lack of basketball success, its coach, Dom Perno, and its athletic director, John Toner. The audience seemed united in support of UConn's Big East affiliation but annoyed that the basketball team had three straight losing seasons and was on the verge of a fourth. They pummeled Toner for going on record that UConn's goal was to finish in the top five of the Big East within three years rather than winning the conference. When the academic ramifications did receive attention, some speakers noted that Georgetown and Villanova effectively competed in the league without downgrading their academic standards. UConn needed to do something to improve, and, they argued, it should look to such models. David Camaione, head of the university's Sports and Leisure Studies Department and a former athlete at Ohio State, compared his place of work with his alma mater. Ohio State had tremendous resources, while UConn had "second-third-fourth-rate resources. That's a sin. There are 500 athletes here, one academic advisor with one assistant. They just can't do the job. When you go to Ohio State, you're impressed. When you go to Connecticut, you're depressed. It's a dirty campus."[88]

That last remark referred to UConn's deferred maintenance, which during the 1980s put off physical improvements in the buildings and grounds at Storrs. The remainder of Camaione's comment spoke to the reality of the situation affecting Connecticut's resources in general. On May 9, 1986, the President's Task Force on Athletics issued its final report. It operated under the following premises: that the university's central mission was education and providing excellence in teaching, research, and service; that the development of excellence in athletics did not contradict such a mission; that excellence in academics and athletics mutually reinforced each other; and that those situations that prevented the attainment of athletic excellence could be rectified. The task force found a malaise infecting the attitude toward, and operation of, athletics at the university and recommended that the president and board of trustees make clear to the university community, the alumni, and the people of the state that they were committed to excellence in athletic programs and that a winning tradition is compatible with the institution's academic goals. It found that the athletic director had not been formally evaluated and urged an annual evaluation as well as an annual structured evaluation of each coach, sport, and program. It advocated a new mission statement for the Division of Athletics after finding that goals for athletic programs had been "poorly stated and evaluated." The task force noted that graduation rates for participants in all intercollegiate athletics at UConn actually were slightly higher than for the student body as a whole, but in select sports (football and men's basketball), they lagged significantly behind the institutional average. It recommended improvement at least to the student body norm for the laggards and an ideal goal of a 100 percent graduation rate within five years of matriculation. The academic advising program also required improvement, and the task force recommended that a new program that provided appropriate academic support and tutoring for athletes be put in its place. A staff member should be specifically charged with monitoring and assisting the academic progress of men's basketball. On the other hand, the task force recommended against separate dormitories or eating facilities for student athletes but advocated designated areas within "mainstreamed" facilities and dining facilities for the service of the late meals required by practices. It advocated a goal of providing financial assistance to all recruited athletes, and those in the most demanding sports should receive aid for summer school or for continuing academic programs after the completion of athletic eligibility. It remarked on the inadequacy of the Sports Medicine Program and recommended that a well-developed one be put in its place, with a medical director in charge. It called for improved public relations with a director who oversaw a comprehensive program including athletics, and for improving the appearance of the campus (which would help in recruiting athletes). These and other recommendations ultimately became standard for UConn as it attempted to reach national prominence in both academics and athletics.[89]

The Coming of Calhoun

Another move toward national prominence, although one not fully predictable at the time, occurred almost simultaneously with the issuance of the task force's report. The search for a successor to Dom Perno as basketball coach came to a close. The fourteen-member committee headed by John Toner, which had met for approximately eleven hours in three meetings, selected its short list on Monday, May 5, with the goal of choosing a new coach by May 18, the day before the start of the Big East basketball meetings in Puerto Rico. The three leading candidates were Mitch Buonaguro, who served in his first year as head coach of the Fairfield University Stags after having been an assistant to Rollie Massimino for eight years at Villanova; Nick Macarchuk, the successful nine-year coach of Canisius, who had previously worked with Big East Commissioner Dave Gavitt at Providence; and Jim Calhoun. Calhoun, the fourteen-year coach at Northeastern, had brought New England's others Huskies to the NCAA tournament five times in six years and had a won-loss record of 250 and 137; the professional National Basketball Association (NBA) had also drafted five of his players. The search committee ranked him as top candidate "due to his lengthy experience, his grasp and understanding of UConn, and his familiarity with large institutions." It added, "He's intelligent, very industrious, and is a problem solver." While he was not likely to be able to recruit in-state athletes as quickly as Buonaguro, the committee believed that "Calhoun *is* perceived to be one who will find a way to get the job done."[90]

Calhoun understood that the school didn't expect immediate miracles, even if the fans demanded them. He believed that he had at least six years to rebuild and stabilize. After his first season, he might have wondered if that would be long enough. Calhoun listed his program expectations for 1986–87: (1) improve relationship between academics and basketball; (2) improve actual and public perception of type of student-athlete representing UConn; (3)maintain current squad and implement new style and perception of play. The team finished with nine wins and nineteen losses. Worse still from the perspective of his stated goals, the two star players, Cliff Robinson and Phil Gamble, despite the efforts of a new Counseling Program for Intercollegiate Athletes, were declared academically ineligible for the final eleven games of the season. Men's basketball seemed to implode, but the athletic director, not the new coach, took the fall. President Casteen reassigned John Toner to new duties while denying that he fired him and brought in Todd Turner from the University of Virginia to replace him. Calhoun, while suffering the 1986–87 season, began the recruiting that would change Connecticut's fortunes. He signed Chris Smith, the state's best player and a national top-25 standout. The following season, 1987–88, the Cinderella Huskies won the NIT, followed the next year by an 18–13 record and their advance to the quarterfinals of the NIT. For the first time in school history, UConn produced victories in national tournament play in back-to-back seasons. By 1990 Calhoun's Huskies, in a "Dream Season," shared the regular season Big East title, won the Big East postseason championship, and ended the year with thirty-one victories and a trip to the elite eight of the NCAA tournament. Led by Smith, Israeli Nadav Henefeld, Tate George, and Scott Burrell, the Huskies held the number-one seed in the Eastern Region of the NCAA. They beat Boston University and California to advance to the "sweet sixteen" at the Meadowlands in New Jersey. There, with a second left in the game, Burrell pitched the basketball ninety-four feet to George, who sunk "the shot," which defeated Clemson University. In a subsequent game, Christian Laettner of Duke was equally impressive when he hit a jump shot with 2.8 seconds left to give the North Carolina school a 79–78 victory over Connecticut and eliminate the Huskies from the tournament. UConn men's basketball, however, would never be the same. It came big onto the national scene. Its leader, Jim Calhoun, four years after coming to UConn, was named Coach of the Year by the Big East, UPI, the AP, and the *Sporting News*.[91]

The Arrival of Auriemma

A year before Connecticut hired Calhoun, a new women's basketball coach had also arrived in Storrs. The team had suffered for quite some time, with a 9–18 overall and 3–13 Big East record in 1984–85; it had failed to achieve even one winning season in the eleven years since it had become a varsity sport as part of the Division of Athletics. Hence, the new women's coach faced a definite challenge. On May 17, 1985, John Toner announced the appointment of thirty-one-year-old former University of Virginia assistant coach Geno Auriemma. At Virginia, Auriemma's main responsibilities included recruiting, practice planning, and working with players in practice. Before Auriemma's arrival in Charlottesville, the Lady Cavaliers had been last in the Atlantic Coast Conference (ACC). In his four years there, he helped them achieve a 75–39 record and make the NCAA tournament during his final two years. Pat Meiser, the female administrator most responsible for UConn women's sports at the time, remarked that Auriemma's attractiveness as a candidate stemmed from his ability to build a program from the ground up. She remarked, "We weren't looking for someone who was successful at an established program, but someone who turned a losing program around." Approximately one hundred people applied for the job and six were interviewed. Meiser continued, "We had a sense that Geno was the person who could bring us from mediocre to successful. He understood what it would take to get the job done."[92]

The job did get done. Auriemma began to build a winning tradition. In light of the momentous success he would have later, his goals for 1987–88 now appear modest. He aspired to being one of the top three teams in the conference; he wanted to improve the team's overall record; he desired to increase attendance to five hundred people per game; and he hoped to continue to graduate all of his players. By 1989 the women's team, led by Big East Player of the Year Kerry Bascom, won its first Big East Conference regular season and tournament championship. For the first time, the women went to the NCAA tournament, something that would become perennial over the next two decades. Auriemma offered his wisdom: "I try to instill in our team the philosophy that you have to work hard and there is no easy way to do anything." While beginning to enjoy the fruits of victory, the coach showed some frustration with the status of women's athletics. He complained, "The worst part of coaching is the perception that it is just women's sports and if you were really good you would be coaching men's."[93]

Title IX Taken Seriously

Women's sports, however, increasingly received respect, especially at UConn, but change did not come easily. In 1965, basketball, field hockey, and gymnastics comprised the only permanent women's intercollegiate teams at UConn, and they shared a budget of $1,700. This compared to twenty-six men's varsity and sub-varsity teams, which consumed a $750,000 budget. Women fielded eighty-two intramural teams, as compared to 415 for men; they were barred from the Field House and relegated to the old Hawley Armory. By 1974–75, John Toner diverted funds originally allocated for a new scoreboard and track and field improvements to a projected and enhanced but still insufficient $25,000 women's sports budget. The Field House opened to both sexes during recreational hours. At the beginning of that academic year, Toner appointed Rita Custeau to be coordinator of women's athletics, which was transferred from the financially strapped Physical Education Department to the previously all-male Athletics Division. Much of this was in response to Title IX of the federal government's Higher Education Act of 1972, which stated, "No person in the United States shall, on the basis of sex, be excluded from participation in, be denied the benefits of, or be subjected to discrimination under any education program or activity receiving federal financial assistance." This meant that facilities, equipment, and coaching had to be comparable for intercollegiate athletes of both sexes. Despite this, Mary Kovacik, the captain of the women's basketball team, complained in January 1975 about interruptions in the varsity game against Springfield because men were lifting weights and practicing free throws on an adjacent court, activities that were forbidden when the men played. The only time the hoop women could perform before a large audience occurred when they were permitted to play during the halftime of men's games. The women's softball team complained that they lacked a coach, the hockey team expressed dismay about inadequate dressing facilities, and the women skiers felt discriminated against because they lacked uniforms, which the men on the same team had.[94]

At the end of September 1977 female athletes at UConn protested when they were forced off their already poor-quality softball field by football coach Walt Nadzak, whose team would further degrade the grassy surface. They told the *Connecticut Daily Campus*, "Our point is this—women's athletics are coming of age at the University of Connecticut. We no longer will settle for second best.

We are improving in every aspect of every sport. We've come a long way, but . . . we still have a long way to go." Three years later, the Athletic Advisory Committee released a report on the progress in implementing Title IX. Between the academic years 1975–76 and 1979–80, total expenditures for athletics had increased 73.5 percent, but those for women's sports had risen by 154.3 percent. The Athletic Division had also hired three new fulltime coaches for women's teams. Most tellingly for students, in 1975–76 UConn offered one grant-in-aid for $350 to a woman athlete; in 1979–80, forty-two women received grants-in-aid totaling $62,868. While the allocation for males still dwarfed that for females, the gender equity situation had improved. With the new financial assistance, the number of women athletes increased from 153 in 1975 to 220 in 1979–80, at a time when the number of men had decreased because of the elimination of some sub-varsity men's sports. The progress, however, hid ongoing problems. In 1979 Rita Custeau, joined by all of the women coaches, brought allegations of unequal treatment of women coaches and varsity teams within the Department of Athletics. The complaints involved unequal assignments and access to facilities. Men's visiting teams could pre-empt locker rooms assigned to women's teams; poor maintenance adversely affected playing fields for field hockey, softball, and the practice gym for basketball; office space was unequally apportioned, and women coaches had inadequate clerical support. Other complaints involved salary inequities, unequal teaching loads, lack of formal, written job descriptions, and a lack of scholarships for players. The director of the Office of Affirmative Action Programs found a desire in the administration to resolve the issues but suspected men were favored by John Toner, the athletic director. She remarked, "The old boys' network mentality is very much alive in the department." Efforts to remedy the situation ebbed and flowed during the remainder of the decade. In May 1984 the State of Connecticut's Permanent Commission on the Status of Women voted unanimously to commend President DiBiaggio for his "position supporting the spirit and the intent of the Federal Title IX Legislation." By February 1990 the women's basketball team broke an attendance record by attracting 3,151 spectators to its game with Georgetown—far more than Coach Auriemma's goal of 500 that he had set just three years earlier. The new interest prompted him to remark, "I want to develop a following. I want this to be the beginning of something."[95]

Under the Dome: The Opening of Gampel Pavilion

The attraction may not simply have been the team. The crowd came to the new Gampel Pavilion when the Student Union Board of Governors, in cooperation with the Athletic Department, gave away tickets in order to break the attendance record for a Big East women's basketball game. A few days earlier, the men opened Gampel with their game against St. John's. For those who couldn't get tickets for that, or wanted to see Gampel from a better seat than they had had for the men's contest, the women Huskies versus Georgetown provided the opportunity. One student, sitting in the front row for the tipoff, said, "This is the first women's game I've ever been to. I came to the [men's game] against St. John's, but tonight I came to see what's it's like to get a good seat . . . and to see the girls play." The Sports Center, of which Gampel stood out as the most prominent part, had been long in the making. Discussions to develop expanded athletic facilities had begun as early as 1968. A project request for a new sports center went to the board of trustees in 1975 but was put on hold because of other pressing needs, notably the new university library. In the summer of 1978 the Board of Higher Education approved planning funds, and in 1979 the trustees endorsed the project for full funding. After that, a bumpy path over the next decade finally led to the opening of Gampel Pavilion in January 1990.[96]

UConn officials offered many reasons to justify the new facility. Most simply, the Field House had become outmoded and overused. As a journalism student described the situation in 1974, the student population in Storrs had more than doubled, from 6,510 in 1953, when the Field House opened, to 15,806. He recalled, "The only addition to the complex since its construction has been an interior coat of paint." The American Association of Health, Physical Education, and Recreation prescribed 162,480 square feet as the minimum covered floor space required in 1974 for an adequate facility; the Field House offered 77,000. By the next decade, when Gampel was under construction, the student population had increased even more and the ratio called for even greater square footage. The University of Rhode Island, which was two-thirds the size of UConn in the mid-1970s had half again as much gym space; the University of Maine counted the same amount of covered playing space as UConn but enrolled half the number of students. John Toner didn't hesitate to point out that between 1961 and 1974, the State Legislature spent $13 million on indoor facilities at the four state colleges but nothing at Storrs. The coming of Title IX further necessitated a new venue for UConn indoor sports. Finally, the Big East Conference found that four league facilities, including the Field House, did not meet its standards of excellence for basketball games. Thus by 1987 plans called for a domed building of approximately 171,000 square feet, which included a handicapped-accessible arena with seating for 8,000 (in order not to compete with the larger Hartford Civic Center), locker rooms for men and women, offices for the Division of Athletics, and classrooms, research labs, and offices for the academic department of Sports and Leisure Studies. Also planned was a 39,000-square-foot adjoining natatorium with a fifty-meter, Olympic-size swimming pool, a separate diving well, and seating for five hundred spectators.[97]

Not everyone agreed with the priority reflected in the building of the Sports Center. When UConn sought design money in 1983 from the state, WFSB

Channel Three television station editorialized about the shortage of library books and buildings with leaking roofs that forced "students to run an obstacle course around buckets on the floor. . . . We urge the legislature to cut the arena from its budget, and to put that money where it's really needed—into books and maintenance." President John DiBiaggio responded publicly that some of UConn's best academic programs benefitted from the laboratories and equipment in the new center. He pointed out that instruction and research programs that train the state's future teachers and coaches, fitness and nutrition experts, and rehabilitation therapists would be strengthened. He added that students required new facilities because the Field House operated twenty hours a day during much of the year. The president concluded, "I agree with this station that none of these factors is any *more* important than library books, or repairs to other campus buildings. But neither are they any *less* important to maintaining the quality of an education at the University of Connecticut."[98]

Aside from overcoming such criticism as WFSB's, UConn officials had to deal with rising costs and make good on a pledge to raise private funds in support of the pavilion. At the beginning of 1987 a spokesman for the Department of Public Works announced that far-reaching cost miscalculations by the architects required an additional $5 million in state bonding to cover a new projected total cost of $21.1 million; in 1985, they had estimated a total of $14 million, and then in April 1986 the figure had jumped to $17.1 million. As a consequence, Donald Cassin, the deputy commissioner of the Department of Public Works, acknowledged that the need to return to the legislature for added funds was embarrassing. The *Hartford Courant* claimed that "anyone can make a mistake, but the recently revealed $5 million error . . . is too much." The Republican senate minority leader, Reginald J. Smith of New Hartford, said, "At some point, you have to consider pulling the plug on this sort of thing when it starts getting too expensive. And this is rapidly approaching that point." Despite such doubt, the Senate voted 33–3 to issue the additional $5 million in bonding, clearing the way for construction. After a visit to Florida from President Casteen and Lois Post of the UConn Foundation, the requirement for private funding received assistance from an unprecedented $1 million contribution by Harry A. Gampel, who had received his undergraduate business degree from UConn in 1943. In one of his first jobs after graduation Gampel, a Connecticut and Florida real estate developer, worked on the structural steel of the Field House that the pavilion would replace. His gift was the largest private contribution to UConn up to that time and won him the naming rights in perpetuity to the pavilion, which officially opened to acclaim and "Huskymania" on January 27, 1990, when twentieth-ranked UConn beat fifteenth-ranked St. John's 72–58 in basketball. A new era in UConn sports exploded under the domed arena that sat like a flying saucer in the midst of the Storrs campus.[99]

The turn in athletics coincided with the beginning of an era in which UConn reached for national prominence. It represented the first leg of a three-legged stool that would bring the institution national recognition. The other two, a handsomely rebuilt campus and an enhanced academic atmosphere, emerged as UConn continued to soar athletically. The end of one millennium and the beginning of the next would witness the institution's extending its reach far beyond the dreams of the small agricultural school of its beginnings or even of the modern institution of mid-century. The university in Storrs was ready to make its mark nationally.

6

Creating a National University: 1990–2006

$\mathcal{U}$Conn, at the close of the millennium and immediately after, would finally achieve new prominence, transcending its status as both a state and a regional institution to win national recognition. Two presidents of very different styles, Harry J. Hartley and Philip E. Austin, each in his own way presided over the dramatic changes that occurred. The physical transformation of the campuses, the attraction of students who were more academically qualified and more nationally diverse than ever before, the addition of leading faculty, unprecedented private fundraising, the rising stature of the athletic teams, particularly in basketball, and the upgrade in football all promoted a new regard for the university despite its weakened operating budgets. Research successes, as in the field of reproductive genetics, attracted national and international attention and brought research funding to all-time highs. By 2006, as the University of Connecticut celebrated its 125th anniversary, this once modest agricultural school and later regional university would emerge as a national institution.

The Hartley Years

John Casteen departed UConn as a respected, if not always liked, *outsider,* never having established a warm relationship with the university community. Consequently, many looked to a known quantity, an *insider,* to succeed him. When it came time to appoint an interim president, several familiar names captured attention, particularly Provost Thomas J. Tighe, James E. Mulvihill, vice-president and provost at the UConn Health Center, and Anthony T. DiBenedetto, former graduate and academic vice-president. Others considered included Peter Mc-

Fadden, the former dean of engineering and acting provost and, at the time, Casteen's executive assistant and secretary to the board of trustees, and Harry J. Hartley, who had served twice as financial vice-president from 1975 to 1978 and 1984 to 1987 and very briefly as acting president when Casteen was abroad in 1987. In early April 1990 the trustees, despite some quiet opposition to such an appointment from Casteen, selected the fifty-two-year-old Hartley. Earlier, Hartley had been approached by David McQuade, Governor William O'Neill's assistant, and encouraged to accept the post. He seemed to have broad support among students and had served as president of the AAUP in 1980–81, which suggested that he would have good relations with the union. As a consequence, the trustees were assured of Hartford's support for their choice. Canzonetti told the public, "It won't take long to bring Harry up to speed. Currently our fiscal problems are of paramount importance to the university. Our experience with Harry says we will continue to make progress with him in the interim instead of sitting still until a new president is appointed." He added, in an attempt to prevent outside candidates from being discouraged about applying for the permanent position, that the appointment would remove Hartley from consideration for that. The trustees, however, did not vote on the matter, and Hartley never promised he would not be a candidate. By August, when Hartley officially took over for Casteen, rumors raced around that he had been nominated for the permanent job. Two other individuals familiar to Connecticut, Lewis B. Rome and State Education Commissioner Gerald Tirozzi, also received attention as possible candidates. Tirozzi's candidacy appeared less serious than Rome's. On the other hand, Rome, the former Connecticut legislative leader and 1982 Republican gubernatorial candidate who had entered UConn as a sixteen-year-old freshman, earning a BA degree in 1954 and his LLB from the university's Law School in 1957, confirmed his interest in the position as early as May 1990. He had maintained close ties with his alma mater and believed because of his political experience that he could give it a strong voice in Hartford if he were selected president. Despite that, in mid-October the *Daily Campus* editorialized that Hartley should be chosen as the university's next president. As the semester drew to a close in early December, the paper reported that Hartley would be the top selection from a pool of 117 candidates that included twelve minority individuals, six women, and twenty college presidents. The report proved accurate. The trustees selected Harry J. Hartley as the university's twelfth president. On December 12, 1990, before the start of the UConn basketball game against New Hampshire in Gampel Pavilion, the public address announcer introduced Hartley, who stood at center court, as the new president. The student section started chanting "Harry! Harry!" and the sellout crowd gave him a several-minute standing ovation that brought UConn's new leader to tears.[1]

Not long after, in 1992, Governor Lowell Weicker appointed Lew Rome to be chair of the University of Connecticut Board of Trustees, making for a complicated, but ultimately workable, relationship between the two former rivals. Rome's ascendancy followed the shifting political winds within the state. Andrew Canzonetti was a very visible surgeon and active Democrat from New Britain. When independent Lowell Weicker won the governorship in 1990, his roots in the state Republican Party gave him solid ties to Lew Rome, whom he appointed to replace the New Britain Democrat. In doing so, he installed an activist board chair who on occasion placed the new president in an awkward position. The line between policymaking and administration blurred on matters such as the transfer of the Hartford campus from West Hartford to downtown Hartford or the building of a football stadium in Hartford, and Rome would move out in front of his president *and* his board. When the *Hartford Courant* ran a series of articles on downtown Hartford and examined the move to downtown and the stadium, Hartley found himself peppered with questions he couldn't answer. As a consequence, he took the unprecedented step of inviting the chairman of the board of trustees to address the University Senate. Rome began by noting his long involvement with the university and said that the time had come to consider some perhaps controversial moves, such as the initiatives to shift the Hartford and Stamford campuses to downtown sites. He stated that it was not the role of the board to be administrators, pointing out, "The Chairman tries not to cross the line (or else steps back if, in his enthusiasm, he has). Academics are the function of the administration, not the board; *growth opportunities, however, are the board's prerogative*" (emphasis added). For him, a growth opportunity would be a new initiative, such as a stadium or a downtown move. Many of his initiatives remained outside of Storrs, although he played a leading role in the demolishing of the decrepit South Campus dorms (in which he had lived many years earlier as a student) and their replacement with what proved to be the very popular, handsome, new South Campus residences, one of which would be named in his honor. He also was central to establishing the Nutmeg Scholarships, which brought outstanding students to UConn regardless of financial need. While some faculty and administrators found Rome too willing to make pronouncements without consultation, others thought him a tonic in comparison to President Hartley, who appeared to be cautious and to accepting of the university's status as just another state agency rather than a special part of Connecticut's institutional hierarchy. At the senate meeting, Rome diplomatically spoke highly of Hartley, especially praising his dealing with the legislature. He assured the senators that he himself had no interest in the presidency.[2]

President Hartley's personality differed greatly from that of his predecessor. Casteen, the remote medievalist, had been replaced by what one observer called "a pump-your-hand kind of guy." Frequently walking around campus in a UConn sweat suit, Hartley made himself accessible to all members of the university community. He cracked jokes and responded to "hey's and hi's" as admirers greeted him. Students came to love him, and politicians and the public felt comfortable with this president, who was without pretense. On the other hand, some faculty resented what they believed to be his lack of formality and his detachment from scholarship and academic life, as well as his undue emphasis on sports. In response, Hartley reaffirmed his academic commitment and explained that he was charged by the board of trustees to strengthen the school's athletics. The athletic upgrade, he said, did not come at the expense of academics, and he pointed out that federal research funding increased from $77 million in 1990 to $109 million in 1996. "Most of the top ten schools you see in basketball rankings are also first-rate academic institutions—Duke, Stanford, University of North Carolina. Academic success and athletic success are absolutely compatible," he contended. While his view earned him criticism from some faculty as a "gym rat," Hartley's argument gained support as UConn achieved increased success in national athletic competition. He agreed with jogging companion Jim Calhoun, UConn's very successful men's basketball coach, who asserted, "Basketball and athletics are the front porch to the mansion. If you're attracted to the front porch, you might look inside the mansion." Athletics brought national attention and students—ideally, good students—would follow. Hartley argued that he didn't determine society's values. "If it was the philosophy department that the world was hungry for and was being televised on a national basis and was being honored with a parade of 100,000 people in Hartford, I'd be there in my Plato-Aristotle-Hegel T-shirt saying, 'I love philosophy.'" To the chagrin of many faculty, probably philosophers foremost, the world, or at least the society in the United States, did not hunger for philosophical learning. From Hartley's tenure onward, however, the university's enrollment strategy, building on his playbook, assumed that successful teams attracted positive attention to Storrs.[3]

Born in Aliquippa, Pennsylvania, a blue-collar steel-mill town outside of Pittsburgh, the new UConn president shared his birthplace with sports stars Mike Ditka, player with and then coach of the Chicago Bears professional football team, and pro basketball standout "Pistol Pete" Maravich. Hartley's parents were teachers, but the young Harry aspired to be a stockbroker. He studied economics at Geneva College and later at the University of Pittsburgh, became a substitute teacher, and went on for his doctorate in educational administration at Penn State. He taught at SUNY-Buffalo and then moved to NYU as associate dean. A workshop Hartley conducted that emphasized program budgeting, for which he earned a national professional reputation, brought him on a visit to Storrs. In 1972, he was appointed dean of the UConn School of Education. Hartley claimed to have loved living in Greenwich Village near NYU, but Storrs won his heart. He remarked, "When I came to UConn, I came home. I bought my first house, a dog. I put down roots." The roots went deep, and he remained in Storrs for thirty-two years until his retirement to Florida in 2004, eight years after he stepped down as president.[4]

Budget Blues

His first year in the presidency included what for him was the low point of his entire tenure in that office. Budgetary problems swept all state government like a great wave. In April 1991 the university laid off sixty-seven workers in response to the state budget crunch. By the summer, matters took a turn for the even worse. Governor Weicker became embroiled in an ultimately successful, but politically wrenching, battle to bring an income tax to Connecticut. On July 1, Weicker directed all state agencies to send home everyone who was not an essential employee. Hartley remained in Gulley Hall by himself, manning the console of telephones. When Kate Farrish, a *Hartford Courant* reporter, arrived, she asked, "Where is everybody?" The president responded, "I'm it. The staff went home as directed." Hal Brody, the new engineering dean, who had begun work that day, was told to stay home, after having been recruited based on what a great place UConn was to work. Weicker threatened to close the summer school, and Hartley had to plead with the governor for a special exception because the program was not dependent upon state funds. He had to convince him to permit the holding of major conferences that paid their own way, such as the Confratute, which brought seven hundred people from thirty nations in the field of gifted and talented education to Storrs. Hartley also considered the possibility of declaring financial exigency, a contractual term that permitted the reduction of staff without the usual legal constraints. With the attorney general and the AAUP, Hartley reluctantly reviewed the circumstances under which he could lay off tenured professors, something he later termed his "worst nightmare." When the income tax became law and the budget crisis subsided, such a draconian measure appeared unnecessary. The university, like the rest of the state government, escaped irreparable damage but not the blow to its morale.[5]

The Year of the Woman

To offset the increasing malaise, Hartley decided to pursue "an exciting theme to counteract the negatives." In August, as freshmen swarmed to campus to begin the new academic year, the president declared 1991–92 the "Year of the Woman" and appointed Cynthia H. Adams, a professor of allied health, to head the "100 Years of Women at UConn" celebration. Research had uncovered Nellie Louise Wilson of Mansfield and Louise Jane Rosebrooks as the first women to attend the Storrs Agricultural School in the spring of 1891; the next fall, Anna Mabel Snow of Storrs and Grace Everill Colburn of Mansfield Depot took courses, although women were not welcome officially until 1893, when the institution became the Storrs Agricultural College. The 1891 female presence marked the catalyst for the centennial. Early in the celebration, English professor and humorist Regina Barreca became the first woman to address an opening university convocation. Barreca lauded the administration's support for the celebration and remarked that Hartley created something of a stir when he appointed her to be the fall speaker: "There were men who were much taller and much older who had a lot more stuff hanging off their academic gowns who were really listening to what I had to say." Symposia, seminars, exhibits, and conferences celebrated UConn's women throughout the year. Eight hundred fifty people attended an awards banquet honoring a dozen women at the Aqua Turf Club in Southington. The university established a scholarship fund to commemorate "100 Years of Women at UConn" and conferred honorary degrees on five women. Hartley ended the year by anointing Adams to be the spring undergraduate commencement speaker. She earlier had pointed out that despite the strides made by women, only two of UConn's trustees were women, the university had never had a woman president, few women held administrative posts, and salaries remained higher for men. She had confidence, however, that Hartley did not merely offer lip service and remarked, "We bring things to his attention, and he fixes them."[6]

Racial Tension

If women saw him as *their* president, Hartley also tried to reach out to minorities. In assessing his top twenty major achievements, he included promoting "diversity through cultural centers and ethnic studies programs." He took pride in creating in 1992 the university's first associate provost's position with the express purpose of promoting multiculturalism, and the creation of the Asian American Cultural Center and Asian American Studies Institute in 1993, and the Institute for Puerto Rican Studies in 1994. He did not, however, fully escape the pressure that minority issues had placed upon his predecessors. A series of racial incidents plagued the institution in 1992. In April of that year, African American animal science professor Acie C. Murry found a rope hanging from the doorknob of his office. He interpreted it as a symbol to mark him for lynching. Hartley condemned the incident and ordered a police investigation, but critics nevertheless found the president to be too weak in his dealing with racial issues. Black faculty members stated that they were disturbed, shaken, and outraged by the incident. Affirmative Action Programs Director Thomasina Clemons remarked, "I don't think many faculty are sleeping too well." A black resident assistant complained that a racial harassment suit he filed was badly handled; a number of foreign students took cultural insult from the interim dean of students' comment regarding their hygiene and sanitary conditions. In total, approximately sixty people subsequently marched on Hartley's office. The president and other administrators thought the critics unfair, with Hartley commenting, "I think we're trying. My goal is to have a bias free campus . . . to eradicate tension."[7]

Tension, however, did not fully abate during Hartley's presidency, as the racial issue took an unexpected turn. When his office in 1994 published a brochure entitled "Introductions: A Resource Guide to UConn's Asian, Black, Hispanic, and Native American Faculty and Staff," the *Daily Campus* attacked what it termed "Hartley's List." It minced no words, editorializing, "Whether this project is borne of a fit of P.C. [politically correct] hysteria, or the same sentiments that gave us Apartheid cleverly disguised as ethnic sensitivity, it misses the mark by a mile when it comes to the stated purpose. It will be a great day indeed when a person's racial background simply doesn't matter. To get there, we need to emphasize what we have in common more than what sets us apart." A few weeks later, a *Campus* staff columnist pursued a similar path when she accused the university's Center for Academic Programs (CAP), which assisted minority students with tutoring and other academic services, of being discriminatory because other students could not receive the same help. The writer claimed CAP students didn't have to meet normal admission standards and asked, "Imagine what it would do to your ego to know the only reason you got into college is because your [*sic*] are poor or black or your mother speaks Spanish?" In response, more than seventy students, faculty, and staff rallied in protest at the *Daily Campus* offices and charged the newspaper with racism. Protesters claimed that the *Campus* had a long history of bias and suggested cutting the paper's budget, which came partly from undergraduate fees. The publisher and the editor countered that the article represented a columnist's opinion, to which she was entitled under the First Amendment; the paper also published letters opposing the column. Karru Martinson, the student publisher, then offered to attend a forum to be held at the African American Cultural Center (AACC).[8]

The meeting drew over one hundred people to the AACC. Administrators, including the dean and associate dean of the College of Liberal Arts and Sciences, stressed their confidence in the CAP program. Harry Hartley took the opportunity to reaffirm his support for the program and the students enrolled in it and directed his attention to the *Daily Campus*'s criticism of his efforts on behalf of diversity. He agreed with the columnist that it would be a great day when a person's racial background did not matter but regretted that such a day had not yet arrived. He encouraged the paper to emphasize greater diversity on its staff and to offer greater balance in its editorial perspective. He was not alone. Two weeks after the AACC forum, David Garnes, a library staff member, wrote to Carol Wiggins, the vice-president of student affairs and services, with copies to Hartley and Peter Halvorson, the chair of the University Senate Executive Committee. Garnes noted his dismay at what was happening at the *Campus* and directed his ire at the column on the CAP program and one on gay orientation, which "smelled of racism, bigotry and hate." At the end of the fall 1995 semester, the College of Liberal Arts and Sciences Curricula and Courses Committee approved a controversial new course, White Racism, to be taught on an experimental basis. Its instructor, sociologist Noel A. Cazenave, explained that "'White racism' are fighting words because they acknowledge the existence of a color- and race-based system of group privilege. In a society that holds both equality and the superiority of the so-called 'white' race as core but conflicting values, such recognition is extremely unpopular." The development of the course reflected the concern about racism that continued to occupy the campus community.[9]

Gay Pride

Like racism, the gay issue had percolated on campus for some years and also captured attention. In May 1992 Hartley, at the request of the board of trustees, wrote to then Secretary of Defense Richard Cheney explaining that the board had passed a motion stating that the Department of Defense policy of barring homosexuals and lesbians from receiving ROTC scholarships or being commissioned as officers was incompatible with the anti-discrimination policy of the university. He pointed out that the Undergraduate Student Government and the University Senate passed resolutions condemning the policy and argued for its revision. As with race, the question of gays in the military did not die easily. In 1994, Colonel David Fairclo, head of UConn's air force ROTC, pointed to a new law signed by President Clinton that instituted the "don't ask, don't tell policy" and claimed, "Focusing on the issue is a red herring that is unlikely to benefit anyone at UConn." In 1995, however, the University Senate recommended the discontinuance of UConn's ROTC program because of its discrimination in opposition to institutional policy. Although the trustees voted to continue the ROTC, albeit while requesting a change in the Department of Defense policy, when Hartley resigned in February 1996 he had won the gratitude of the gay community. Paula Liseo and Edward Eggleton, co-presidents of Bisexual, Gay, Lesbian Association (BiGALA), complimented him for helping to create an academic environment that embraced diversity and stressed UConn as a family. They thanked him for his efforts on behalf of UConn's gay, lesbian, and bisexual community and continued, "You have been a constant supporter of us, and our needs. We only hope that our next president is as open minded as you, and welcomes all individuals into the UConn family."[10]

The Strategic Plan

If UConn seemed a "family," a term Hartley often employed, some in the community advocated long-range family planning. Strategic planning was well known to corporations, and UConn joined other institutions of higher education in using it. Hartley, as a management consultant, had assisted with planning and budgeting in forty states. Before coming to UConn, he had published a book on educational planning, so it wasn't surprising that when he became president he immediately recognized a need for planning. In 1991, when Andrew Canzonetti still served as board of trustees chairman, Hartley proposed the development of a strategic plan, which became the subject of several trustee retreats. At a meeting in August 1992 chaired by Trinity College President Tom Gerety (because Hartley wanted an outsider to preside), Hartley presented a vision statement and proposed twenty goals for the year 2000 to the trustees. Four years later, he recalled his thoughts at the time, which amounted to "All right, I'll see if I can get my board interested in thinking about the future." The board, according to Hartley, didn't get very excited about the process. Then came the change in board chairs, with Rome replacing Canzonetti. Hartley still wanted to move forward and announced to the trustees that he would present them with the outline of a strategic plan in September 1993. He began inviting people, including a representative of the AAUP, some deans, and others such as engineering professor David Jordan, whom he asked to chair the group, to serve on his President's Task Force on Strategic Planning, but this effort would be short-lived.[11]

Lew Rome phoned Peter McFadden, then Hartley's executive assistant, to discuss a variety of topics. He concluded by saying "Would you mind telling Harry not to go forward on his strategic plan?" and then he explained that strategic planning would be a board activity. When Hartley learned of the decision, he considered stepping down as president, but despite his belief that Rome's direction was administratively wrong, and despite likely feeling insulted, he decided to wait and see how the process would evolve. He had to explain to those he invited to serve that he was no longer in charge. Rome, with support from Governor Weicker, appointed a Strategic Planning Management Committee (SPMC) chaired by Weicker-appointed trustee William Berkeley, a wealthy Greenwich insurance entrepreneur, and co-chaired by David Jordan, Hartley's original choice for the job. Many faculty and staff expressed uneasiness about a process that might lead to radical changes and possibly to cuts in selected programs. Berkeley, in response to such concern, told the SPMC's organizational meeting, "I want everyone to be uncomfortable. But I want advocates, not people trying to point fingers at others. I want everybody . . . ready to explain why we exist, what we do, and what we contribute. I want everything on the table. Anyone can say cut, but tell me what you can give. I want to hear people singing for their supper." In establishing the committee, Rome stressed the need to examine the university at a time of limited resources and to accomplish a great deal in spite of budget constraints. Berkeley added that UConn needed to demonstrate how it contributed to the state in order to justify the resources it received. The SPMC set a timetable for public forums, discussions and hearings, draft reports, and other activities that culminated in a package to be presented to the board of trustees on December 9, 1994. The board finally adopted the plan on February 10, 1995.[12]

The adoption came after much discussion and some controversy. Hearings in Storrs and Stamford and a University Senate meeting in November 1994 raised issues for the SPMC to reconsider, such as the balance between teaching and research. The senators inquired about shared governance; the AAUP asserted that the plan was too concerned with vocationalism and didn't leave room for "learning for learning's sake"; students joined a crowd of four hundred at the four-hour hearing at the Bishop Center in Storrs to protest the removal of the vice-president for student affairs from the President's Council, a measure that was ultimately reversed. After making changes in response to both criticism and friendly suggestions, and following an additional hearing, the SPMC unanimously recommended the plan to the board of trustees, which then adopted "Beyond 2000: Change," a ten-year strategic plan that offered a bold vision statement, which, if it seemed inflated to some, marked a major turn for the University of Connecticut. It began: "The University of Connecticut will be perceived and acknowledged as the outstanding public university in the nation—a world-class university." The next ten years would be spent working toward that goal.[13]

The top priorities of "Beyond 2000: Change," all of which came to fruition in one form or another, included the following: establishment of an Office of Multicultural Affairs within the senior administration; the creation of an Office of Enrollment Management to centralize admission activities including recruitment, enrollment, retention, and the graduation of students; the development of a University Center where graduates, undergraduates, faculty, and community residents could gather for events, generally enhancing the undergraduate experience; the updating of computer communications between the main campus at Storrs and UConn's satellite campuses; and the elimination of automobiles in the campus center near the Homer Babbidge Library. The trustees assigned the job of implementation of the plan to the president. Dissatisfied with the process but putting his ego aside, Hartley thought the plan "a pretty damn good report." He remarked, "I liked the mission statement. I liked the vision. I liked the strategic goals. I liked most of the action plan—not all of it. I'm not sure I could have prepared a better strategic plan." One of the first things he began working on was creating a chancellor structure at Storrs, and in Farmington at the Health Center. The trustees desired the president to spend more time out of Storrs, fundraising, developing corporate relations, and working with alumni chapters. The two chancellors, on the other hand, would oversee activity at the main and the Farmington campuses. While Hartley saw the new organizational model as having some advantages, he worried that it could make the

UConn president into a "phantom." He enjoyed being known as the "students' president" and believed that "Any president who is not visible on the Storrs campus will not be popular or effective. The core of the university is the student body at Storrs." The model, however, proved attractive to Mark Emmert, who had been recently hired as provost to replace Thomas Tighe, who was forced out by the trustees over the issue of the strategic plan. Tighe was reluctant to move quickly and disagreed with a number of the plan's priorities. Emmert's authority would be increased, and Hartley found the new arrangement acceptable, because he claimed that when first appointed he had intended to serve for only five years and would not be president much longer. According to him, he stayed for a sixth year only to host President Clinton, the first sitting U.S. president to visit UConn, when he inaugurated the Thomas J. Dodd Research Center in October 1995, and to help get "UConn 2000" passed, which was to transform the campus infrastructure.[14]

UConn 2000 Initiated

Hartley recalled, "I was well aware that this (UConn 2000) would be my legacy at UConn." Others argued that the cautious Hartley was the last one to agree to lobby for the legislation, and his own testimony reveals his wary approach. When Hartley heard, during the fall 1994 election campaign, the initial figure of two billion dollars that would be needed to repair the campus infrastructure, he worried that the Republican candidate for governor, John Rowland (who ultimately won office), was running on a platform to reduce taxes and state bonding. Once Rowland prevailed, Hartley believed it was the wrong time for UConn to be discussing the issue publicly. He did, however, claim to encourage private discussion. House of Representatives Republican Minority Leader Robert Ward, a devoted UConn alumnus, credited Hartley with establishing a good relationship with the legislature in the years before the consideration of UConn 2000 and thereby paving the way for the initiative. However, the most active players in achieving passage of the legislation appeared to be Scott Brohinsky, then in charge of governmental relations for the university, Edward Allenby, UConn's new vice-president for institutional advancement, and Speaker of the Connecticut House of Representatives Tom Ritter, a UConn Law Graduate and avid Huskies basketball fan. Jonathan Pelto, a former legislator from Storrs turned communications strategist with the Hartford law firm of Robinson and Cole, developed a public relations campaign. Pat Sheehan, television news anchor and president of the UConn Foundation, Ed Marth, executive director of the AAUP, and Roger Gelfenbien, a managing partner in Andersen Consulting and Lew Rome's successor as chair of the university's board of trustees, all participated. Other people involved included Athletic Director Lew Perkins and Denise

Merrill of Storrs, Pelto's newly elected successor as representative from the Fifty-fourth General Assembly District. All of them contributed to the success of the campaign for UConn 2000.[15]

During the summer of 1994 Merrill, fearing severe cuts to UConn's budget, approached Brohinsky and others about the need to come up with some aggressive measure to counteract them. Brohinsky, who had been bothered by the deterioration of the facilities at Storrs, responded that nothing could be done without the assistance of Tom Ritter and wondered whether the speaker could be drawn into some sort of committee to consider UConn's long-term needs. Merrill visited Ritter at his office and asked about his participation. His enthusiasm surprised Merrill, who understood that political leaders usually are more cautious in their promises to colleagues. Not only agreeing to participate, Ritter said he would help make it "the year of UConn," suggesting that such an initiative might be one of the most positive things that could be done for the state. Merrill returned to UConn and brought back the good news to Brohinsky. They arranged to meet together with Ritter in September 1994, and he then reiterated his support. When Brohinsky suggested a long-term ten-year program for infrastructure renewal and threw out a figure of between one and two billion dollars, Ritter replied, "You know, sometimes it's harder to get two million than two billion, and I'd be interested." He also indicated that he would confer with Bob Ward, because the approach had to be bipartisan. Brohinsky and Merrill returned again to Storrs, and Brohinsky, after discussing the matter with Allenby and getting the green light from Hartley and Lew Rome, formed the UConn 2000 Task Force. Merrill, in turn, who was relatively new to the legislature and seen already as the "UConn Representative," moved to the background, wanting to insure that the initiative appeared to have wide support and was not simply another Storrs project. She helped to round up votes among both Democrats and Republicans, but the heavy lifting started in the speaker's office.[16]

Tom Ritter acted with as much enthusiasm as he had shown in his meetings with Brohinsky and Merrill. He quarterbacked strategy and tactics for the legislative success of what was to become Public Act 95–230, "An Act to Enhance the Infrastructure of the University of Connecticut." To make his colleagues take the matter seriously rather than laugh at a request for so much money, Ritter initiated the idea for a bipartisan press conference to be held on January 30, 1995, at the beginning of the legislative session in the Old Judiciary Room of the State Capitol. Driving into what would be a major media event, Hartley seemed understandably nervous. Right before he left Storrs for Hartford, the Governor's Office had phoned. The call raised fears that Rowland might tell him to back off, but Hartley, by that time, claimed nothing would stop him. He was committed. He spoke with the governor's representative, who explained that Rowland had made no commitment but would not stop Hartley's press conference. The governor's representative added that at some point, UConn and the

Governor's Office had to talk. The press conference, which displayed varying levels of support from legislative leaders of both parties, went on as planned and attracted a great deal of media attention. UConn unveiled a ten-year building and thirty-year financing plan for sixty-two major construction projects. M. Adela Eads, Republican senate president pro tem from the Torrington area, announced, "I think the concept of UConn 2000 is absolutely wonderful. We all realize this can't be done overnight, but this is our flagship university and we should maintain it. Unfortunately, that has not been done." Democratic Senate Minority Leader William DiBella of Hartford was more cautious. He lauded UConn for planning and prioritizing construction projects but warned that the details of the process still had to be worked out. Republican Senator William Nickerson, co-chair of the Finance Committee and a member of the State Bond Commission, did not attend the press conference. While he supported some aspects of the proposal, he acidly remarked, "When they come down from the clouds and hand in a piece of paper, I will compare it with Gov. John Rowland's piece of paper. He has yet to be heard from." A great deal of work still had to be done.[17]

Ritter spent hours and hours with the bond counsel and other legislative and UConn staff. The bill they drafted, which changed many powers, was long and complex, comprising approximately seventy-five pages in length. In the middle of snowstorms, they sat working on the draft in Richard Sigal's law office in Hartford's CityPlace. Huddled around a table, the group commented on every paragraph, readying it for the Finance Committee's deadline. They then moved it through the Education Committee, and it began to take on a life of its own. Ritter reached out to touch all bases—the Treasurer's Office, the Governor's Office, rank and file legislators—and asked for comment on the bill. In order to build a wide coalition of support, the bill's advocates determined to keep all aspects of the proposal together in their legislation, including the transfer of the Stamford campus from its suburban site to the city's downtown, improvements at Avery Point, and changes at the Hartford regional campus, as well as the initiatives in Storrs. Only the timing of the construction projects would differ. On February 1 Hartley visited Stamford and gave assurance of the university's backing for the downtown move. He spoke at Champion International Corporation headquarters, whose chief executive officer was L. C. "Whitey" Heist, a UConn trustee, and told an audience of city officials and business leaders, "It is important we unite as a single university." Stamford Democratic State Representative Moira Lyons stated that Hartley's comments "guaranteed we will have a downtown campus. It takes out of the political debate the pitting of one region against another . . . Stamford against Storrs." This strategy ultimately won the support of Republican Nickerson, a resident of Greenwich who strongly desired the move to downtown Stamford.[18]

The legislature and the governor could not help but be influenced by the grassroots postcard and media campaign launched from Storrs. In a first mailing, over eight thousand postcards in support of UConn 2000 inundated legislators. More would come. The campaign, developed in large part by the politically savvy Jonathan Pelto, emphasized targeted databases to assure the effectiveness of the effort. Over $100,000 of privately raised money from sources such as the Alumni Association, the UConn Foundation, and the AAUP (which contributed $25,000) funded the campaign. Letters went to the Governor as well as legislators. One day before an important March 3 joint hearing of the General Assembly's Education Committee and Finance, Revenue, and Bonding Committee, Governor John Rowland responded to a family that had written in support of UConn 2000. He told them that he believed UConn to be a tremendous resource for the state and that he had as a priority the rebuilding of the crumbling main campus infrastructure. The governor explained that his budget included $93 million in bond funds, more than double the amount of previous years, toward that goal, and remarked, "When it comes to the University of Connecticut, in my administration all roads lead to Storrs. The main campus of UConn is the trunk of the University tree; if the trunk is not healthy, the branches cannot survive." He did not, however, come out in support of UConn 2000.[19]

At the six-hour hearing before a large audience in the hallowed hall of the House of Representatives, the UConn group and its supporters made their case, and the legislators asked difficult questions. They probed both widely and deeply, asking about the enormous amount of money involved, the university's autonomy in constructing projects, the concern that funds would be used to build a football stadium and to move the Hartford campus to downtown (two of board chairman Lew Rome's desires), and the effect of assisting UConn at the expense of other public institutions of higher learning in the state. Democratic Representative Frederick A. Gelsi, co-chairman of the Bonding Subcommittee, who was concerned about losing control of spending, complained, "You've made our university a sovereign nation." The deputy secretary of the state's Office of Policy and Management, Lorraine M. Aronson, who would later become UConn's chief financial administrator and a leading supporter of the institution, claimed that the project's far-reaching costs would do serious harm to the state's cash flow and its credit rating. She remarked, "UConn's needs are very important, but they cannot take absolute precedence over all other needs." If such comments tried to take the air out of the Storrs balloon, word from Dennis J. Nayden, president of the Stamford-based GE Capital and a UConn School of Business alumnus, gave it additional inflation. He announced a million-dollar commitment to the School of Business Administration, provided the legislature supported the UConn 2000 plan. The money would provide an endowment for faculty development, student scholarships, and long-distance learning at both the Storrs and Stamford campuses. Such support did much to demonstrate the viability of the initiative.[20]

The lobbying blitz continued after the hearing, with additional supportive cards, letters, and phone calls directed to legislators and the governor. UConn trustee William Berkeley used his influence with John Rowland to persuade him of the proposal's value, and the politically attuned governor did not need much coaxing to understand the popularity of the measure. A week before UConn 2000 came to a vote in the Finance Committee on May 1, Rowland and legislative leaders of both parties, particularly Ritter and Ward, announced their support for the $1 billion, ten-year plan. After two and a half hours of debate, the proposal passed, 35–9. Ten days later, the entire House of Representatives voted in support, 138–10, with Speaker Ritter remarking that the bill's passage was "probably my proudest moment in fifteen years" in the legislature.[21]

Not everyone shared his enthusiasm. Belton Copp, a member of the state's Board of Governors of Higher Education, resigned, saying too much money was going to UConn, shortchanging the other public colleges in the state. He pointed out that only 17 percent of the state's public higher-education students attended school in Storrs and the regional campuses, while 52 percent attended the community colleges and 31 percent Connecticut State University. He thought the other 83 percent deserved the benefits of state funding as well. He also charged in his letter of resignation that Rowland supported UConn 2000 because he was "piggybacking" on the popularity of the women's national-championship basketball team "for personal political influence with the public and the legislature." The governor's spokesman denied the charge.[22]

The impact of UConn's basketball success, however, cannot be discounted, although it would be an oversimplification to think it the only reason for UConn 2000's adoption. The planning, the lobbying, the targeted public relations campaign, and the enthusiastic efforts of alumni all combined to bring about the bill's passage. The success of both the men's and the women's teams simply created "an era of good feelings." In mid-February 1995, when both teams were ranked number one in the nation, the first time in NCAA history when the same school stood atop the world of men's and women's basketball simultaneously, Rowland, still not completely signed on to UConn 2000, recognized the impact of what became known as "Huskymania" in the state. He told a press conference that Huskymania "gives us some real morale boost that we need. . . . So we'll do our part—the state—in terms of taxpayer dollars, and you'll see in my [budget] speech. . . . We need to make sure that we rebuild that campus . . . and make sure that it's the bright, shining example that we want it to be for the rest of the UConn system." It was then that he put in his request for $93 million for UConn. On April 26, after the women's team, behind the leadership of Rebecca Lobo and Jennifer Rizzotti, went undefeated in a 35–0 championship season, and the men ended with a 28–5 record and an appearance in the NCAA's "elite eight" tournament round, Speaker Ritter and the legislature hosted the annual Husky Day at the State Capitol. That morning Rowland, Hartley, and Lew

Rome met. The governor agreed to support the billion-dollar proposal, which he announced at a hastily called press conference at 12:30 P.M., shortly before the arrival of the teams. As legislators and their families lauded the teams and sought autographs, Geno Auriemma, the women's basketball coach, told them that their accomplishments would go down in the history books just as the women's team's perfect season did. He remarked, "By supporting UConn 2000 . . . you've made sure we will be No. 1 in the country. Hopefully, our basketball team will never be better than our university." House Minority Leader Bob Ward, a fan, implicitly agreed. He recognized that basketball made people more aware of UConn but that the university should have a first-rate reputation for other reasons. Before the voting, he showed his colleagues a recent *New York Times* article about NYU and how an improvement of its facilities helped to bring an improvement in the quality of the institution generally. Clearly, more than basketball brought about UConn 2000. Belton Copp may have complained about the governor's "piggybacking" on the hoop success, but few joined him. In fact, in the "era of good feelings" generated in part by Husky-mania, no real organized opposition to UConn 2000 emerged. When the measure came to the State Senate on Tuesday, June 6, it passed 35–0.[23]

The legislation gave UConn unprecedented authority, which would be questioned a decade later, to issue its own bonds and spend nearly a billion dollars over ten years for sixty-two projects to rebuild the main campus and also impact the regional campuses. These included a new chemistry building and science quadrangle at Storrs, the expanded downtown campus in Stamford, and a Marine Sciences Center at Avery Point in Groton. The board of trustees would not need approval from the State Bond Commission for any of the sixty-two, but the governor would have veto authority. In the staged plan, the trustees would be able to issue up to an average of $100 million in each of the next ten years, two and a half times more than UConn had been receiving on an annual basis. To permit legislative oversight, the law split the projects into two phases, the first one lasting four years and the second, six. After the first phase, the General Assembly would review the project and, if successful, would have to vote, which it ultimately did, for the second phase. An agreement between Ritter and Rowland hammered out $20 million in state funds for an endowment to match private contributions. Edward Allenby, chief UConn fundraiser, was delighted with the outcome and commented, "It gives the university the opportunity to do some things it never could have done before. It gives us the tools to get the job done. Now, we've got to go out and do it."[24]

The governor quickly signed the bill into law and, on a warm, sunny Thursday, June 22, came to Storrs, along with many other dignitaries, for a ceremonial signing. Jubilant in their praise, they all saw the day as marking a renaissance for the university. The student pep band played the UConn fight song and a cheerleader dressed as the Husky pumped up enthusiasm. With the guests encamped before the still plastic-wrapped library, the symbolism could not be missed. Lew Rome told Hartley, "Harry, I think we can take the scaffolding down now." In keeping with the strategic plan's vision statement, he added, "This will give us the opportunity to be the No.1 public university in the United States." Rowland proclaimed that the future new facilities were an excellent investment, because they would keep students in Connecticut rather than have them attend colleges out-of-state, perhaps never to return. The legislative achievement won national attention for Connecticut. Peter M. Buchanan, the president of the Council for Advancement and Support of Education, told the *New York Times,* "UConn 2000's approval is a benchmark for public higher education in this country. No other state has taken such decisive action to strengthen its flagship university." Tom Ritter, who engineered the state's decisive action, looked to the future. He remarked, "We look forward to being your partner over the next 10 years. Let's come back in 10 years and see it all done." Within the decade, the campus would indeed be dramatically changed, and more students would stay in state and view the school in Storrs as one of first choice; it appeared that the legacy of UConn 2000 would prove as attractive as its promise, although later problems with managing the construction would take their toll.[25]

The Football Upgrade

Part of the strategy for the adoption of UConn 2000 called for the omission of a football stadium among the planned projects. Some people saw a stadium as a luxury that detracted from the needs of a campus that had suffered too long from deferred maintenance. The argument for a stadium intensified, however, because the NCAA required one with a seating capacity of at least 30,000 for the university's inclusion in Division I-A, the major athletic program classification. During President Hartley's tenure, the board of trustees decided to upgrade Husky football from I-AA to I-A. Hartley saw this coming when he first became president and then hired Athletic Director Lew Perkins in 1990, knowing that Perkins had guided Division I-A football at Maryland. It did not hurt that basketball coaches Calhoun and Auriemma also favored his appointment, but the football factor played an important role in the hiring. In April 1994 an ad hoc trustees' committee reviewing the possibility of an upgrade held hearings in Storrs, Stamford, and at the UConn Health Center in Farmington. The board charged the committee with identifying the advantages and disadvantages of elevating to Division I-A, investigating the financial impact on UConn and the state, considering the implications for gender equity, and determining the conditions under which the university could build a high-quality, successful program. The hearing in Storrs, as expected, brought out both supporters and detractors.[26]

David Ivry, an emeritus professor of insurance and an outspoken critic of the upgrade, asked, "How can people of good will put football above the needs of the University?" Besides, he said, "There is no tradition of football here. Where is the great joy of being clobbered 70–0 by Florida State?" A UConn admissions officer and former football staff member, Brian Usher, extolled the upgrade's value in terms of spirit and pride. AAUP President Ronald Taylor commented on the expansion's poor timing in light of UConn's recent fiscal problems and declining state support. A Class of 1972 alumnus, Ben Grzyb, argued that the upgrade would improve family entertainment opportunities for the state, attract more qualified athletes, and "greatly enhance the image of UConn nationally." He added that the increased media coverage of football would attract more students and donations. Professor of molecular and cell biology James Knox, citing the work of outstanding researchers, countered that it was an error to think that national recognition and glory came only through sports. Cynara Stites of the UConn Mental Health Services feared that more resources for football would increase the disparity in athletics between men and women and be a step in the wrong direction under Title IX. "If the decision [were] up to me, I would not only not expand football, I would abolish it altogether," she concluded. After hearing the divergent opinions, committee chair Gerard Lawrence ended the meeting by stating that the committee was still looking for answers and that it did not want the audience to leave "without the sense that we're committed to the academic mission" of UConn. A headline in the *UConn Advance* summed up the session: "Hearing On Potential for Football Upgrade Ends in a Tie."[27]

The trustees' committee broke the "tie" at the board meeting of October 14, 1994, held at Constitution Plaza in Hartford, a site chosen by board chair Lew Rome and challenged by upgrade foes, who thought a Storrs location would give students and faculty a better chance to attend. The committee recommended that the trustees approve Division I-A status for the football team, which would take about five years and require a new stadium and additional funds for women's athletics to ensure gender equity under Title IX. Lawrence announced, "The ball is in play." Rome pointed out that upgrading the athletic program was a "major opportunity used all over the country" at schools known for both athletics and academics. The committee's report invoked the strategic plan and argued that Division I-A athletics "should be viewed as a means to help attain the goal of establishing the University of Connecticut as the premier public university in the nation." It contended that playing against major research universities would improve UConn's academic reputation. Division I-A would also assist in reaching out to alumni, attract private funding, and encourage the state's economic development. The committee did not disregard the realities of big-time sports in America. It argued that the upgrade would assure that UConn was a major player in the NCAA and position it effectively to deal with a system of realigned megaconferences. Lew Perkins saw the issue as a business decision and warned that if football did not move to Division I-A, the university's twenty-one other programs could be adversely affected, and especially men and women's basketball, because of NCAA restructuring. Harry Hartley, who supported the committee's recommendation, recognized that some risk existed in the implementation but stated, "There is a greater risk if we didn't consider it at all." A campus survey found that 67 percent of students, 39 percent of faculty, and 46 percent of the overall community backed the upgrade. The division spilled over to the University Senate.[28]

At its meeting of October 24, the senate by a count of hands rejected a motion endorsing the committee's report to upgrade, although moderator Harry Johnson, a business professor, initially held that a voice vote supported it. The motion to endorse originally included three stipulations, with a fourth added during debate. The stipulations held that the decision must not divert funds from the university's other capital and operating budgets; that it must not contribute to an increase in tuition and fees; that it must be accompanied by programs and expenditures that insured compliance with gender equity under Title IX; and that an academic enhancement fund must be established to provide one dollar to upgrade existing academic programs and initiate new academic programs for every dollar spent on the football upgrade. The heated debate rehashed the same arguments made earlier. Advocate Gary English of the School of Fine Arts commented, "It's easier to raise money when you have highly visible programs. The traditional ways don't work. The ceilings in Beach Hall are still bad; the floors in other buildings are still bad. It's a huge risk, but the enhanced public face of the University will enhance our fundraising." Economics professor Peter Barth attacked the premise that under the upgrade football would lose less money than it did in Division I-AA. He suggested, "I think it would be very hard to make the argument with a straight face in the real world." The trustees, however, claimed to understand the "real world" very well, and the relatively close vote in the senate did not persuade them.[29]

If the faculty-dominated senate did not demonstrate great enthusiasm for the upgrade, resolutions by the Undergraduate Student Government and the Alumni Association did. A feasibility study by Coopers and Lybrand, a Big Six accounting firm, also lent support. This did not fully convince board vice-chair Andrew Canzonnetti, who while favoring the plan worried that university funds might be better spent elsewhere, such as on adding faculty and strengthening academic programs. The AAUP agreed with his concern and voiced others, but the trustees voted unanimously to upgrade the football program to Division I-A status and asked Hartley to develop a detailed plan to accomplish the purpose. This president so identified with sports could add the new status for football to the women's and men's basketball successes during his tenure in office, 1990–96, which he termed "a golden era for UConn athletics."[30]

Hartley Resigns

The Hartley era, then, encompassed a number of important initiatives that would have a major impact on UConn's future. The strategic plan, UConn 2000, and the football upgrade all marked significant steps. While Harry Hartley may not always have been the most significant actor in their development, he supported all of them and they occurred on his watch. With the division of powers between a chancellor and the president in the waning months of his presidency, Hartley became less visible. When the State Bond Commission considered UConn 2000 for a crucial vote in December 1995, Mark Emmert, the chancellor, represented the university. A television reporter asked what was on the minds of many: "Where's Harry?" When he announced his resignation in mid- February 1996, a day after Governor Rowland proposed cutting ninety university positions in addition to its existing eighty-three vacancies, the strains of years of cost cutting on the university's operating budget could not be camouflaged by the bonding generosity of UConn 2000. Bricks and mortar meant a great deal for the university's continued progress, but during Hartley's tenure UConn's staff had been reduced by about 10 percent. Like his immediate predecessors, the stewardship of the finance expert Hartley could not escape such fiscal troubles.[31]

A contentious University Senate meeting, at which senators peppered the president with questions about the budget and a decision to spend $2 million on equity between the sexes in athletics, preceded the resignation by a couple of days. Despite flagging faculty morale, Hartley's resignation brought forth praise for his affability and approachability. The head of the university's Journalism Department, Maureen Croteau, remarked, "It's been nice to have a president that people all over the state feel they're on a first name basis with, and I really think that's very important to the school, and very important to students." Ed Marth, the AAUP's executive director, countered those who thought Hartley too informal and too unpresidential by commenting, "Some people look at him and complain that he doesn't show up in a three-piece suit and say he isn't the world's greatest philosopher, but you have to say he is genuine." A student, Katie Fitzpatrick, thought him very personable. "He's always at football and basketball games and Jorgensen [Auditorium] events. You smile, you wave. He seems very friendly," she exclaimed. The *Hartford Courant* editorialized that none of his immediate predecessors generated the passion on campus that Hartley had, reminding its readers that "Not since Homer Babbidge has a UConn president been so visible, so likeable." The affable Hartley believed the timing of his resignation was right for the institution and for him personally. In his letter of resignation, he explained that his successor could lead the university into the twenty-first century, using as a foundation the strategic plan and UConn 2000.

He concluded, "Now it is time for the trustees to identify a new leader who can transform our vision into reality." The governor urged the trustees to move rapidly.[32]

John Rowland said the state would begin a national search for a successor, a process that could take at least six months. The trustees would choose the next president, but Rowland suggested that he would be involved in the search process. In fact, the governor, who later events would show was hard strapped for cash, after learning of the president's $185,000 salary as compared to his of $78,000, joked that he thought about applying for the job himself, continuing with tongue in cheek, "But after careful consideration I have ruled myself out." Lew Rome chaired both the thirty-six-member search committee and the eleven-member steering committee that did most of the work in selecting a new president, with the help of Korn/Ferry International, a consulting firm. By the end of June 1996 the steering committee planned to interview eleven candidates, narrowed from a field several times that size. Ten were university officials— presidents, chancellors, or provosts—and one a corporate executive, a category encouraged by the governor. Some thought the steering committee showed too much of his influence, because six of its members had ties to the governor's office. UConn AAUP Executive Director Ed Marth commented, "I think that is too many. I don't think . . . being elected governor is necessarily the best credential for being able to start appointing people to the presidency of a major university. We want what's best for the institution—not somebody giving out jobs as a favor for friendship." David O'Leary, the governor's chief of staff, who sat on the board and was a steering committee member, denied that the process would be political, and Lew Rome backed his assertion. He explained that although he consulted with Rowland's office as he named committee members, the governor didn't try to steer the search in any one direction. If there were a direction, the *Journal Inquirer* newspaper editorialized that the times called for "vision, academic excellence, a passion for greatness. . . . The new president should not be a long-time UConn administrator, a politician whose legs have given out, or a person who has been head of a faculty senate somewhere. . . . This is the moment for UConn to reach for greatness."[33]

The Austin Years

During the third week of July, the trustees unanimously voted to approve the selection of the Presidential Search Advisory Committee at a meeting at the School of Law, where those present greeted Philip E. Austin with enthusiastic applause. The fifty-four-year-old Austin became the thirteenth president of the University of Connecticut. Just as the insider Harry Hartley replaced the outsider John Casteen, outsider Austin in turn replaced insider Hartley. Austin, a native of Fargo, North Dakota, came to UConn after serving seven years as chancellor of the University of Alabama System. Educated in his home state, he received his bachelor's and master's degrees in agricultural economics from North Dakota State University and his Ph.D. in economics from Michigan State University. He served in the U.S. Army between 1969 and 1971 and worked with General Creighton Abrams as an economist at U.S. military headquarters in Saigon, where he attained the rank of captain and earned the Bronze Star and other commendations. From 1971 to 1974 he served as an economist in the director's office of the U.S. Office of Management and Budget, and for three years after that he was a deputy assistant secretary for education. His academic work took him to New York City and CUNY's Baruch College as provost and vice-president for academic affairs, and from 1984 through 1989 he served as president of Colorado State University, before moving to Alabama. In Alabama, he had forged strong ties to the business and political communities. The trustees looked forward to his doing the same in Connecticut. Harry Hartley wished him well in leading UConn into the twenty-first century. John Casteen offered congratulations and confided, "You are going to a great and exciting university." Austin responded, "I look forward to the challenges that await me, and I am convinced that the opportunity that exists now in Connecticut is unique in American public higher education."[34]

He particularly saw UConn 2000 as offering great potential for the institution's progress. Austin told his initial press conference attendees that at the end of ten years the university would have one of the most magnificent infrastructures in the United States. He saw that as the beginning of a process that would assure UConn's status as a major national public research university, although he recognized that the quality of the faculty and how they interacted with students determined whether a school achieved and maintained national stature. Improved facilities—comprehensive libraries, clean, safe, state-of-the art classrooms and dormitories, advanced instrumentation and laboratories—would encourage faculty and help attract superior students. He vowed to increase the university's visibility in the state and to make UConn a school of first choice for Connecticut's students. He expressed the need for increased legislative and corporate support and looked forward to visiting "every nook and cranny of [the] state" in support of his newly adopted institution.[35]

Building an Endowment

Austin's employment agreement with the university listed first among his duties "Fund raising, development, public and alumni relations." After a month on the job, the new president, consistent with the intent of the division of powers with a chancellor, explained to the *Daily Campus* that he planned to spend a lot of time with the business leadership throughout the state, and in particular Fairfield County. He also emphasized that all of the elements of the university—the regional campuses and Storrs—were a single unit, and a "we-they" division was "suicidal [and] self-destructive." The university ranged throughout the state and extended beyond Storrs. Implicitly, Austin's presidency would not be tethered to the main campus. He surprised that community when he chose to reside in Farmington rather than in the president's Oak Hill Road house on campus, although he used the Storrs house for official functions and came to live there a few years later. Initially, he viewed the more central location as a better staging ground to meet with political and corporate leaders. His success in meeting with private donors, supported all the while by the work of the UConn Foundation, quickly became apparent.[36]

Despite questions about the propriety of foundation fundraising and spending, which emerged early in Austin's presidency in 1997 and focused upon what seemed to the *Hartford Courant* to be excessive expenditures for the Athletic Department during the Hartley administration, the university went on to develop an immensely successful capital campaign. At its conclusion in the summer of 2004, Austin could tell John Rowland's successor as governor, M. Jodi Rell, that while the campaign's goal was $300 million, the final tabulation came to approximately $470 million, which included an in-kind $146 million cutting-edge software gift from EDS PLM Solutions to the School of Engineering. Along the way came a number of generous individual gifts that had long-range impacts on the university, ranging from the establishment of the Lodewick Visitors Center, which became a UConn welcome point, to seed money from alumnus Gary Gladstein for the institution's signature program in human rights. None, however, exceeded the unprecedented $23 million gift of Raymond Neag, Class of '56, whose niece Sally Reis taught in the School of Education. In thanking Neag, for whom the school would be named, Austin assured him that the "gift will transform UConn and the School of Education in ways that I hope and expect will exceed our greatest aspirations." The gift, the largest ever given to any public university in New England, was also the largest for its purpose in the nation. By 2005, *U.S. News and World Report* ranked the Neag School twenty-ninth among the top schools of education. The magazine's guidebook of the best graduate programs acclaimed the Neag School's five-year integrated bachelor/master's approach as "one of three innovative schools grooming grads for the long haul by requiring lengthy in-classroom internships." Private foundations invested in the Neag School as well. The Bill and Melinda Gates Foundation awarded it a $3 million grant, and the Carnegie Corporation of New York granted $5 million and designated the Neag School one of its eleven "Teachers for the New Era" schools. In 2004 the UConn Health Center also dedicated the Carole and Ray Neag Comprehensive Cancer Center. A plaque there included the Neags' philosophy: "Our hope is to leave this world a little better for our being here."

The University of Connecticut, which not long before had had an anemic endowment, could boast of a respectable fund and, in keeping with a national trend for public universities, a sea change in its approach to private giving.[37]

UConn 2000 Implemented

If Austin brought a successful track record in fundraising to Storrs, the opportunity that UConn 2000 presented served as the magnet that attracted him. The program was scheduled to expire in 2005, and by August 2003 over $900 million had been expended. New buildings had sprung up for chemistry, biology/physics, music, marine sciences, the Stamford campus, and information technology, among others; new residence halls provided five hundred beds in suites, five hundred apartments in the Charter Oak complex, and three hundred beds in Husky Village designed for fraternities and sororities. Significantly more, however, had to be done to bring the campus to a world-class standard. It did not take much to convince the governor, who recognized the success and popularity of the building program. A few months before the 2002 legislative session, Austin visited John Rowland and asked him if he would be willing to consider an extension of UConn 2000. The president stressed that this would be seen as Rowland's legacy, something very tangible that he would leave to the people of Connecticut and something in which he could take great pride. Those with more immediate matters on their minds thought that an extension of the building program would be an attractive plank on which to run if the governor sought a fourth term in office. With John Rowland's encouragement, both houses of the legislature approved by wide margins 21st Century UConn.[38]

That program added $1.3 billion dollars more of bonding over the ten years following UConn 2000's expiration in 2005. While UConn 2000 involved the construction of about fifty new buildings and the renovation of approximately fifty more, 21st Century UConn would finance an additional twenty new buildings and focus on the renovation of existing buildings, many dating from the early and mid-twentieth century. Significantly, the UConn Health Center in Farmington, omitted from the first plan, received $300 million, including $60 million for a new research tower, which included more than thirty laboratories, a new Nuclear Medicine Research Program, and additional funds for numerous renovations. The Law School in West Hartford and regional campuses in Waterbury, Torrington, and Groton benefited as well. Karla Fox, a business professor who served at the time as associate vice-chancellor for university affairs and oversaw the university's master plan, remarked, "In UConn 2000 we addressed absolutely critical needs, the issues that needed immediate attention because we had basic decaying infrastructure. Now, 21st Century UConn will allow us to move forward, to really plan a state of the art campus for the future." The university sold the first bonds for 21st Century UConn in March 2005. Lorraine Aronson, the chief financial officer, recognized this as a significant milestone that marked "the end of one of the most significant university building programs ever undertaken, nationally or internationally," and the beginning of a new one. The success in terms of improving and beautifying the campus infrastructure and serving as a magnet for students and faculty could not be questioned, although it had to be tempered by the impact in 2005 of concerns regarding the issuance of contracts, cost overruns, and building-code violations. A series of articles in the *Hartford Courant* damaged the university's reputation for managing the massive construction projects and led to a number of investigations and changes in UConn's building policy. President Austin quickly instituted a seven-point corrective program that strengthened oversight of projects, restructured reporting relationships, and established a new University Office of Fire Marshall and Building Inspector under UConn's Division of Public Safety. However, as an increasing number of construction problems and safety violations surfaced at summer's end 2005, criticism intensified. A commission appointed by the governor recommended that control be left with the UConn board of trustees but called for greater outside oversight of the building process and criticized the university for inattention to audits and general mismanagement. Nevertheless, as the university approached its 125th anniversary, its campuses would be transformed, with much of the construction done in a grander style that had been absent from the austere red brick edifices of the past. An innovative competition for a fine arts complex that would tie the campus to a planned new downtown for Storrs brought world-renowned architects to UConn during the spring of 2003. Judges selected Frank O. Gehry, famed for his Guggenheim Museum in Bilbao, Spain, as well as other works, to design the complex at the Storrs campus's east end. Twenty million dollars would come from 21st Century UConn, with the remainder of the $70 million project to be raised through private donations. High aspirations came at a high price and posed a new challenge for UConn.[39]

Society's Problems in a Campus Context: Racial Tension Continued

The Austin presidency did not escape other challenges also familiar to his predecessors. New issues as well as those already familiar occupied the campus. Just as the nation grappled with matters of race, ethnicity, gender, and the environment, so did the university at the end of one millennium and the beginning of another. UConn could not avoid questions raised by the September 11, 2001, attack on the World Trade Center and anti–Iraq War protests. Nor did it escape the increasingly important issues of corporatization and globalization.

Two incidents in April 2001 inflamed tensions and exposed the fragility of race relations on campus, despite years of effort to alleviate such problems. By their very nature, universities have a large turnover of population each year as students graduate. Racial lessons learned by one class may be lost on those who newly arrive, particularly when society at large has not resolved such issues. On April 17 the University Police received a report of graffiti on the men's room wall in the Institute of Material Sciences Building. The message was threatening, racist, and anti-Semitic. Two days later an unrelated, but similarly incendiary, situation arose when the campus newspaper, on free speech grounds, printed a full-page advertisement paid for by former leftwing radical-turned-neoconservative writer and activist David Horowitz, who sought to have it printed in college newspapers throughout the nation. The title of the ad read "Ten Reasons Why Reparations for Slavery Is a Bad Idea—and Racist Too" and tapped into a growing controversy about whether contemporary African Americans should be compensated for the enslavement of their ancestors. When the advertisement appeared at Brown University in Providence, protesters destroyed four thousand copies of the student newspaper; elsewhere, printings by the *Duke Chronicle* and the University of Wisconsin *Badger Herald* met protest as well. At UConn, students at the African American Cultural Center held a press conference to publicize their concerns about the advertisement and the graffiti. Then about sixty students marched to President Austin's office, where, with Austin out of town, they squeezed together to meet with administrator Thomas Callahan. That night a racially diverse crowd marched on the *Daily Campus* office to proclaim that they no longer wanted their student fees to go to the paper because of the advertisement. Editors, who that day had published an editorial urging students to show restraint in debating the advertisement and also ran a lengthy commentary disputing Horowitz's views, countered with an argument for free speech. The following day, President Austin condemned the graffiti but defended the newspaper's right to print the advertisement, declaring, "The free expression of ideas is a value worth preserving even when the ideas presented are obnoxious or offensive, as long as they are not directly threatening." His statement of the high ideals necessary for a university to function as a free marketplace of ideas did little to soothe the feelings of the aggrieved students.[40]

Echoing sentiments he had expressed as a young assistant professor of sociology a quarter of a century before, Ronald L. Taylor, now vice-provost for multicultural affairs, pointed out that many students arrive on campus as freshmen either from suburban schools that are mostly white or urban schools that are mostly black and Hispanic—a recipe for tension and misunderstanding. "Many have virtually no experience with each other," he concluded. The complexity of racial relationships did not escape a white sophomore from Windsor, who remarked that even trying to make acquaintances with other students could be awkward. He elaborated, "It's almost as if I had ulterior motives for being nice—that I was patronizing. . . . It's a very confusing situation." Despite the fact that UConn spent over $3 million a year on multicultural programs, including its cultural centers, society's tensions remained those of the campus. Two years later, when a *Daily Campus* columnist wrote that the centers propagated rather than ended racism, the article not only brought a rash of letters to the editor in reply, but almost nine thousand copies of the newspaper were stolen from the *Daily Campus* building and various other distribution points. The incident underlined the continuing tensions in UConn's race relations, despite the university's best efforts.[41]

The Aftermath of 9/11

If the history of slavery and twentieth-century racial injustices took their toll, contemporary events could also fan the flames of ethnic tension. When terrorists struck New York's World Trade Center on September 11, 2001, some UConn students expressed concern over how Muslims would be treated in the aftermath of the attack, in light of a growing number of incidents across the country. One fifth-semester business major who was not a Muslim said that although he didn't feel personally threatened, he found himself looking over his shoulder and questioning the motives of others. The suspicious student commented, "You stop trusting other countries, you stop trusting other people." UConn's Islamic Center and the Muslim Student Association, along with other Muslim organizations in the region, issued appeals for "solidarity and swift response." Abdul Hamadan, a Saudi Arabian and president of the association, condemned the tragedy. Reda A. Ammar, president of the board of directors of UConn's Islamic Center, feared a backlash against innocent Muslims. He said he received a call from the Office of Student Affairs telling him that any Muslims who are harassed should contact an on-campus Muslim or university organization. Mark Wentzel, the director of the Department of International Services and Programs, pointed out that many Muslim students attempted to remain active, despite fearing for their safety. They participated in a candlelight vigil at the Student Union, and in the following weeks a number of campus women, in solidarity with their Muslim counterparts, donned the traditional hijab, headscarves worn by Muslim females. Art history and women's studies professor Anne D'Alleva, who promoted the hijab wearing, remarked, "I felt we had a very troubled campus with Muslim students getting harassed. I felt like I had to do something. This is a very visible anti-racist movement[;] it is no longer us and them[,] it's everybody."[42]

At the end of September, nine students of Muslim, Asian, and European descent who claimed to represent thousands of concerned students wrote to Austin, suggesting what needed to be done "to ensure the safety and well-being of all students on campus." In a thoughtful letter, they advocated several measures to encourage understanding. The president endorsed their goals of working toward "campus safety, assuring an atmosphere free of bigotry, and enhancing understanding of the issues surrounding the tragic events of September 11." He explained that he had met with a group of Muslim students, faculty, and staff to hear their concerns, and that the chancellor would convene a university group to coordinate educational activities over the course of the semester that focused on political, social, and cultural matters in an effort to cultivate more global understanding and awareness among members of the university community. Austin particularly welcomed the call for a day of awareness and unity, which could be relatively easily translated through existing mechanisms into a "Metanoia," a time of contemplation and consideration. As the events of September 11 transformed America, they penetrated the consciousness of University of Connecticut students for that semester too—and long after.[43]

The Iraq War: Protest and Support

Events following September 11 brought U.S. President George W. Bush's "War on Terror." When in March 2003 that war moved from Afghanistan to Iraq, the controversial decision engendered protests on campus. Nor did UConn stand alone, as over 230 college campuses, schools, and organizations participated in a nationwide walk-out/strike organized by the War Resisters League and spread by the National Youth and Student Peace Coalition Web site. At 11:30 A.M. on Wednesday, March 5, in a scene reminiscent of Vietnam War teach-ins, more than 350 students, faculty, and staff members rallied in front of Babbidge Library despite the rain to hear three professors and several students speak against the war. History professor Paul Goodwin told the crowd that the war had no justification—"The case for war has not been made. The evidence presented just doesn't stand up." Many agreed, but not the group of prowar students who counterdemonstrated and were heard to say, "Go home hippies." One, a junior history major who echoed President Bush, argued, "I am in favor of war if Saddam [Hussein] does not completely and totally give up all of his weapons." The rally organizers promised to have weekly meetings and planned on writing letters to congressmen and senators. War Resisters League member Sarah Lust exclaimed, "This is in our hands. If we want to stop the war, we need to have our voices heard."[44]

In order to communicate their position to as many people as possible, about twenty-five antiwar protesters pitched tents on the rolling lawn sloping up to the main campus, alongside Route 195, which carried major local traffic. For several weeks, they camped overnight in the "Tent City," but not without being pelted by an occasional apple or water bomb tossed by vandals. The UConn police arrested the miscreants and, unlike the days of the Vietnam War, assisted the demonstrators, who chose a less confrontational approach than their predecessors had three decades earlier. The police, however, occupied with Spring Weekend reveling, could not prevent the destruction of the "Tent City" in late April. On the last Saturday night of that month, attackers slashed the unprotected tents and spread the personal effects of the owners across the lawn in front of Route 195. While the 2003 protest came to a bad end, in 2005, on the second anniversary of the war in Iraq, a group called Strike One reestablished the Tent City in the same location. It called for the university to end its involvement with companies or state organizations that aided the war effort and to end military recruiting on campus. It also asked President Austin and student government organizations to publicly denounce the war. Geoff Traugh, one of the group's leaders, perhaps exaggerated the continuity of history when he stated, "If it seems as though we are expressing ourselves in the language of a bygone era, it is because nothing has changed."[45]

Gay and Straight Allies

If the age of terror made itself felt in Storrs, the cultural wars over sexual orientation also had their impact at UConn. When Philip Austin first assumed his presidency, the Bisexual, Gay, and Lesbian Association (BiGALA) celebrated its second Month of Pride in October 1996. The group's head said she expected the month to go smoothly. There had been no problems the previous year and she foresaw none in 1996, but she added that some people thought "We shouldn't be doing this, but those are just individuals, not the majority." The following year, the student co-chairperson of BiGALA acknowledged hatred toward homosexuals in the United States but confessed that he hadn't seen it on campus. Matters took a different turn in 1998. In February, in what police, after some convincing from the victim, termed a hate crime, someone burned the office door of a dramatic arts professor who was active in BiGALA. He had joined UConn eighteen months before the incident and until that time had found the campus to be conservative but not hostile. Concern then rose that gay and lesbian groups were being targeted.[46]

The situation exploded a year and a half later when vandals chalked anti-gay graffiti on campus sidewalks and Sprague Hall. On Monday, October 25, 1999, a crowd of approximately one hundred gathered at the Student Union mall to offer a united front against intolerance. The previous week, those opposed to the messages of the original graffiti scrawled their own pro-gay and anti-hate messages across the main pedestrian walkways on campus. At the rally, one speaker, enraged by the anti-gay epithets, said she understood why the *Princeton Review* listed UConn among the twenty least homosexually tolerant universities in the nation. With Duke University ranked first, she quipped, "I don't want to be on the *Princeton Review* [list] again. I'd rather compete with Duke on the basketball court." President Austin condemned the anti-gay incidents and in a letter to the campus community pointed out that it was cold comfort to note that almost every university in America had witnessed its own crimes of hate and vandalism. He asked whether society was giving young people license to act on their ugliest impulses. UConn, he said, must be "a haven from hate." "Vicious, anonymous attacks" were not an exercise in the free speech, which he vowed to protect. He continued, "No, the graffiti that appeared here recently was vandalism pure and simple. It was cowardly, because it was anonymous. It was not an invitation to dialogue and it did not contain even the germ of an idea. It was about as intellectual an act as smashing someone's windshield, and very possibly more dangerous."[47]

Martha Nelson, director of the Rainbow Center, recognized the importance of Austin's statement but told a reporter Austin "can plead with people until he's blue in the face. What needs to change is the environment around here." She said that a University Town Meeting that would be held on Tuesday, November 2, would be an opportunity for the community to voice its concerns. Nearly two hundred people showed up for the meeting to offer words of support and to suggest ways to promote tolerance and civility. Hundreds affirmed their support for gays when they picked up and wore "Ally" buttons distributed by the Rainbow Center and BiGALA. The Undergraduate Student Government allocated money to purchase two thousand additional pins and expressed their support in other ways as well. The UCForum, UConn's e-mail listserv, filled with messages condemning the vandalism. When two traveling evangelists visited campus one day during the last week in October to speak at the Student Union Mall against gays, rock and roll, communists, and most organized religions, students responded negatively. The events had raised UConn's consciousness about sexual orientation and revealed a sincere condemnation of homophobia, although it did not eliminate it completely on campus.[48]

The Battle of Horsebarn Hill

Economic and environmental issues proved equally contentious, and one seemed particularly costly for the university. High hopes greeted the announcement in March 1998 that UConn and Pfizer, Inc., a major international pharmaceutical company with its research and development headquarters based in Groton, Connecticut, would join to create a "Center for Excellence in Animal Vaccine Research." Under the ultimate terms of the agreement, UConn would grant to Pfizer, for one dollar a year, a thirty-five-year lease to land on which the company promised to construct a $35-million, 90,000-square-foot building with mixed office and animal health research space. In turn, Pfizer would lease one-fifth of the building back to the university, also for one dollar a year. The facility, which would add to the town of Mansfield's tax rolls, would support basic and applied research on vaccines to improve the health of swine, sheep, and cows. The principals expected the new partnership to lead to breakthroughs in the prevention of livestock diseases that compromised food safety, endangered farm animal welfare, and increased animal production cost. Governor Rowland declared the proposed center to be an outstanding example of public-private partnerships and heralded Connecticut's leadership in biomedical research. Austin saw the initiative as advancing the state's economic development, "a vital part of a land grant university's mission." George M. Milne Jr., Pfizer's president of central research, recognized that "What is unusual about this is that scientists from the University and Pfizer will be working side by side. What we're doing will become a model for the rest of the country." Optimism reigned.[49]

But opposition, based mainly on the scenic Horsebarn Hill site of the center, quickly developed, although concern about the university's emerging corporate ties also played a role. The opposition involved demonstrations and freedom of information complaints and lawsuits, and it sometimes exceeded the expected. At one Town of Mansfield organizing meeting, an enthusiastic gun collector remarked, "If they build it there, they're going to be able to see my gun collection in action!" One speaker at a public hearing referred to Horsebarn Hill as Mansfield's "spiritual town green." As the dispute grew, the location increasingly took on iconic proportions.[50]

Early in the battle that ensued, Ayla Kardestuncer, the head of Mansfield Common Sense, a local citizens' group, wrote to Pfizer, "If you insist on building anything like the proposed monstrosity on Horsebarn Hill, you probably will have to fight the entire Town of Mansfield, its people and its government. . . . We think such a fracas would be messy and costly even if you did win." That warning in December 1998 did not exaggerate the intensity of the opposition that developed and the difficult road the center would face, until Milne called Austin in August 1999 to tell him that Pfizer's corporate headquarters informed him that they had to "pull the plug." They didn't doubt the commitment of the state or the university, but the town's opposition could keep them tied up in court for another two to three years. In the meantime, Pfizer's vaccine sat on the shelf, untested. The company, in an economic move, was simultaneously cutting back on hundreds of millions of dollars in capital projects, so perhaps the project would have ended without the opposition of the local groups. However, the protestors certainly made it easier to do so.[51]

Students joined local citizens and environmentalists to form the Coalition to Save Horsebarn Hill. At an April 1999 meeting of the board of trustees, bongo-drum-playing demonstrators with homemade signs, life-sized puppets, and horse costumes made their opposition known. A student leader of the group, Lisa Terezakis, presented board chair Roger Gelfenbien with a thick sheaf of papers containing 3,500 signatures opposed to the location. Emeritus professor David Ivry, who visited President Austin frequently attempting to persuade him to change his mind about the location, told the trustees, "This is a different place—not for buildings, not for industry, but for the beauty of life. Do not transform Horsebarn Hill. It should be for our children and our grandchildren." An eleven-year-old carried a sign, "We will save the hill." Despite the fact that UConn and Pfizer complied with Mansfield's request to move the building thirty feet north, so that it would be less visible from Route 195, the town's Planning and Zoning Commission voted 5–4 against the proposed site and advocated one away from the hill. Subsequent to the trustees' meeting, Austin asked the university's Master Plan Committee to review alternative sites expeditiously. It held a heated five-and-a-half-hour hearing at which all sides offered arguments for and against the location on Horsebarn Hill. UConn administrators stressed the extraordinary opportunity for research in conjunction with Pfizer, which would be of value to students, faculty, and the community at large. The president of the UConn Alumni Association, Andrea Dennis-LaVigne, a veterinarian, thought the UConn-Pfizer partnership could put the university "on the map." On the other hand, one Mansfield resident contended that building on the hill was like "building Walmart in the Grand Canyon." Another, Peter Newcomer, warned that the coalition had hired a lawyer and would "make every delay possible happen if you don't get this building off Horsebarn Hill." For Quentin Kessel, a physics professor whose father had headed the English Department during the Jorgensen era, the university stood on the horns of a dilemma. "We will either lose the hillside or lose Pfizer," stated Kessel, whose parents, buried near the site of the proposed center, had long ago sold the university 120 acres on Horsebarn Hill in the hope that it would be preserved.[52]

The Master Plan Advisory Committee recommended that if moving the site delayed the project significantly or otherwise jeopardized the partnership with Pfizer, the original site should be used. In mid-July Austin announced the siting of the center as originally planned. Around the same time, the coalition filed suit in Hartford Superior Court. Within a month, Pfizer ended its participation. The initiative for the center originated with faculty in the College of Agriculture, and its demise presented a great disappointment to them and the loss of an opportunity for research and partnering with a major corporation with enormous resources; it also led to the departure of some leading but discontented faculty members. It did not, however, end the university's relationship with Pfizer, which in 2004 established the School of Pharmacy's first endowed chair with a gift of $2 million. The loss of the vaccine center, however, resonated in 2005 when the issue of state funding for stem cell research emerged. A Yale postdoctoral fellow in molecular biophysics and biochemistry who held his doctorate from UConn complained about "Connecticut's dysfunctional attitude toward science" and offered as an example the "neo-Luddite locals driving

Pfizer away from building a multimillion-dollar research lab next to the University of Connecticut campus in Storrs. The state lost out to Terre Haute, Ind[iana], which welcomes the jobs and investment."[53]

Sweat Shirts, Sweat Shops, and Justice for Janitors

One columnist claimed that while the objections to the Pfizer project were nominally aesthetic and environmental, even if they had been met the coalition members would have objected to any cooperation between the university and a corporation. A very specific form of cooperation involved the manufacture by large corporations such as Nike and Reebok of apparel bearing the UConn logo. The issue had global implications and brought attention to fair labor standards. In May 1997 Duke University's head of marketing, with the support from Students Against Sweatshops, encouraged the drafting of a code of conduct to set standards for the manufacture of sportswear. Other institutions followed Duke's lead. By the winter of 1999, the *Daily Campus* informed the UConn community of protests about sweatshop labor in the making of logo-bearing apparel at several Ivy League universities and at the Universities of North Carolina and Wisconsin as well as Georgetown. In April, President Austin met with the student Labor Action Coalition to discuss UConn's affiliation with clothing manufacturers who used sweatshop labor. In 1998 UConn athletics had already earned $400,000 from licensing and merchandising. By 2003–4 it would take in more than $1 million in royalties, placing the university among the twenty-five highest-earning schools.[54]

At his meeting with the students in April 1999 Austin pledged to try to find ways to avoid the exploitation of the labor involved in manufacturing apparel carrying UConn's logo. A few days later, he issued a statement explaining the university's position. UConn was strongly committed to the enforcement of fair labor standards in its own workplace and expected all establishments with whom it had a commercial relationship to share that commitment. With a number of other institutions, the school participated in the Collegiate Licensing Company (CLC), a licensing agent that administered trademark licensing for colleges and universities. The CLC had drawn up a Code of Conduct, which UConn felt did not yet meet appropriate standards, and disclosure and monitoring processes. It would work with other universities to change the code rather than do so by itself. In its final form, Austin argued that the code should incorporate a number of fair labor principles. If the CLC did not adhere to such principles, Austin suggested that UConn would consider alternative licensing arrangements. He also stated that he would shortly appoint a special university panel to monitor the issue, maintain worksite information, and recommend further appropriate courses of action.[55]

In the fall, he appointed a Task Force on College Licensing Issues, to be headed by Jeremy Paul, associate dean of the Law School. Over the next six months the group reviewed UConn's existing contractual agreements, consulted with other universities, held a public hearing, and met with two workplace monitoring organizations, the Fair Labor Association and the Workers Rights Consortium. The task force recommended that the university join other schools and sign on to the CLC code but also ask for a rider calling for special protection for women workers. Austin accepted the recommendation and as of May 1, 2000, UConn required all licensees to disclose factory locations. As on so many campuses across the nation, UConn continued to grapple with this dilemma, which pitted human rights against corporate profits. In 2005, as the issue reemerged, students established a Coalition for a Sweat-Free UConn, which began negotiations with the UConn Coop to establish a "sweat-free" zone that would carry only union goods made in the United States. By April of that year, students could purchase merchandise in a special "union made" section that carried only goods manufactured under fair labor conditions.[56]

The corporate issue played out in another way in 2001, during what became known as the "Justice for Janitors" campaign. A small but vocal group, "Students Concerned about UConn Janitors," wrote to Austin about what they believed to be the university's lack of "respect for human dignity" because of the "poverty wages" paid to some university employees. In actuality, the employees in question worked for a private contractor, Capitol Cleaners. The students, however, felt their pleas had been neglected in the past and as "the conscience of the University" thought it hypocritical on the part of the then-chancellor, John Petersen, to announce a "Human Rights Semester" for the next term while not "respecting human rights on campus." Because they did not want to have to point out the hypocrisy at every event related to human rights during the next semester, they demonstrated at the opening celebration of Campaign UConn (the capital campaign). NBC weekend television anchor Brian Williams, a main speaker at the event, recognized that the protesters were exercising their right of free speech and assembly. The *Daily Campus,* on the other hand, chastised the demonstrators for embarrassing the university. Its editorial went as far as to argue that "UConn administrators should be praised for their humanitarian actions" because they provided jobs for individuals who in many instances did not speak English and in some cases had criminal records. The polarization reflected end-of-the-school-year tension, with the drama still to have another act.[57]

The protestors distributed a flyer entitled "Decorp UConn" that began, "Some students are concerned about the increasing corporatization of UConn. There is a clear pattern at UConn, as at most major universities today, of running the University more like a corporation. This extends all the way from day to day operations, which is the reason why we're forced to run the Justice for Janitors campaign, all the way up to the level of curriculum and budget." They asked why the university had a new Business School Building (a "multi-million dollar shrine to business," as they termed it), but, pointing to the impact of UConn's diluted operating budgets, which had accompanied the unprecedented funding for bricks and mortar, class sizes had increased dramatically without any comparable growth in faculty and staff. They questioned the university's fundraising and investment policies and advocated the "decorporation" of UConn so that it no longer would be a "servant of corporations."[58]

Rhetoric fused into action on Tuesday, May 8, when nine students, calling themselves the Gulley Hall 9, occupied the president's office shortly after noon. The UConn protest began on the same day that Harvard students ended a twenty-day sit-in demanding a livable wage for workers, which prompted observers to wonder whether this signaled nationally a new age of student activism. On the second day of the protest, the directors of the university cultural centers wrote to Austin in support of the occupiers. They claimed to represent the UConn community and urged agreement with the students' demands for workers, "so we can stand proud next fall at the beginning of our Human Rights Semester and show our community that UConn truly believes in, and practices, the ideals of human rights." Austin, a staunch believer in academic freedom, met briefly with the students, whom he believed to be disruptive, and then reacted to what he saw as "thuggish threats and behavior." He told them that final exams were starting and if there were further disruption they would be arrested and removed. Philosophically, there was little disagreement with the "Justice for Janitors" goals. Long before the students' occupation of Gulley Hall, the university's budget request already included funds to improve wages, and when the state did not cover the added costs, UConn did. Ultimately, Thomas Callahan, Austin's special assistant, and the occupiers signed an agreement in which UConn promised that all contracts with private providers of maintenance service would reflect prevailing wages and benefits levels effective July 1, 2001. In addition, the university promised that in the event that it privatized future work performed by unionized employees (although it had no plans to do so), it would initiate consultations with the union representative at least six months prior to implementation. The agreement ended the occupation as students campus-wide attended to their final examinations. Many just a few days earlier had been less occupied with social activism and more concerned with UConn's annual rite of spring, seen as fun and as "blowing off steam before finals" but instead often a senseless and destructive event unfortunately not uncommon to campuses nationwide.[59]

Spring Weekend: "Kill-A-Kegs," Bonfires, and Car Flipping

While Alabama spared Philip Austin the experience of Spring Weekend, he had encountered the celebration during his tenure heading Colorado State University. As the drinking and destruction worsened over the years in Fort Collins, Austin brought together the Chamber of Commerce, the mayor and city council, faculty leadership, and the school's trustees to develop a plan to control the event. He believed the conditions there, which included media and commercial support and the city's larger size, offered a better chance of success than in Storrs. When he arrived at UConn, a long tradition had already been established. A few months prior to his arrival, at the end of April 1996, some students issued the "Spring Manifesto." They importuned their fellows to observe tradition and advised that "Spring Weekend is the one event all year that makes the mediocrity of the rest of the semester seem worth it." To celebrate, they invited everyone to the Carriage House Apartments on Hunting Lodge Road on Thursday, May 2, to partake in an all-day "Kill-A-Keg," and they instructed potential participants to deliver their kegs on Wednesday in order to "preempt the 'authorities'"— and to arrive early on Thursday. The off-campus but nearby apartment complex attracted thousands of carousing students and non-students. Year after year, it morphed into a bacchanalian revelry.[60]

After the 1996 celebration, which included police using pepper spray and dogs against students throwing rocks, bottles, and cans during a South Campus bonfire, university officials established a Spring Weekend Work Group consisting of students and staff to examine the issues surrounding the event and to make recommendations for the future. The group determined that the atmosphere created both on and immediately off campus was unacceptable. It made a number of suggestions, ranging from the well-intentioned but naïve attempt to change the name of the weekend in an effort to disguise it to separating the major spring concert from the weekend in order to discourage non-student visitors from attending. The change of the name to "University Weekend" fooled no one, and non-students continued to flock to Storrs during future celebrations. A Town/University Relations Committee Rental Properties Work Group did not have much success either in its effort to control rowdiness at the off-campus properties. The 1997 "Spring Manifesto" advised students to avoid another South Campus incident but feared for the life of the annual rite because of the name change, the absence of a band, and the dwindling financial support. It wondered whether the event would vanish into obscurity or emerge with renewed vigor and urged readers to "go forward with unprecedented safety, intelligence, and sound judgment while exercising our right to publicly assemble in our common pursuit of happiness." It concluded, "May our preparations culminate in the greatest Bacchanalia this university has ever seen."[61]

Over the next several years, and especially in 1998, students, and more likely non-students, continued to find ways to perpetuate Spring Weekend merriment and havoc. Despite a change in the Student Conduct Code that applied the university's disciplinary process to off-campus activities, the extensive reports after significant deliberation of the Chancellor's Special Task Force on Community and Civility (1999), and President Austin's appointment of a Task Force on Substance Abuse (2003), UConn's efforts to curb drinking fell short of success. In 2004, after the unprecedented dual national basketball championships of the men's and women's teams, the celebration turned "dangerous and destructive," with much of the damage being done off-campus, less at Carriage House and more at nearby Celeron Square Apartments. Between April 3 and April 7 the police arrested forty-one people, twenty-three of whom were UConn students. The courts made examples of several in an effort to dampen the drunken troublemaking. Shortly afterward, that year's Spring Weekend, according to the UConn Police, attracted 20,000 people to X-Lot and 8,000 to 10,000 to Celeron. They blamed much of the unlawful rowdiness on non-student visitors and noted that the number of visitors attending Spring Weekend had increased substantially between 1999 and 2004. By September 2004, fall partying at Carriage House and Celeron Square caused Mansfield officials to complain of the weekend disturbances, which increasingly outraged residents who lived in the neighborhood of the apartments. The town threatened to strictly enforce its ordinance regulating the possession of alcohol by minors. By March 2005 Mansfield Police, state police, and state liquor control agents raided a local bar, the Civic Pub, and arrested thirty-two patrons found to be under twenty-one. Mansfield's mayor, Betsy Paterson, made clear the town's position when she stated, "As a community, we want to let students know we do not tolerate underage drinking." Town and gown did not disagree, but the problem persisted during the 2005 Spring Weekend. An increased police presence, intense rain, the wearing of wristbands to identify students, and no kegs at the Carriage House "Kill-A-Keg" on Thursday night still did not deter the rowdiness, although it appeared more subdued than the previous year. More arrests were made than in 2004, although most of the people arrested identified themselves as non-UConn students. A UConn "night court" that had the authority to issue temporary suspensions ordered two students off campus on the first night of festivities. Liquor control agents cited two near-campus package stores for selling to minors. The state commissioner in charge of such sales proclaimed, "All liquor retailers must be part of the solution in reducing the problems associated with underage drinking." Despite such efforts, as UConn emerged as a national university it had to contend with a national problem that had no easy remedy.[62]

National Champions, a New Stadium, and a Bowl Victory

National prominence came more positively through athletics, as the university gained recognition during the Hartley and Austin eras. Its men's and women's basketball successes and the move from regional to national competition in football, along with a new stadium and a bowl game victory, attracted the attention of many people around the country. The unprecedented athletic success in the period between 1990 and 2005, and particularly since 1995, enhanced UConn's public recognition as it emerged academically and its attraction to students nationwide. While basketball dominated the attention and football began to compete for a wider audience, other sports won recognition for the Huskies as well. Men's soccer coach Joe Morrone retired in 1996 after twenty-eight years at UConn as the second most-winning coach in Division I men's soccer history. His successor, Ray Reid, led the team to regular season and Big East tournament titles in 1999, when the booters advanced to the NCAA "Final Four," and ended the season ranked fourth in the nation. In 2000, he was named National Coach of the Year after the Huskies won the NCAA Division I National Championship and key player Chris Gbandi received recognition as the top collegiate men's soccer player in the country. Women's coach Len Tsantiris had achieved the same honor as Reid three years earlier when he brought his soccer players to the NCAA championship game. Three-time all-American Sara Whalen earned National Player of the Year honors in 1997. A year earlier, highly successful baseball coach Andy Baylock, who retired in 2003, was elected to the American Baseball Coaches Association Hall of Fame; he posted his five-hundredth victory during his twenty-second season at UConn in 2001. Connecticut made Big East conference history when it emerged in 1998 as the first school to win regular season titles in four separate fall sports: field hockey, men and women's soccer, and volleyball. The next year, the field hockey team ended its season in the Final Four and ranked third in the nation. By 2000, UConn's twenty three varsity intercollegiate teams combined to win 71 percent of their games. During the 1999–2000 academic year, athletic fundraising surpassed the $10 million level for the first time in school history. Overall athletic success had become commonplace, but the big story rested with basketball and football.[63]

The hiring of Geno Auriemma and Jim Calhoun, the women's and men's basketball coaches, in 1985 and 1986, respectively, ushered in a golden era of UConn major sports. Both earned unprecedented success during the 1990s and the first years of the new millennium. In 2005 the university rewarded them with generous contracts, making Auriemma the highest-paid women's basketball coach in the nation, while Calhoun earned more than any other men's coach in the Big East conference. Handsome but controversial deals with Nike, the athletic apparel company, supplemented their contracts, and their faces graced advertising billboards across the state. It could be argued that the coaches emerged as the two most prominent celebrities in Connecticut at the turn of the twenty-first century.[64]

In 1991, as noted, the women's basketball team earned its first-ever trip to the NCAA Final Four. From February 1, 1994, when the Lady Huskies first moved into the Top-10 national rankings, to the second poll of the 2004–5 season, they never ranked lower than sixth and remained in the top five for all but nine weeks.

In ninety-three of those weeks, UConn was ranked number one. Their perfect 35–0 season record in 1994–95 and the national championship began a decade of dominance in women's basketball, unparalleled except perhaps at the University of Tennessee, which became the Huskies' archrival. Rebecca Lobo, a star of the 1994–95 team, captured its mystique when she recalled, "That season, we were on angel's wings. A force greater than anything we could control was taking care of us, pushing us along that path. We had no thoughts of going undefeated or what it would lead to in Connecticut or anywhere else in the universe of women's basketball. . . . It was a magical time." Lobo, who epitomized UConn women's basketball, went on to become National Player of the Year in 1995, with the same honor bestowed on scrappy point guard Jennifer Rizzotti in 1996 and center Kara Wolters in 1997. Geno Auriemma was named National Coach of the Year in 1995 and 1997, and would repeat the honor in 2000 after a 36–1 season and another national championship. His teams in the new millennium and the old, studded with stars such as Nykesha Sales, Shea Ralph, Svetlana Abrosimova, Sue Bird, Swin Cash, and Diana Taurasi, who was considered by some to be the best women's basketball player in the history of the game, added to the luster of the accomplishment. Between 2000 and 2005, in addition to dominating the Big East conference, the Lady Huskies won twenty straight games in the NCAA tournament, appeared in five Final Fours, and brought home three national championships. Sellout crowds filled Gampel Pavilion and the larger Hartford Civic Center to watch a team that had won the hearts of fans throughout the state. A contract with Connecticut Public Television (CPTV) signed in 1995 and renewed throughout the period allowed fans all over the state to see the games, and women's basketball emerged as the station's most popular program. When the national success ended with a loss to Stanford in the 2005 NCAA tournament Sweet Sixteen and the derailing of a bid for a fourth title, the *New York Times* reported, "UConn Campus Quiet for This Time of Year." At most other universities, a 25–8 season would be seen as something to celebrate. UConn, however, had come to expect perfection from its women's team.[65]

Perfection had come the year before, in 2004, when both the men's and the women's basketball teams won national championships, an unprecedented achievement in NCAA history. The men's team, playing in a more competitive environment, did not dominate nationally as consistently as the women, but by March 1996 they had won their third consecutive Big East tournament and compiled a record-setting league mark of 49–5. Two years later they played in the NCAA tournament's Elite Eight and ended with a 32–5 record. As the millennium wound down, the team peaked. In the November 1998 early-season polls, both the men and the women's teams ranked number one in the nation, the second time in NCAA Division I history that the same school led in both categories (the first time occurred on February 13, 1995, when the Huskies initially accomplished the feat). The men began their 1998–99 season with nine-teen consecutive wins and were ranked number one for ten straight weeks. They proved themselves worthy by sweeping the Big East regular season and tourna-ment and going on to win the national championship by beating Duke 77–74 while compiling a 34–2 record. By then Jim Calhoun had surpassed Hugh Greer as UConn's winningest coach. In December 1997, he had already won his five-hundredth career victory; he would join the exclusive 700 club at the end of the 2004–5 season and be named to the Basketball Hall of Fame. Calhoun brought his players to a second national championship in 2004 with future NBA stars Emeka Okafor, as renowned for his academic abilities as for his basketball prowess, and Ben Gordon leading the way against Georgia Tech in an 82–73 vic-tory. His teams had become perennial NCAA tournament contenders and fre-quently appeared on national television, carrying the UConn banner through-out the nation. The coach emerged as a respected and dependable developer of NBA talent, not only with Okafor and Gordon, but with athletes Ray Allen, Scott Burrell, Caron Butler, Khalid El-Amin, Tate George, Richard Hamiliton, Travis Knight, Donny Marshall, Donyell Marshall, Chris Smith, Charlie Vil-lanueva, and Jake Voskuhl. In the Calhoun era, a regional team had exploded into a national basketball powerhouse.[66]

Husky football did not reach the same pinnacle around the turn of the mil-lennium, but planning and support did propel it toward national recognition. By the middle of the 1990s the intent to upgrade to Division I-A stood firmly in place. Skip Holtz, an enthusiastic and successful young coach, was hired in December 1993 and by the Huskies one hundredth season in 1998 he led them to a school record of ten victories and, for the first time, a postseason trip to the NCAA Division I-AA quarterfinals. Holtz, born in Willimantic when his more famous father, Lou, was an assistant coach at UConn in the 1960s, left Storrs in 1999 to work with his father at South Carolina after the elder Holtz left Notre Dame. At that time, it appeared that attaining one ingredient for I-A status, a stadium with a capacity for 30,000 people, might be elusive.[67]

In 1997, President Austin supported the upgrade and building of such an arena as part of UConn's step from regional to national institution, provided that the funding would not be at the expense of academic programs or UConn 2000 money. He told legislators in November, "The real issue is the transfor-mation of the University of Connecticut from a very good state university to one of the preeminent public institutions of higher education in the United States. . . . Football is not, in and of itself, a central University priority. Nor is athletics in general. The proposed football upgrade is important to the Univer-sity because, and only because, it will help us mightily to reach goals that do represent central priorities. It will, for example, help us build a more exciting campus—one that can attract more of Connecticut's best students." Possible locations included an expansion of Memorial Stadium, the abandoned UCEPI site, the vacated Mansfield Training School, or downtown Hartford. Those arguing in support of the stadium claimed that it would rejuvenate the campus, increase school spirit, enhance fundraising, and attract additional applications and enrollment. The opposition argued that it would adversely affect academic programs by siphoning off funds, attract burdensome traffic on game days to Storrs if built on or near campus, and have a negative environmental impact.[68]

Two years later, in November 1999, when the United Technologies Corporation offered to donate seventy-five acres of land at East Hartford's Rentschler Field, formerly used as a Pratt and Whitney airfield, the state and the university jumped at the opportunity. Despite his comment in 1997 that a stadium should be built on campus because "We shouldn't create the biggest magnet to the university 40–50 miles away [from campus]," Governor Rowland felt confident that the move to East Hartford would be good for all involved, "a win-win-win situation." Athletic Director Lew Perkins agreed and stated, "It is an exciting location which is easily accessible and still part of the overall economic development of the riverfront communities of Hartford/East Hartford." Perkins thus touched upon the main reason for building the stadium, which suited the economic needs of the state and the Hartford region and filled the void left by an earlier aborted attempt to lure the professional New England Patriots. The 40,000-seat arena, which cost the state $90 million and included thirty-eight luxury boxes and parking for 12,000 cars, opened as scheduled on August 30, 2003, when the football Huskies beat Indiana 34–10 before a sellout crowd. The opening of Rentschler Field assured UConn's I-A status, and the institution became the first in the nation to move from Division I-AA to membership in a Bowl Championship Series (BCS) Conference, the Big East, which promised big dividends as a result of conference revenue sharing.[69]

According to Lew Perkins, maintaining UConn's basketball Big East affiliation depended upon the football upgrade. The university's athletic administrators feared that the league would be divided between the Division I-A football-basketball schools and the basketball-only schools, with the former having more clout in the conference. The latter, including UConn, if it didn't upgrade, and the private Catholic institutions—Georgetown, Providence, St. John's, Seton Hall—would be placed into an inferior position or excluded altogether. The new stadium guaranteed UConn's eligibility to play football as well as basketball in the Big East and contest against national gridiron powerhouses such as Miami, Boston College, Virginia Tech, Syracuse, and Pittsburgh. However, just as UConn readied for "big-time" Big East football, the league seemed about to unravel. The successful Atlantic Coast Conference (ACC) in the late spring of 2003 tried to lure Miami away, and rumors suggested that Boston College and Syracuse also were in play. Miami had flirted with the ACC earlier, but Austin remembered that Miami's president had promised other Big East leaders that the school would not engage in discussion for the "foreseeable future," which was interpreted as four to five years. When Miami accepted the ACC bid, ill feelings prevailed, and then Virginia Tech went with them. Later, Boston College, which initially appeared rejected by the ACC and expressed fealty to the Big East, jumped leagues, creating additional hard feelings on the part of those still in the league, especially UConn. The remaining schools, concerned that they would be financially hurt by losing the football giants, brought a lawsuit. More significantly, they recognized the need to rebuild and did so by adding five teams: Louisville, Cincinnati, and South Florida, which played football and basketball, and Marquette and DePaul for only basketball. In this manner, as UConn approached its 125th anniversary, its basketball conference promised to be premier in the nation, while the Big East in football would at least remain nationally competitive.[70]

At the moment that things seemed most uncertain for UConn in the Big East, the departure of Athletic Director Lew Perkins complicated the situation and temporarily shook UConn's confidence. On Friday, June 6, 2003, he had joined the governor, Attorney General Richard Blumenthal, and President Austin at the State Capitol and announced the lawsuit against Miami, Boston College, and the ACC. Three days later, the *Hartford Courant* carried a first-page banner headline announcing his impending departure for the University of Kansas. *Courant* columnist Jeff Jacobs captured the feeling of many when he wrote that it was understandable to want to seek a new opportunity, "But damn, Lew, the timing is lousy for Connecticut." Under his tenure, beginning in 1990, UConn athletics had achieved unprecedented success: six national championships, the football upgrade and new stadium, impressive increases in the athletic budget and fundraising, and the Title IX enhanced programming in women's sports, to almost half of the athletic budget. Under ordinary circumstances, it would be hard to replace him, but immediately the search for a new director focused exclusively upon Jeff Hathaway, Perkins's second-in-command between 1990 and 2001 before he left to become athletic director at Colorado State University. Despite some faculty concern about the lack of a broad national search, the efficiency of the appointment and the choice of an individual with experience at UConn won praise. The forty-three-year-old Hathaway eased into the position and provided a continuity that few, if any, could. His otherwise successful tenure was shaken in 2005 when ethical and legal questions arose regarding his relationship with a local automobile dealer who had a contract with the university. He and his defenders pointed to earlier precedent and prior approvals by the state's Ethics Commission and many on campus continued to recognize Hathaway as a person of strong integrity. Undistracted sports fans, however, celebrated the university's increasing gridiron success under Coach Randy Edsall, whom Perkins had appointed to replace Skip Holz. Edsall shepherded the Huskies into the Big East in 2004, a year earlier than originally scheduled. Not only did he and his star quarterback, Dan Orlovsky, lead the team to an 8–4

record, they brought UConn its first Division I-A bowl victory, a 39–10 triumph over the University of Toledo Rockets before 52,552 spectators at the
Motor City Bowl in Detroit two days after Christmas. Football began to successfully vie for parity with basketball in Storrs. Huskymania proffered enough
enthusiasm for both.[71]

Academic Accomplishment

Athletic success and the significant physical changes to the campus complemented the academic accomplishment of the new UConn. The new and renovated buildings changed the face and character of the university and made it
more inviting for scholars to engage in teaching and research. A new hotel, the
Nathan Hale Inn, facilitated the holding of national and international conferences that previously could not easily be arranged. An impressive Alumni House
welcomed those graduates returning to their alma mater and helped build
support for the university. Open vistas were complemented by a pedestrian-
friendly campus, and well-equipped buildings demonstrated the university's
emphasis on academic improvement. New buildings offered a home to scientific research, engineering, business, and education. Research-oriented faculty
attracted more federal and other grant monies to support their work. Sponsored awards received by the university exclusive of the Health Center increased
from $61 million in 1994 to $92 million in 2004. The Health Center in 2004
brought in another $99 million, for a total of $191 million. It played an important role in UConn's increasing research success and under Austin's leadership
was brought into closer collaboration with the main campus. Like other academic health centers nationwide, though, it suffered from severe financial problems during the final years of the twentieth century. These were caused by reduced payments from managed care companies and drastic reductions in
Medicare disbursements due to the U.S. Balanced Budget Act of 1997. Under the
leadership of its dean, Peter Deckers, and a special $20 million allocation from
the legislature in 2000 to overcome its deficit and invest in research, the Health
Center went on to prosper during the early years of the new millennium. UConn
vied with other universities for leading status as a research institution.[72]

By discipline, 39 percent of the 2004 sponsored funds at Storrs and the regional campuses went to the life sciences, 35 percent to the physical sciences and
engineering, and 22 percent to the social sciences. Humanities and fine arts received only 1 percent. The importance of the humanities and their contribution
to society, however, did not go unrecognized or unappreciated. In 2001 Dean
Ross MacKinnon of the College of Liberal Arts and Sciences established the
University of Connecticut Humanities Institute (UCHI), with historian Richard
D. Brown as its first director and anthropologist Francoise Dussart as associate

director. The institute developed a series of fellowship, seminar, and workshop programs and became a gathering place for humanistic scholarship on campus. It brought together UConn faculty residential fellows and external residential fellows recruited from other institutions, all selected through competitive processes, and provided them with the time and resources to complete projects that were often unavailable to historians, philosophers, and literary scholars. It established study groups and co-sponsored conferences. The UCHI appointed graduate and undergraduate fellows to support dissertation research and to give UConn undergrads a sense of the research experience. While the humanities brought in only a tiny fraction of UConn's external funding, they played an important role on campus, and the UCHI demonstrated the university's desire to foster the generation of knowledge in all disciplines.[73]

To recognize, and thereby further encourage, excellence in scholarship and teaching, the trustees approved a plan in 1998 to establish a program of Board of Trustees Distinguished Professorships. The designation awarded the university's highest academic honor, which was reserved exclusively for recognizing full professors who had achieved exceptional distinction in three areas—scholarship, teaching, and service—while at the University of Connecticut. Recipients were granted the title for life, and only 5 percent of the active faculty could hold the distinction at any one time. The trustees selected the first six designees in 2000, and the group represented very diverse disciplines. Accounting professor Stanley Biggs was internationally known for his work in the behavioral audit process and had been named the KPMG Professor Of Accounting, a title held by only forty-five professors across the country. The English Department's Lynn Bloom came to UConn in 1988 to fill the first endowed professorship at Storrs, the Aetna Chair in Writing. Her many publications included a biography of Dr. Benjamin Spock. Howard Lasnik of the Linguistics Department was widely regarded as one of the world's most influential linguists. Joseph Renzulli was widely recognized as an international authority on gifted education; he served as Raymond and Lynn Neag Professor of Gifted and Talented Development and also director of the National Research Center on the Gifted and Talented. Renzulli received almost $14 million in research grants between 1990 and 2000 from the U.S. Department of Education. His "Revolving Door Identification Model" and "Schoolwide Enrichment Model" were two innovative programs to increase educational opportunities for children. Psychology professor Michael Turvey, a native of Surrey, England, co-founded the Center for the Ecological Study of Perception and Action in 1987. The American Psychological Association selected him as a Distinguished Scientist Lecturer in 1998. Turvey had a reputation at UConn as a legendary teacher and was Distinguished Alumni Professor from 1994 to 1997. Each year between 2001 and 2005, the trustees annually designated four or five additional Distinguished Professorships as they continued to emphasize academic accomplishment.[74]

Those selected continued to reflect the breadth of research and scholarship conducted in Storrs, the regional campuses, and the professional schools. William Fitzgerald, a professor of marine sciences and founder of the Mercury Laboratory at the Avery Point campus, joined the distinguished group in 2004. He developed an interest in mercury poisoning during the 1960s while he studied at MIT and worked at the Woods Hole Oceanographic Institution in Massachusetts. In the vanguard of such efforts, Fitzgerald earned the sobriquet "the father of mercury research." His studies emphasized mercury's environmental impact on both local and global levels, and he employed Long Island Sound, which neighbored his campus, to study the marine cycling of mercury. In 2003 Fitzgerald received the Geochemical Society's highest honor, the Patterson Award and Medal, which recognized contributions to environmental geochemistry. The first two Health Center faculty to be selected as Distinguished Professors, Lawrence Raisz and Howard Tennen, were chosen the same year as Fitzgerald. Raisz came to UConn in 1974 to head the Division of Endocrinology and Metabolism, which he developed into a major center with an important interdisciplinary research program in bone biology. His early research developed new methods of studying bone formation, and for four decades the National Institute of Health supported his work on factors influencing bone metabolism. Raisz also served as the scientific editor of the Surgeon General's Report on Osteoporosis and Bone Health. Tennen, a professor in the Department of Community Medicine and Psychiatry, held affiliation in the university's Department of Psychology and offered an example of the increasing collaboration between Storrs and the Health Center's Farmington campus. His research focused on how people adapt to major health crises and everyday stressful situations. In 2003 the Health Center established its own prize, which carried a substantial financial reward, to recognize and celebrate the excellence of its faculty members. Dr. Peter Albertsen, professor and chief of urology in the Department of Surgery, won the Health Center Board of Directors Faculty Recognition Award in 2005. Albertsen, a nationally and internationally renowned practioner and researcher, undertook many studies related to prostate cancer and excelled as a clinician and teacher as well as a researcher. At the time of his selection, he was president-elect of both the New England Section of the American Urologic Association and the American Association of Clinical Urologists. In addition, he was given the prestigious honor of a five-year trustee's appointment with the American Board of Urology, which certifies urologists in the United States.[75]

Academic accomplishment at the University of Connecticut was diverse and impressive, fitting well with the choice of John W. Rowe to chair the board of trustees in 2003. Rowe, who previously served on the Health Center's board of directors, was a physician, an internationally recognized scientist and member of the National Academy of Sciences, former president of the Mount Sinai Hospital and Mount Sinai School of Medicine, and at the time of his appointment chairman and CEO of Aetna, Inc. As President Austin stated, "Dr. Rowe [brought] to the Board both a clear understanding of UConn's mission as Connecticut's premier public research institution of higher education and a deep appreciation of the University's potential." His extraordinary credentials epitomized the standard of achievement sought by UConn in the new millennium.[76]

To reach that standard, the university determined to create additional endowed chairs and professorships. In 2001 UConn had a total of forty-seven endowed chairs and twelve endowed professorships, including twenty-four chairs at the Health Center and one chair and three professorships at the School of Law. This lagged behind endowed positions at other major public research universities such as Ohio State, which added seventy-nine during a successful fundraising campaign. Robert R. Birge, the first Harold S. Schwenk Sr. Distinguished Chair in Chemistry, who came to UConn in 2000, said, "If you look at the top departments in the world, they all have three or four endowed chairs in them. So, it's very important for UConn to offer the same competitive advantage." A chair offered eminent scholars greater flexibility than typical research grants might provide. Birge continued, "You can try out new things—very 'high risk' research that you otherwise couldn't get funded. It's that high-risk research that has the high payoffs." By 2005, the university supported seventy-four endowed chairs and professorships. It honored fourteen faculty members named to chairs and professorships at an April 2005 reception in Jorgensen Center for the Performing Arts. These included scholars in a variety of disciplines: the Northeast Utilities Foundation Chair in Experimental Oncology (Carolyn D. Runowicz); the Thomas F. Gallivan Chair of Real Property Law (Jeremy Paul); the Yuji Hayashi Distinguished Chair in Plasma Chemistry (Steven L. Suib); the James L. and Shirley A. Draper Chair of Early American History (Robert Gross); the Treibick Family Chair for the Connecticut Information Technology Institute (James R. Marsden); the Marsha Lilien Gladstein Distinguished Chair in Human Rights (Richard A. Wilson); the Marianne E. Klewin Professorship in Engineering (Yaakov M. Bar-Shalom); the Ray Neag Professorship in Adult Learning (Barry G. Sheckley); and the United Technologies Corporation Chair in Fuel Cell Technology (Nigel Sammes). As a consequence, the thrust for national recognition brought a new prominence to the faculty.[77]

As it transcended its local and regional heritage, though, UConn did not forget its agricultural roots. One of the university's leading research accomplishments came in the field of animal science, the school's original focus. Cloning (the science of regenerative biology) and stem cell research made their mark at Storrs. Xiangzhong "Jerry" Yang, who grew up in Mao's China, came to UConn from Cornell University, where he had begun study in 1983. After receiving his Ph.D. and working in Ithaca, he arrived in Connecticut, the same year that a team of Scottish scientists birthed Dolly the sheep, the first cloned mammal. On June 10, 1999, as head of UConn's Transgenic Animal Facility, Yang led a team of animal scientists that announced the birth of a ninety-four pound calf, Amy, the first large animal cloned from genetic material extracted from an adult farm animal in the United States. He explained, "We took a simple ear skin biopsy (a simple minute-long procedure) and used the cells for cloning." It took seven days to culture the embryo in a lab and transfer it to the surrogate mother on October 5. The successful birth came eight months later and, based on this effort, within a few years thousands of cloned animals were developed worldwide. The scientific breakthough offered the possibility of expanding herds of high milk–producing cows or improving the breeding of beef cattle to obtain higher-quality beef. The world took notice of Yang's achievements, and so did UConn's administrators. In 2001, when he contemplated moving to a peer institution, Rutgers, UConn agreed to provide him with a new lab and staff. He was named founding director of the Center for Regenerative Biology, which further propelled UConn into the vanguard of cloning and stem cell research; officials dedicated UConn's Advanced Technology Laboratory in the fall of 2003, an arc-shaped building that served as home to the center's five research labs, two resource labs for the College of Agriculture and Natural Resources, and the Technology Incubation Program, which sought to encourage the development of high-tech businesses. Yang first collaborated with the Japanese Cattle Breeding Development Institute and then with the Institute of Zoology of the Chinese Academy of Science in his native land. In 2005 Yang, with his Japanese colleagues, participated in a pioneer study that revealed that beef and dairy products from cloned cattle are safe for human consumption. With the Chinese scientists, he appeared ready to move from studying stem cells in cows to creating human embryonic cells to fight the battle against Parkinson's disease, Alzheimer's, and other human inflictions. At the eighth Annual Immigrant Day held at the State Capitol on April 14, 2005, Connecticut honored Yang and nineteen other naturalized citizens for their contributions. He and UConn stood on the threshold of even greater achievements as the state in 2005 allocated $100 million over ten years for stem cell research.[78]

As UConn upgraded its research efforts, it also changed its list of academic peers. While recognized as the number-one public university in New England during the early years of the new millennium, it still aspired to the heights of institutions such as Virginia, Michigan, and Berkeley. A list of peers drawn up in 2004 included Iowa State, the Universities of Iowa, Missouri, Georgia, and Minnesota, Rutgers, Ohio State, and Purdue—all nationally respected state institutions. By 2005, UConn's schools and departments and their graduate programs showed improvement in the *U.S. News and World Report* rankings. In a separate 2005 evaluation, the Health Center received recognition as a "Top 100 Hospital Performance Improvement Leader." Two years earlier, the UConn School of Dental Medicine stood first in the nation based on student test scores on part 2 of the National Board Dental Examinations, which focused on applied dental science and clinical judgment and decision making; it rated second on the first part, which measured basic medical sciences. Undergraduate education proved increasingly popular with UConn's freshman applicant pool, which rose from 9,874 applications for admission in 1995 to 18,597 in 2005. More than half of the applications came from students who lived outside of Connecticut and who made up 30 percent of the actual 2005 entering class. Average SAT scores of incoming freshmen increased from 1113 in 1995 to 1192 ten years later. While forty valedictorians and salutatorians came to UConn in 1995, 115 entered in 2005. More than 1,000 of the 3,250 students entering in 2005 were graduated in the top 10 percent of their high school classes, up from 860 the previous year. Concluding their undergraduate education in 2004, graduates declared high satisfaction with their experience at Storrs; 94 percent said they would recommend UConn to others. The school at Storrs had achieved national prominence and now served as a magnet for an increasing number of students from inside Connecticut and from the world beyond.[79]

While Yang and many other UConn scholars in diverse disciplines met the challenges of the twenty-first century, students in the school's Forestry and Wildlife Club built a one-room wooden cabin on the outskirts of campus, off Horsebarn Hill Road. A sign for "100 percent Connecticut Maple Syrup" hung on the door. Inside the cabin one found an evaporation machine, three sugar-holding tanks, and tubing that allowed club members to make seven gallons of syrup in 2005. Edward Belinsky, the club's president and a junior majoring in natural resources management and engineering, said, "We just do as much as the club can handle and that's it. We hang out, we have a good time, and when it all boils out, we go home." In Connecticut, "the land of steady habits," these sentiments would probably have been very understandable to the "boys" who came to Storrs Agricultural School in 1881, one hundred twenty-four years earlier. On the other hand, cloning and stem cell research would have seemed like science fiction, if they were understood at all. At Connecticut's red brick university, tradition and progress marched in tandem as UConn achieved its goal of national prominence.[80]

As it did during the institution's first fifty years, questions continued to arise regarding the mission of the school. Rather than the old debate between "agricultural" and "cultural," between a school for farmers or for those who lived and worked in cities, in June 2005, the local newspaper, the *Chronicle* of Willimantic, raised a new question that ironically recognized UConn's success in improving its national standing. An editorial headline asked, "Is UConn Too Elite for a State School?" The editors stated, "It appears that UConn has been traveling down a path that would make it a more elite university—similar to some of the private schools it competes against in athletics—by enticing quality students from out of state and the better educated (and often more affluent) students from Connecticut, leaving the rest of the students out of the loop." UConn continued to shape its destiny as it moved forward. Could it be "elite" and distinguished in all respects, as other institutions are, while carrying out the charge of a state university to be widely accessible? To even have to ask this question suggests the educational progress the University of Connecticut has made in its first 125 years.[81]

Appendixes

Appendix A:

Facts about UConn, 1881–2004

Unless otherwise noted, all of the information in the following six tables is taken from "Facts About the University of Connecticut since 1881," second edition, edited by Christine Rocco, printed by the Office of Institutional Research, and based on "Connecticut's Own University: The First Proud Century, 1881–1981" (unpublished working paper, ECH).

Facts about UConn, 1881–1934

	1881	1893	1899	1909	1918	1928	1934
Residing president	Solomon Meade	Benjamin Koons	George Flint	Charles Beach	Charles Beach	Charles Beach/George Works	Charles McCracken
Enrollment	13	113	124	196	201	521	787
Undergraduate	13	113	124	196	201	515	749
Graduate	0	0	0	0	0	6	38
Storrs undergraduate men	51 (1890)	119 (1895)	77 (1900)	153 (1910)	285 (1920)	395 (1930)	564 (1935)
Storrs undergraduate women	0 (1890)	19 (1895)	33 (1900)	22 (1910)	67 (1920)	164 (1930)	240 (1935)
Storrs undergraduate male/female ratio	N/A	6.3:1	2.3:1	7.0:1	4.3:1	2.4:1	2.4:1
Degrees conferred	0	15	19	29	11	75	104
Undergraduate	0	15	19	29	11	74	101
Master's	0	0	0	0	0	1	3
Cost (tuition, fees, room, board, misc. expenses)	$154	$120–125	$125–200 (1903)	$125–200	$210 (1917)	$520 (1927)	$500 (1935)
Percent of factory worker's yearly wage	38%	26–27%	27–28% (1897)	23–36% (1910)	28% (1920)	39% (1925)	54% (1930)
Number of volumes in the library	300	3,943 (1895)	8,127 (1900)	11,650 (1910)	17,000 (1920)	19,000 (1925)	24,000 (1930)

Facts about UConn, 1935–45

	1935	1940	1945
Residing president	Charles McCracken/ Albert Jorgensen	Albert Jorgensen	Albert Jorgensen
Enrollment	844	1,457	3,264
Undergraduate	804	1,338	3,145
Graduate	40	69	119
Storrs undergraduate men	564	901	1,802
Storrs undergraduate women	240	487	1,343
Storrs undergraduate male/female ratio	2.4:1	1.9:1	1.3:1
Degrees conferred	96	186	236
Undergraduate	92	176	205
Master's	4	10	31
Cost (tuition, fees, room and board, misc. expenses)	$500	$425–$525	$460–$560 (1942)
Percent of factory worker's yearly wage	41%	30–41%	23–28% (1942)
Number of volumes in the library	35,000	60,000	95,000

Facts about UConn, 1946–1959

	1946	1950	1955	1959
Residing president	Albert Jorgensen	Albert Jorgensen	Albert Jorgensen	Albert Jorgensen
Enrollment	5,944	7,505	8,829	9,761
Undergraduate	5,462	6,518	7,714	8,249
Graduate	288	700	844	1,216
Law	194	287	271	296
Storrs undergraduate men	1,802 (1945)	4,487	4,074	4,170 (1960)
Storrs undergraduate women	1,343 (1945)	1,578	1,950	2,476 (1960)
Storrs undergraduate male/female ratio	1.3:1 (1945)	2.8:1	2.1:1	1.7:1 (1960)
Degrees conferred	289	1,740	1,396	1,803
Undergraduate	278	1,570	1,067	1,367
Master's	11	119	242	337
Ph.D.	0	7	32	48
JD	0	44	55	51
Cost (tuition, fees, room and board, misc. expenses)	$550–$700 (1948)	$585–$710	$695–$860	$900–$1,000
Percent of factory worker's yearly wage	18–23% (1948)	18–21%	16–20%	17–19%
Number of volumes in the library	95,000 (1945)	125,000	200,000	231,000 (1960)

266

Facts about UConn, 1962–72

	1962	1967	1972
Residing president	Albert Jorgensen/ Homer Babbidge	Homer Babbidge	Homer Babbidge
Enrollment	11,877	15,775	20,514
Undergraduate	9,842	12,136	15,392
Graduate	1,720	3,185	4,225
Law	315	454	658
Medical/Dental	0	0	239
Storrs undergraduate men	4,170 (1960)	4,608 (1965)	4,170 (1970)
Storrs undergraduate women	2,476 (1960)	3,685 (1965)	5,124 (1970)
Storrs undergraduate male/female ratio	1.7:1 (1960)	1.3:1 (1965)	0.81:1 (1970)
Degrees conferred	1,703	2,665	4,340
Undergraduate	1,289	1,725	2,954
Master's	300	720	978
Ph.D.	47	119	204
JD	67	101	163
DMD	0	0	12
MD	0	0	29
Cost (tuition, fees, room and board, misc. expenses)	$1,500 (1961)	$1,700 (1966)	$2,400
Percent of factory worker's yearly wage	27% (1961)	25% (1966)	25%
Number of volumes in the library	451,368 (1963)	680,370	1,154,172

	1973	1979	1985	1990
Residing president	Glenn Ferguson	John DiBiaggio	John DiBiaggio/ John Casteen	John Casteen/ Harry Hartley
Enrollment	20,945	22,510	23,878	26,478
Undergraduate	15,452	15,131	16,096	17,999
Graduate	4,536	5,911	6,264	6,791
Law	673	608	703	707
Medical/Dental[1]	284	860	815	981
Storrs undergraduate men	6,809 (1975)	6,228 (1980)	6,083	6,640
Storrs undergraduate women	6,062 (1975)	6,114 (1980)	6,613	6,932
Undergrad male/ female ratio	1.1:1 (1975)	1:1 (1980)	0.92:1	0.96:1
Minority enrollment	844 (1974)	1,285	1,685	2,600
Degrees conferred	4,548	4,630	4,404	4,677
Undergraduate	3,191	3,072	2,929	3,163
Master's	947	1,058	972	979
Ph.D.	176	161	181	217
JD	186	210	202	205
DMD	17	44	37	36
MD	31	85	83	77
Cost (tuition, fees, room and board, misc. expenses)	$2,400 (1972)	$3,700	$5,750	$8,250
Percent of factory worker's yearly wage	25% (1972)	22%	29%	36%
Number of volumes in the library	1,235,502	1,710,546	1,960,607	2,271,849
Endowments[2]	N/A	$1,679,000	$1,992,000 (1984)	$23,361,000 (1991)
Federal research-and-development funding in the sciences and engineering[3]	$7,618,000	$23,938,000	$38,944,000	$43,477,000

1. Figures include interns and residents.

2. Office of Institutional Research provided this information from the annual National Association of College and University Business Officers Endowment Study of member institutions with endowments greater than $1 million. Endowments of University of Connecticut until 1984. Endowments of University of Connecticut Foundation beginning fiscal year 1987. The figures include growth from gifts and returns on investments, as well as reductions from expenditures and withdrawals.

3. Office of Institutional Research provided this information from the annual *Survey of Research and Development Expenditures at Universities and Colleges* by the NSF Division of Science Resources Statistics. Prior to fiscal year 1996: the annual *Survey of Scientific and Engineering Expenditures at Universities and Colleges* by the same NSF Division. Figures cover only research-and-development expenditures in science and engineering and exclude spending in such disciplines as the arts, education, the humanities, law, and physical education.

Facts about UConn, 1992–2004

	1992	1996	2000	2004
Residing president	Harry Hartley	Harry Hartley/ Philip Austin	Philip Austin	Philip Austin
Enrollment	25,190	22,316	23,419	27,579[1]
Undergraduate	16,407	14,454	16,681	20,151
Graduate	7,058	6,717	5,625	6,053
Law	666	634	629	727
Medical/Dental[2]	1,059	511	484	485
Pharmacy	0	0	0	163
Storrs undergraduate men	8,169	7,082	7,317	7,266[1]
Storrs undergraduate women	8,238	7,372	8,292	7,994[1]
Undergrad male/female ratio	0.99:1	0.96:1	0.88:1	0.91:1
Minority enrollment	2,621	3,013	3,844	4,424[2]
Degrees conferred	5,119	4,718	4,561	5,445[1]
Undergraduate	3,441	2,839	2,802	3,673
Master's	1,146	1,328	1,145	1,111
Ph.D.	206	239	275	257
JD	205	196	209	174
DMD	36	32	44	35
MD	85	84	86	68
LLM	0	0	0	18
Pharmacy	0	0	0	79
6-year education	0	0	0	40
Cost (tuition, fees, room and board, misc. expenses)	$9,298	$10,276	$11,658	$14,894[1]
Percent of factory worker's yearly wage	39%	39%	39%	N/A
Number of volumes in the library	2,372,350	2,626,066	2,987,772	3,211,431
Number of faculty (Excluding Health Center)[3]	1,157	1,148	1,147	1,243
Number of tenured faculty (Excluding Health Center)[3]	805	852	784	752
Endowments[4]	$27,814,000	$56,773,000	$179,483,000	$196,971,000
Federal research-and-development funding in the sciences and engineering[5]	$45,967,000	$53,009,000	$66,144,000	$93,326,000 (2002)

1. "University of Connecticut 2004–2005 Fact Book" provided this information.
2. Figures include interns and residents.
3. Office of Institutional Research provided this information.
4. Office of Institutional Research provided this information from the annual National Association of College and University Business Officers Endowment Study of member institutions with endowments greater than $1 million. Endowments of University of Connecticut until 1984. Endowments of University of Connecticut Foundation beginning FY87. The figures include growth from gifts and returns on investments, as well as reductions from expenditures and withdrawals.
5. Office of Institutional Research provided this information from the annual Survey of Research and Development Expenditures at Universities and Colleges by the NSF Division of Science Resources Statistics. Prior to FY96: the annual Survey of Scientific and Engineering Expenditures at Universities and Colleges by the same NSF division. Figures cover only research-and-development expenditures in science and engineering and exclude spending in such disciplines as the arts, education, the humanities, law, and physical education.

Appendix B:

Honorary Degrees Awarded by the University of Connecticut, 1982 – 2005*

Doctor of Letters Awarded	*Year*
Barbara Tuchman	1982
Malcolm Cowley	1983
John Hope Franklin	1984
Isaac B. Singer	1985
Virgil Thomson	1985
Ann Petry	1987
Maurice Sendak	1990
Fred Rogers	1991
Barbara Chase-Riboud	1996
Laurel T. Ulrich	1996
Rex M. Nettleford	1997
Antonia Pantoja	1997
Frank McCourt	1998
David McCullough	1999
Noam Chomsky	1999
Philip Roth	2001
Bobbie Ann Mason	2002
Les Payne '64	2003

Doctor of Humane Letters Awarded	*Year*
Clifton R. Wharton Jr.	1983
John H. Filer	1983

* In 1980, the University of Connecticut Board of Trustees authorized the granting of honorary degrees, the first of which was awarded at commencement on May 23, 1982. Earlier, two honorary M.S. degrees were awarded to Robert M. Landers and Robert Scoville in 1918, and Edwina M. Whitney received an honorary M. of Letters degree in 1934. *Source: Office of the President.*

John F. Welch Jr.	1984
Rafael Caldera	1986
Josef A. Gierowski	1986
Stanley Popiel	1987
Gladys Tantaquidgeon	1987
Marian Anderson	1987
Elie Wiesel	1988
Denis Mullane	1988
Robin Morgan	1992
Samuel Birnbaum	1993
W. Randall Pinkston	1993
Kevin V. Dowling Jr.	1993
Alice Heilig	1994
Charles Heilig	1994
Richard Hayward	1994
Ronald Compton	1994
William Jefferson Clinton	1995
Frances M. Visco	1996
Simon Konover	1996
Sanford Cloud Jr.	1996
Helen Waichen Rogow	1996
Aaron Feuerstein	1997
Robert W. Fiondella	1997
Raymond Sackler	1998
Beverly Sackler	1998
Robert G. Burton	2000
Ray Neag	2001
Her Royal Highness Princess Irene of Greece	2002
John W. Kluge	2003
Daniel C. Dennett	2003
Linda Darling-Hammond	2004
Eduardo Aguirre	2005

Doctor of Fine Arts Awarded	*Year*
Robert Motherwell	1982
Victor Borge	1983
Ray Bolger	1986
Susan Saint James	1987
Ronald William Howard	1993
Peter Guber	1994

Betty Allen	1995
Michael Bolton	1995
Julie Harris	1995
William H. Cosby Jr.	1996
Quincy Jones	1996
Larry Aldrich	1996
Samuel Goldwyn Jr.	1997
Jack Paar	1998
Tomie dePaola	1999
Joseph Volpe	2002
Frederick Fennel	2003
Gordon Parks	2003
David Macaulay	2004
Tim Page	2005

Doctor of Science Awarded	*Year*
Dr. Frank Press	1982
Howard Green	1985
Roger Tory Peterson	1987
Nicholaas Bloembergen	1988
John Archibald Wheeler	1989
Franklin Chang-Diaz	1990
Mildred Dresselhaus	1992
Bernadine Healy	1992
Torsten N. Wiesel	1993
Peter H. Raven	1993
Sylvia Earle	1994
Edith Martin	1994
Chang-Lin Tien	1994
Anthony Fauci	1994
Thomas M. Sutherland	1995
Edward O. Wilson	1995
Patrick A. McKeown	1996
Norman Hascoe	1997
David M. Lee	1997
Alvin M. Liberman	1997
William C. Steere Jr.	1997
Varro E. Tyler	1998
Alphonse Chapanis	1998
Harold C. Slavkin	1999

Rita R. Colwell	2000
Sheila E. Widnall	2000
Harvey Sadow	2000
Lester R. Brown	2001
Shirley Ann Jackson	2001
Charles H. Thornton	2001
Judah Folkman	2002
Edmund Pellegrino	2002
William Wulf	2002
Fujia Yang	2002
Henry C. Lee	2003
Philip Leder	2003
Gene E. Likens	2004
Iognaid G. O'Muircheartaigh	2004
Gerhard Giebisch	2004
Roger S. Newton	2005
Henry B. C. Low	2005

Doctor of Laws Awarded	*Year*
Harry J. Gray	1982
Homer D. Babbidge	1984
John J. Driscoll	1985
Charles H. Kaman	1985
Charles S. Robb	1987
Dorothy Goodwin	1988
James McNally	1989
Thomas P. Melady	1990
Edward H. Budd	1990
Constance Baker Motley	1990
Harold Seidman	1991
Arpad Goncz	1991
James Comer	1991
Alice Cook	1992
Ellen Peters	1992
Harry A. Gampel	1993
T. Emmet Clarie	1993
Phillip Blumberg	1994
Adbou Diouf	1994
A. Leon Higginbotham Jr.	1995
Stephen Gerald Breyer	1996

Jose A. Cabranes	1998
George Bush	1998
Harry T. Edwards	1999
Frank Rich	1999
Christopher J. Dodd	2000
Harold Hongju Koh	2000
Jules B. LaPidus	2000
Lionel H. Olmer	2000
Mary Frances Berry	2001
Thomas D. Ritter	2001
Frene Ginwala	2002
Patricia McGowan Wald	2002
Arthur Levitt	2003
Jonathan F. Fanton	2005
Morris Sheppard Arnold	2005

Notes

Introduction (pp. xiii–xix)

1. For Connecticut's nicknames, see http://www.netstate.com/states/intro/ct_intro.htm; for an explanation of Great Britain's "red brick" universities, see http://www.nationmaster.com/encyclopedia/Red-Brick-universities. The original six civic or "red brick" universities were the Universities of Birmingham, Bristol, Leeds, Liverpool, Manchester, and Sheffield.
2. Walter Stemmons, *Connecticut Agricultural College—A History* (Storrs, Conn.: Connecticut Agricultural College, 1931) is a useful and detailed account of the college's first fifty years. Mark J. Roy, *University of Connecticut* (Charleston, S.C.: Arcadia, 2001) offers a more recent photo history.
3. Herman F. Eschenbacher, *The University of Rhode Island: A History of Land Grant Education in Rhode Island* (New York: Appleton-Century-Crofts, 1967); Robert V. Daniels, ed., *The University of Vermont: The First Two Hundred Years* (Burlington, Vt.: University of Vermont, 1991). Connecticut's state universities have had several institutional histories published. A fine example is Herbert F. Janick, *A People's University: The Centennial History of Western Connecticut State University, 1903–2003* (Danbury, Conn.: Western Connecticut State University, 2002).
4. George H. Callcott, *A History of the University of Maryland* (Baltimore, Md.: Maryland Historical Society, 1966); Robert C. Alberts, *Pitt: The Story of the University of Pittsburgh, 1787–1987* (Pittsburgh: University of Pittsburgh Press, 1986).
5. Thomas G. Dyer, *The University of Georgia: A Bicentennial History, 1785–1985* (Athens, Ga.: University of Georgia Press, 1985); William D. Snider, *Light on the Hill: A History of the University of North Carolina at Chapel Hill* (Chapel Hill, N.C.: University of North Carolina Press, 1992); Alan Bogue and Robert Taylor, eds., *The University of Wisconsin: One Hundred and Twenty-five Years* (Madison, Wisc.: University of Wisconsin Press, 1975); Verne A. Stadtman, *The University of California, 1868–1968* (New York: McGraw-Hill, 1970).

Chapter 1. In the Beginning: 1881–1935 (pp. 1–29)

1. For a list of the institution's leadership and its changes of name, see Office of Institutional Research, "Facts about the University of Connecticut since 1881" (2nd edition, Christine Rocco, editor), vii, 13; "C.A.C. Conditions: One Who Has Had Chances to Know Writes of Them," *New Haven Register,* undated, President's Office–Flint (hereafter POFl), box 1, file 1, Thomas J. Dodd Research Center (hereafter DRC).

2. For a useful overview of Gold's activity, see Joseph A. Bongiorno, "In Pursuit of Intelligent Cultivation: Theodore Sedgwick Gold and Agriculture in Nineteenth-Century Connecticut," *Connecticut History* 44:1 (spring 2005): 48–76; Walter Stemmons, *Connecticut Agricultural College—A History* (Storrs, Conn.: Connecticut Agricultural College, 1931, hereafter *CAC*), passim. *CAC* was written for the college's fiftieth anniversary and is the standard and most detailed work on the first five decades of the educational institution at Storrs. This chapter offers a brief overview of that era and adds material on Charles McCracken's presidency, 1930–35, which was not covered in detail by Stemmons.

3. *CAC,* 29–35; Roy, *University of Connecticut,* 9–10; Mark J. Roy, "Historical Story of the Storrs Brothers," *University of Connecticut Advance* (October 20, 1997). This brief article is part of the series "A Piece of UConn History" by Mark Roy, which appeared occasionally in the *UConn Advance* and offered a capsule account of the university's early development; Bongiorno, "In Pursuit," 67.

4. *CAC,* 38–41. Those students enrolled during the first term were Frederick B. Brown, Gilead, Tolland County; Frank D. Case, Barkhamsted, Litchfield County; Charles H. Elkins, Brooklyn, N.Y.; Charles S. Foster, Bristol, Hartford County; John M. Gelston, East Haddam, Middlesex County; George C. Gilbert, Georgetown, Fairfield County; William H. Gillette, East Haddam, Middlesex County; Samuel B. Harvey, Mansfield, Tolland County; Henry R. Hoisington, Coventry, Tolland County; Burke Hough, Weatogue, Hartford County; Arthur S. Hubbard, Glastonbury, Hartford County; Andrew K. Thompson, West Cornwall, Litchfield County; and F. M. Winton, Bristol, Hartford County.

5. *CAC,* 38–41 and 83; *Lookout* (May, 1899).

6. H. P. Armsby, "The Storrs Agricultural School: Course of Study," from the Report of the Secretary of Conn. Board of Agriculture, 1882, President's Office–Mead (hereafter POM), folder 1, DRC.

7. *CAC,* 40, 44, 97, 128–29; "Shake Up at Storrs," *Hartford Courant,* June 2, 1897, President's Office–Koons (hereafter POK), file 5, DRC.

8. *CAC,* 49–57; Roy, *University of Connecticut,* 10.

9. "The Land Grant Tradition," www.uwex.edu/ces/depthead/landgranttrad.pdf, based on a chapter in the 1962 Department of Health, Education, and Welfare's "Land-Grant Colleges and Universities, 1862–1962," by Henry S. Brunner (the history was adapted and updated in February 1995 by the Office of Public Affairs of the National

Association of State Universities and Land-Grant Colleges); *CAC*, 58–71; Mark J. Roy, "Land Grant Status Acquired through Struggle: A Piece of UConn History," *UConn Advance* (November 24, 1997), www.advance.uconn.edu/112497hs.htm. For the establishment of the Storrs Agricultural Station and the contributions of W. O. Atwater, see *CAC*, 217–23. Atwater Laboratory on the Storrs campus, built in 1930 and expanded in 1958, was named in his honor.

10. *CAC*, 71–77; "Storrs Agricultural School," *Willimantic Journal,* July 2, 1886, POK, box 1, file 5, DRC; "C.A.C. Conditions: One Who Has Had Chances to Know Writes of Them," *New Haven Register,* undated, POFl, box 1, file 1, DRC.

11. *CAC*, 78–81; Roy, *University of Connecticut,* 10, 15; *Lookout,* October 1896, April 1899.

12. Office of Institutional Research, "Facts about the University," 94; *Hartford Courant,* June 2, 1897, undated, 1897, July 7, 1899, POK, box 1, file 5, DRC. Information on sports comes from timelines prepared by Tim Tolokan, Division of Athletics, University of Connecticut.

13. *Hartford Times,* undated, 1898, June 13, 1900, POF, box 1, file 1, DRC; "Anarchy at Storrs," undated and unidentified newspaper article, POF, box 1, file 1, DRC, includes information on salaries; *CAC*, 97–98; Roy, *University of Connecticut,* 16.

14. "C.A.C. Conditions," *New Haven Register,* undated, POFl, box 1, file 1, DRC (For a full account of the "War of the Rebellion," see *CAC*, 97–110); *Hartford Courant,* July 22, September 13, 1901, President's Office–Stimson (hereafter POS), box 1, file 4, DRC.

15. *CAC*, 94–96, 111.

16. *CAC*, 111–12; Stimson to Graduates and Friends, undated, 1901, POS, box 1, file 1, DRC.

17. Stimson to D. W. Shurtleff, March 9, 1904, POS, box 1, file 1, DRC.

18. *CAC*, 116–20; *Lookout,* December 1904, February 1905, March 1906.

19. *C.A.C. Lookout,* January 1907, March 1908; *Hartford Courant,* February 10, 1908, President's Office–Beach (hereafter POBe), box 7, file 109, DRC; *CAC*, 130–31.

20. *C.A.C. Lookout,* October 1906, March 1908, April, 1908; *CAC*, 132; for a useful but sometimes overly laudatory profile of Charles Lewis Beach, see the pamphlet by James H. Barnett entitled "'Mr. Beach': A Profile of Charles Lewis Beach, President, Connecticut Agricultural College, 1908–1928" (University of Connecticut Publications Series, 1969). Between April 25 and September 15, 1908, Professor E. O. Smith served as acting president.

21. *Hartford Times,* January 5, 1914, and *Willimantic Chronicle,* undated, 1917, POBe, box 7, file 110, DRC; Beach to Robert Scoville, July 9, 1919, POBe, box 9, file 144; *CAC*, 133–40, 155–57, 174–75, 196; University of Connecticut Division of Student Affairs and Services, Department of Residential Life, "What's in a Name? A Fact Book about Residence Halls at UConn," 6–7, undated, but likely 1998, in possession of the author. For examples of Beach's building plans, see Charles N. Lowrie to Beach, May 22, 29, 1917, POBe, box 6, file 87, DRC; "Summary: Appropriations Asked for Buildings and Improvements, 1917–1919 and 1919–1923," POBe, box 11, file 170, DRC; Beach to Ralph J. Averill, President, Alumni Association, June 4, 1920, POBe, box 6,

file 98, DRC; "Statement of Appropriations for Land, Buildings and Improvements During Period of 43 Years—1881–1924," POBe, box 2, file 19, DRC; "Buildings and Improvements, Needs for 1927–29," POBe, box 4, file 57, DRC.

22. Barnett, "'Mr Beach,'" 9, 31–32; the figures taken from Barnett's pamphlet may not be entirely accurate, however. Tara Latawic of the Office of Institutional Research indicates that Barnett may have double-counted individuals on the faculty and in the Agricultural Experiment Station; Albert E. Waugh Journal (hereafter AEW), pp. 446–47, Tuesday, November 4, 1947, box 16, file October 7–November 8, 1947, DRC; out of eighteen professional staff members in 1912, Waugh counted two with doctorates, seven with master's degrees, and nine with bachelor's degrees; Roy, "A Piece of UConn History," *UConn Advance,* June 12, 2000.

23. AEW, p. 466, Monday, November 19, 1945, box 15, file November 16–December 6, 1945; AEW, p. 367, Wednesday, November 25, 1959, box 17, file November 11–December 31, 1959; AEW, pp. 11–12, Monday, January 8, 1968, box 19, file January 1–February 4, 1968, DRC; James H. Barnett, "Three Storrs Pioneers" (Storrs, Conn.: University of Connecticut, 1981), 69–72, 86; *CAC,* 146–47.

24. *Connecticut Campus,* November 16, 1917, May 19, 1919; *CAC,* 162–66; Stemmons, in *CAC,* 159, writes that the 1919–20 college catalogue lists the names of 426 students who entered service, and the *Campus* gave the number as 583 immediately after the Armistice.

25. *Connecticut Campus,* November 16, 1917, December 14, 1917, May 19, 1919.

26. *Connecticut Campus,* May 19, 1919, November 29, 1918; AEW, "Walter Stemmons Talk to Golden Age Club," June 19, 1962, box 11, publications, DRC; *CAC,* 166.

27. Roy, *University of Connecticut,* 34; Armistice Day Proclamation, POBe, box 6, file 89, DRC; *Connecticut Campus,* January 10, 1919, February 7, 1919.

28. M. Estella Sprague to Mr. Slate, Chairman of Administrative Committee of CAC, POBe, box 9, file 149, DRC; William F. Kirkpatrick to Beach, February 6, 1923, POBe, box 10, file 164; Ralph M. Grant to Beach and responses, March 27, 31, April 12, 1926; *Hartford Times,* April 7, 1923, POBe, box 7, file 111.

29. For a history of the School of Economics and Family Studies, see Michele Palmer, *Decades of Pride* (Storrs, Conn.: University of Connecticut, 1981); *Connecticut Campus,* January 19, 1922, and Office of Institutional Research, "Facts About the University," 2. The two women trustees were referred to by their husband's names or initials, with Mrs. always preceding, not by their own first names. M. E. Sprague to Beach and reply, January 25, 1922, April 5, 1922, POBe, box 9, file 155, DRC.

30. Roy, "A Piece of UConn History," *UConn Advance,* February 9, 1998, and September 27, 1999. Alan T. Busby served as grand marshal of the annual UConn homecoming parade in 1990. "Fraternity Membership at Storrs," "Report of a Faculty Committee Regarding Policy of Control of Fraternities," and "Rules Governing Fraternities," POBe, box 4, file 55, DRC; *Connecticut Campus,* January 15, September 20, 1921, October 22, 1925, December 2, 1927, May 26, 1928.

31. *Connecticut Campus,* September 20, 1921, February 2, 1923. While championships

were not the purpose of the conference, during 1924 CAC had an undefeated football season and beat Rhode Island on November 15 before the largest crowd ever to
that time in the history of Storrs. See *CAC*, 197.

32. Beach to A. W. Manchester, January 17, 1924, POBe, box 6, file 90, DRC.

33. *Connecticut Campus*, May 26, 1922, October 30, 1925; Statement of trustees, undated,
probably 1921, POBe, box 1, file 13, DRC; Chamber of Commerce Committee on
Storrs College Report, May 11, 1925, POBe, box 3, file 35, DRC; for a detailed account
of the criticism of the college during this era, see *CAC*, chapter 9. Regarding salaries,
when Albert E. Waugh arrived as a young scholar in 1924, he received $900 per year,
far from the $3,000 maximum. See AEW, January 21, 1969, box 19, file January 1–
February 4, 1969, DRC. The limitation of five hundred students was changed in 1929
to five hundred who would reside in dormitories. See *CAC*, 201.

34. AEW, November 25, 1959, p. 367, box 17, file November 11–December 31, 1959, and
August 1, 1946, box 15, file July 23–August 30, 1946, DRC; Oral History Interview with
Albert E. Waugh, February 12, 1981, p. 4, Center for Oral History (hereafter COH),
DRC (hereafter Waugh Interview); Barnett, "'Mr Beach,'" 26–36; Roy, "A Piece of
UConn History," *UConn Advance*, November 3, 1997; *Connecticut Campus*, Septem-
ber 27, 1928.

35. For a portrait of Gentry's life and career, see James H. Barnett, *"Mr. Gentry": A Profile of Charles Burt Gentry, Professor of Education and Dean of the University, 1920–
1950* (Storrs, Conn.: University of Connecticut Publication Series, 1971) and for
material cited above, see esp. 23 and 35–56; AEW, Friday, April 11, 1969, box 19, file
March 20–May 5, 1969, DRC.

36. *Connecticut Campus*, April 12, 1929; Waugh Interview, pp. 10, 20; *CAC*, 201–2.

37. *Connecticut Campus*, December 13, 1929, March 7, 1930; *CAC*, 202.

38. Works to Harry G. Manchester, June 9, 1930, President's Office–Works (hereafter
POW), box 2, file 39, DRC; *Hartford Courant*, June 13, 1930, POW, box 3, file 41; C. E.
Hough to Works, October 24, 1929, Works to Hough, October 28, 1929, and Hough
to Works, October 30, 1929, POW, box 1, file 24, DRC.

39. AEW, July 30, 1942, pp. 292–94, box 15, volume 1942, DRC; Waugh Interview,
pp. 21–24.

40. *Connecticut Campus*, September 26, 1930; Waugh Interview, p. 18. As a consequence
of this incident, Waugh stopped attending church because he did not want his work
to be judged on the basis of his attendance. From the beginning of the SAS through
its transformation into the college, the Storrs Congregational Church played an important role in the university community. It served as a place of prayer as well as a location for social gatherings. For the first twenty-five years of the school and college's
existence, attendance at chapel was compulsory for students. See *CAC*, 129, 189–90.

41. Waugh Interview, pp. 25, 28–29.

42. AEW, August 1, 1946, p. 268, box 15, file July 23–August 30, 1946, DRC; Waugh Interview, pp. 25–26; *Connecticut Campus*, May 21, 1935; McCracken to Board of Trustees,
May 15, 1935, President's Office–McCracken (hereafter POMc), box 17, file 386, DRC.

43. *Connecticut Campus,* December 12, 1930; Guy H. Holliday to McCracken, April 22, 1931, POMc, box 7, file 154, DRC; McCracken to Alice Hure, October 7, 1931, POMc, box 3, file 68, DRC. Throughout McCracken's tenure, the college unsuccessfully struggled to obtain membership in the AAU, which first raised questions about student and faculty quality and then emphasized the hobbling instability that had been created by the turnover of presidencies after Beach's resignation. See McCracken to R. M. Hughes, October 18, 1932, POMc, box 7, file 156, DRC, and McCracken to Roy Denslow, October 7, 1933, POMc, box 13, file 288, DRC.

44. *Connecticut Campus,* October 30, 1931.

45. *Hartford Courant* and *Waterbury Republican,* February 19, 1931, POMc, box 2, file 50, DRC.

46. *Hartford Courant,* April 28, 1931, POMc, box 2, file 50, DRC; Bert Wright to Mc-Cracken, April 28, 1932, POMc, box 7, file 150, DRC. A similar statement later was issued by alumni and students. See POMc, box 8, file 176, DRC.

47. "General Statement" of Change-of-Name Committee, undated minutes of Board of Trustees meeting, Change-of-Name Committee to Governor Cross, November 8, 1932, Minutes of the Meetings of the Change-of-Name Committee, S.B. 136, all in POMc, box 8, file 176, DRC; *Connecticut Campus,* March 3, 1933.

48. McCracken to R. M. Hughes, October 18, 1932, POMc, box 7, file 156, DRC; Mc-Cracken to Fernandus Payne, August 21, 1934, POMc, box 17, file 383, DRC; *Connecticut Campus,* January 9, 1934, January 8, 1935; Office of Institutional Research, "Facts About the University," 95–96, 105. For salaries, see *Connecticut State College Bulletin* 30, no. 3 (November 1934), Public Document 29, Biennial Report, "Division of Resident Instruction/Storrs Experiment Station/ Extension Service for the Two Years Ending November 30, 1934." Of the fourteen New England colleges, all but three of them within a radius of one hundred miles of Storrs, CSC's assistant professors were fifth from the bottom in median salary, while associate and full professors were third from the bottom. For the husky, see *Connecticut Campus,* November 27, 1934; Roy, *University of Connecticut,* 53–55. The original Jonathan died a few weeks after arriving on campus as a result of being hit by an automobile in North Windham, where he was kept at the home of music professor Herbert France. He was buried in February 1935 at a ceremony presided over by the four class presidents and President McCracken. Jonathan II came to replace him in November 1935; Oral History Interview with Barbara Isham Potterton, Class of 1935, October 31, 2003, pp. 19–22. Her husband, George Potterton, was one of the class presidents who buried the first Jonathan.

Chapter 2. From State College to University: 1935–45 (pp. 30–60)

1. The topics referred to, along with others, are discussed and documented in this chapter.

2. James Wechsler, *Revolt on the Campus* (New York: Corici Friede, 1935), 310.

3. Wechsler, *Revolt on Campus*, viii, 310–12; Elizabeth Upham to Education Committee, February 1935, President's Office–Jorgensen (hereafter POJ), series 2, box 35, file 8, DRC; Capt. William L. Ritter to McCracken, March 9, 1935, POJ series 2, box 35, file 3, DRC.

4. *Hartford Courant*, April 13, 1935, Evan Hill Collection (hereafter EHC), box 3, 1896–1944, Blue Binder, DRC; Board of Trustees Minutes, April 17, 1935, p. 861, EHC, box 3, 1896–1944, Blue Binder, DRC.

5. *Hartford Courant*, April 18, 1935, EHC, box 3, 1896–1944, Blue Binder, DRC; McCracken to Professor Hornell Hart of Hartford Theological Seminary, April 22, 1935, POJ, series 2, box 35, file 3, DRC.

6. Walter Landauer to Gen. C. G. Dawes, April 24, 1935, and Dawes to McCracken, May 5, 1935, POJ, series 2, box 35, file 4, DRC; President of MIT to Walter Landauer, May 13, 1935, POJ, series 2, box 35, file 8, DRC.

7. POJ, series 2, box 35, file 1, DRC; ACLU to Wilbur Cross, April 29, 1935, POJ, series 2, box 35, file 5, DRC; Wilbur Cross to Oswald Garrison Villard, June 3, 1935, POJ, series 2, box 35, file 12, DRC.

8. *Connecticut Campus*, April 23, 1935, EHC, box 3, 1896–1944, Blue Binder, DRC.

9. *HC*, May 3, 8, 1935, EHC, box 3, 1896–1944, Blue Binder, DRC; Marjorie W. Smith, Secretary of the Faculty, to McCracken, May 1, 1935, POJ, series 2, box 35, file 6, DRC. Twenty faculty signed petitions opposing the majority faculty resolution. See Petitions, POJ, series 2, box 35, file 6, DRC.

10. Harrington Littell to McCracken, May 2, 1935, and McCracken to Littell, May 7, 1935, POJ, series 2, box 35, file 4, DRC; McCracken to R. A. Pearson, May 6, 1935, POJ, series 2, box 35, File 4, DRC.

11. *HC*, May 11, 12, 1935, EHC, box 3, 1896–1944, Blue Binder, DRC.

12. *HC*, May 14, 1935, EHC, box 3, 1896–1944, Blue Binder, DRC; *Connecticut Campus*, April 23, 1935.

13. POJ, series 2, box 35, file 1; *HC*, May 15, 1935, EHC, box 3, 1896–1944, Blue Binder, DRC.

14. *Connecticut Campus*, May 21, 1935, EHC, box 3, 1896–1944, Blue Binder, DRC; Wechsler, *Revolt on Campus*, 323.

15. Board of Trustees Minutes, May 15, 1935, EHC, box 3, 1896–1944, Blue Binder, DRC; C. B. Gentry to Chase Kimball, September 23, 1935, POJ, series 2, box 35, file 7, DRC; McCracken to Justice Charles Garside, May 17, 1935, POJ, series 2, box 35, file 4, DRC; Fletcher D. Parker to McCracken, May 17, 1935, and McCracken to Parker, May 20, 1935, POJ, series 2, box 35, file 4, DRC. For other details regarding McCracken's resignation, see the previous chapter.

16. P. R. Brammell to C. B. Gentry, October 9, 1935, POJ, series 2, box 35, file 7, DRC; undated transcript of meeting between Jorgensen and Board of Trustees, POJ, series 2, box 35, file 7, DRC.

17. Jorgensen to H. W. Tyler, AAUP national vice-president, November 11, 1935, POJ,

series 2, box 35, file 7, DRC; Roger N. Baldwin to Jorgensen, October 31, 1935, POJ, series 2, box 35, file 7, DRC.

18. Undated, unlabeled clipping from EHC, box 6, Jorgensen folder, DRC; *News Bulletin,* Connecticut State College, September 19, 1935, vol. 6, no. 1-A, POJ, box 1, file 46, DRC.

19. Board of Trustees Minutes, September 12, 1935, p. 883, September 18, 1935, p. 884, box 3, file 1935, September 4–August 18, 1936, DRC; EHC, box 6, file 2, DRC.

20. James E. Brinckerhoff to Jorgensen, June 15, 1936, POJ, box 1, file Bi–Brm, DRC; *News Bulletin,* Connecticut State College, September 19, 1935, vol. 6, no. 1-A, POJ, box 1, file 46, DRC; undated 1935 clipping, "Agriculture Not To Lose At College," *Hartford Courant,* November 26, 1935, EHC, box 6, Jorgensen file, DRC.

21. *Campus,* October 15, 1935, ECH, box 6, Jorgensen file, DRC; *HC,* undated, 1935, and November 26, 1935, EHC, box 6, Jorgensen file, DRC; "Statement by the Trustees of the Minimum Outlay Needed by the Connecticut State College to Provide for Its Present Enrollment—Including Proposed Requests to the General Assembly," undated (probably 1936), EHC, box 6, Jorgensen file, DRC, pp. 3–5; table 5 of the same document reveals that the number of volumes in the CSC library were thirty thousand, as compared to Massachusetts State (100,625), New Hampshire (80,645), Maine (116,000), Vermont (138,000), Wesleyan (193,561), Trinity (125,000), or Connecticut College for Women (60,000).

22. Information form for the *National Cyclopedia of American Biography,* POJ, box 4, file 23, DRC.

23. *Hartford Daily Times,* November 28, 1936, and *HC,* March 11, 1937, EHC, box 6, Jorgensen file, DRC.

24. November 6, 1941, list prepared for the *Bridgeport Post,* POJ, box 4, file 51, DRC; also see *New York Times,* December 16, 1940, "Storrs Will Build Two Dormitories," EHC, box 6, Jorgensen folder, DRC.

25. From draft version of unpublished seventy-fifth-anniversary history of the University of Connecticut by Walter Stemmons, DRC; *HC,* December 21, 1938, EHC, box 6, Jorgensen folder, DRC.

26. Stemmons draft; *Campus,* May 26, 1939, EHC, box 6, Jorgensen file, DRC; unidentified clipping in EHC, box 6, Jorgensen file, DRC.

27. *Register,* November 14, 1939, POJ, box 3, file 85, DRC; Jorgensen to Samuel R. Spencer, January 10, 1940, POJ, box 3, file 94, DRC; Mrs. H. F. Peck to Jorgensen, May 5, 1941, POJ, box 4, file 16, DRC; D. H. Horton to Jorgensen, January 11, 1941, and Jorgensen to Horton, January 14, 1941, POJ, box 4, file 45, DRC.

28. Board of Trustees Minutes, February 21, 1940, pp. 977–82, September 20, 1939–July 10, 1940, file, DRC; Stemmons draft, 37–38, DRC.

29. Jorgensen to Gen. George Marshall, December 8, 1939, POJ, box 3, file 80, DRC; Major G. H. Passmore to Colonel Frederick F. Black, July 5, 1939, POJ, box 3, file 80, DRC; Jorgensen to Gov. Raymond E. Baldwin, July 11, 1940, POJ, box 4, file 22, DRC.

30. *Connecticut Campus,* September 5, 1940.

31. "University of Connecticut War Activities," POJ, box 5, file 54, DRC; *Connecticut Campus*, September 5, October 9 and 30, 1940.

32. *Connecticut Campus*, October 23, 1940, April 16, 1941.

33. "University of Connecticut War Activities," POJ, box 5, file 54, DRC; *Connecticut Campus*, October 23, 1940.

34. AEW, December 7–15, 1941, pp. 516–29, box 15, DRC.

35. Jorgensen to Al Jr., December 11, 1941, POJ, box 5, file 20, DRC.

36. *Connecticut Campus*, December 17, 1941, January 7, 1942; Jorgensen to James W. Hook, December 17, 1941, POJ, box 5, file 17, DRC; AEW, February 10, 1942, p. 61, January 9, 1942, p. 16, box 15, DRC.

37. *Connecticut Campus*, January 7, 16, March 31, April 3, October 9, 16, 20, November 20, December 11, 1942.

38. *Connecticut Campus*, January 7, 1942.

39. AEW, January 28, February 10, March 18, 1942, pp. 41–42, 61, 111, DRC; Lt. Col. G. H. Passmore to Headquarters First Corp Area Commanding General, February 4, 1942, POJ, box 5, file 27; *Connecticut Campus*, March 4, 25, October 16, 1942.

40. Col. Walter J. Reed to Jorgensen, January 21, 1942, POJ, box 5, file 27, DRC; Stemmons, unpublished 75th anniversary manuscript, 47; *Connecticut Campus*, December 8, 1942.

41. Stemmons unpublished 75th anniversary manuscript, 46–48; *Connecticut Campus*, January 26, 1944.

42. Stemmons, unpublished 75th anniversary manuscript, 46–48; *Connecticut Campus*, January 26, 1944; *Connecticut Alumnus*, vol. 22, no. 4, p. 1, DRC.

43. AEW, June 16, 1943, p. 247, DRC.

44. AEW, June 16, 1943, pp. 246–47, DRC.

45. *Connecticut Campus*, February 28, March 6, 20, May 8, 1940.

46. *Connecticut Campus*, March 13, April 24, May 1, October 16, 1940.

47. Mildred P. French to Jorgensen, July 18, 1940, and Jorgensen to French, July 22, 1940, POJ, box 4, file 40, DRC; *Connecticut Campus*, October 2, December 18, 1940, March 12, 1941.

48. Jorgensen to William J. Haggerty, March 14, 1941, POJ, box 4, file 46, DRC; correspondence between Jorgensen and Mary H. Smith, Secretary, AAUW Committee on Membership and Maintaining Standards, February 5, 10, 17, May 5, 8, 1941, POJ, box 4, file 17, DRC; "Staff Members Eligible for Membership in AAUW," November 12, 1941, POJ, box 4, file 89, DRC.

49. *Connecticut Campus*, March 12, 1941.

50. AEW, September 22, 24, 1942, pp. 369, 371, box 15, DRC; Beatrice Fox Auerbach to Jorgensen, March 5, 1942, POJ, box 4, file 95, DRC; J. H. Lampe to Jorgensen, March 31, 1942, POJ, box 5, file 22, DRC; *Connecticut Campus*, October 30, 1942.

51. *Connecticut Campus*, December 4, 1942, January 22, February 2, 1943.

52. *Connecticut Campus*, January 15, 1943.

53. *Connecticut Campus*, March 19, 23, 1943. During World War I and the 1917–18

academic year, the lowest enrollment figures registered revealed forty-nine men and six women.

54. *Connecticut Campus,* November 20, 1942, April 20, 1943, October 25, November 1, 1944, March 7, 1945.

55. For a basic exploration of Japanese American internment, see Alice Yang Murray, *What Did the Internment of Japanese Americans Mean?* (Boston: Bedford/St. Martin's, 2000); FDR's role in issuing Executive Order 9,066 can be found in Greg Robinson, *By Order of the President,* (Cambridge, Mass.: Harvard University Press, 2001); Stemmons unpublished 75th anniversary manuscript, 45; George M. Fukui '45 (College of Liberal Arts and Sciences/CLAS) told his story to Howard V. Sann in the University of Connecticut alumni magazine *UConn Traditions* (summer 2003): 31–33, 50; Dr. Fukui also compiled a compact disc, "Japanese American Students at the University of Connecticut During World War Two, 1943–1948," for the sixtieth anniversary reunion, October 16–18, 2003; according to Dr. Fukui, the following Japanese American students matriculated: Shiro Aisawa, Tetsuo Fuchigami, George Fukui, Tokuo Furuta, Toshi Hamasaki Kato, William Hayakawa, Kei Hori, Tomoko Ikeda Wheaton, Ben Iwakiri, Kay Kiyokawa, Don Kawasaki, Jim Nakano, Ken Nakaoka, Luther Ogawa, Satoshi Oishi, Yoneo Ono, Edna Sakamoto White, Kazuo Yamaguchi, and Terry Yeya Yatsu. Not all of the students were assigned to UConn by the NJASRC. For instance, Kazuo Yamaguchi was from Long Island and was unfamiliar with the internment camps until he served in the army's Japanese American 442nd regiment (Oral History Interview, October 16, 2003). George Fukui first moved to New York with his sisters, who had employment there. He applied to UConn from New York (Oral History Interview, October 15, 2003). Jim Nakano did come from the Topaz camp. After a three-day train trip, he arrived in Mansfield but thought it strange to see bars on the windows of the dormitories. His image of Connecticut came from the film "White Christmas," and he expected a beautiful place. He quickly learned that he was at the "Mansfield Institute for the Feeble Minded," later the Mansfield Training School. He walked from there to UConn, which he found very much more to his liking (Oral History Interview, October 17, 2003).

56. E-mail from Greg Robinson to the author, October 18, 2002, based on his exploration of War Relocation Authority Papers in the National Archives and the records of NJASRC at the Hoover Institution; AEW, May 1, 1943, p. 175, box 15, DRC; *Connecticut Campus,* March 23, 1943.

57. E-mail from Greg Robinson to the author, October 18, 2002; *Connecticut Campus,* March 17, April 14, May 17, 1944; Oral History Interview with Kay Kiyokowa, October 17, 2003; George M. Fukui (as told to Howard Sann), "Internment: UConn Was a Way Out," *UConn Traditions,* summer 2003, pp. 30–33, 50.

58. Fukui, "Internment," 30–33, 50; Fukui, compact disk; Larry Bloom, "Tumbling Tumbleweeds," *Northeast (Hartford Courant Magazine),* March 14, 1999, p. 9; ECH, box 6, Jorgensen folder 2, notes, p. 7, 1945, p. 56.

59. *Connecticut Campus,* April 14, 1944, April 24, 1940.

60. *Connecticut Campus,* May 14, 1943; AEW, May 17, 1943, p. 203.

61. For details on the Croteau-Siegel dispute, see AEW, December 3, 8, 9, 11, 14, 17, 18, 24, 1943.

62. *Connecticut Campus,* April 14, 1944; AEW, January 27, 1944, p. 49, January 16, 1945, p. 17, January 20, 1945, p. 28, box 15, DRC; *Connecticut Campus,* February 14, 1945; EHC, box 6, Jorgensen file 2, p. 54, notes, p. 6; Stemmons unpublished 75th anniversary manuscript, insert 49.

63. Stemmons, unpublished 75th anniversary manuscript, p. 46; *Connecticut Campus,* January 5, 12, 1944; AEW, January 7, 1944, p. 7, box 15, DRC.

64. For faculty complaints about Jorgensen, see AEW, February 2, April 5, May 9, July 8, September 30, 1943; for the AAUP committee, see December 17, 1943, pp. 488–90; for the resignation, see January 21, 1944, p. 39, box 15, DRC.

65. AEW, February 2, 1943, p. 59, May 31, 1944, July 22, p. 305, 25, p. 308, 26, p. 313, August 12, 1944, p. 349, box 15, DRC.

66. Jorgensen to N. L. Whetten, August 5, 1940, POJ, box 4, file 82, DRC; Stemmons, unpublished 75th anniversary manuscript, pp. 38–insert 41, DRC.

67. AEW, September 29, 1944, pp. 435–36, September 22, 1944, pp. 419–20, April 19, 1943, p. 159, box 15, DRC.

68. AEW, September 22, 1944, pp. 418–23, February 5, 1945, p. 59, October 4, 1943, p. 361, box 15, DRC; EHC, box 6, Jorgensen file 2, DRC.

Chapter 3. The Jorgensen Transformation: 1946–62 (pp. 61–99)

1. For a succinct summary of the G.I. bill, the "Servicemen's Readjustment Act of 1944," see the Web site www.gibill.va.gov/education/GI_Bill.htm; Walter Stemmons to Jorgensen, who received the article on December 6, 1946, POJ, box 5, file 56b, DRC.

2. Board of Trustees Minutes, May 15, 1946, box 3, p. 1355, DRC; AEW, May 23, 1946, p. 175, DRC; Jorgensen to Gov. Raymond E. Baldwin, June 25, 1946, Board of Trustees Minutes, July 17, 1946, pp. 1374–75, box 3, DRC.

3. Jorgensen to Commandants of U.S. Coast Guard and U.S. Maritime Service, June 14, 1946, Board of Trustees Minutes, July 17, 1946, p. 1376, box 3, DRC; for registration figures and reference to the fence, see "Fort Trumbull, 1946–1948: A Report to the Connecticut Taxpayers," POJ, box 6, file 2, DRC; the 1947 *Nutmeg,* box 7, Fort Trumbull File, Evan Hill Collection (hereafter EHC), DRC, sizes the campus at eleven acres with twenty-three buildings; interview with Morton Tenzer, August 18, 2003, p. 26 (first draft); *Hartford Courant Magazine,* March 20, 1949, EHC, box 7, Fort Trumbull file, DRC.

4. "Fort Trumbull, 1946–1948: A Report to the Connecticut Taxpayers," POJ, box 6, file 2, DRC.

5. Ibid.; 1947 *Nutmeg,* EHC, box 7, Fort Trumbull file, DRC; *Connecticut Campus,* October 29, 1946, 1945–1982, Blue Binder, box 3, EHC, DRC; *New Haven Sunday*

Register Magazine, February 23, 1947, EHC, box 7, Fort Trumbull file, DRC; AEW, September 12, 1947, p. 350, DRC.

6. *New Haven Sunday Register Magazine,* February 23, 1947, EHC, box 7, Fort Trumbull file, DRC; AEW, September 12, 1947, p. 350, DRC; *Hartford Courant Magazine,* March 20, 1949, EHC, box 7, Fort Trumbull file, DRC.

7. Jorgensen to C. A. Weber, January 25, 1950, POJ, box 6, file 48; for the problems with obtaining equipment, see Jorgensen correspondence, May 15, 1950, POJ, box 6, file 48, May 23, 1951, POJ, box 6, file 97, June 13, 1951, POJ, box 6, file 107, DRC; draft cover letter for, "Fort Trumbull 1946–1948," POJ, box 6, file 2, DRC; apparently, Jorgensen did not permit this report to go forward; see Jorgensen to E. A. Adler Jr., September 25, 1948, which is appended to the report; *Connecticut Campus,* May 20, 1954.

8. *Hartford Courant,* October 26, 1946, *Connecticut Campus,* September 27, October 8, 31, 1946, EHC, 1945–1982, Blue Binder, box 3, DRC; *Connecticut Campus,* April 12, 1956; AEW, June 7, 1945, p. 229; September 28, 1945, p. 392; April 13, 1946, p. 121, DRC.

9. AEW, October 16, 1945, pp. 419–20, DRC. Although the president agreed with the policy, it is not entirely clear how widely it was implemented, if at all.

10. AEW, November 25, 1946, pp. 410–13, DRC.

11. AEW, November 25, 1946, p. 414, DRC.

12. Gerson's view is in the *Connecticut Campus,* February 10, 1948, EHC, box 3, 1945–1982, Blue Binder, DRC; for a revision of the "Silent Generation," see, for example, Joanne Meyerowitz, ed., *Not June Cleaver: Women and Gender in Postwar America, 1945–1960* (Philadelphia, Pa.: Temple University Press, 1994).

13. AEW, February 6, 1952, pp. 37–38, box 16, file January 1–February 18, 1952; *Hartford Courant,* February 7, 1952; for letters with anti-Semitic content, see Jorgensen to Harry S. Ganders, November 18, 1935, POJ, box 1, file 46, DRC, and Jorgensen to Stanhope Bayne-Jones, December 9, 1935, and response, December 11, 1935, POJ, box 1, file 51, DRC; for Jorgensen winning a B'nai B'rith Americanism Award in 1951, see POJ, box 6, file 113, DRC.

14. *Connecticut Campus,* February 8, 11, March 26, 1952. For a brief history of the Druids, see Mark J. Roy, "A Piece of UConn History: UConn's Secret Society," *UConn Advance,* March 21, 2005. He writes: "Over the 31 years that the Druids existed, 159 students were tapped as members. With two exceptions all were white males; the exceptions were one woman and one Japanese American. At least three members, over the years, were Jewish."

15. *Connecticut Campus,* May 25, 1937, EHC, box 3, 1896–1944, Blue Binder, DRC; AEW, January 28, 1946, pp. 36, box 15, DRC.

16. *Connecticut Campus,* February 14, 1947, EHC, box 3, 1945–1982, Blue Binder, DRC; *Connecticut Campus,* January 17, February 24, 1950.

17. POJ, series 2, box 36, file 1949, Resolution, Discrimination in Fraternities, March 15, 16, 1949, DRC; *Connecticut Campus,* March 18, 1949, EHC, box 3, 1945–1982, Blue Binder; *Connecticut Campus,* January (4, 5, or 6), 1949; *Connecticut Campus,* March 4, 1949, EHC, box 3, 1945–1982, Blue Binder, DRC. At its July 21, 1948, meeting, Pres-

ident Jorgensen presented to the board of trustees an earlier Student Senate resolution on discrimination related to establishing new Greek chapters on campus. The
board voted to approve in principle the Student Senate recommendation and requested the president to present at a later meeting a carefully worded resolution incorporating in principle the intent and purpose of the students; Minutes, July 21,
1948, box 3, DRC. The board adopted the Bryzman-Blawie resolution on May 17,
1950. However, Chairman of the Board James W. Hook wrote, "Personally I think we
were on sound ground when we limited our denial to honorary, professional, recognition or other scholastic groups, but I would question the wisdom of interfering
with social or fraternal groups except in cases where an individual complained of
being barred only for racial, religious or color reasons. It is very easy to warp the
conception of civil rights in an effort to make them conform to certain social patterns and wake up to find that more rights have been denied to one than have been
extended to the one it was desired to help." James W. Hook to Jorgensen, April 18,
1950, POJ, box 6, file 56, DRC.

18. *Hartford Courant,* September 27, 1950; Interview with Alfred R. Rogers, Daniel
Blume, and Marvin Lapuk, May 28, 2003. While Lapuk had a sense that pledging
Rogers would create a precedent, Blume wasn't aware of the issue until the national
"blackballed" Rogers; pp. 20–21 (first draft). Not everyone on campus believed the
pledging of Rogers to be without motive. Student Senate President John H. Bannan
suggested that the Upsilon chapter pledged Rogers in order to break the discriminatory clause in the national's constitution and that the whole matter was a publicity
stunt. He opposed discrimination but felt that Rogers was being used inappropri-
ately. Upsilon's president, Irving Chaneles, challenged Bannan's remarks, and a
number of observers pointed to Bannan's connection with the Independent Student
Organization (ISO), a non-fraternity, perhaps anti-fraternity, group, as the reason
for his comments. *Connecticut Campus,* October 11, 13, 1950; also see Jim H. Smith,
"The Measure of Character," *UConn Traditions,* spring 2000, pp. 30–33.

19. *Hartford Courant,* September 27, 2003; *Connecticut Campus,* September 29, 1950;
Chester Bowles to Phi Epsilon Pi executive secretary, October 26, 1950, POJ, box 6,
file 87, DRC.

20. *Connecticut Campus,* October 9, 1950, January 3, 1951; interview with Rogers, Blume,
and Lapuk, May 28, 2003, pp. 31, 36–37, 49, 64 (first draft); telegram, Irving R. Chaneles to Jorgensen, December 28, 1950, POJ, box 6, file 95, DRC.

21. Jorgensen to Donald Fairweather, President, Upsilon Chapter, Alpha Gamma Rho,
October 23, 1951, to David S. Cook, Grand President, Alpha Gamma Rho, October 31,
1951, Cook to Jorgensen, November 5, 1951, Fairweather to Jorgensen, May 30, 1951,
Jorgensen to Fairweather, June 26, 1951, POJ, box 6, file 95, DRC.

22. AEW, September 25, 1952, pp. 251–52, box 16, file September 22–November 1, 1952,
DRC; Mrs. J.M. to Jorgensen, undated but received November 16, 1954, POJ, box 10,
file 41, DRC; J. O. Christian to Athletic Advisory Committee, with copy to Jorgensen,
April 24, 1956, and Jorgensen response, May 2, 1956, POJ, box 11, file 25, DRC. This

was not the first time Connecticut's African American basketball players encountered discrimination. On January 28, 1934, Harrison "Honey" Fitch, the first African American to play for Connecticut, when it was still Connecticut State College, was kept out of a game with the U.S. Coast Guard Academy probably because of the academy's objections based on race, an issue that would arise at most of the games in which he participated. See Mark J. Roy, "Son of UConn's First Black Basketball Star Recounts Father's Story," *UConn Advance,* February 2, 2004; *Connecticut Daily Campus,* January 4, 1957, December 6, 1957.

23. For the effect of McCarthyism on the nation's campuses, see Ellen Schrecker, *No Ivory Tower: McCarthyism and the Universities* (New York: Oxford University Press, 1986); for a graduate student's interpretation of McCarthyism at UConn, see University of Connecticut Department of History 402 research paper by Mark Sattler, Spring 2003; "A- Member-of-the-Faculty" to Jorgensen, January 5, 1938, POJ, box 2, file 45, DRC; Florien Heiser to S. A. Dole, January 12, 1938, POJ, box 2, file 74, DRC.

24. AEW, January 30, 1947, pp. 37–38, box 16, file January 1–February 5, 1947, DRC; AEW, May 12, 1947, pp. 165–66, box 16, file May 3–June 6, 1947, DRC.

25. William A. Ward to Jorgensen, March 24, 1949, Jorgensen to Ward, March 31, 1949, POJ, box 6, file 25, DRC; J. H. Trumbull to *Connecticut Campus,* October 18, 1950, EHC, box 3, 1945–1982, Blue Binder, DRC. The charges against Owen Lattimore regarding subverting Far Eastern policy to advance communism received a great deal of publicity during the McCarthy era and made him one of the symbols of the age; AEW, June 13, 1949, p. 173, box 16, file May 2–July 18, 1949, DRC.

26. *Connecticut Campus,* March 2, 10, 1953; AEW, March 11, 1952, pp. 72–73, February 14, 1953, p. 56, February 6, 1953, p. 47, file February 10–March 20, 1953, DRC.

27. AEW, March 13, 1953, p. 88, box 16, file February 10–March 20, 1953, DRC.

28. AEW, March 13, 1953, pp. 89–90, box 16, file February 10–March 20, 1953, DRC.

29. AEW, March 18, 1953, pp. 95–97, box 16, file February 10–March 20, 1953, DRC.

30. AEW, March 18, 1953, pp. 97–98, box 16, file February 10–March 20, 1953, DRC.

31. AEW, March 18, 1953, pp. 99–100, box 16, file February 10–March 20, 1953, DRC; Waugh to Jorgensen, June 29, 1953, in Report of Committee of Five, POJ, series 2, box 35, file "Communism 1953," DRC.

32. AEW, March 20, 23, 1953, pp. 102–3, 108–9, box 16, files February 10–March 20, 1953, March 21–April 22, 1953, DRC; Board Minutes, March 23, 1953, pp. 2,055–58, box 4, file January 26–July 27, 1953, DRC. A month later, when the board's policy became public, Jorgensen claimed that it was general policy and not a response to a specific case. This led to a dispute between the president and James W. Hook of the board of trustees. See *Hartford Courant,* April 20, 1953, and AEW, April 21, 1953, pp. 150–56, box 16, file March 21–April 22, 1953, DRC; for the AAUP, see *Connecticut Campus,* April 20 and 22, 1953. When Zilsel asked that his case be brought by the local AAUP to the national's attention, local officers thought it unwise and advised Zilsel to refer the case himself. They would assist him as individuals, but not as an organization. See AEW, April 24, 1953, pp. 163–64, box 16, file April 23–May 21, 1953, DRC.

33. AEW, March 26, 30, 1953, pp. 113, 116, box 16, files March 21–April 22, 1953, DRC; for Harry Marks's testimony before HUAC, see Testimony of Harry J. Marks, June 22, 1953, pp. 1843–74, "Communist Methods of Infiltration" (Education—part 6), Hearings before the Committee on Un-American Activities, House of Representatives, Eighty-third Congress, First Session, USGPO, Washington, D.C., 1953.

34. AEW, April 1, 9, 20, 1953, pp. 120, 129, 147, box 6, file March 21–April 22, 1953, DRC.

35. Committee of Five to Board of Trustees, June 15, 1953, in Report of Committee of Five, POJ, series 2, box 35, file "Communism, 1953," DRC; AEW, April 23, 1953, box 16, file April 23–May 21, 1953, DRC; Testimony of Paul Rudolph Zilsel, "Communist Methods of Infiltration" (Education—part 3), Hearings before the Committee on Un-American Activities, House of Representatives, Eighty-third Congress, First Session, April 21 and 22, 1953, quotes from pp. 1036–37, *Hartford Courant* reference, pp. 1041–42, entire testimony, pp. 1036–45, Government Printing Office, Washington, D.C., 1953.

36. Report to the Board of Trustees of the University of Connecticut by the Committee of Five, Report on Paul R. Zilsel, pp. 3–4, POJ, series 2, box 35, file "Communism 1953," DRC; AEW, April 23, 1953, pp. 159–61, box 16, file April 23–May 21, 1953, DRC.

37. AEW, April 23, 24, 1953, pp. 162–63, box 16, file April 23–May 21, 1953, DRC.

38. Report of Committee of Five, Report on Paul Zilsel, p. 4 and exhibit G, "Statement on Invoking the Fifth Amendment," POJ, series 2, box 35, file "Communism, 1953," DRC.

39. *Connecticut Campus,* May 6 and 7, 1953; for the full AAUP statement, see Report of Committee of Five, exhibit S, p. 70, POJ, series 2, box 35, file "Communism, 1953," DRC.

40. Report of Committee of Five, pp. 30–64, Marks, Kogan, Gerson, Beck testimony, pp. 60–61, POJ, series 2, box 35, file "Communism, 1953," DRC.

41. Report of the Committee of Five, pp. 65–66, POJ, series 2, box 35, file "Communism, 1953," DRC; AEW, June 22, October 19, 1953, pp. 232, 353, May 14–15, 1954, pp. 165–69, box 17, files May 22–July 11, 1953, October 19–November 30, 1953, May 2–June 18, 1954, DRC; Board of Trustees Minutes, p. 2, 115, box 4, September 16, 1952–November 18, 1953, DRC; Waugh to Harold P. Knauss, March 3, 1954, POJ, box 7, file 12, DRC; Minutes of Special Meeting, July 27, 1953, pp. 2090–91, box 4, file January 26–July 27, 1953, DRC; AEW, July 14, 27–28, 30, 1953, pp. 253, 265–67, 270–71, box 17, file July 12–September 1, 1953, DRC.

42. AEW, September 27, 29, 1946, pp. 339–342, file August 31–October 11, 1946, and October 2, 1948, p. 309, file August 22–October 4, 1948, box 16, DRC; *Connecticut Campus,* October 1, 1948, EHC, box 3, Blue Binder, 1945–1982, DRC.

43. Stemmons unpublished 75th anniversary manuscript, 56, DRC.

44. Ibid.; AEW, September 29, 1946, p. 342, box 16, file August 31–October 11, 1946, DRC; almost five years after Waugh's ruminations about the president's athletic bias, he again wrote about his warning to Jorgensen of the faculty's grave concern that he admitted an athlete who did not meet the university's admission requirements. Critics

threatened a University Senate investigation. See AEW, February 15, 1951, p. 52, box 16, file February 14–April 6, 1951, DRC.

45. Richard D. Robertson to Jorgensen, October 19, 1949, and Jorgensen to Robertson, November 3, 1949, POJ, box 6, file 50, DRC.

46. "Notes Concerning the Proposed Evaluation of the Athletic Situation at the University of Connecticut," December 2, 1949, POJ, box 6, file 50, DRC.

47. The Committee to Jorgensen, December 28, 1949, POJ, box 6, file 50, DRC.

48. Ibid; for cynicism about the other recommendations, see "Notes Concerning the Proposed Evaluation of the Athletic Situation at the University of Connecticut," December 2, 1949, p.1, POJ, box 6, file 50, DRC.

49. Draft of press release, January 8, 1950, POJ, box 6, file 7, DRC; Stemmons unpublished 75th anniversary manuscript, p. 62, DRC; AEW, January 4, 1950, p. 5, box 16, file January 1–February 19, 1950, October 10, 1953, p. 343, box 17, file September 2–October 18, 1953, DRC; Office of Institutional Research, "Facts about the University of Connecticut since 1881," 45–46; information on basketball from "University of Connecticut Men's Basketball Historical Timeline," supplied by Timothy M. Tolokan.

50. Stemmons unpublished 75th anniversary manuscript, 57, 69, DRC; AEW, January 7, 1953, pp. 9–10, March 15, 1951, p. 83, DRC; "Basketball Historical Timeline"; "The University of Connecticut Statement of Athletic Policy," February 1, 1950, POJ, series 2, box 35, file "Athletic Policy," DRC.

51. See appendix B, "Selected Chronology," of an unpublished manuscript for a history of the University of Connecticut Health Center, in possession of the author; AEW, November 29, 1945, p. 484, box 15, file November 16–December 6, 1945, DRC.

52. *Connecticut Campus*, April 14, 1952; Gov. John D. Lodge to James W. Hook, July 26, 1950, POJ, box 6, file 107, DRC.

53. Appendix B, "Selected Chronology;" AEW, September 25, 1952, p. 253, box 16, file September 22–November 1, 1952, June 9–10, 1955, pp. 239–41, box 17, file May 5–June 21, 1955, DRC.

54. Appendix B, "Selected Chronology;" AEW, March 2, 1955, p. 68, box 17, file February 14–March 30, 1955, AEW, March 5, 1957, pp. 66–67, box 17, file February 16–April 10, 1957, DRC.

55. AEW, March 5, 1957, p. 67, box 17, file February 16–April 10, 1957, DRC; for examples of Jorgensen's quiet lobbying, see Jorgensen to Mary H. Mahoney, November 1, 1955, and attachment, "Connecticut's Needs for Additional Facilities for Medical, Dental, and Veterinary Education," POJ, box 12, file 9, DRC, and Jorgensen to Sen. Joseph S. Longo, Chair of the Judiciary Committee, and Rep. Erving Pruyn, Chair of the Judiciary Committee, March 25, 1955, POJ, box 9, file 14, DRC; Report to President Jorgensen by Provost Waugh, March 30, 1955, "Notes on Hearings Before the Education Committee, March 23, 1955," POJ, box 9, file 14, DRC; Waugh to Legislative Committee on Education, April 14, 1955, POJ, box 9, file 15, DRC; letters of endorsement, March 21, April 25, May 16, 1955, May 21, 1956, POJ, box 12, file 45, DRC.

56. Report to the General Assembly about House Joint Resolution No. 9, POJ, box 9,

file 15, DRC; James H. Kinsella to Lester E. Shippee, Chair, Board of Trustees, University of Connecticut, October 31, 1955, POJ, box 13, file 59 (Shippee); Jorgensen to Shailer Peterson, Secretary, Council of Dental Education, December 28, 1955, box 12, file 16, DRC.

57. Jorgensen to Joseph A. Adorno, December 21, 1956, POJ, box 13, file 37, DRC; "A Study of Available Sites and Clinical Facilities for a Medical and Dental School—A Report to the General Assembly by the Board of Trustees of the University of Connecticut and State Board of Education," January 9, 1957, POJ, box 14, file 52, DRC; Jorgensen to Rep. Nelson Brown II of Groton, March 1, 1957, POJ, box 14, file 51, DRC; Jorgensen to Creighton Barker, Executive Secretary, Connecticut State Medical Society, October 24, 1957, POJ, box 16, file 84, DRC.

58. For sample letters seeking foundation support and their disposition, see "Foundation Replies to Medical-Dental Request Letter," POJ, box 32, file 12, DRC; "Proposal for the Establishment of a Two-Year Medical School at the University of Connecticut," marked "Board Meeting," July 20, 1960, box 20, file 34, DRC; news release, August 25, 1960, POJ, box 26, file 5, DRC; notes of meeting between Jorgensen and Citizens Committee for a Connecticut Medical-Dental School, April 4, 1961, by Keith B. Hook, POJ, box 28, file 12, DRC.

59. W. K. Kellogg Foundation, undated press release, POJ, box 32, file 46, DRC; notes of meeting between Jorgensen and Citizens Committee for a Connecticut Medical-Dental School, April 4, 1961, by Keith B. Hook, POJ, box 28, file 12, DRC.

60. Appendix B, "Selected Chronology"; Oral History Interview with Helen Loy by Whitney W. and Edna E. Jacobs, p. 3, University of Connecticut Health Center Records (1963–97), box 123, DRC. The poor relationship between Jorgensen and Ribicoff is documented in Waugh's journal; see particularly AEW, December 22, 1958, pp. 480–81, box 17, file December 4–31, 1958, and November 12, 1960, pp. 342–43, box 18, file October 3–November 16, 1960, DRC. In the first instance, the two argued about a proposed increase in Jorgensen's salary. The argument was heated and the governor, who threatened to bring the issue to the public, told Jorgensen he would be made an example of before the media. "They'll cut your balls off," Ribicoff asserted. The president responded, "Not unless you give them a knife." The second example described how Ribicoff, scheduled to preside at the president's twenty-fifth-anniversary convocation, cancelled his appearance on short notice.

61. Appendix B, "Selected Chronology"; Memorandum for the Education Committee of the General Assembly, April 13, 1961, POJ, box 28, file 12, DRC; Gov. John Dempsey to Jorgensen, September 7, 1961, POJ, box 32, file 25, DRC; Oral History Interview with Helen Loy, pp. 4–5; Jorgensen to John M. Bailey, May 23, 1962, POJ, box 31, file 33, DRC; Western Union Telegram, Jorgensen to Congressmen, August 16, 1962, President's Office Babbidge (hereafter POB), box 2, file 39, DRC.

62. "Educational Programs," Finding Aid, University of Connecticut Health Center Records (1963–97), pp. 5–6, DRC.

63. Board of Trustees Minutes, November 20, 1957, pp. 2,493–94, box 4, file September

18, 1957–July 16, 1958, DRC; *Hartford Courant* and *Hartford Times,* October 28, 1948, POJ, box 6, file 6, DRC.

64. Office of Institutional Research, "Facts About the University of Connecticut since 1881," pp. 28–29. Ackerman also served as dean of the School of Insurance (called "the College" until 1961) between 1943 and 1963; AEW, November 22, 1957, p. 312, box 17, file November 13–December 10, 1957, DRC; "Plan for the Development of the School of Law of the University of Connecticut," July 1957, p. 4 and chart 5, POJ, box 16, file 62; Jorgensen to Bert E. Hopkins, August 2, 1954, POJ, box 9, file 3, DRC; Waugh to Hopkins, April 20, 1955, POJ, box 9, file 14, DRC.

65. Bert E. Hopkins to John G. Hervey, Esq., November 7, 1957, POJ, box 16, file 62; Waugh and Hopkins to Jorgensen, March 7, 1958, POJ, box 16, file 62, DRC. The Law School certainly drew on students from high-quality colleges. The first-year class in the 1958–59 academic year admitted sixty-three students, one of whom was female. Twenty-eight were from UConn; the others came from Yale (five), Fairfield (four), Brown (three), two each from Boston University, Middlebury, Notre Dame, the University of Pennsylvania, and Trinity, and one each from Dartmouth, Duke, Fordham, Georgetown, the University of Hartford, Harvard, Holy Cross, Lehigh, Princeton, St. Anselm's, Tufts, Wells, and Wesleyan (Report of the [Law School] Dean, 1958–59, July 1, 1959, p. 4, POJ, box 21, file 65, DRC.

66. AEW, November 22, 1957, pp. 312–15, box 17, file November 12–December 10, 1957, DRC.

67. AEW, January 20, 1958, pp. 37–38, box 17, file January 1–25, 1958, DRC; AEW, January 31, 1958, pp. 61–62, February 6, 1958, p. 70, box 17, file January 26–February 22, 1958, DRC; AEW, February 23, 1958, pp. 99–100, box 17, file February 23–April 3, 1958, DRC; Waugh to Jorgensen, January 28, 1958, POJ, box 16, file 102, DRC; Chair of the Board of Trustees to Members of the Council Section on Legal Education and Admissions to the Bar, ABA, February 20, 1958, POJ, box 16, file 62, DRC; Waugh and Hopkins to Jorgensen, March 7, 1958, POJ, box 16, file 62, DRC.

68. Report of the [Law School] Dean, 1958–59, July 1, 1959, p. 4, POJ, box 21, file 65, DRC; Hopkins to Jorgensen, May 4, 1960, POJ, box 21, file 65, DRC; Hopkins to John G. Hervey, Esq., January 24, 1961, POJ, box 27, file 40, DRC; John J. Budds to Albert E. Saunders Jr., Assistant Counsel, Phoenix Mutual Life Insurance Co., May 4, 1961, POJ, box 27, file 40, DRC; T. J. Murphy Jr. to John J. Budds, Chair, Board of Trustees, July 3, 1961, POJ, box 29, file 30, DRC; Henry D. Gray, Chair, Commission on the City [of Hartford] Plan to Court of Common Council, March 24, 1961, POJ, box 27, file 40, DRC; C. F. Sharpe, Hartford City Manager, to Jorgensen, May 15, 1961, POJ, box 27, file 40, DRC; "Memorandum by Dean Hopkins Concerning Site for New School of Law Building," May 29, 1962, POJ, box 32, file 31, DRC; W. M. Pickett Jr., President, Law School Alumni Association, to John J. Budds, May 24, 1962, POJ, box 32, file 31, DRC; John G. Hervey, Adviser, ABA, to Hopkins, May 18, 1962, POJ, box 32, file 31, DRC.

69. AEW, March 7, 1958, p. 118, box 17, file February 23–April 3, 1958, DRC; AEW, July 24, 1958, p. 293, box 17, file June 23–August 2, 1958, DRC.

70. Waugh to Dean F. Roy Brammell, June 18, 1955, POJ, box 7, file 13, DRC.
71. Charles Waring to Waugh, May 25, 1954, POJ, box 7, file 9, DRC.
72. Waugh to Waring, June 2, 1954, POJ, box 7, file 9, DRC; Waugh to Marjorie D. Farmer, July 29, 1953, POJ, box 7, file 10, DRC; Waugh to Whetten, October 20, 1960, POJ, box 32, file 9, DRC.
73. *New Englander Magazine,* August 1960, POJ, box 31, file 49, DRC; *Connecticut Daily Campus,* October 20, 1961.
74. *Hartford Courant,* April 9, 10, 1961. According to Elliot Wolk, the stories were published without the knowledge of the editor, who probably would have prevented publication. Conversation with the author, May 15, 2003.
75. Elliot Wolk to Jorgensen, October 20, 1960, POJ, box 31, file 21, DRC.
76. POJ, Administrative Council File, box 31, inserted between files 22 and 23, DRC; Jorgensen to John J. Budds, December 18, 1961, POJ, box 31, file 40, DRC; AEW, October 20, 1960, box 18, file October 3–November 16, 1960, DRC; Minutes of Dean's Council, April 11, 1962, POJ, box 32, file 2, DRC.
77. Jorgensen to John J. Budds, December 18, 1961, box 31, file 40, DRC; Waugh to Walter Wardwell, May 19, 1954, POJ, box 7, file 13, DRC; *AAUP Newsletter,* 2, no. 1 (October 1961), box 31, file 21, DRC.
78. Waugh to Dorothy Goodwin, January 25, 1961, POJ, box 31, file 9, DRC.
79. *Hartford Times,* October 21, 1961; Jorgensen to William Benton, November 6, 1961, POJ, box 31, file 34, DRC.
80. Jorgensen to Benton, December 29, 1961, POJ, box 31, file 34, DRC.
81. Babbidge to Jorgensen, March 23, 1962, and Jorgensen to Babbidge, April 10, 1962, POJ, box 31, file 32, DRC.
82. Babbidge to John W. Gardner, President of the Carnegie Foundation, December 4, 1962, POB, box 1, file 16, DRC.

Chapter 4. Homer's Odyssey—The Babbidge Years: 1962–72 (pp. 100–58)

1. F. Robert Paulsen to Provost Waugh, January 12, 1962, POJ, box 32, file 7, DRC; Inaugural Program, October 20, 1962, POB, box 2, file 30, DRC; J. H. Arjona to Babbidge, June 1, 1963, POB, box 1, file 7, DRC; Joe Marfuggi to Babbidge, June 20, 1963, box 3, file 46, DRC; Robert E. Dunn to Babbidge, June 26, 1963, POB, box 22, file 2, DRC; Sumner Dole to Babbidge, March 17, 1963, box 1, file 20, DRC; Telegram, John F. Kennedy to Babbidge, June 15, 1963, box 2, file 34, DRC.
2. Board of Trustees Minutes, March 16, 1962, p. 2992, box 5, file January 17–August 7, 1962, DRC; John J. Budds to Jorgensen, March 22, 1962, POJ, box 31, file 32, DRC; Budds to Members of the Faculty and Staff, March 26, 1962, POJ, box 31, file 32, DRC; Jorgensen to W. B. Young, May 25, 1962, POJ, box 32, file 32, DRC; AEW, February 16, 1962, pp. 49–50, box 18, file January 1–February 16, 1962, March 12, 1962, pp. 72–73, and March 17, 1962, p. 77, box 18, file February 17–April 11, 1962, DRC. The faculty

members on the Search Committee were David Ivry, associate professor of insurance, Paul J. Jannke, professor of pharmacy, Albert I. Mann, professor of dairy husbandry, W. Howard Martin, professor of education, Victor E. Scottron, professor of civil engineering, and Philip Taylor, head of the Economics Department, who served as committee secretary; the two administrators in addition to Dean Whetten were Hugh Clark, director of the Institute of Cellular Biology, and Bert L. Hopkins, dean of the Law School; John J. Budds, chair, Guy B. Holt, and Elmer S. Watson represented the board of trustees; see AEW, November 16, 1961, p. 381, box 18, file October 26–December 3, 1961, DRC, and *Connecticut Daily Campus,* November 29, 1961; AEW, March 26, 1962, p. 85, and April 4, 1962, p. 94, box 18, file February 17–April 11, 1962, DRC. Apparently Jorgensen, during a visit to Washington, D.C., well before he announced his intention to retire, tested Babbidge's interest in becoming a university president and, particularly, the president of the University of Connecticut. When Babbidge showed interest, Jorgensen duly noted it for future consideration and probably passed it on to the Search Committee. See AEW, July 8, 1963, p. 223, box 18, file June 15–August 3, 1963, DRC.

3. *Connecticut Daily Campus,* May 3, 1962.
4. Waugh for the Inaugural Committee to all members of the professional staff, May 4, 1962, POJ, box 31, file 32, DRC; Waugh to Jorgensen, May 11, 1962, POJ, box 31, file 32, DRC.
5. Jorgensen to Budds, April 10, 1962, POJ, box 31, file 40, DRC; Board of Trustees Minutes, October 18, 1961, pp. 2952–54, and April 18, 1962, p. 3000, box 5, DRC; Telegram, Jorgensen to Budds, May 25, 1962, POJ, box 31, file 40, DRC; AEW, April 13, 1962, p. 103, April 18, 1962, p. 111, May 23–25, 1962, pp. 144–48, box 18, file April 12–May 27, 1962, DRC; *Hartford Times,* May 24 and 25, 1962, and *Hartford Courant,* May 25, 1962.
6. AEW, July 5, 1962, p. 187, box 18, file May 28–July 18, 1962, and August 30, 1962, p. 642, box 18, file July 19–September 5, 1962, September 4, 1962, p. 247, box 18, DRC.
7. AEW, September 24, 1962, p. 272, October 1, 1962, p.279, October 10, 1962, p. 289, box 18, file September 6–October 20, 1962, DRC; *Connecticut Daily Campus,* October 1, 1962; anecdote undated from President's Office–DiBiaggio (hereafter PODiB), box 34, file 1,162; William T. O'Hara, ed., *Fitted to the Burden: Selected Speeches of Homer Daniels Babbidge Jr.* (Storrs, Conn.: University of Connecticut Alumni Association, 1972), "The Difference Between the Good and the Great," pp. 39–44.
8. AEW, October 20, 1962, p. 300, box 18, file September 6–October 20, 1962, DRC; *Connecticut Daily Campus,* October 20, 1962; O'Hara, *Fitted to the Burden,* "Inaugural Address," pp. 17–21.
9. *Connecticut Daily Campus,* October 20, 1962; biographical sketch, "Homer D. Babbidge, Jr.," November 10, 1970, POB, box 115, file 1,739, DRC.
10. Biographical sketch, "Homer D. Babbidge, Jr." See also the review in the *Washington Star,* June 24, 1962, of Homer D. Babbidge Jr. and Robert M. Rosenzweig, *The Federal Interest in Higher Education* (New York: McGraw-Hill, 1962), POB, box 14, file 208, DRC; "From Storrs," May 1972, POB, box 162, file 2,488, DRC.

11. Babbidge's statement at budget hearing, December 7, 1962, POB, box 1, file 15, DRC; University of Connecticut Administrative Report, 1962–1963, POB, box 1, file 2, DRC.

12. AEW, October 5, 1962, p. 285, box 18, file September 5–October 20, 1962, DRC; Waugh to Babbidge, May 6, 1963, POB, box 2, file 40, DRC.

13. Statement at Budget Hearing, December 7, 1962, and Mimeograph of University of Connecticut Legislative Request, 1963–1965, POB, box 1, file 15, DRC.

14. "Library Statistics of Colleges and Universities, 1960–1961," POB, box 1, file 15, DRC.

15. AEW, October 3, 1962, p. 281, box 18, file September 6–October 20, 1962, DRC; AEW, January 21, 1963, p. 31, February 4, 1963, pp. 49–50, box 18, file January 1–February 5, 1963, DRC; AEW, February 12, 1963, pp. 59–60, box 18, file February 6–March 16, 1963, DRC; Advisory Committee on Division of the Library to Babbidge, October 10, 1962, POB, box 3, file 44 ("Skipper"), DRC; John P. McDonald to Babbidge, April 19, 1963, POB, box 3, file 44, DRC; McDonald to Babbidge, July 12, 1963, POB, box 24, file 357 ("Library"), DRC; *Hartford Times*, January 3, 1971, *Meriden Record*, January 6, 1971, *New Haven Register*, January 3, 1971, clippings, POB, box 143, file 2,167 ("Library–John McDonald"). A new addition to the Wilbur Cross Library was dedicated on October 16, 1964; see AEW, October 16, 1964, p. 300, box 18, file October 16–December 6, 1964, DRC. In 1968, McDonald was joined by Norman Stevens, who came as associate university librarian. They teamed up as the two key library administrators, and Stevens succeeded McDonald as director of university libraries when the latter retired in 1986.

16. Oral History Interview with Wilfred B. Young, January 18, 1974, pp. 107–8, COH, DRC. Young tells about how the first fight he had with the administration occurred when Babbidge arrived and said that someone in the Extension Program couldn't be a full professor because he didn't teach and do research: "He had little conception of what constituted a land grant state university. His total experience had been in a private college." Young then went on to say that he felt Babbidge's understanding improved in his later years as president; Milton R. Stern to Babbidge, January 10, 1963, and Babbidge's reply, January 21, 1963, POB, box 1, file 17, DRC.

17. "Grad Students Confront Novelists in English Seminar," *University Newsletter*, June 1963, POB, box 7, file 91 ("President's Newsletter"), DRC; conversations with Milton R. Stern and R. Kent Newmyer.

18. Press release on Wallace Stevens lecture, April 24, 1964, POB, box 30, file 438, DRC; *University of Connecticut Newsletter*, October 1963, POB, box 13, file 202, DRC; Press release, November 11, 1963, POB, box 24, file 364, DRC; Press release, March 24, 1965, POB, box 47, file 670, DRC; Press release, February 22, 1966, POB, box 58, file 908, DRC; Press clippings, November 1967, POB, box 86, file 1,314, DRC; Press release, November 15, 1968, POB, box 105, file 1598, DRC. Prior to Babbidge's arrival, McMahon lecturers included Sir John Maud, Hans Morgenthau, Henry Kissinger, John K. Fairbank, Glenn Seaborg, and Adolph Berle.

19. "Art Comes to 'The Beanery,'" *Providence Sunday Journal*, March 26, 1967, POB, box 178, file 3,116 ("Museum of Art"), DRC; press release for Sternbach and Rheaume

Architects, April 25, 1966, POB, box 56, file 869 ("Fine Arts, School of"); Nathan Knobler to Babbidge, November 30, 1966, POB, box 66, file 1,031 ("Fine Arts, School of"), DRC; Frank B. Cookson to Clark Bailey, May 25, 1967, POB, box 66, file 1,030 ("Fine Arts, School of"), DRC; "Storrs, Connecticut: Hardly a Wilderness," ECH, box 4, DRC.

20. AEW, May 23, 1963, pp. 174–75, box 18, file May 1–June 12, 1963, DRC; AEW, May 12, 1964, p. 137, box 18, file April 9–May 23, 1964, DRC.

21. AEW, May 23, 1963, pp. 175–76, box 18, file May 1–June 14, 1963, DRC.

22. AEW, May 23, 1963, pp. 177–80, box 18, file May 1–June 14, 1963, DRC.

23. Oral History Interview with John G. Rohrbach, March 22, 2004; Minutes of the Council of Deans, September 11, 1963, POB, box 19, file 202 ("Dean's Council"); press release, October 21, 1964, POB, box 45, file 615 ("Fuller, Alfred, Trustee"), DRC.

24. Press Release, October 21, 1964, POB, box 45, file 615 ("Fuller, Alfred, Trustee"), DRC; Report of the Secretary, University of Connecticut Foundation, May 24, 1965, POB, box 52, file 760 ("University Foundation"), DRC.

25. Report of the Secretary, University of Connecticut Foundation, May 24, 1965, POB, box 52, file 760 ("University Foundation"), DRC; Suggested Introduction, POB, box 61, file 940 ("University Foundation"), DRC; *The Measure of a University: A New Film in Color,* POB, box 61, file 939 ("University Foundation"); AEW, December 21, 1965, box 18, file December 20–31 1965, DRC.

26. AEW, September 12, 1966, p. 296, box 19, file August 4–September 19, 1966, DRC; Report of the Secretary, University of Connecticut Foundation, May 24, 1965, POB, box 52, file 760 ("University Foundation"), DRC; *Hartford Courant,* June 5, 1966, box 61, file 939 ("University Foundation"), DRC; Francis H. Horn to Babbidge, December 20, 1965, POB, box 56, file 866 ("Faculty Alumni Center"), DRC; Reports of the Foundation Secretary, May 15, 1967, box 74, file 1,129 ("University Foundation"), and October 25, 1969, box 134, file 2,032 ("University Foundation"), DRC.

27. Bylaws of the Faculty Club of the University of Connecticut, adopted January 11, 1965, POB, box 44, file 600(F), DRC; Oral History Interview with John G. Rohrbach, March 22, 2004; Leonard Orzech to Babbidge, October 22, 1964, POB, box 36, file 509 ("Babbidge Personal–6"), DRC.

28. Minutes of Meeting of Council of Deans, September 11, 1963, POB, box 19, file 202 ("Dean's Council"), DRC; AEW, April 24, 1964, p. 118, file April 9–May 23, 1964, and October 6 and 15, 1964, pp. 290 and 298–299, file August 28–October 15, 1964, DRC. Albert Waugh's father, who ended his career at what became the University of Massachusetts, replaced Gulley at Vermont when he came to Storrs. AEW, October 18, 1963, p. 335, December 15, 1963, p. 396, and March 28, 1964, p. 91, box 18, files September 23–November 1, 1963, November 2–December 31, 1963, and February 12–April 8, 1964; *Connecticut Daily Campus,* October 5, 1967, POB, box 173, file 2,824 ("Blue Bike Brigade"), DRC; *Hartford Times,* November 23, 1967, p. 18B, POB, box 173, file 2,824 ("Blue Bike Brigade"), DRC; *Connecticut Daily Campus,* December 16, 1969, POB, box 175, file 2,933 ("Ducks"), DRC, which describes the problems

caused by the proliferation of the ducks, the propensity of people to feed them, and the effect of winter weather.

29. AEW, September 24, 1964, p. 284, and March 19, 1965, p. 90, box 18, files August 28–October 15, 1964, and February 12–March 29, 1965, DRC. While usually very approving of Babbidge, Waugh complained that on his final day as provost, the president read his mail most of the time that Waugh tried to talk to him. This was a "bad habit" Waugh had also noted earlier. See AEW, June 30, 1965, pp. 212–13, box 18, file June 18–July 31, 1965, DRC; "Chronology: The Babbidge Years," supplement to *From Storrs,* May 1972, POB, box 162, file 2,488 ("Resignation—Printed Material"), DRC.

30. "Wrong Way Babbidge" and "A Warm Athletic Supporter," PODiB, box 34, file 1,162 ("Babbidge, Homer"), DRC. For Babbidge's relationship to Gov. John Dempsey, see Oral History Interview with Kenneth G. Wilson, COH, DRC, January 4, 1982, p. 42.

31. Athletic Overview by Tim Tolokan, in possession of the author; AEW, September 25, 1965, pp. 313–14, box 18, file September 16–October 20, 1965, DRC.

32. AEW, January 14, 1963, pp. 18–20, January 24, 1963, p. 37, box 18, file January 1–February 5, 1963, DRC.

33. AEW, March 9, 1964, p. 73, box 18, file February 12–April 8, 1964, DRC; AEW, March 9, 1965, pp. 76–77, box 18, file 12, February 12–March 29, 1965, DRC; Tim Tolokan, "University of Connecticut Men's Basketball Historical Timeline," in possession of the author; "Shabel Was Abel," *Hartford Courant,* December 4, 2003; AEW, February 4, 1967, p. 54, box 19, file February 2–March 12, 1967, DRC.

34. O'Hara, *Fitted to the Burden,* p. 66; University Senate Committee on General Scholastic Requirements, "Intercollegiate Athletics and Academic Standards," March 8, 1965, POB, box 52, file 768 ("University Senate"), DRC; Minutes of the Adjourned Meeting of the University Senate, March 15, 1965, p. 171, POB, box 52, file 768 ("University Senate"), DRC; AEW, March 5, 1965, p. 73, box 18, file February 12–March 29, 1965, DRC.

35. Minutes, Athletic Advisory Committee, February 19, 1970, POB, box 173, file 2,784 ("Athletics Advisory Committee"), DRC; Alan J. Barth to Babbidge, March 25, 1971, POB, box 147, file 2,243 ("Student Senate"), DRC; Mark J. Roy, *University of Connecticut* (Charleston, S.C.: Arcadia, 2001), 53–55 and 102 (tri-corner hats).

36. Elizabeth T. Noftsker to Mr. Goodale, October 4, 1962, and notice to "All Women Students, Fall, 1962," POB, box 4, file 59(N), DRC. For the changing cultural attitudes of the 1960s, see, for example, Alexander Bloom and Wini Breines, eds., *"Takin' It to the Streets": A Sixties Reader* (New York: Oxford University Press, 1995).

37. Oscar Fox to Babbidge, June 29, 1964, POB, box 34, file 490 ("Young, W. B., Dean College of Agriculture"), DRC; *Connecticut Daily Campus,* October 21, 1965, POB, box 177, file 3,077 ("Liquor"), DRC.

38. AEW, March 24, 1965, pp. 95–96, box 18, file February 12–March 29, 1965, DRC; *Connecticut Daily Campus,* February 17, 1966, POB, box 177, file 3,093 ("Marijuana and LSD"), DRC; V. S. Comella to Brian Klitz, Security Report on Drug Abuse, July 14, 1971, POB, box 154, file 2,530 ("Drugs"), DRC.

39. "Confidential Memorandum to the Board of Trustees," March 25, 1966, POB, box 38, file 527 ("Board of Trustees"), DRC.

40. Undated press release, "September," and excerpts from reports, POB, box 80, file 1,202 ("Committee—Conditions of Student Life"), DRC; Student Life Recommendations, October 18 (?), 1967, POB, box 180, file 3,275 ("Student Life Committee"), DRC; AEW, December 29, 1969, p. 542, box 19, file December 5–31, 1969, DRC.

41. W. J. Rorabaugh, *Berkeley at War: The 1960s* (New York: Oxford University Press, 1989), ix; Todd Gitlin, *The Sixties: Years of Hope, Days of Rage* (New York: Bantam Books, 1987), 241, 306–9; Mark Kurlansky, *1968: The Year That Rocked the World* (New York: Ballantine Books, 2004), 192–208; Robert A. McCaughey, *Stand Columbia: A History of Columbia University in the City of New York* (New York: Columbia University Press, 2003), 423–61; *Chronicle of Higher Education,* November 25, 1968. President Richard M. Nixon appointed a Commission on Campus Unrest. Its report, known as the Scranton Report after commission chair William W. Scranton, explores the development of, and causes for, student unrest. Sections of it were published in the *Chronicle of Higher Education,* October 5, 1970.

42. *Connecticut Daily Campus,* September 22, 1967.

43. *Connecticut Daily Campus,* October 3, 6, 1967.

44. *Connecticut Daily Campus,* November 1, 1967; AEW, November 1, 1967, box 19, file October 30–November 30, 1967, DRC; at its national convention in July 1967 the SDS decided to direct its efforts toward reducing military involvement on university campuses. The UConn demonstration was in alignment with this decision. See *Connecticut Daily Campus,* November 8, 1967.

45. *Connecticut Daily Campus,* November 2, 3, 1967, POB, box 167, file 2,655 ("Dow Chemical Documents 1967"), DRC; Alumni Council Resolution, November 6, 1967, which included a chronology of events, pp. 1–6, POB, box 89, file 1,351 ("Recruitment Policy"), DRC.

46. Alumni Council Resolution, November 6, 1967, pp. 1, 6–8; *Connecticut Daily Campus,* November 8, 1967.

47. Alumni Council Resolution, November 6, 1967, pp. 8–11; Report of the Select Faculty Committee of the University Senate, November 13, 1967, POB, box 89, file 1,351 ("Recruitment Policy"), DRC; *Hartford Times,* November 14, 1967, POB, box 167, file 2,655 ("Dow Chemical Documents 1967"), DRC.

48. Connecticut Resistance Movement, November 8, 1967, Babbidge to the Board of Trustees, November 10, 1967, and "A Dissenting Faculty Member" to Babbidge and the Board of Regents [*sic*], November 17, 1967, POB, box 89, file 1,351 ("Recruiting Policy"), DRC; *Connecticut Daily Campus,* November 8, 16, 1967.

49. *Connecticut Daily Campus,* November 12, 14, December 11, 1967; *Hartford Times,* December 9, 1967; The New Haven Police Department's version of events can be found in the *Connecticut Daily Campus,* February 7, 1968.

50. *Hartford Times,* December 14, 1967, POB, box 167, file 2,655 ("Dow Chemical Documents, 1967"), DRC; *Connecticut Daily Campus,* December 15, 1967.

51. A Resolution Condemning the Punitive Use of Selective Service in the Case of J. David Colfax; Telegram, Babbidge to Lewis B. Hershey, May 2, 1968; Concerned Faculty to Colfax, Senate, and Babbidge, May 3, 1968; *Hartford Times,* May 3, 1968; all in POB, box 79, file 1,193 ("Colfax Statement"), DRC.

52. Anonymous report of SDS meeting of September 17, 1968, POB, box 108, file 1,699 ("Recruitment Policy"), DRC. It would appear that the report was written for the administration by an observer or "infiltrator."

53. "State of the University," September 30, 1968, POB, box 108, file 1,644 ("Recruitment Policy"), DRC.

54. *Connecticut Daily Campus,* October 29, 30, 31, 1968.

55. *Connecticut Daily Campus,* October 31, 1968.

56. Ibid.; Statement of Homer D. Babbidge Jr., October 30, 1968, POB, box 166, file 2,624 ("Babbidge Statement, 10/30/68"), DRC.

57. "Chronology: The Babbidge Years," supplement to *From Storrs,* May 1972, POB, box 162, file 2,488 ("Resignation Printed Material"), DRC; *The President's Newsletter* 7, no. 4 (November 5, 1968), POB, box 167, file 2,655 ("Dow Chemical, Documents 1967"), DRC; *Connecticut Daily Campus,* November 7, 11, 12, 1968.

58. Statements by Gant and Babbidge, November 12, 1968, Statement by Leo Mulcahy, POB, box 167, file 2,660 ("Dow Chemical Statements, 1968"), DRC; *Connecticut Daily Campus,* November 13, 1968.

59. *Connecticut Daily Campus,* November 13, 1968.

60. *Connecticut Daily Campus,* November 15, 1968; "Chronology: The Babbidge Years," supplement to *From Storrs,* May 1972, p. S6, POB, box 162, file 2,488 ("Resignation Printed Material"), DRC.

61. Flyer, POB, box 108, file 1,644 ("Recruitment Policy"), DRC.

62. Provost's summary of events of November 25–26 and president's statement of November 26, 1968, POB, box 140, file 2,132 ("Gant, Edward V."), DRC; Report of the Committee on Recruitment and Placement, November 22, 1968, POB, box 112, file 1,694.6 ("Extra—University Senate"), DRC.

63. Provost's Statement to Students and Faculty, POB, box 140, file 2,132 ("Gant, Edward V."), DRC; Report of the Committee of Five, December 22, 1968, POB, box 108, file 1,642 ("Recruitment Policy"), DRC; *Hartford Times,* November 26, 1968; *Hartford Courant,* November 27, 1968. An SDS spokesman contradicted many of the points about the incident made by the provost. For instance, he claimed that the injured security officer was hit by another officer's riot stick, not by something thrown at him by a demonstrator. He denied that the student interviewee who tried to enter the building on Gilbert Road was "tackled" by demonstrators and claimed he was struck down by security officers. He also contended that the reading of the riot act was inaudible and that the arrests were directed by Dean Hewes, who was carrying a "list." SDS leaders termed the arrests a "purge," an attempt to rid the campus of radical leaders. See *Connecticut Daily Campus,* December 4, 1968; on Emanuel Margolis, see *Willimantic Chronicle,* March 5, 1969, EHC, box 6, DRC.

64. *Hartford Times,* November 26, 1968; *Hartford Courant,* November 27, 1968; *Connecticut Daily Campus,* December 4, 1968; for the events of 1968, see note 41.

65. *Hartford Courant,* December 18, 1968; Kenneth G. Wilson to Edward Gant, December 2, 3, 5, 1968, POB, box 100, file 1,645 ("Recruitment Policy"), DRC.

66. Statement from Professor Leggett dictated to the *Hartford Times,* January 22, 1969, POB, box 108, file 1,642 ("Recruiting Policy"), DRC. For the Federation of University Teachers critique of the disciplinary procedural safeguards, see "To the Faculty— A Statement of Concern," January 1969, POB, box 167, file 2,664 ("Federation of University Teachers"), DRC, and Anita D. Fritz, federation president, to Babbidge, January 10, 1969, POB, box 108, file 1,642 ("Recruitment Policy"), DRC.

67. Minutes of the special meeting of the Board of Trustees, January 25, 1969, POB, box 166, file 2,636 ("Budds, John J.—Statement, Special BOT Meeting, January 25, 1969"), DRC.

68. "What Ever Happened to the Facts? Annotated Chronology," POB, box 109, file 1,648 ("Recruitment Policy"), DRC; Jack L. Roach to Babbidge, January 29, 1969, POB, box 109, file 1,647 ("Recruitment Policy"), DRC; No. 12395, State of Connecticut v. Jack L. Roach, Superior Court, Tolland County, February 5, 1969, and *Hartford Times,* May 26, 1969, POB, box 168, file 2,693 ("Roach, Jack"), DRC.

69. *The Husky Handjob* 1, no.1 (February 23, 1969), EHC, box 6, DRC; *The Husky Handjob* 1, no. 2 (March 3, 1969), EHC, box 4 (?), DRC.

70. *Connecticut Daily Campus,* March 4, 1969.

71. *Connecticut Daily Campus,* March 20, 1969 (the board of trustees minutes for March 19, 1969, reveal nothing of the turmoil that occurred, except that Larry Smyle and Howard Reed were invited to speak to the board. It lists who received tenure, promotion, and reappointment, but not who had been refused); "Join the Finger In," POB, box 168, file 2,694 ("SDS Complaints"), DRC. While the Department of Sociology and Anthropology committee had recommended tenure for Colfax, in January at least one senior professor in the department vehemently disagreed, seeing the "democratic" committee as an attack on the department's legitimate structure. See Floyd W. Dotson to Dean Kenneth G. Wilson, January 7, 1969, POB, box 109, file 1,649 ("Recruitment Policy"), DRC.

72. *Connecticut Daily Campus,* March 25, 26, 1969; Colfax to Members of the University of Connecticut Community, March 23, 1969, POB, box 109, file 1,648 ("Recruitment Policy"), DRC; Evan Hill, "The Revolution (Cont.): At the University of Connecticut," *New York Times Magazine,* February 23, 1969.

73. Memo of the Strike Committee on Commencement, POB, box 117, file 1,772 ("Commencement"), DRC; "Chronology: The Babbidge Years," supplement to *From Storrs,* May 1972, POB, box 162, file 2,488 ("Resignation Printed Material"), DRC.

74. "Chronology: The Babbidge Years," supplement to *From Storrs,* May 1972, POB, box 162, file 2,488 ("Resignation Printed Material"), DRC.

75. *Connecticut Daily Campus,* September 22, 26, 29, October 4, 6, 1969; University Senate Resolution, Office of the Provost, October 7, 1969, POB, box 128, file 1,938 ("Mora-

torium, October 15, 1969"), DRC; *The President's Newsletter* (October 9, 1969), POB, box 130, file 1,973 ("President's Newsletter"), DRC; Schedule of Events, October 15, 1969, POB, box 128, file 1,938 ("Moratorium, October 15, 1969"), DRC; *New Haven Register,* New England Newsclip stamp, October 31, 1969, POB, box 117, file 1,767 ("Clippings"), DRC. The evening before the events of October 15, Rennie Davis, one of the "Chicago Seven" defendants who had been tried for fomenting disorder at the 1968 Democratic National Convention, and Doug Miranda, a leader of the Black Panthers, spoke to an audience of two thousand at the Jorgensen Auditorium. See *Hartford Times,* October 15, 1969. President Babbidge returned from his sabbatical early because of a racial incident on October 9, 1969, that will be discussed subsequently. The unity that developed on October 15 coalesced around the antiwar issue, while racial matters were instead becoming increasingly sensitive.

76. *New Haven Register* and *Milford Citizen,* December 16, 1969, POB, box 117, file 1,767 ("Clippings"), DRC; editorial, *Hartford Courant,* December 17, 1969, POB, box 167, file 2,667 ("General Electric Interviews, December 15, 1969"), DRC; *Connecticut Daily Campus,* February 4, 1970; for a description of events concerning the GE demonstration and identification of those involved, see the Affadavit of John J. Manning, Associate Dean of Students, December 22, 1969, POB, box 166, file 2,639 ("Campus Disorders"), DRC.

77. Strike Chronology, May 1970, POB, box 116, file 1,752 ("Board of Trustees"), DRC. This was issued by the board of trustees and includes the key documents related to the strike. For another perspective, see the *Connecticut Daily Campus,* May 6, 1970, and the *Hartford Times,* May 6, 1970.

78. Strike Chronology, May 1970, POB, box 116, file 1,752 ("Board of Trustees"), DRC.

79. Ibid.; *Connecticut Daily Campus,* May 8, 1970.

80. Strike Chronology; *Connecticut Daily Campus,* May 9, 1970.

81. Strike Chronology; *Connecticut Daily Campus,* May 11, 1970.

82. Strike Chronology; in April 1972 students again marched on the ROTC hangar. See *Connecticut Daily Campus,* April 20, 1972.

83. Strike Chronology; see document J; author's conversation with Elliot Wolk, May 12, 2004.

84. Student Senate Press Release, POB, box 173, file 2,783 ("Associated Student Government"), DRC; Student Senate Resolution, box 168, file 2,706 ("Strike Material June 1970"), DRC.

85. John F. Kennedy to John J. Budds, July 12, 1963, and Budds to Kennedy, July 24, 1963, POB, box 15, file 229 ("Budds"), DRC.

86. Dictated version of *New York Times* article of October 5, 1963, POB, box 17, file 249 ("Comm. on Higher Education"), DRC; Minutes of Meeting of Council of Deans, December 4, 1963, POB, box 19, file 282 ("Dean's Council"), DRC; Robert M. Rosenzweig to Babbidge, December 4, 1964 and Babbidge to Rosenzweig, December 28, 1964, POB, box 36, file 505 ("Babbidge Personal 1"), DRC. In June 1966 an Equal Employment Opportunity report showed that of 2,418 employees, only twenty-one were

"Negro," twelve men and nine women; nine employees, four men and five women, were listed in the professional (including technicians) category, which totaled 1,290 people. See POB, box 68, unnumbered K file ("K" for H. J. Kammer, director of Personnel Services), DRC. When the Atomic Energy Commission raised issues of "affirmative action" in 1967, Kammer indicated surprise at the "inordinate attention being paid to the University of Connecticut" and explained that the surrounding labor market also had a very small percentage of non-whites.

87. *Connecticut Daily Campus,* February 10, 1967; Gwendolyn Sebastian to Babbidge, April 27, 1967, with the conference program and statement of objectives, POB, box 71, file 1,088 ("Organization of Afro-American Students"), DRC.

88. Ronald Lanier to Babbidge, April 20, 1968, POB, box 78, file 1,177 ("Board of Trustees"), DRC; *Connecticut Daily Campus,* April 17, 18, 1968; "The President's Newsletter," April 18, 1968, POB, box 88, file 1,343 ("President's Newsletter"), DRC; Resolution on Human Rights and Opportunities Adopted by the Board of Trustees of the University of Connecticut, April 17, 1968, POB, box 175, file 2,908 ("Council on Human Rights and Opportunities"), DRC. The board also asked that requests for student leaves of absence to participate in community action programs be received sympathetically by appropriate university officials and honored when feasible.

89. Press release, September 15, 1968, and "The Urban Semester," October 9, 1968, POB, box 112, file 1,699 ("Urban Semester"), DRC; press release, June 27, 1969, and "Proposal for the Establishment of a Center for Black Studies," March 28, 1969, POB, box 96, file 1,467 ("Center for Black Studies"), DRC.

90. "A Memorandum of Necessary Changes at the University of Connecticut," December 13, 1968, POB, box 130, file 1,957 ("Organization of Afro-American Students"), DRC; Transcript of Babbidge Interview with Mike Whalen, pp. 41–42, POB, box 81, file 1,232 ("Daily Campus"), DRC; Babbidge to Enamidem Ubok-Udom, Chairman, OAAS Committee on Necessary Changes, June 4, 1969, POB, box 106, file 1,620 ("Organization of Afro-American Students"), DRC; OAAS Committee on Necessary Changes to Babbidge, July 8, 1969, POB, box 130, file 1,957 ("Organization of Afro-American Students"), DRC.

91. University Council on Human Rights and Opportunities Report to the Board of Trustees, April 16, 1969, POB, box 99, file 1,514 ("Council of Human Rights and Opportunities"), DRC; *Connecticut Daily Campus,* March 25, 1969; The Committee Formed to Investigate the Possibility of Racial Discrimination at the University of Connecticut to Babbidge, June 5, 1969, and Report of June 3, 1969. Norman Davis, Joseph N. Grant (chair), Rev. Joseph Quinn, Morton Tenzer, and Clarence Williams comprised the committee, with Steve Abramson of the Department of Men's Affairs serving as a consultant.

92. Summary Information on Six Incidents of Disruption on the University of Connecticut Campus during Academic Year 1969–70, Attachment B, POB, box 137, file 2,079 ("Campus Disorders"), DRC; *Connecticut Daily Campus,* October 10, 1969.

93. *Connecticut Daily Campus,* October 10, 1969; "Statement of Homer D. Babbidge, Jr.,

October 10, 1969," and "Statement of the Board of Trustees, Executive Session, October 12, 1969," in *The President's Newsletter* 8, no. 3 (October 13, 1969), POB, box 130, file 1,973 ("President's Newsletter").

94. *Connecticut Daily Campus,* October 15, 16, 1969; "Report of Investigation and Recommendation of the Ombudsman: Case No. 1015 Sousa House, POB, box 168, file 2,699 ("Sousa House Incident"), DRC.

95. Report of Investigation and Recommendation of the Ombudsman: Case No. 1015 Sousa House, POB, box 168, file 2,699 ("Sousa House Incident"), DRC; *Hartford Times,* April 21, 1970, POB, box 167, file 2,651 ("Disturbances on Campus"), DRC; "Summary Information on Six Incidents of Disruption on the University of Connecticut Campus during Academic Year 1969–1970," Attachment B, POB, box 137, file 2,079 ("Campus Disorders"), DRC. On May 6 a Metanoia took place on the topic of racial respect, just prior to the Cambodia–Kent State Strike of the next day. See POB, box 128, file 1,935 ("Metanoia"), DRC. The May 13 Gulley Hall occupation had both antiwar and racial overtones. The Black Student Union sought amnesty for the black students believed to be singled out by the dean of students during the class exam disruption of that day.

96. Neil Olcott to Senator Abraham Ribicoff, March 6, 1970, with appended petition to U.S. Commissioner of Education; Ribicoff to Babbidge, March 13, 1970; Babbidge to Ribicoff, April 1970; all in POB, box 128, file 1,923 ("Legislation-Federal"), DRC.

97. Oral History Interviews with Elizabeth "Betty" Roper, August 20, 1997, and Susan Weldon, August 11, 1997, Women's Center Oral History Project, Center for Oral History (hereafter COH), DRC. These interviews are among the few in the COH collection that are not transcribed. *Connecticut Daily Campus,* March 9, 1966; "The Women's Center: Herstory," January 1983, in Women's Center Oral History Project.

98. *Connecticut Daily Campus,* May 4, 1970.

99. *Connecticut Daily Campus,* September 29, 1970; *Hartford Courant,* June 18, 1970, POB, box 178, file 3,152.5 (extra), DRC.

100. *Hartford Courant,* June 18, 1970, POB, box 178, file 3,152.5 (extra), DRC; *Connecticut Daily Campus,* November 13, 1970.

101. Claire M. Berg to Babbidge, box 165, file 2,514 ("Women"), DRC.

102. Ibid.; *Connecticut Daily Campus,* February 16, 1972.

103. Berg to Babbidge, March 29, 1972, and News Release, May 5, 1972, POB, box 165, file 2,514 ("Women"), DRC; University Senate Faculty Standards Committee—A Report on the Status of Faculty and Professional Women, May 11, 1972, POB, box 165, file 2,514 ("Women"), DRC; The Women's Center Herstory, January 1983, Women's Center Oral History Project, DRC. Title VII of the Civil Rights Act of 1964 prohibited discrimination in employment on the basis of race, color, religion, national origin, or sex. The Women's Equity Action League used it to lodge sex discrimination charges against universities. As a consequence, the Department of Health, Education, and Welfare began investigations and insisted on the filing of affirmative action plans. Executive Order 11246 required any company doing business or holding

federal contracts with the government to rectify sex discrimination in its hiring and employment practices. At UConn there were 2,438 fulltime faculty and professionals, of whom 394, or 16.1 percent, were women in 1972; the national average was 20 percent. Few women filled administrative positions, except in divisions traditionally associated with women, such as home economics, nursing, or physical therapy. Only one woman held a university-level administrative position. See the University Senate status report cited above.

104. Babbidge to Gordon Tasker, October 1, 1971, POB, box 163, file unnumbered ("Tasker, Gordon W., Trustee"), DRC; "A Campus Revolt," undated, POB, box 178, file 3,138 ("NET Show—letters regarding it"). This comment was made during Babbidge's discussion of the film "The Diary of a Campus Revolt," made at the University of Connecticut by National Educational Television (NET) in December 1968, at the time of the Dow Chemical recruiting protests. Two camera crews came to campus. One followed Babbidge, the other the protestors.

105. Petition distributed by Associated Student Government, October 4, 1971, POB, box 162, file unnumbered ("Resignation—Student Petition, October 4, 1971"), DRC; AEW, May 14, 1971; "Chronology: The Babbidge Years," supplement to *From Storrs,* May 1972; POB, box 162, file 2,488 ("Resignation—Printed Material"), DRC; *Connecticut Daily Campus,* January 3, 1963. In-state tuition of $350 and out-of-state tuition of $850, effective the spring semester of 1972, moved UConn from seventy-seventh to thirteenth most expensive among one hundred state universities and land-grant colleges in the nation; Oral History Interview with John G. Rohrbach, March 22, 2004, p. 34, COH, DRC.

106. Remarks of Homer D. Babbidge, Jr., University of Connecticut Foundation Dinner, April 12, 1972, POB, box 150, file 2,284 ("Babbidge, Homer D.—Biogaphical Information"), DRC; "Chronology: The Babbidge Years," supplement to *From Storrs,* May 1972, POB, box 162, file 2,488 ("Resignation—Printed Material"), DRC; *The Day,* New London, Conn., March 28, 1984; John P. McDonald, Director of University Libraries, Letter to the Editor, *Hartford Courant,* April 23, 1984, EHC, box 6, Babbidge file, DRC. The Babbidge Library's electronic catalogue is appropriately named Homer.

Chapter 5. Holding Its Own—UConn's Years of Consolidation: 1973–90 (pp. 159–211)

1. For Alvin Liberman's election to the National Academy of Sciences, see President's Office–Ferguson (hereafter POF), box 21, file 746, DRC; Ferguson's comment in POF, box 21, file 741 ("Press Releases, G.W.F."), DRC.

2. John W. Vlandis to Babbidge, April 10, 1972, with undated news clipping; and Press Release, April 12, 1972, POB, box 150, file 2,300 ("Campus Community Carnival"), DRC; clipping, *Hartford Courant,* May 24, 1972, POB, box 155, file 2,375 ("Gant,

Edward V., Provost"), DRC; *Hartford Courant,* May 2, 1973, POF, box 8, file 332 ("Ferguson's Appointment"), DRC.

3.   *Connecticut Daily Campus,* October 4, 1972; *Hartford Courant,* May 2, 3, 1973, POF, box 8, file 332 ("Ferguson's Appointment"), DRC; *New Haven Register,* May 6, 1973, POF, box 8, file 332 ("Ferguson's Appointment"), DRC.

4.   *Hartford Courant,* May 2, 3, 1973, POF, box 8, file 332 ("Ferguson's Appointment"), DRC; Interview with Kenneth G. Wilson, January 4, 1982, pp. 45–49, Center for Oral History Collection, DRC.

5.   UCPEA Newsletter, October 1972, POF, box 7, file 268 ("Professional Employee Association"), DRC.

6.   FUT Newsletter, September 1973, with attachments, POF, box 4, file 206 ("Federation of University Teachers"), DRC.

7.   "Prospects for Collective Bargaining and a Proposal for Action," undated AAUP statement, POF, box 3, file 155 ("AAUP"), DRC. This document in the president's files is marked, in handwriting, "Excellent. It's time the AAUP took the lead in this matter."

8.   Ibid.; A. T. DiBenedetto to Ferguson, November 18, 1974, POF, box 11, file 398 ("AAUP"), DRC.

9.   Faculty Standards Committee Report on Collective Bargaining, December 9, 1974, POF, box 14, file 497 ("Collective Bargaining"), DRC.

10.   *AAUP Newsletter,* April, 1975, POF, box 11, file 398 ("AAUP"), DRC; *AAUP Newsletter,* February 18, 23, 27, 1976, POF, box 14, file 498 ("Collective Bargaining"), DRC; *FUT Newsletter,* February 23, 25, March 4, 1976, POF, box 14, file 501 ("Collective Bargaining"), DRC. While the inclusion of the librarians was the key sticking point, the administration on February 9, 1976, agreed to drop its original objection to including department heads and county extension agents in the units. The administration initially claimed that department heads were administrators rather than faculty. The AAUP and FUT, on the other hand, agreed to drop their insistence on the inclusion of special payroll lecturers.

11.   *AAUP Newsletter,* February 27, 1976, POF, box 14, file 498 ("Collective Bargaining"), DRC. In 1971–72 dollars, corrected for inflation, the budget went from $42.5 million in 1971–72 to $50.6 million in 1975–76; see the statements on collective bargaining presented to the University Senate (FUT by Elliot Wolk; AAUP by William Rosen, Anthony DiBenedetto, and Emiliana Noether), March 29, 1976, POF, box 14, file 496 ("Collective Bargaining"), DRC.

12.   Statements on collective bargaining presented to the University Senate, March 29, 1976, POF, box 14, file 496 ("Collective Bargaining"), DRC; *AAUP Newsletter,* March 22, 1976, POF, box 11, file 398 ("AAUP"), DRC; AAUP statement on "A Visualization of How Collective Bargaining Will Work at the University of Connecticut," POF, box 31, file 1,042 ("Collective Bargaining"), DRC.

13.   Joseph Cusker to Presidents, Land Grant Universities of New England, April 14, 1976, PODiB, box 33, unnumbered file ("NELGU Council of Presidents Joint Operations Committee, January–June 1976"), DRC; Board of Trustees Minutes, June 11, 1976,

PODiB, box 8, file 161 ("Collective Bargaining"), DRC. In November 1976, non-teaching professionals selected UCPEA as their bargaining agent and became a unit that included the librarians. See Office for the Vice President of Academic Affairs, Collective Bargaining Status Report #1, November 19, 1976, POF, box 14, file 496 ("Collective Bargaining"), DRC. It should be noted that this book's author was president of the FUT during this period.

14. *FUT Newsletter,* 9/76, received in President's Office, September 27, 1976, POF, box 14, file 501 ("Collective Bargaining"), DRC; Board of Trustees Minutes, September 10, 1976, p. 6,173, PODiB, box 8, file 161 ("Collective Bargaining"), DRC; *AAUP Newsletter,* received in the Vice-President for Academic Affairs Office on March 3, 1977, POF, box 13, file 495 ("Collective Bargaining"), DRC.

15. *AAUP Newsletter,* received in the Vice-President for Academic Affairs Office on March 3, 1977, AAUP News Report, March 4, 1977, and Collective Bargaining Council to Kenneth G. Wilson, February 23, 1977, POF, box 13, file 495 ("Collective Bargaining"), DRC; *Connecticut Daily Campus,* March 3, 1977.

16. Interview with Kenneth G. Wilson, January 4, 1982, pp. 63–66, COH, DRC; Kenneth G. Wilson to AAUP Collective Bargaining Council, March 4, 1977, and Joan T. Geetter to Members of the Faculty Unit, March 4, 23, 1977, POF, box 13, file 495 ("Collective Bargaining"), DRC; Interview with Joan Geetter, October 1, 1997, passim, COH, DRC.

17. Interview with Anthony T. DiBenedetto, August 6, 1997, pp. 12–13; Interview with William Rosen, July 14, 1997, pp. 23–27, COH, DRC.

18. Interview with William Rosen, July 14, 1997, pp. 27–29; Interview with Anthony T. DiBenedetto, August 6, 1997, p. 13, COH, DRC; for the contract see Agreement Between the University of Connecticut and the University of Connecticut Chapter of the American Association of University Professors, July 1, 1977–June 30, 1979, POF, box 14, file 498 ("Collective Bargaining"), DRC.

19. Interview with Philip E. Austin, August 9, 2002, p. 22 (first draft); Interview with Anthony T. DiBenedetto, August 6, 1997, pp. 15–16; Interview with William Rosen, July 14, 1997, pp. 25–26, COH, DRC; *Chronicle of Higher Education,* June 9, 1975, April 23, 1986, April 12, 1996.

20. Coalition Flyers and Statement, March 1974, and Ferguson to the Faculty, Students, and Staff, "Response to the Demands of 'The Coalition,'" March 29, 1974, POF, box 6, file 237 ("Mass., University of—Collective Bargaining"), DRC. According to the "Response" document, the Coalition was composed of the following groups: Anthropologists for Radical Political Action; Attica Brigade; Committee Against Racism; Committee to Stop Cut-Backs; FSSO Central Committee; FSSO Chairperson's Office; Inner College; New Vocations Center; Political Collective of the Women's Center; Puerto Rican Student Movement; SDS; and the Women's Radical Union. The Coalition's publication, *Forward Motion,* April 1974, lists the UConn Gay Alliance, the Political Collective of the UConn Cooperative Buyers Club, and the Anthropology Club also as members. See POF, box 6, file 237 ("Mass., University of—Collective Bargaining"), DRC.

21. *Forward Motion,* April 1974, box 6, file 237 ("Mass., University of—Collective Bargaining"), DRC; Ferguson to Faculty, Students, and Staff, "Response to the Demands of 'The Coalition,'" March 29, 1974, box 6, file 237 ("Mass., University of—Collective Bargaining"), DRC.

22. *Forward Motion,* May 1974, in possession of the author, and College of Liberal Arts and Sciences, Special Committee on Demands, Report: October 1, 1974, p. 4, POF, box 20, file 681 ("Library Sit-In"), DRC; Board of Trustees Minutes, April 19, 1974, p. 5,489, DRC. Strong impetus for the Coop came from "radical" philosophy professor Len Krimmerman, who drafted a blueprint for how it would function. See Krimmerman et al., Bookstore Proposal, March 4, 1974, POF, box 3, file 175 ("Bookstore"), DRC. Ironically, once in operation, the Coop itself would become the object of a protest when it was decided to site it on the Hawley Armory Field. One argument against that choice contended that building on the field would harm women's athletics when Title IX should be enforced. See Peter Ellner to Edward V. Gant, November 14, 1978, and Joyce Mordenti to John Bynoe, November 15, 1978, POF, box 15, file 539 ("Co-op"), DRC.

23. Report to the Faculty of the College of Liberal Arts and Sciences from the Faculty Committee to Investigate the Reorganization of the Department of Anthropology, September 18, 1974, POF, box 11, file 400 ("Anthropology"), DRC.

24. Ibid.

25. Ibid.; Benson Ginsburg and William Laughlin to Ferguson, October 1, 1973, POF, box 30, file 1,009 ("Biobehavioral Sciences, Department of"), DRC. The University Senate took six weeks of debate to pass an amended resolution by Professor John C. Greene on academic freedom arising out of the Laughlin-Ginsburg situation. See the *University of Connecticut Chronicle,* May 3, 1973, and *Challenge,* April 19, 1973, POF, box 7, file 272 ("Racism"), DRC; also see Attachment #63, Communication to the University Senate Concerning the Subject of Racism, April 19, 1973, signed by forty-eight faculty members.

26. Report to the Faculty of the College of Liberal Arts and Sciences from the Faculty Committee to Investigate the Reorganization of the Department of Anthropology, September 18, 1974, POF, box 11, file 400 ("Anthropology"), DRC; Jean S. Aigner to Ferguson, April 30, 1974, flyer, "The Attack on Anthropology at U. Conn: The Issue Is Racism" circulated at Clark University at the Northeast Anthropological Association, April 27, 1974, POF, box 7, file 272 ("Racism"), DRC; Ferguson to the Faculty, Students, and Staff, "Response to the Demands of 'The Coalition,'" March 29, 1974, POF, box 6, file 237 ("Mass., University of—Collective Bargaining"), DRC; Board of Trustees Minutes, March 15, 1974, p. 5,465, DRC.

27. Ferguson to the Faculty, Students, and Staff, "Response to the Demands of 'The Coalition,'" March 29, 1974, POF, box 6, file 237 ("Mass., University of—Collective Bargaining"), DRC; Julius Elias to Faculty of the College (of Liberal Arts and Sciences), Report on Anthropology, December 2, 1975, POF, box 11, file 400 ("Anthropology"), DRC.

28. John G. Bynoe, Regional Civil Rights Director, Office for Civil Rights, Department

of Health, Education, and Welfare, to Edward V. Gant, November 2, 1972, and attached Report of Findings for the University of Connecticut at Storrs, POF, box 4, file 184 ("Commission on Human Rights and Opportunities"), DRC. This report covered only the Storrs campus. On January 19, 1973, the Federal Office of Contract Compliance removed the exemption originally afforded public universities under Executive Order 11246. See Bynoe to Gant, April 3, 1973, POF, box 1, file 5 ("Affirmative Action Plan"), DRC.

29. Bynoe to Gant, April 3, 1973, POF, box 1, file 5 ("Affirmative Action Plan"); *Connecticut Daily Campus,* April 13, 1973, POF, box 34, file 1,252 ("Kitty Hawk Unlimited"), DRC; Office for Civil Rights, March 12, 1974, Report of Findings and Recommendations, Complaint No. I-HEIV-31, Filed by Willie J. Hagan (KHU), and letters Bynoe to Ferguson, March 8, 20, 1974, POF, box 3, file 149 ("Affirmative Action Plan"), DRC. At the end of 1976, Bynoe wrote to Ferguson that the university had been responsive to the recommendations made by the federal agency and was "currently in compliance with Title VI of the Civil Rights Act of 1964." See Bynoe to Ferguson, December 15, 1976, POF, box 10, file 371 ("Affirmative Action/Brubaker/Kitty Hawk Utd."), DRC. A number of years later, Hagan became an administrator at UConn and then at the California State University, Fullerton.

30. The University of Connecticut Organization of Faculty and Professional Women, "On the Status of Faculty and Professional Women at the University of Connecticut," March 1972, POF, box 4, file 189 ("Commission on Human Rights and Opportunities"), DRC; *Connecticut Daily Campus,* May 8, 1972. As a precursor of the future problems, board of trustees chair Gordon Tasker voted against Shea's appointment. See Board of Trustees Minutes, May 17, 1972, p. 4,875, DRC.

31. *Connecticut Daily Campus,* May 8, 1972.

32. Announcement of Gail Shea Legal Defense Fund, POF, box 8, file 312 ("Women's Council"), DRC; Robert L. Hirtle Jr. to Gordon W. Tasker, June 13, 1973, POF, box 2, file 131 ("Gail Shea"), DRC; Babbidge Deposition Received in President's Office, July 13, 1973, and Babbidge remarks on *Face the State* television program, September 2, 1973, POF, box 34, file 1,261 ("Legal Matters"), DRC; Board of Trustees Minutes, June 20, 1973, p. 5,230, DRC.

33. "Tenure Denied," EHC, box 6, file "The Trouble Years: 1960–70s," DRC; *Connecticut Daily Campus,* February 22, 1973, September 18, 1974. The Lieberman case trial did not conclude until May 1978 and judgment was rendered for the university in June 1979. The U.S. Court of Appeals for the Second Circuit affirmed the judgment in July 1980. The case required fifty-two trial days, four hundred exhibits, and nearly ten thousand pages of transcript, as well as docket entries that stretched over thirty-two pages. See John F. McKenna to Arthur Gillis, November 18, 1981, PODiB, box 7, file 107 ("Attorney"), DRC.

34. Gail Shea to Glenn Ferguson, August 13, 1973, and response, September 5, 1973, and Claire Berg to Ferguson, October 25, 1973, POF, box 8, file 311 ("Women's Concerns"), DRC.

35. Reply to President Ferguson from Members of the Women's Council, January 10, 1974, POF, box 8, file 312 ("Women's Council"), DRC; Women's Council Press Release, October 9, 1974, and appended material, POF, box 25, file 880 ("Women's Council"), DRC. An African American male, Bertram Wilson, served as equal employment opportunity officer. He was noncommittal about the feminists' request for a woman in his position and said, "I feel I could work with anyone, because we are all working for the same thing, non-discriminatory practices. But the administration has backed me all the way and I will back president (Glenn) Ferguson 110 percent. He's trying." See *Hartford Times,* February 5, 1974, POF, box 4, file 204 ("Equal Employment Opportunity"), DRC.

36. *Connecticut Daily Campus,* December 4, 1973, and February 21, 1974.

37. The Black Students of the University of Connecticut to Ferguson, April 11, 1974, POF, box 3, file 171 ("Black Students"), DRC.

38. Ferguson to Rodney Bass, April 16, 1974, Denise Baker to Ferguson, April 17, 1974, POF, box 3, file 171 ("Black Students"), DRC.

39. Timetable of Actions Re: Library Sit-Ins and Evacuation, May 2, 1974, POF, box 6, file 248 ("NAACP"), DRC.

40. Ibid.; D. M. Kinsman to Ferguson, April 30, 1974, POF, box 6, file 250 ("NAACP"), DRC; *Contac,* May 1974, in possession of the author; Committee Against Racism Flyer, April 24, 1974, POF, box 6, file 237 ("Mass., University of—Collective Bargaining"), DRC; Donald Gibson, Chair of the Council on Human Rights and Opportunities, to Ferguson, April 25, 1974, POF, box 6, file 250 ("NAACP"), DRC; William Olds, Executive Director of the CCLU, to Ferguson, April 30, 1974, and response, June 14, 1974, POF, box 4, file 186 ("CCLU"), DRC; Ben F. Andrews Jr., Executive Director, Connecticut NAACP, to Ferguson, April 25, 1974, POF, box 6, file 248 ("NAACP"), DRC, and NAACP's Fact Finding Report, May 1974, POF, box 6, file 249 ("NAACP"), DRC. The state's charges against the demonstrators were *nolled,* but some were subject to university discipline. Dismissal charges were dropped for some white faculty members who were evicted in the second demonstration, but they were denied merit salary increases for two years. Ferguson instituted the punishment in opposition to the Committee of Five, which recommended no penalty. See *Hartford Courant,* December 27, 1974, POF, box 19, file 664 ("Krimmerman and McCarthy"), DRC; Committee of Five to Ferguson, April 2, 1975, POF, box 14, file 513 ("Committee of Five"), DRC; Ferguson to Florence McCarthy and Leonard Krimmerman, April 14, 1975, POF, box 19, file 664 ("Krimmerman and McCarthy"), DRC. For examples of university efforts to deal with racial issues, see *Connecticut Daily Campus,* November 16, 1976, "Minority Program Nears Completion," October 5, 1977, "Minority Affairs Funds Slated to Create 7 New Positions," and March 7, 1979, "AACC to Receive UConn Support."

41. *Connecticut Daily Campus,* April 6, 1976; *Willimantic Chronicle,* April 22, 1976, POF, box 36, file 1,371 ("Regents"), DRC; AAUP Executive Committee, "An Open Letter to All Connecticut Legislators," April 6, 1976, POF, box 36, file 1,371 ("Regents"), DRC.

42. *Willimantic Chronicle,* April 22, 1976, POF, box 36, file 1,371 ("Regents"), DRC; Meriden, Conn., *Morning Record,* April 30, 1976, PODiB, box 22, file 768 ("Board of Regents"), DRC; *Norwich Bulletin,* April 21, 1976, POF, box 36, file 1,371 ("Regents"), DRC; *Hartford Times,* May 6, 1976, PODiB, box 22, file 768 ("Board of Regents"), DRC; Ferguson to Coordinating Council, September 15, 1977, POF, box 27, file 935 ("Coordinating Council"), DRC.

43. J. G. Rohrback, fiscal planning document for the new library, March 22, 1972, POF, box 9, file 356 ("Trustee Material"), DRC; John P. McDonald to John G. Rohrbach, July 20, 1973, POF, box 20, file 679 ("New Library"), DRC.

44. Ferguson to Warren G. Hill, October 5, 1973, POF, box 8, file 330 ("Correspondence, August 1973"), DRC; Statement on Bill 238, undated, probably early 1974, POF, box 5, file 233 ("Legislative Concerns"), DRC; Stuart M. Chase, "The Library at the Limit," *Connecticut Alumnus,* December 1973, POF, box 34, file 1,286 ("Library"), DRC; Catherine Seelye to Ferguson, December 4, 1973, POF, box 20, file 677 ("Library-Misc."), DRC; Ferguson to Jay O. Tepper, April 17, 1975, and attached statement by Norman Stevens, "Summary Statement of Programmatic Impact of Further Delay in Library Construction," box 20, file 679 ("New Library"), DRC; Remarks for Mr. Tasker, Library Groundbreaking, July 10, 1975, Topping Off Press Release, December 1, 1976, POF, box 20, file 678 ("Library Dedicated"), DRC; undated news clipping, "UConn Library Accepted as Ready," POF, box 20, file 679 ("New Library"), DRC; *Connecticut Daily Campus,* September 20, 1977; Kenneth Wilson to Ferguson, January 24, 1977, and attachments regarding naming of the library, and Norman Stevens to Ferguson, February 15, 1977, POF, box 20, file 680 ("Library Name"), DRC; RFE-RL Press Release, April 20, 1978, and UConn Press Release, April 19, 1978; Board of Trustees Minutes, July 11, 1975, pp. 5,907–5,908, DRC.

45. *New Haven Register,* July 31, 1978, *Willimantic Chronicle,* August 24, 1978, Editorial, *The Day* of New London, POF, box 22, file 789 ("Search, Presidential Ads"), DRC; *Connecticut Daily Campus,* January 24, March 20, 1979; Oral History Interview with Kenneth G. Wilson, January 4, 1982, pp. 57–59, COH, DRC.

46. Biography of DiBiaggio, PODiB, box 1, file 3 ("Inauguration Committee"), DRC. The Schools of Nursing, Pharmacy, and Allied Health and the Student Health Service gave DiBiaggio a direct link to the Storrs campus. He also attended Ferguson's cabinet meetings. See "John A. DiBiaggio: New Directions," *University of Connecticut Chronicle,* September 6, 1979, PODiB, box 3, file 22 ("Newspaper clippings"), DRC.

47. *Willimantic Chronicle,* September 10, 1979, and *Bristol Press,* September 11, 1979, PODiB, box 21, file 749 ("Board of Higher Education"), DRC.

48. *Bristol Press,* September 11, 1979, PODiB, box 21, file 749 ("Board of Higher Education"), DRC; Finding Aid, John A. DiBiaggio President's Office Records, p. 5, DRC.

49. Inaugural Address of John A. DiBiaggio, September 8, 1979, PODiB, box 38, file 1,617 ("Inaugural Address"), DRC; *Hartford Courant,* September 9, 1979, PODiB, box 1, file 1 ("Cazel, Fred A."); *Willimantic Chronicle,* September 10, 1979, PODiB, box 3, file 22 ("Newspaper Clippings"), DRC.

50. Richard Stephenson to DiBiaggio, September 19, 1980, and response, September 23, 1980, PODiB, box 16, file 563 ("School of Engineering"), DRC.

51. *Hartford Courant,* February 3, 1980, PODiB, box 21, file 751 ("Board of Higher Education"), DRC; DiBiaggio to Christopher H. Shays, March 26, 1980, PODiB, box 26, file 880 ("Legislative Inquiries-A"), DRC.

52. *Hartford Courant,* February 3, 1980, PODiB, box 21, file 751 ("Board of Higher Education"), DRC; *Connecticut Daily Campus,* October 4, 1983; John McDonald to Mr. and Mrs. Paul S. Koda, PODiB, box 12, file 364 ("Homer Babbidge Library"), DRC.

53. A. T. DiBenedetto to Faculty and Staff, April 14, 1983, PoDiB, box 5, file 31 ("Academic Planning"), DRC; Report of Progress on Recommendations in the Academic Plan, "Opportunities for the 1980s," President's Office–Casteen (hereafter POC), box 1, file 8 ("Inaugural Symposium [October 11]"), DRC. The twelve academic programs singled out for augmented support were the Schools of Business Administration and Law, the Cooperative Extension Service, the Departments of Animal Genetics, Communication Sciences, Economics, History, Linguistics, Metallurgy, Nutritional Sciences, and Psychology, and the Biological Sciences Group.

54. *Hartford Courant,* May 1977, special section on the UCHC; Appendix B, Selected Chronology, unpublished history of UCHC, in possession of the author; *Hartford Courant,* eleven-part series on the UCHC, December 27, 1970–January 6, 1971; *Hartford Times,* February 19, 1974.

55. Health Center Report, September 1978, box 7, EHC, DRC; Appendix B, Selected Chronology, unpublished history of UCHC, in possession of the author.

56. Memo on New School of Law Facility forwarded by Phillip I. Blumberg to DiBiaggio, February 6, 1980, PODiB, box 10, file 304 ("Finance and Administration, Hartford Seminary"), DRC.

57. *University of Connecticut Advance,* September 6, 1984; George Schatzki to Governor William A. O'Neill, December 5, 1984, PODiB, box 12, file 399 ("L-Miscellaneous"), DRC; Chapter 1, History [of the School of Law], unmarked, undated (likely 1994 or 1995) manuscript, in possession of the author; http://www.law.uconn.edu/about/.

58. Harry Hartley to Senator Kevin P. Johnston, *Connecticut Technology Park: History and Background,* March 15, 1985, POC, box 8, file 264 ("New York Times"), DRC; Ilze Krisst to ConnTech Advisory Committee, Rationale Behind Establishing Research Park, April 9, 1986, POC, box 11, file 422 ("ConnTech Advisory Committee"), DRC. The Nathan Hale Inn, a hotel, was built later and was unrelated to the research park proposal.

59. Arthur Gillis to William Weaver, December 14, 1981, PODiB, box 15, file 519 ("Research Park"), DRC; Ilze Krisst to ConnTech Policy Advisory Committee, Background Material, February 3, 1986, POC, box 11, file 424 ("ConnTech Advisory Committee"), DRC; unnamed UConn publication, February 26, 1981, PODiB, box 15, file 520 ("Research Park"), DRC; *Connecticut Daily Campus,* February 28, 1983; Press Release, February 25, 1983, PODiB, box 19, file 683 ("UCEPI"), DRC.

60. A. J. R. Guttay to E. J. Kersting, February 2, 1983, and Kersting to Arthur Gillis,

February 23, 1983, PODiB, box 15, file 520 ("Research Park"), DRC; Harry Hartley to Senator Kevin P. Johnston, March 15, 1985, POC, box 8, file 264 ("New York Times"), DRC; "Notice and Warning," POC, box 6, file 170 ("UCEPI"), DRC; UCEPI Minutes, December 17, 1987, POC, box 25, file 1,173 ("UCEPI"), DRC; "The University and Its Park," POC, box 25, file 1,174 ("UCEPI"), DRC.

61. DiBiaggio to Members of the Board of Trustees Ad Hoc Committee on the Evaluation of the President, March 5, 1984, PODiB, box 7, file 110 ("B, Misc."), DRC; *Connecticut Daily Campus,* September 12, 1983; 1985 *Nutmeg* Dedication, POC, box 6, file 134 ("President"), DRC. From Michigan State, DiBiaggio moved to Tufts University, from which he eventually retired as president.

62. Andrew J. Canzonetti M.D. to Casteen, June 7, 1985, and response, July 2, 1985, POC, box 6, file 134 ("President"), DRC; *Daily Campus,* July 1, 1985; Connecticut Commissioner of Higher Education Norma Glasgow, quoted in the *UConn Advance,* October 17, 1985, POC, box 1, file 15 ("Newspaper articles"), DRC.

63. *Daily Campus,* July 1, September 11, 1985; *UConn Advance,* October 10, 1985, POC, box 1, file 15 ("Newspaper Articles"), DRC; Inaugural Address of John T. Casteen III, October 12, 1985, POC, box 1, file 7 ("Inaugural Address—Casteen"), DRC.

64. *Daily Campus,* September 17, 24, 1986.

65. *Daily Campus,* April 24, September 17, 1986; Fred Carstensen to Casteen, May 22, November 6, 1986, POC, box 11, file 445 ("Economics: Fred Carstensen"), DRC.

66. *Daily Campus,* May 2, 1986.

67. *Daily Campus,* May 7, November 4, 1987; March 20, 1990; *Hartford Courant,* March 10, 1990, POC, box 2 ("Biographical Information"), no folders, DRC.

68. Arthur L. Green to Casteen, February 19, 1987, Governor William A. O'Neill to Casteen, March 18, 1987, Karen Grava Williams to Casteen, undated but received in the President's Office on March 4, 1987, all in box 26, file 1,206 ("Commission on Human Rights and Opportunities—Affirmative Action Plan"), DRC; *Willimantic Chronicle,* October 10, 1987, POC, box 19, file 804 ("Admissions"), DRC.

69. "Report of Victims on the Incident at the Belden-Watson Semiformal," Thomasina Clemons to Carol A. Wiggins, December 8, 1987, Robert S. Hudd to Sallie A. Giffen, December 11, 1987, with police report of Case #87–4653, POC, box 25, file 1,151 ("Student Affairs: Disciplinary Actions, Landolfi/Doyle"), DRC. For lengthy published accounts of the incident, see the *Daily Campus,* May 5, 1988, and David Morse, "Prejudicial Studies," *Northeast Magazine* of the *Hartford Courant,* November 26, 1989. The Morse article is a particularly useful account that helped in reconstructing the incident and its consequences.

70. There were 14,533 undergraduates, with 530 blacks and 340 Hispanics as well as the 450 Asian Americans (*Daily Campus,* May 5, 1988).

71. Frank P. Ardaiolo to Sean Doyle, December 22, 1987, and Ardaiolo to Mark A. Landolfi, same date, POC, box 25, file 1,151 ("Student Affairs: Disciplinary Actions, Landolfi/Doyle"), DRC; Report of the Subcommittee on Discriminatory Harassment to the Student Welfare Committee and the University Senate, April 5, 1989, POC,

box 43, file 2,041, DRC. The committee was chaired by Professors Peter Halvorson and Glenda Price; Morse, "Prejudicial Studies." On March 21, 1988, Landolfi wrote an apology in which he stated, "I now understand the effects of racism, bigotry, and prejudice, and as I go through life I will always work toward eliminating this situation." See Mark A. Landolfi to Fellow Students, March 21, 1988, POC, box 33, file 1,560, DRC. For the Athletic Division's assessment of whether Landolfi should have been permitted to play football, see Todd Turner to Casteen, August 25, 1988, POC, box 33, file 1,566, DRC; Paul Shapiro to Debra Burns, August 30, 1988, John Allen to Casteen, August 31, 1988, Debra Burns to John Allen, September 6, 1988, Todd Turner to Casteen, September 6, 1988, all in POC, box 25, file 1,151 ("Student Affairs: Disciplinary Actions, Landolfi/Doyle"), DRC.

72. *Daily Campus,* April 6, 1988; Morse, "Prejudicial Studies."

73. For Bock's memos and materials related to his activities, see POC, box 33, files 1,558, 1,561, 1,562, and 1,566, passim; his hunger strike was featured in the article "Fasting Professor Meets with UConn," *Hartford Courant,* August 19, 1988; see also Morse, "Prejudicial Studies."

74. Statement of John T. Casteen III, President, University of Connecticut, May 20, 1988, POC, box 33, file 1,560, DRC; Open Letter to the University Community, June 29, 1989, Casteen, box 43, file 2,042, DRC; Bruce M. Stave to Casteen, July 31, 1989, and response, August 3, 1989, POC, box 38, file 1,814, DRC; Morse, "Prejudicial Studies."

75. *New York Times,* December 11, 1989, POC, box 43, file 2,041, DRC. Wu denied using the word "homos" but asked the court to assume she did, for the purpose of the case was to test the issue.

76. Ibid.; Mark Abrahamson to Casteen et al., December 5, 1989, POC, box 43, file 2,041, DRC; Paul M. Shapiro to Casteen, December 12, 1989, and notes of December 8, 1989, phone conversation with Paul Bock, POC, box 44, file 2,083, DRC.

77. Casteen to David McQuade, December 14, 1988, and Sallie A. Giffen to Patrons of the Babbidge Library, December 14, 1988, POC, box 33, file 1,532, DRC.

78. John P. McDonald to Casteen, November 14, 1985, and Casteen to Anthony T. DiBenedetto, November 19, 1985, POC, box 5, file 111 ("Library"), DRC; Thomas G. Paterson to Casteen, October 28, 1985, Paterson to Sen. Christopher Dodd, October 19, 1985, John McDonald to Paterson, November 18, 1985, Paterson to Casteen, October 6, 1986, Paterson to Galvin Gall, December 12, 1986, all in Thomas G. Paterson Papers, box 31, file 786, DRC.

79. Casteen to Senator Christopher Dodd, October 21, 1987, Randall C. Jimerson, "Preliminary Proposal: Archives Research Center," September 21, 1987, and Jimerson to Casteen, October 13, 1987, all in POC, box 19, file 848 ("Archives Building"); Draft of Case Statement: Archival Research Building, POC, box 38, file 1,815, DRC. Simon Konover initially pledged $250,000, and Sigmund Strochlitz $50,000.

80. *Hartford Courant,* July 30, 1989; for Julius Elias's extended critique of Casteen, see Oral History Interview with Julius Elias, January 10, 1995 session, pp. 47–58 (first draft), DRC.

81. *Daily Campus,* February 7, 1990; Casteen to Dr. Andrew J. Canzonetti, March 9, 1990, POC, box 2 ("Biographical Information"), no files, DRC; *Hartford Courant,* March 11, 1990, POC, box 2 ("Biographical Information"), no files, DRC.

82. Roger A. Bradlau to Edward V. Gant, November 8, 1972, POF, box 1, file 20 ("Athletics"), DRC; "University of Connecticut: Accomplishments since 1980," POC, box 2 ("Biographical Information"), no folders, DRC.

83. *Connecticut Daily Campus,* April 22, 1975; Ferguson to John Toner, January 6, 1975, POF, box 11, file 311, DRC; Attachment A, Agenda, Council of Presidents, New England Land Grant Universities, October 10, 1979, PODiB, box 33, file 1,129 ("NELGU Council of Presidents"), DRC; *Burlington Free Press,* October 25, 1979, PODiB, box 7, file 104 ("Athletics, Yankee Conference"), DRC.

84. John Toner to Edward V. Gant, May 31, 1979, PODiB, box 6, file 79 ("Athletics—Big East Conference"), DRC; *Summer Campus,* June 7, 1979; *Connecticut Daily Campus,* October 19, 1979.

85. *Summer Campus,* June 7, 1979; *Connecticut Daily Campus,* October 19, 1979, February 27, March 3, 1980.

86. Tim Tolokan, "Athletic Overview" and "University of Connecticut Men's Basketball Historical Timeline" in possession of the author; *Daily Campus,* May 2, 1986; "UConn Sports News," April 14, 1986, POC, box 9, file 349 ("Basketball Coach Search"), DRC.

87. *New Haven Register,* February 27, 1986, and Owen Canfield, "The Mood at UConn: Clean House," *Hartford Courant,* February 26, 1986, POC, box 15, file 692 ("DHE: March"), DRC; "A Study of Graduation Rates of Participation in Intercollegiate Athletics at the University of Connecticut: Executive Summary," June 1985, POC, box 9, file 342 ("Athletics"), DRC; A. T. DiBenedetto to Casteen, November 20, 1985, POC, box 4, file 41 ("Athletics"), DRC.

88. *Hartford Courant,* January 26, 1986, POC, box 10, file 359 ("Athletics—Press Clips"), DRC; Owen Canfield, "The Mood at UConn: Clean House," *Hartford Courant,* February 26, 1986, POC, box 15, file 692 ("DHE: March"), DRC.

89. The President's Task Force on Athletics: Final Report, Executive Summary, May 9, 1986, POC, box 10, file 365 ("Task Force on Athletics—Final Report"), DRC; A Study of Graduation Rates . . . , June 1985, POC, box 9, file 342 ("Athletics"), DRC.

90. *Hartford Courant,* May 7, 11, 16, 1986; Search Committee Evaluation, May 12, 1986.

91. *Daily Campus,* November 17, 1987, May 4, 1989, January 27, 1990, May 3, 1990; goals for major sports, 1986–87, undated, POC, box 9, file 341 ("Athletics"), DRC; Randy Smith, "Does UConn Really Expect Us to Bury This?," *Journal Inquirer,* January 24, 1987, Bob Casey, "Toner Release Unfair," *New Haven Register,* January 24, 1987, *UConn Sports News,* January 23, 1987, all in POC, box 20, file 852 ("Athletics"), DRC.

92. *Summer Campus,* July 1, 1985; *Daily Campus,* December 10, 1985; *Hartford Courant,* November 22, 1985.

93. Division of Athletics Annual Report, 1986/1987, POC, box 9, file 345, DRC; *Daily Campus,* March 21, May 4, 1989.

94. Jan Zieger, "UConn Women's Athletics on Upswing," *Hartford Courant,* April 6, 1975, and *Connecticut Daily Campus,* January 30, 1975, POF, box 12, file 424 ("Athletics—Women"), DRC; "Laws and Regulations Affecting Equal Opportunity Programs at University of Connecticut as of July, 1976," POF, box 16, file 577 ("Equal Employment Opportunities Office"), DRC.

95. Patricia J. Bresser, Joanne L. Burruano, and Karen Mullins to Editor, *Connecticut Daily Campus,* received in President's Office on September 29, 1977, POF, box 12, file 424 ("Athletics—Women"), DRC; A. J. Pappanikou to DiBiaggio, August 1, 1980, with attached Progress Report on Title IX, PODiB, box 6, file 95 ("Athletics—Title IX"), DRC; "Report to the President: Current Allegations of Unequal Treatment of Women Coaches/Varsity Teams Within Department of Athletics," February 24, 1981, PODiB, box 6, file 96 ("Athletics—Title IX"), DRC; Susan Bucknell and Tina Cunningham to DiBiaggio, May 16, 1984, PODiB, box 27, file 932(W), DRC; *Daily Campus,* February 1, 1990.

96. *Daily Campus,* February 1, 1990; "University of Connecticut Sports Center Chronology of Major Planning Activities," POC, box 20, file 866 ("Athletics—Sports Center"), DRC.

97. Jack Sharry, "Final Draft—UConn Athletic Inadequacies," Journalism 112 L1, April 26, 1974, POF, box 11, file 411 ("Athletics"), DRC; "The University of Connecticut Sports Center Update," University of Connecticut Alumni Association, February 10, 1987, POC, box 20, file 866 ("Athletics—Sports Center"), DRC; *Daily Campus,* February 13, 1986. The relatively small size of the arena seating may have been dictated by a fear of competing with the Hartford Civic Center and a new convention center that was being planned at the time. See Ann L. Huckenbeck to Casteen, June 16, 1988, POC, box 29, file 1,375, DRC, and Stephen M. Lombardi to Todd Turner, January 25, 1989, POC, box 38, file 1,829, DRC.

98. WFSB Editorial, March 16, 1983, and DiBiaggio Response, March 21, 1983, PODiB, box 37, file 1,401 ("Response of JAD to a WFSB editorial"), DRC.

99. *Hartford Courant,* February 6, 1987, POC, box 10, file 363 ("Athletics—Sports Center Presentation, February 11"), DRC; *Hartford Courant,* January 28, February 25, 1987, POC, box 20, file 868 ("Athletics—Sports Center"), DRC; *Daily Campus,* January 26, 29, 1990; Program for Ground-Breaking Ceremony, June 29, 1987, POC, box 20, file 867 ("Athletics: Sports Center"), DRC. On March 4, 1987, Casteen thanked Gampel for his "magnificent gift of $1 million." On August 21, 1989, Gampel wrote that he never received anything in writing about the name of the pavilion and other matters. Casteen responded on October 16, 1989, guaranteeing the name in perpetuity, and also answered satisfactorily Gampel's other requests, such as that all event tickets would say Harry A. Gampel Pavilion. See Casteen to Gampel, March 4, 1987, POC, box 20, file 868 ("Athletics—Sports Center"), DRC, and Gampel to Casteen, August 21, 1989, and response, October 16, 1989, POC, box 40, file 1,888, DRC.

Chapter 6. Creating a National University: 1990–2006 (pp. 212–60)

1. *Hartford Courant,* March 12, 1990, and *Chronicle,* Willimantic, Conn., April 4, 1990, POC, box 2 ("Biographical Information"), no folders, DRC; *Daily Campus,* August 6, October 17, December 7, 1990; *Journal Inquirer,* May 16, 1990; for a comment on the Rome-Hartley relationship, see *Hartford Courant,* February 15, 1996, "Hartley Quits UConn Presidency" and Oral History Interview with Harry Hartley, May 21, 28, 1996, pp. 146–50, COH, DRC (hereafter Hartley Interview.) For McQuade's intervention, Casteen's opposition, and Hartley's making no promise not to be a candidate for the permanent position, see the same interview, pp. 95–96 and 99; "University of Connecticut: President Hartley's Five Year Report," p. 8, in possession of the author.
2. Hartley Interview, pp. 146–50; University Senate Minutes, October 10, 1994, pp. 5–6, DRC.
3. A perceptive portrait of Hartley's tenure as UConn president can be found in Jackie Fitzpatrick, "At UConn, How It Was with Harry at the Helm," *New York Times,* March 24, 1996; Hartley Interview, p. 118.
4. Fitzpatrick, "At UConn"; Hartley Interview, pp. 1–4 and passim.
5. University of Connecticut *Traditions,* spring 1996, p. 12; Hartley Interview, pp. 105–107.
6. Hartley Interview, p. 107; *Hartford Courant,* August 18, 1991, in President's Office Papers–Austin (hereafter POA); *New York Times,* January 26, 1992, POA; Hartley to Board of Trustees, July 10, 1992, "Significant Activities: University of Connecticut, 1991–92," in possession of the author.
7. "University of Conecticut: President Hartley's Five Year Report," pp. 11 and 15; "UConn Police Probe Unusual Incident," *Hartford Courant,* April 16, 1992; "Case Reopens Racial Wounds at UConn," *Hartford Courant,* May 15, 1992; "UConn Offers Reward for Info in Race Case," *Chronicle* (Willimantic), April 21, 1992, all in POA.
8. "Hartley's List," *Daily Campus,* September 14, 1994, POA; J. A. Nielsen, "Discrimination, by Any Other Name . . . ," *Daily Campus,* October 3, 1994, POA; Editorial, Letters to the Editor, and page 1, *Daily Campus,* October 6, 1994, POA; "Student Protesters at Rally Accuse UConn Newspaper of Racism," *Hartford Courant,* October 6, 1994, POA.
9. *Daily Campus,* October 11, 1994; Hartley's comments at AACC forum, October 10, 1994, POA; David Garnes to Carol A. Wiggins, October 27, 1994, POA; Noel A. Cazenave, "Why I Will Teach a Course on White Racism," *Hartford Courant,* February 18, 1996, POA.
10. Hartley to Richard Cheney, May 15, 1992, POA; Peter McFadden to Thomas Tighe, March 11, 1994, Judith W. Meyer to Peter McFadden, March 27, 1994, Judith W. Meyer to Carol Flynn, April 19, 1994, Col. David Fairclo to Judith W. Meyer, April 6, 1994, and Judith W. Meyer to Paul Shapiro and Karen Molitor, April 15, 1994, all in POA; Kevin Kean (and Darryn DiFrancesco) to Board of Trustees, undated, and Peter Mc-

Fadden to Kevin Kean, April 19, 1995, POA; Paula Liseo and Edward Eggleton to Hartley, March 3, 1996, POA; University Senate Minutes, February 13, 20, 1995, DRC; Board of Trustees Minutes, May 8, 1992, p. 7,762, and April 21, 1995, pp. 7987–88 and Attachment M, DRC.

11. "University of Connecticut: President Hartley's Five Year Report," p. 23; Hartley Interview, pp. 139–41.

12. Hartley Interview, p. 142; *UConn Advance*, November 19, 1993. Others on the SPMC were trustees Louise Berry, Claire Leonardi, Jennifer Smith, and student trustee Thomas Mika; faculty members Maureen Croteau and Devendra Kalonia; Provost Thomas J. Tighe, Vice-President for Institutional Advancement Edward T. Allenby; Mary Jo Blanchard, president of the Undergraduate Student Government; David McQuade, a staff member at the legislature; Stanley A. Twardy, an attorney and former counsel to Gov. Lowell P. Weicker; and Lester Baum, a businessman and alumnus. Memo on "Beyond 2000: Change"—The University of Connecticut Strategic Plan, from William R. Berkeley to Board of Trustees, February 10, 1995, POA; Board of Trustees Minutes, February 10, 1995, pp. 7976–77, DRC.

13. *UConn Advance*, December 2, 1994; William R. Berkeley to Board of Trustees, Memo on "Beyond 2000: Change"—The University of Connecticut Strategic Plan, February 10, 1995, POA; Students to Board of Trustees, Memo Received in President's Office on December 19, 1994, POA; University of Connecticut—President Hartley's Five Year Report, p. 24. The vision statement was originally approved by the trustees on June 10, 1994. See Board of Trustees Minutes, June 10, 1994, p. 7,919, DRC. The present author was president of the AAUP at the time of the hearings and made its presentation at the hearing of November 18, 1994.

14. *Hartford Courant*, February 11, 1995, POA; President Hartley's Annual Report, 1995–96, pp. 6–7, in possession of the author; William R. Berkeley to Board of Trustees, Memo on "Beyond 2000: Change—The University of Connecticut Strategic Plan, February 10, 1995, POA; Hartley Interview, pp. 143–45. Leslie Cutler was appointed chancellor at the Health Center. The position of Chancellor was eliminated several years later, during the administration of Philip Austin, Hartley's successor. For the forcing out of Tighe, see the *Hartford Courant*, September 10, 1994, in Harry J. Hartley, "UConn 2000: Planning, Politicking, and Managing a Billion Dollar Campus Transformation" (2000), p. I-16, DRC, which is Hartley's personal account of the events leading up to and following the passage of UConn 2000 (hereafter Hartley, "UConn 2000").

15. Hartley Interview, pp. 185, 125–26; *Hartford Courant*, February 15, 1996; Interview with Scott Brohinsky, May 4, 2004, p. 20–25, COH, DRC (hereafter Brohinsky Interview). Brohinsky suggests that Hartley remained reluctant for quite a while after the process got started and came on board only after Speaker of the House Tom Ritter wrote to him, saying, "I think this can happen, but it cannot happen without your aggressive, enthusiastic support"; Interview with Robert M. Ward, July 12, 1995, pp. 15–16, COH, DRC (hereafter Ward Interview); Hartley, "UConn 2000," p. I-1;

Interview with Denise Merrill, July 3, 1995, passim, COH, DRC (hereafter Merrill Interview).

16. Merrill Interview, pp. 10–16; Brohinsky Interview, pp. 18–22.

17. Interview with Tom Ritter, August 14, 1995, p. 25, COH, DRC (hereafter Ritter Interview); Brohinsky Interview, p. 24, 30; *Hartford Courant,* January 31, 1995, in Hartley, "UConn 2000," p. II-1.

18. Ritter Interview, pp. 27–28; Interview with Kevin Sullivan, August 14, 1995, p. 31, COH, DRC; *Advocate,* "United UConn," February 2, 1995; Hartley, "UConn 2000," p. II-10.

19. Hartley, "UConn 2000," pp. 32–44, II-29.

20. Hartley, "UConn 2000," pp. 52–53, and *Hartford Courant* and *Journal Inquirer,* March 4, 1995, in Hartley, "UConn 2000," II-25, 26. The present author testified on behalf of the AAUP at the hearing.

21. Ritter Interview, pp. 28–29; *Hartford Courant,* May 2, 11, 1995, in Hartley, "UConn 2000," pp. II-31 and II-33.

22. Hartford Courant, May 11, 1995, in Hartley, "UConn 2000," p. II-33.

23. For the impact of basketball on UConn 2000's passage, see "Huskeymania and Votes" in Hartley, "UConn 2000," pp. 49–52 and newspaper stories, pp. II-15–22; Ward Interview, pp. 13–15.

24. *Hartford Courant,* June 7, 1995, in Hartley, "UConn 2000," p. II-35; Ritter Interview, p. 30.

25. *Chronicle,* Willimantic, June 23, 1995, and *New York Times,* June 23, 1995, in Hartley, "UConn 2000," pp. II-36, II-39–40, 61. Although the library served as the backdrop for the ceremonial signing of the UConn 2000 legislation, the funds to repair it came from a separate appropriation.

26. Hartley Interview, p. 117; *UConn Advance,* April 15, 22, 1994.

27. *UConn Advance,* April 22, 1994. The present author also testified at the hearing, raised concerns about gender equity, and urged the committee to consider the impact of the upgrade on academic standards.

28. *UConn Advance,* October 14, 21, 1994; Board of Trustees Minutes, October 14, 1994, pp. 7,948, 7,953–54 and Attachment 7,955–0, box 93, 1994–95, DRC.

29. *UConn Advance,* October 28, 1994; University Senate Minutes, October 24, 1994, pp. 9–10, box 10, file 1994–95, DRC. The present author introduced the academic enhancement fund stipulation.

30. *UConn Advance,* November 11, 18, 1994; Board of Trustees Minutes, November 11, 1994, pp. 7958–59 and Attachment J, box 93, file 11/11/94, DRC; Hartley Interview, p. 117.

31. *Journal Inquirer,* February 14, 1996, front page; *Hartford Courant,* February 15, 1996, front page.

32. *Hartford Courant,* editorial, February 15, 1996; Hartley's letter of resignation was published in *UConn Advance,* February 16, 1996.

33. *Hartford Courant,* February 15, 1996; "For the Record," *Hartford Courant,* February

16, 1996. Governor John Rowland resigned from his position during his third term in office and as the legislature was conducting impeachment proceedings. He later pled guilty to a federal corruption charge and was sent to prison. His need to enhance his personal finances and maintain a lifestyle that his governor's salary could not support was seen as one reason for the corruption in his administration. *Daily Campus,* March 20, 1996; *UConn Advance,* May 24, June 21, 1996; *Hartford Courant,* June 23, 1996. Steering Committee members with ties to the governor's office included O'Leary; Mary Ann Hanley, Rowland's legal counsel; Lt. Gov. M. Jodi Rell; James Abromaitis, a UConn trustee and former Husky basketball player who was a personal friend of Rowland; and Hartford businessman Michael Martinez, whom the Governor's Office suggested as a committee member. Athletic Director Lew Perkins also sat on the steering committee, and his daughter served as O'Leary's summer intern in Rowland's office. *Journal Inquirer,* June 5, 1996.

34. *Hartford Courant,* July 20, 1996; *UConn Advance,* July 22, 1996; Oral History Interview with Philip E. Austin, Session One, July 30, 2002, passim (draft version), COH, DRC (hereafter Austin Interview); John T. Casteen III to Austin, August 8, 1996, and response, August 13, 1996, POA.

35. *UConn Advance,* July 22, 1996.

36. University of Connecticut President's Employment Agreement, section 1.2.1, POA; *Daily Campus,* November 1, 1996. For Austin's move to Farmington, see the *UConn Advance,* February 28, March 7, 1997. For the reaction to the move, see the *Hartford Courant,* March 2, 1997; Austin moved into the campus president's house five years later. When a much-needed renovation to the house caused by deferred maintenance cost one million dollars, the *Hartford Courant* carried the story on the first page, and an editorial in the student paper was very critical of the expenditure. The *Courant's* editorial was more forgiving but a Willimantic *Chronicle* editorial cartoon was unkind. See *Hartford Courant,* January 30, 2005, and February 2, 2005, *Daily Campus,* February 1, 2005, and *Chronicle,* February 24, 2005.

37. For an investigative reporter's inquiry into the UConn Foundation and the Athletic Department, see Alan Levin, "UConn Sporting Entourage Travels in Style," *Hartford Courant,* February 9, 1997, which among other issues cited the $73,000 bill, including $1,540 for one day's supply of orange juice and $75 for three chicken club sandwiches, at New York City's Four Seasons Hotel during the men's basketball tournament in March 1996; Austin to M. Jodi Rell, July 19, 2004, POA; Austin to Mr. and Mrs. Philip H. Lodewick, January 16, 2001, POA; News Release, April 23, 1999, "Alumnus' Gift to Create Human Rights Chair," and Edward T. Allenby to Gary Gladstein, April 10, 2000, POA; Austin to Raymond Neag, February 5, 1999, and Allenby to Members of the UConn Foundation Board of Directors, February 23, 1999, POA; *UConn Advance,* March 1, 1999, and April 19, 2004. Twenty-one million dollars of Neag's gift went to the School of Education and two million to the Health Center, to be used for a distinguished chair in the School of Medicine. The *U.S. News and World Report* rankings were recognized by Richard Schwab, the dean of the Neag

School, as being only a rough barometer of quality but a welcome index of the school's rising reputation.

38. *UConn Advance*, August 25, 2003; Austin Interview, fourth session, May 13, 2003, pp. 1–7, draft version; Brohinsky Interview, pp. 46–47. Before Governor Rowland resigned at the end of June 2004 the board of trustees approved a resolution expressing deep appreciation for all he had done for the university, and President Austin wrote to him that "with regard to our physical infrastructure we know that by the conclusion of 21st Century UConn" the university would be counted among the nation's top public universities. See Austin to John Rowland, June 24, 2004, POA.

39. *New York Times*, January 5, 2003; *Journal Inquirer*, August 22, 2003; *Hartford Courant*, August 22, 2003; *Chronicle*, August 22, 2003; *UConn Advance*, August 25, 2003, February 10, 2003, February 14, 2005. For *Hartford Courant*'s articles concerning UConn 2000 contracts, cost overruns, and building violations, see the issues of March 25, 29, 30, April 5 (news story and editorial), 13, 14 (news story and editorial cartoon), 17, 2005; for UConn's response, see Austin's e-mails to all UConn employees, March 28 and April 14, 2005, and the articles in *UConn Advance*, April 4, 18, 2005. For a balanced editorial concerning UConn's progress under UConn 2000 and the difficulties that arose, see the *Journal Inquirer*, April 27, 2005. For the Governor's Commission report, see *Hartford Courant*, September 2, 2005.

40. Ron Schurin to Board of Trustees, April 19, 2001, POA; *Hartford Courant*, April 20 and 21, 2001, POA; *Daily Campus*, April 20, 2001.

41. *Hartford Courant*, April 21, 2001, POA; *Daily Campus*, February 27, 28, March 3, 7, 2003.

42. *Daily Campus*, September 13, 14, and October 2, 2001.

43. Kathy Hoang, Sage Radachowsky, Joe Therrien, Khalid Alyahya, Shireen Moidu, Miriam Lee, Abdul Alhamdan, Becky Maran, and Jenny Lai to Austin, September 27, 2001, and response, October 2, 2001, POA.

44. *Daily Campus*, March 6, 2003.

45. *Daily Campus*, March 28, April 15, 28, 2003, March 21, 2005. In 2005, Strike One found the following companies listed as sponsors on the UConn Booth Engineering Center for Advanced Technology home page and complained that they all were involved with the manufacturing of military weapons: Lockheed Martin, Northrop Grumman Corporation, and the Ballistic Missile Defense Organization.

46. *Daily Campus*, October 4, 1996, October 3, 1997, February 11, 1998.

47. *Daily Campus*, October 26, 28, 1999; "Statement by President Philip E. Austin on Anti-Gay Incidents at UConn," October 27, 1999, POA.

48. *Daily Campus*, October 28, 29, November 4, 30, 1999, February 8, 2002; *UConn Advance*, November 8, 1999.

49. *UConn Advance*, March 9, 1998, and April 19, 1999; *Daily Campus*, March 6, 1998; Austin to the University Community, April 14, 1998, in possession of the author.

50. Austin Interview, August 8, 2002, first draft, pp. 33–45; *UConn Advance*, March 9, 1998; *Daily Campus*, December 11, 1998.

51. *Daily Campus,* December 11, 1998, September 7, 1999; Austin Interview, August 8, 2002, first draft, pp. 33–45.

52. Board of Trustees Minutes, pp. 8,236–37 and attachments, April 13, 1999, box 103, DRC. Twenty-four individuals addressed the board about the Pfizer building site. Also see *Daily Campus,* April 14, 1999; *UConn Advance,* April 19, May 3, 1999.

53. *UConn Advance,* July 19, 1999; Austin Interview, August 8, 2002, first draft, pp. 33–45; Letters to the Editor, *Hartford Courant,* February 26, 2005; University of Connecticut Press Release, June 23, 2004. The university found itself dealing with a number of other environmental and preservation issues at the beginning of the new millennium, including the preservation of Farwell Barn and twenty-five surrounding acres and matters related to hazardous waste and water pollution. For the barn, see the *Daily Campus,* February 24, October 18, 2000, and Robert T. Molleur to Austin, March 11, 2000, POA; Thomas Q. Callahan to Mansfield Town Council, January 24, 2002, Mayor Elizabeth C. Paterson to Callahan, February 6, 2002, Callahan to Paterson and Mansfield Town Council, March 1, 2002, POA; for hazardous waste and water pollution, see the *Daily Campus,* November 29, 2000, October 24, 2001. In September 2002 the university appointed Richard Miller, who had been manager of environmental regulatory affairs at Northeast Utilities, as its director of environmental policy. He was charged with overseeing compliance issues and developing an enhanced environmental awareness. See *UConn Advance,* September 23, 2002.

54. Chris Powell, "Failure of Pfizer Deal Leaves Power at UConn in Question," *Daily Campus,* September 7, 1999, reprinted from unsigned editorial, *Journal Inquirer,* August 11, 1999; Ken Krayeske, "Huskies, Swooshes and Sweatshops," *Hartford Advocate,* 1998, http://old.hartfordadvocate.com/articles/bball98h.html; *Daily Campus,* April 27, 1999; Matthew Kauffman and Lisa Chedekel, "As Colleges Profit, Sweatshops Worsen," *Hartford Courant,* December 12, 2004.

55. *Daily Campus,* April 27, 1999; "Statement Regarding Collegiate Licensing Company Code of Conduct," by President Philip E. Austin, April 29, 1999, POA.

56. Matthew Kauffman and Lisa Chedekel, "As Colleges Profit, Sweatshops Worsen," *Hartford Courant,* December 12, 2004. In 2005, the Connecticut General Assembly considered a bill to ensure that all apparel purchased by the state would be produced in factories and washed in laundries where workers earn a living wage and their rights were respected. See e-mails at the listserv Humanrights-L@listserv.uconn.edu, February 22, March 3, 2005; announcement about Coop at "Slaves to Fashion" presentation, Konover Auditorium, Thomas J. Dodd Reseach Center, March 16, 2005, and articles in the *Daily Campus,* March 16, April 21, 2005, the *Hartford Courant,* March 26, 2005, and the *Chronicle,* March 30, 2005.

57. "Students Concerned about UConn Janitors," care of Sage Radachowsky to Austin, May 2, 2001, POA; *Daily Campus,* May 4, 2001. The *Daily Campus* editorial explained that janitors in the university dormitories were state employees paid a starting wage of $9.50 per hour and receiving state benefits. In contrast, non-dormitory janitors

were contracted for with Capitol Cleaners and paid $6.50 an hour without benefits. The Student Labor Coalition protestors objected to the inequality.

58. "Decorp UConn: Whose University?" May 2, 2001, POA.

59. *Hartford Courant* and *Chronicle*, May 10, 2001; Kathleen Holgerson (Women's Center), Willena Kimpson Price (African American Cultural Center), T. R. Richardson (Rainbow Center), Isnoel Rios (Puerto Rican/Latin American Cultural Center), Angela Rola (Asian American Cultural Center) to Austin, May 9, 2001, POA; Austin Interview, August 9, 2002, pp. 4–6 (first draft); signed agreement by Thomas Callahan and students on prevailing wages, POA.

60. Austin Interview, first draft, August 8, 2002, pp. 50–52; "Spring Manifesto," received in the Office of Greek Life on April 30, 1996, POA. The Greek letters Pi Epsilon Pi were initialed at the bottom of the typed "Manifesto."

61. "Recommendations for Spring Weekend," August 19, 1996, POA; *Daily Campus*, September 19, October 23, 1996, and April 10, 25, 1997; "Spring Manifesto," 1997, http://www.internet-95.com/personal/richv/springweekend.htm, POA.

62. Chancellor's Special Task Force on Community and Civility: Interim Report and Recommendations, January 27, 1999, POA; Final Report, President's Task Force on Substance Abuse, March 21, 2003, POA; Ronald C. Schurin to Harold Grinspoon, April 16, 2001, POA; *Daily Campus*, April 9, 26, September 17, 29, 2004, March 22, April 25, 2005; *Chronicle*, March 21, 2005, April 25, 26, 2005.

63. Tim Tolokan, "UConn Athletic Timeline from 1978 to Present," in possession of the author.

64. *Hartford Courant*, January 15, 2005; according to newspaper reports, Calhoun's contract totaled $1.4 million and Auriemma's $825,000 in 2005, and their extended averages over six and five years, respectively, were even higher. Their deals with Nike drew controversy because of state ethics policies regarding compensation resulting directly from one's state position, and also the charges that Nike employed sweatshop labor. The state Ethics Commission had approved the deals and critics asked why others, who may not have had the celebrity given to the coaches, did not receive similar approval. See *Hartford Courant*, February 19, 2005, editorial, February 23, 2005, Jeff Jacobs, "Truth Should Be Out There," February 26, 2005, Michele Jacklin, "A Different Brand of State Employee," February 27, 2005, letters to the editor, February 22, 27, March 4, 2005; *Chronicle*, March 8, 2005, editorial, March 12, 2005.

65. Tim Tolokan, "UConn Athletic Timeline from 1978 to Present," in possession of the author; *Hartford Courant Courtside*, December 28, 2004; Jeff Jacobs, "Day of Joy, Heartache," *Hartford Courant*, March 7, 2005; *New York Times*, March 29, 2005.

66. Tim Tolokan, "UConn Athletic Timeline" and "University of Connecticut's Men's Basketball Historical Timeline"; *Hartford Courant*, April 5, 2005; *UConn Advance*, April 11, 2005; Ira Berkow, "Calhoun Makes Developing Talent a Specialty," *New York Times*, February 9, 2005. The luster of UConn's basketball success dulled in the shadow of its graduation rates for players, however. A 2004 study by the University of Central Florida's Institute for Diversity and Ethics in Sport found that only 27 per-

cent of the UConn men's team graduated over a six-year period. According to the NCAA's academic reform plan, introduced in 2005, teams with less than 50 percent graduation rates would face penalties that would include the loss of scholarships and a ban on postseason play. One problem for athletically successful teams like the Huskies was that the Academic Progress Rate (APR), as initially designed, subtracted points for players who left school early to play professionally. Successful coaches like Jim Calhoun would suffer from their own success if their players moved on to the pros after one, two, or three years of college play. Of course, professional play did not explain all—or most—of the attrition, which is an issue that institutions continue to deal with today. See the *Daily Campus,* March 30, 2005, the *Journal Inquirer,* March 1, 2005, the *Hartford Courant,* March 2, 5 (Jeff Jacobs, "APR Needs Some Fixing"), 8 (editorial), 2005.

67. Tim Tolokan, "UConn Athletic Timeline," "Football," "Athletics." Including the playoffs, the 1998 football record was 10–3. See the *Hartford Courant,* November 9, 2003; the *Daily Campus,* December 8, 1998.

68. *UConn Advance,* September 19, October 6, 27, November 24, December 8, 1997; *Daily Campus,* October 30, November 6, 18, 20, December 2, 1997.

69. *Daily Campus,* October 20, 1997, December 10, 1998, November 12, 1999; *UConn Advance,* May 8, 2000; *Journal Inquirer,* August 26, 2003.

70. Austin Interview, May 13, 2003, first draft, pp. 32–36; *Hartford Courant,* May 7, 16, November 5, 2003. Temple University played its last Big East football season in 2004. It did not play basketball in the Big East. West Virginia and Rutgers rounded out the football conference.

71. *Hartford Courant,* June 9, 10, July 13, 2003, December 28, 2004; for faculty concern about the search, see e-mail to UConn Forum by Rich Hiskes, June 10, 2003; for Hathaway's ethical and legal problems, see the *Hartford Courant,* April 4, 5, 6, 11, 13, 14, 15, 16, 23, 2005.

72. Information on sponsored awards from Office of Institutional Research and Office of Sponsored Programs, e-mail, June 21, 23, 2005, in possession of the author; "UConn Fact Sheet 2005," in possession of the author. For fiscal year 2002 (later data unavailable) UConn ranked 74th out of 625 among all institutions and 51st out of 374 among public institutions by the National Science Foundation in research and development spending. For the Health Center's special appropriation, see *UConn Advance,* May 8, 2000.

73. "UConn Fact Sheet 2005," in possession of the author; among the sponsored expenditures by discipline, 3 percent went to "other"; UCHI Web site, www.humanities.uconn.edu/about.html.

74. *UConn Advance,* February 28, 2000; *Daily Campus,* March 3, 2000; invitation to April 3, 2000, ceremony honoring the designees, in possession of the author; the author was the sixth individual designated as a Board of Trustees Distinguished Professor in 2000. The others, appointed by year and discipline, follow: 2001—Carl David Benson (English), Robert K. Colwell (ecology and evolutionary biology), Ruth

Millikan (philosophy), Steven L. Suib (chemistry), and Jack Veiga (management); 2002—Yaakov Bar-Shalom (electrical and computer engineering), Richard D. Brown (history), David A. Kenny (psychology), Alexandros Makriyannis (medicinal chemistry and molecular and cell biology), and William C. Stwalley (physics); 2003— Gary English (dramatic arts), Deborah Fein (psychology), Debra Kendall (molecular and cell biology), Philip Marcus (molecular and cell biology), and Robert Weiss (chemical engineering); 2004—William Fitzgerald (marine sciences), Bahram Javidi (electrical and computer engineering), James Marsden (operations and information management), Larry Raisz (medicine), and Howard Tennen (community medicine); 2005—Brenda Murphy (English), Peter Setlow (molecular, microbial, and structural biology at the Health Center), C. F. Sirmans (finance), and Bette Talvacchia (art and art history). See the *UConn Advance*, March 5, 2001, April 22, 2002, April 21, 2003, March 29, 2004, and April 18, 2005.

75. *UConn Advance*, March 29, 2004, June 14, 2005.
76. E-mail, Austin to the University Community, December 8, 2003.
77. *UConn Advance*, April 23, 2001; *UConn Momentum*, summer 2005.
78. *UConn Advance*, June 21, 1999, January 24, 2000, June 17, 2002, April 4, 18, 2005; *Daily Campus*, Freshman/Transfer Mailer '99, April 4, 2005; *UConn Traditions*, spring 2004; "China: Views from the West," *Center for Regenerative Biology Newsletter*, http://web.uconn.edu/crb/China%20voices.htm; *Hartford Courant*, March 25, 2005; *Chronicle*, April 12, 15, 2005; *Journal Inquirer*, March 25, 2005; *People's Daily Online*, http://english.people.com.cn/200504/12/print20050412_180597.html .
79. *Daily Campus*, September 4, 2003, September 14, 2004; *Journal Inquirer*, April 7, June 10, 2005; *UConn Advance*, April 11, May 2, June 14, 2005, March 31, September 3, 2003; e-mail, February 9, 2005, from Dana Wilder to Committee to Study Issues of Retired Faculty and Staff, in possession of the author. The previous set of peer institutions included four on the 2004 list, Iowa State, Iowa, Missouri, and Rutgers, as well as Colorado State, Nebraska, Louisiana State, Tennessee, Massachusetts, and West Virginia, see e-mail from Dana Wilder, April 25, 2005, in possession of the author; *Chronicle*, March 1, 2005. The *U.S. News and World Report* rankings are questioned by academics but have cache with the public. UConn, like other universities, publicizes the ratings when they are favorable and show improvement. Recent graduate satisfaction from "UConn Fact Sheet 2005." While UConn had emerged as a national institution, 96,000 of UConn's 166,000 alumni in 2005 lived in Connecticut.
80. *UConn Advance*, April 4, 2005.
81. *Chronicle*, June 18, 2005.

Sources

Manuscript Collections

All collections except the Philip E. Austin (POA) papers are located in the Thomas J. Dodd Research Center at the University of Connecticut (DRC). The Austin papers, on file in Gulley Hall, were made available by President Austin's office. Harry Hartley did not convey his papers to the Dodd Center and they were not available for this study. The scope of the collections range from one sparse box for Solomon Mead, the principal of the Storrs Agricultural School, 1881–83, to the 48 boxes, 42.5 linear feet, of material in the John T. Casteen III papers. Each box contains many files, and each file many items.

President's Office: Philip E. Austin (POA), Homer D. Babbidge (POB), Charles L. Beach (POBe), John T. Casteen (POC), John A. DiBiaggio (PODiB), Glenn W. Ferguson (POF), George W. Flint (POFl), Albert N. Jorgensen (POJ), Benjamin F. Koons (POK), Charles C. McCracken (POMc), Solomon Mead (POM), Rufus W. Stimson (POS), George A. Works (POW)
Evan Hill Collection (EHC)
Thomas G. Paterson Papers
University of Connecticut Board of Trustees Minutes
University of Connecticut Health Center Records
University of Connecticut Senate Minutes
Albert E. Waugh Journal (AEW)

Speeches

O'Hara, William T., ed. *Fitted to the Burden: Selected Speeches of Homer Daniels Babbidge, Jr.* Storrs, Conn.: University of Connecticut Alumni Association, 1972.

Newspapers and Periodicals

Advocate (Stamford), 1995
Bridgeport Post, 1941

Bristol Press, 1979

Burlington Free Press, 1979

CAC Lookout, 1896, 1899, 1904–8

Challenge, 1973

Chronicle (Willimantic), 1917, 1969, 1976, 1978–79, 1987, 1990, 1992, 1995, 2001–3, 2005

Chronicle of Higher Education, 1967–2004

Connecticut Alumnus, 1944, 1973

Connecticut Daily Campus, 1917–2005

From 1914–56, the campus newspaper was titled the *Connecticut Campus;* it became the *Connecticut Daily Campus* in 1956. From 1914–19, it published twice a month; from 1919–50, it published twice weekly; between 1950 and 1956, the paper published three times weekly; it began daily publication in 1956.

Day (New London), 1978, 1984

Hartford Advocate, 1998

Hartford Courant, 1897, 1899, 1901, 1908, 1930–31, 1935, 1937–38, 1946, 1948, 1950, 1952–53, 1961–62, 1966, 1968–70, 1972–75, 1979–80, 1984–92, 1994–99, 2001–05

Hartford Times, 1898, 1900, 1914, 1923, 1936, 1948, 1961–62, 1967–71, 1974, 1976

Journal Inquirer (Manchester), 1987, 1990, 1995–96, 1999, 2003, 2005

Meriden Record, 1971, 1976

Milford Citizen, 1969

New Englander Magazine, 1960

New Haven Register, 1939, 1969, 1971, 1973, 1978, 1986–87

New York Times, 1940, 1963, 1989, 1992, 1995–96, 2003, 2005

New York Times Magazine, 1969

Northeast (Hartford Courant Magazine), 1949, 1989, 1999

Norwich Bulletin, 1976

Nutmeg, box 7, DRC, 1985

Providence Journal, 1967

Sunday Register Magazine (New Haven), 1947

UConn Traditions, spring 1996, spring 2000, summer 2003, spring 2004

University of Connecticut Advance, 1985, 1993–94, 1996–99, 2000, 2002–5

University of Connecticut Chronicle, 1973, 1979

Washington Star, 1962

Waterbury Republican, 1931

Willimantic Journal, 1886

Government Documents, Reports and Data Lists

"The Storrs Agricultural School: Course of Study." Report of the Secretary of Connecticut Board of Agriculture. 1882.

Christine Rocco, ed. "Facts about the University of Connecticut since 1881." 2nd ed. University of Connecticut Office of Institutional Research. Storrs, Conn., n.d.

"What's in a Name?: A Fact Book about Residence Halls at UConn." University of Connecticut Division of Student Affairs and Services. Department of Residential Life. Storrs, Conn., n.d.

U.S. Congress, House Committee on Un-American Activities. "Hearings before the Committee on Un-American Activities." 83rd Cong., 1st sess., 1953.

Oral Histories

Shiro Aisawa, October 15, 2003

Philip E. Austin, July 30, 2002; August 8–9, 2002; May 13, 2003; June 3, 2005

Daniel Blume, May 28, 2003

Scott Brohinsky, May 4, 2004

Anthony T. DiBenedetto, August 6, 1997

Julius Elias, January 10, 1995

Karla Fox, July 16, 2003

George Fukui, October 15, 2003

Joan Geetter, October 1, 1997

Harry J. Hartley, May 21 and 28, 1996

Toshi Hamasaki Kato, October 16, 2003

Kay Kiyokowa, October 17, 2003

Marvin Lapuk, May 28, 2003

Helen Loy, undated

Denise Merrill, July 3, 1995

Jim Nakano, October 17, 2003

Satoshi Oishi, October 16, 2003

Barbara Isham Potterton, October 31, 2003

Tom Ritter, August 14, 1995

Alfred R. Rogers, May 28, 2003

John G. Rohrbach, March 22, 2004

Elizabeth "Betty" Roper, August 20, 1997

William Rosen, July 14, 1997

Kevin Sullivan, August 14, 1995

Morton Tenzer, August 18, 2003

Robert M. Ward, July 12, 1995

Albert E. Waugh, February 12, 1981

Susan Weldon, August, 11, 1997

Carol A. Wiggins, November 21, 2002

Kenneth G. Wilson, January 4, 1982

Kazuo Yamaguchi, October 16, 2003

Wilfred B. Young, January 18, 1974

Unpublished Manuscripts

Hartley, Harry. "UConn 2000: Planning, Politicking, and Managing a Billion Dollar Campus Transformation."
History of University of Connecticut Health Center
Sattler, Mark. "Sign of the Times: McCarthyism at the University of Connecticut," History 402 Research Paper, University of Connecticut, 2003.
Stemmons, Walter. 75th Anniversary History of the University of Connecticut (DRC).

Web Sites

english.people.com.cn/200504/12/print20050412_180597.html
old.hartfordadvocate.com/articles/bball98h.html
web.uconn.edu/crb/China%20voices.htm
www.advance.uconn.edu/112497hs.htm
www.humanities.uconn.edu/about.html
www.internet-95.com/personal/richv/springweekend.htm
www.law.uconn.edu/about
www.nationmaster.com/encyclopedia/Red-Brick-universities
www.netstate.com/states/intro/ct_intro.htm
www.uwex.edu/ces/depthead/landgranttrad.pdf

Secondary Sources

Alberts, Robert C. *Pitt: The Story of the University of Pittsburgh, 1787–1987.* Pittsburgh: University of Pittsburgh Press, 1986.
Babbidge, Homer D., and Robert M. Rosenweig. *The Federal Interest in Higher Education.* New York: McGraw-Hill, 1962.
Barnett, James H. *"Mr. Beach": A Profile of Charles Lewis Beach, President, Connecticut Agricultural College, 1908–1928.* Storrs, Conn.: University of Connecticut Publications Series, 1969.
———. *"Mr. Gentry": A Profile of Charles Burt Gentry, Professor of Education and Dean of the University, 1920–1950.* Storrs, Conn.: University of Connecticut Publications Series, 1971.
———. *Three Storrs Pioneers: Profiles of Benjamin Franklin Koons, Edwina Maude Whitney, George Stafford Torrey.* Storrs, Conn.: The University of Connecticut, 1981.
Bloom, Alexander and Wini Breines, eds. *"Takin' It to the Streets": A Sixties Reader.* New York: Oxford University Press, 1995.
Bogue, Alan G., and Robert Taylor, eds. *The University of Wisconsin: One Hundred and Twenty-five Years.* Madison, Wisc.: University of Wisconsin Press, 1975.

Bongiorno, Joseph A. "In Pursuit of Intelligent Cultivation: Theodore Sedgwick Gold and Agriculture in Nineteenth-Century Connecticut." *Connecticut History* 44 (spring 2005): 48–76.

Callcott, George H. *A History of the University of Maryland.* Baltimore: Maryland Historical Society, 1966.

Daniels, Robert V., ed. *The University of Vermont: The First Two Hundred Years.* Hanover, N.H.: University Press of New England, 1991.

Dyer, Thomas G. *The University of Georgia: A Bicentennial History, 1785–1985.* Athens, Ga.: University of Georgia Press, 1985.

Eschenbacher, Herman F. *The University of Rhode Island: A History of Land Grant Education in Rhode Island.* New York: Appleton-Century-Crofts, 1967.

Gitlin, Todd. *The Sixties: Years of Hope, Days of Rage.* New York: Bantam Books, 1987.

Janick, Herbert F. *A People's University: The Centennial History of Western Connecticut State University, 1903–2003.* Danbury, Conn.: The University, 2002.

Kurlansky, Mark. *1968: The Year That Rocked the World.* New York: Ballantine Books, 2004.

McCaughey, Robert A. *Stand Columbia: A History of Columbia University in the City of New York, 1754–2004.* New York: Columbia University Press, 2003.

Meyerowitz, Joanne, ed. *Not June Cleaver: Women and Gender in Postwar America, 1945–1960.* Philadelphia: Temple University Press, 1994.

Murray, Alice Yang. *What Did the Internment of Japanese Americans Mean?* Boston: Bedford/St. Martin's, 2000.

Palmer, Michele. *Decades of Pride: A History of the School of Home Economics and Family Studies, the University of Connecticut.* Storrs, Conn.: University of Connecticut, 1981.

Robinson, Greg. *By Order of the President: FDR and the Internment of Japanese Americans.* Cambridge, Mass.: Harvard University Press, 2001.

Rorabaugh, W. J. *Berkeley at War: The 1960s.* New York: Oxford University Press, 1989.

Roy, Mark J. *University of Connecticut.* Charleston, S.C.: Arcadia Publishing, 2001.

Schrecker, Ellen. *No Ivory Tower: McCarthyism and the Universities.* New York: Oxford University Press, 1986.

Snider, William D. *Light on the Hill: A History of the University of North Carolina at Chapel Hill.* Chapel Hill: University of North Carolina Press, 1992.

Stadtman, Verne A. *The University of California, 1868–1968.* New York: McGraw-Hill, 1970.

Stemmons, Walter. *Connecticut Agricultural College—A History.* Storrs, Conn.: Connecticut Agricultural College, 1931.

Wechsler, James. *Revolt on the Campus.* New York: Covici-Friede, 1935.

Index

Illustrations are indexed by figure number. All illustrations follow page 170.